Boulton Paul

since 1915

The Defiant represented 79 per cent of all Boulton Paul designed aircraft with a total of 1,062. The gun turret and under-fuselage retractable aerials are shown well in this low-level fly past view of a Defiant I.

Boulton Paul Aircraft

since 1915

Alec Brew

PUTNAM

© Alec Brew 1993

First published in Great Britain 1993 by
Putnam Aeronautical Books, an imprint of
Conway Maritime Press Ltd,
101 Fleet Street,
London EC4Y 1DE

British Library Cataloguing in Publication Data
Brew, Alec
Boulton Paul Aircraft since 1915
I. Title
623.7

ISBN 0–85177–860–7

Typesetting and page make-up by
The Word Shop, Bury, Lancashire
Printed and bound by the Alden Press, Oxford

CONTENTS

Acknowledgements

Soon after beginning work on this book I came to the conclusion that I should have started 25 years earlier, when so many more of the principals were still alive, not least J D North, and also the company's early archives had not been largely thrown away. That I was able to fill in so many gaps in my knowledge was due to many people, but a few should be highlighted because of their particular assistance.

Les Whitehouse had the foresight to save much archive material from a fiery fate, at a time when he was writing his own HND thesis on the company's engineering history. The section on the Boulton & Paul unbuilt projects could not have been completed to the extent that it has, without that foresight, and his assistance.

Jack Chambers, now chairman of the Boulton Paul Society, worked for the company for 47 years, and has spent most of his retirement researching the company's history. He has been unfailingly helpful, in both providing me with information and useful contacts.

Dave Lockley and Dave James at Dowty Boulton Paul, have been entirely uncomplaining during my frequent visits to the company's photographic library, despite my infringement on their valuable time, and I have to thank Mr E Nugent, the managing director of Dowty Boulton Paul for that access. All photographs reproduced in this book, except where otherwise credited are from Dowty Boulton Paul's archives.

In Norwich Jim Colman has continually ferreted out information for me from the Boulton & Paul archives. I have also to thank Mr D Chenery, the chief executive of Boulton & Paul Plc for his permission to use whatever was left at Riverside of the Aircraft Department's archives.

The last chief test pilot of the company, A E 'Ben' Gunn, has been extremely helpful in answering my numerous questions, and providing details of his log book entries and experiences, as has Mrs Rosemary Middleton, the widow of his unfortunate predecessor, Robin Lindsay Neale.

I have also to thank Peter James and Miss S Carson at the A & AEE, Boscombe Down, the ever helpful staff at the Public Record Office and RAF Museum Library, and Mr J Shore and the staff at the Fleet Air Arm Museum. I must also offer particular thanks to Mr Rick Ewig at the University of Wyoming for fulfilling all my many requests with unfailing efficiency.

Other people who have assisted include Philip Armes, Mrs J Bagshaw, Flg Off F Barker, Wing Commander E Barwell, Denis Bolderston, Chaz Bowyer, Jim Boulton, Peter Brew, Jack Bruce, Ron Cooper, Wing Commander E C Deanesley, F J Endean, Alan Hague, Brian and Jack Holmes, Roger Jackson, Derek James, Philip Jarrett, Charles Kenmir, Gordon Kinsey, Flt Lt A F C Lanning, Harry Law, Colin Manning, Francis K Mason, Geoffrey Monument, Eric Myall, Miss L North, Colin and Ted Penny, Harald Penrose, Cyril Plimmer, Richard Riding, John Stroud, Ray Sturtivant, and certainly not least Wendy Matthiason.

Introduction

Boulton Paul Aircraft, Boulton & Paul Ltd as it once was, or Dowty Boulton Paul as it is now, was never one of the giants of the aircraft industry, never a Hawker, a Bristol or an Avro. It never became a household name as they did, never produced an aircraft, except perhaps the Defiant, which everyone knew as a Boulton Paul product, yet it has been in the aircraft business for over three-quarters of a century since, in October 1915, it flew its first aircraft.

It has managed to survive where more esteemed names such as Handley Page, Gloster and Martinsyde, have fallen by the wayside. Though now part of the TI Group, its factory at Pendeford, Wolverhampton, is still in production, when more famous factories at Hatfield, Kingston and Brooklands are gone. It has survived because it has always managed to find a niche, mostly by innovation and invention. It was a pioneer in metal construction, and other companies sought its expertise, it was a world leader in the development of powered gun turrets, and that led to it currently being a world leader in powered flying controls and fly-by-wire.

Much of the history of the company has also been largely the history of one man, John Dudley North. When only 25 he set up its Aircraft Design Department as chief engineer, and he led it through all the vicissitudes of the aviation industry. The innovation which was to become the key to the company's survival was mainly due to his insight.

J D North, like Boulton Paul Aircraft, is not a household name, yet as much as many of the other great pioneers, and perhaps more than most, he was the guiding influence of one of the main aircraft manufacturers, becoming its managing director and then its chairman. One of his abiding beliefs was that 'If you have a proper organisation, the final purpose of management is thinking'. His own thinking usually concerned 'the things other people in the same line of business would not ordinarily do'.

This thinking helped Boulton Paul avoid the pitfalls which befell many others, and when the rationalisation of the industry was taking place, when a small company could no longer compete with the multi-national giants which were being created, he sought the union with the Dowty Group which enabled the company to survive to this day.

The company built a total of 4,826 complete aeroplanes, including 1,341, of its own design, which is not a great number for over 75 years in the business. In fact Boulton & Paul at Norwich built only 54 aircraft of their own design in the 17 years they built aircraft, and the Defiant represents 77 per cent of all the Boulton Paul aircraft ever built, with the Balliol a further 17 per cent. In spite of that small total there were many significant milestones, the first practical British all-metal aircraft (P.10), the first all-metal aircraft delivered to the Royal Air Force (P.15 Bolton), the biggest 'aircraft' ever built in Britain the (R101), the first aircraft with an enclosed, power-operated gun turret (P.75 Overstrand) and the world's first aircraft powered by a single propeller-turbine (P.108 Balliol T.1).

These accomplishments and the rest of Boulton Paul's record has produced a degree of pride in two quite different towns, Norwich and Wolverhampton, and still continues to do so.

Company History
The Days Before the Aeroplane

The Norwich firm of Boulton & Paul dates back to 1797, when it was founded by William Moore, a 23 year-old farmer's son. In that year he left his father's farm, at Warham, near the port of Wells, and set up an ironmonger's business in Cockey Lane, Norwich. At the time Norwich was a thriving weaving centre, and there was a general influx of people from the countryside into the city.

William Moore's business did well, and he became an emminent citizen. He became Sheriff in 1824, an alderman in 1833 and Mayor in 1835. He had taken John Hilling Barnard as a partner in the firm and when Moore died in 1839, Barnard became the sole proprietor. The company still traded as an ironmongers and stove grate manufacturer.

In 1844 it was Barnard's turn to take a partner, a man of 23 named William Staples Boulton, and the name of the company was restyled Barnard and Boulton. The company expanded into several other shops in the surrounding streets. In 1853 another farmer's son, from Thorpe Abbotts, came into the firm as an apprentice. His name was Joseph John Dawson Paul.

J J Dawson Paul, governing director of Boulton Paul Ltd when the Aircraft Department was started.

1

Dawson Paul did well and rose to the position of works manager, looking after the manufacturing concern at the rear of the ironmongers shop, where they made such things as stove grates, and kettles, and weaved wire netting by hand. William Boulton became sole proprietor when John Barnard died, and he and his young works manager made changes in the company operations. Norwich was going through a period of depression. Cheap imported food had a severe effect on the agriculture of the surrounding countryside, and the invention of the power loom, for which nearby access to coal was essential, meant the weaving industry became wholly centred on the north of England.

Because of the depression there was a large pool of cheap unskilled labour in the town, and Barnard and Boulton aimed to make use of some of it in a new venture. In November 1864 they took a lease on a small works in Rose Lane, Norwich, which contained a foundry, and Dawson Paul became works manager at a salary of £100 a year. The shop was disposed of, but they began to make many of the things which they had formerly sold. They still made grates and kettles, but now added other domestic implements such as sausage and mincing machines, and began to cater for the large local market for agricultural implements, iron railings and garden seats. Most significantly in 1867 they began to weave wire netting in larger quantities. The skills of the weaver could be used, and in fact the first looms they used were very similar to the looms formerly used to weave wool.

The agricultural and horticultural implements remained the most substantial part of the business however, and the firm began to export in large quantities, first to the Continent, but later to the Empire.

In 1869 Boulton made Dawson Paul a junior partner in the company, which was retitled W.S. Boulton & Co, reflecting the fact that Paul only contributed £500 of the £6,000 capital.

The following year steam-powered looms were installed to increase the output of the wire netting side of the business, and the company expanded slowly. In 1874 the capital was increased to £16,000, and Paul was now able to contribute £5,000, which was reflected in a further change of the company name to Boulton & Paul Ltd. The partnership was for life, and the surviving partner had an obligation to buy out the deceased's share, in instalments.

In August 1876 there was a disastrous fire which destroyed the carpenter's shop in the works, and considerably set back the company. William Boulton, who was suffering greatly with his health, took it very badly, and virtually withdrew from the day to day running of the company, leaving Dawson Paul in charge. In 1879 Boulton died, leaving Paul in a difficult position. The fortunes of the company had suffered greatly after the fire, and yet he was obliged to buy out Boulton's widow at a rate which was established at £2,500 a year.

The company was by now quite a large concern, employing 350 men, with an annual turnover of £50,000. To help him run it, Paul elevated one of his employees, a pattern-maker and designer named James Sendall to the position of partner. The partnership was far from a happy one, and eventually it was dissolved, Sendall continuing for a while as works manager until succeeded by Henry Fiske.

Fiske was another farmer's son, who had originally been apprenticed to the ironmongers' in Cockey Lane, but a year later in 1869, his indentures were cancelled so that he could be employed in the Rose Lane Works. He was a large man, with a commanding presence, and had just the sort of personality to run an expanding business.

With Fiske as works manager the company expanded into the country estates market. Wire netting remained one of the main products, and the company exported miles and miles of it to Australia which was being affected by a plague of rabbits. Wrought iron fencing was also still produced in considerable quantities, but the company became better known for an amazing variety of structures which decorated countless country estates. There were summer houses, greenhouses, footbridges, keeper's huts, portable bungalows, aviaries, vineries, conservatories, boat houses, wrought-iron circular tree-seats, galvanised shooting boxes, garden rollers, dog kennels, wheelbarrows and countless other products. They were exported all over the world, but particularly to India.

Henry Fiske was made a partner in 1893, and in 1897 the firm became a limited liability company, with a capital of £168,000, all of which was held by the families. By now Henry Fiske had been promoted to managing director, with Dawson Paul governing director.

There were signs about the turn of the century that the country estate market was changing, but the Boer War brought new opportunities for Boulton & Paul. In 1900 there was an order for a large hutted convalescent camp in Hampshire, and the following year there was a War Office order for £100,000 for portable bungalows to be erected in South Africa for officers' quarters. Three ships were required to deliver this order, and numerous company staff had to travel to South Africa to supervise their erection.

The Fiske family had begun to spell their name in the old style, as ffiske, and Henry's sons William and Guy had come into the firm, to be followed shortly by the youngest, Geoffrey. William, who had served in the Boer War, went on a sales trip to Argentina, taking with him Dawson Paul's son, also named Dawson Paul and just out of school. The sale of company bungalows and other buildings was greatly stimulated right across South America. This was becoming the main work of the company, wooden prefabricated buildings, and large orders were received for relief quarters after earthquakes in Jamaica and Messina, as well as regular orders from all over the world.

The Rose Lane works had by now expanded to twenty times its former size, and the main departments were the wood-working shop, and the wire netting shop, still exporting miles and miles to Australia (7,614 miles in 1905 alone). As well as the original foundry, there was also a smithy in King Street producing the fencing and other wrought iron products, and in 1905 a new department which was located on the other side of the River Wensum at Thorpe Yard, an area leased from the railway and surrounded by marshy ground.

This was a structural steel business, specialising initially in farm buildings, such as steel-framed barns, and was very much the brain-child of Henry ffiske supported by his son William, who was shortly to be invited to join the Board.

The following year another department was started, for the manufacture of motor-boat engines, and it was this more exciting venture which drew the interest of Geoffrey ffiske and Dawson Paul the younger. So much so that they secretly had some of the workmen, who usually built chicken coops, build a small hydroplane. The company's marine engines were four-cylinder units of four-inch bore and six-inch stroke, which was double the number of cylinders required by the racing regulations of the day, and so they cut one in half and fitted it to their new craft, which they named *Dollydo*.

In 1909, in its first race, at Lowestoft, driven by Geoffrey ffiske it won easily at a speed of 21kt, despite being left on the starting line when the engine stalled. *Dollydo* proved to be twice as fast as any other motor boat in the country. The senior members of the firm were not displeased that Boulton & Paul's name was associated with the fastest motor boat in the land, but they still asked the two young conspirators for the £100 cost of it. Their financial embarrassment was relieved when someone offered to buy the *Dollydo* for £150. Boulton & Paul then began building motor boats as a profitable side-line.

The start of the Great War in 1914 caused chaos, with orders cancelled from every part of the world, and teams of building erectors recalled including four brought home from France in a chartered fishing boat without the formality of passports. Almost immediately the company was flooded with orders of a different kind.

There was a naval hospital at Dover, an extra wooden storey on top of the Admiralty in Whitehall, eleven entire hutted camps across East Anglia, a prisoner of war camp in Jersey, hangars for the Royal Flying Corps in Britain and France and military buildings everywhere, even as far afield as Mesopotamia. These orders involved not just the wood-working department but also the structural steel works.

Even the wire fencing department received huge orders, after the War Office had discovered that wire netting was just the thing to hold up the sides of trenches. By the end of the War Boulton & Paul had supplied over 5,372 miles of wire netting for that and other purposes. The smithy produced horse pickets, field kitchens and drum barrows for telegraph wires. The engine department built electric lighting plants for mobile workshops, water pumps for use in the trenches, and engines for naval launches.

Yet in 1915 the company was still producing such items as greenhouses and dog kennels, and the directors decided, on the advice of a local MP, to write to Lloyd George offering the whole of the rest of the works for whatever war production seemed appropriate. Another engineering company in Norwich, Howes and Sons, had also offered its services. An official came from the War Office to inspect the facilities at both firms, but returned to London without comment.

A few days later William ffiske was invited to the War Office. There it was stated that the works had been satisfactorily reported on, with its excellent nucleus of skilled metal and woodworkers with the appropriate plant and equipment. Could they make aeroplanes in Norwich?

The First World War

William ffiske was offered an immediate trial order for twenty-five F.E.2bs on a cost plus profit basis. Drawings and specifications would be supplied, and full access to the Royal Aircraft Factory at Farnborough would be allowed to glean whatever other information might be required. Aeroplanes were something of a mystery to the directors of Boulton & Paul, as well as Howes & Sons, who had agreed to co-operate, with its Chapel Field works. Dawson Paul the elder was reluctant for the company to get involved in anything so revolutionary, which was surprising for the proprietor of a company prepared to make everything from a pre-fabricated wooden bungalow to an iron liquid-manure cart. Boulton & Paul were actually ideally suited to manufacture the wooden aeroplanes of the period. Not only had they been highly skilled wood-workers for fifty years, they were skilled metal-workers in iron and steel and wire, and were even involved in the production of petrol engines. In fact, they eventually very quickly became capable of making every single part of the aircraft they manufactured (except for the engines and armament).

The Board decided that the terms of the contract would not bring any financial loss, and sent an investigating team to Farnborough, including William and Geoffrey ffiske and Stanley Howes. There they discovered that the manufacture of aeroplanes was not such a fine art as they had been led to suppose. They even decided that they could improve on what they saw. Using jigs and press tools they could turn it into a mass production process, providing the initial order was worth the outlay. Geoffrey, who was a trained engineer, and had been removed from a naval posting for this new venture, was to undertake the engineering side. Stanley Howes would organise the erection and assembly, and William ffiske the wood-working and commercial side of the undertaking. The first order, received in late June 1915 had been increased to fifty aircraft and the serials 5201–5250 reserved for them.

A start was soon made preparing templates and jigs, and the wire netting machines were cleared away to create a fuselage production area in the Rose Lane Works. The engines would be installed at Stanley Howes' Coach-building Works in Chapel Field. Extra skilled fitters and tool makers were acquired by combing the military establishments of East Anglia, with the assistance of the War Office.

An aerodrome was required for testing the completed machines. The War Department was building a large one at Snarehill, Thetford, about 26 miles from Norwich, for use as the Aircraft Acceptance Park for Norfolk, and wished the company to use that. Boulton & Paul suggested the use of the Cavalry Drill Ground, just outside Norwich at Mousehold. The War Office was reluctant,

The first F.E.2b completed, 5201, *Bombay No.1*. First flown on 4 October, 1915, and delivered to Farnborough by Howard Pixton on 8 October.

5

believing Mousehold to be too small, but when Boulton & Paul pointed out that the small-holdings surrounding the Drill Ground, as marked on the maps, were in fact grassed over and actually included in the rental paid by the Government to Norwich Corporation, they changed their minds.

A few grass banks were levelled off and Boulton & Paul were given a contract to erect buildings for the use of a Royal Flying Corps School of Flying. On 27 July, 1915, No.9 Reserve Aeroplane Squadron of No.6 Wing was formed at Mousehold with a varied collection of aircraft. The first of a number of RFC training units to use the new aerodrome. Albert Ball VC was one of the pilots to be inducted into the RFC at Mousehold.

The F.E.2bs which Boulton & Paul were to build were urgently needed on the Western Front. In the days of the Fokker scourge, any competent fighting aircraft was a boon to the RFC, and the F.E.2b initially served as a fighter. With its gunner in the nose of the short nacelle, in front of the pilot, and a pusher propeller it overcame the difficulties the Allies were having in developing an aircraft which could fire directly ahead, like the Fokker E III with its interrupter gear.

In March 1915 a new version of the F.E.2b, with the superior 120 hp Beardmore engine, was produced. The Beardmore, a licenced-built version of the Austro-Daimler straight six, was uncowled and drove a two-blade propeller. It was this version which Boulton & Paul had been contracted to build.

Astonishingly, less than 14 weeks after receiving the order the first F.E.2b was nearing completion. The War Office arranged a gala day at Mousehold for the flight of the first aircraft, serial 5201. This was scheduled for 2 October, 1915, a week before the company would have wished, and perhaps an additional way of pressing them for completion. The aircraft was taken to Mousehold the day before, and a team spent all night erecting and rigging it.

General Sir David Henderson, in command of the RFC came to Norwich for the day, along with a large staff. They were given a tour of Rose Lane Works and a splendid lunch, and then the time came for the first flight. The pilot was to be Capt Howard Pixton, a veteran pilot in that he had obtained his Aviator's certificate (No.50) as long ago as January 1911. In 1914 he had won the Schneider Trophy event at Monaco piloting a Sopwith Tabloid seaplane, and had been employed as a test pilot by Sopwith and others. Many hundreds of people had assembled at Mousehold, including major local dignitaries and most of Boulton & Paul's workforce.

The F.E.2b they had all come to see was not only Boulton & Paul's first aircraft it was also proudly inscribed *Bombay No.1*. The cost of it had been raised by the people of Bombay, one of nearly a thousand such presentation aircraft paid for by various organisations and individuals during the 1914–18 War. Another F.E.2b, 5226, which was shortly to follow it from the Chapel Field Works was inscribed *Punjab & Nagra*. Unfortunately for those assembled the engine of 5201 would not start!

After two hours of trying Pixton decided to give up the attempt, having grown rather disillusioned with the whole business. The assembled dignitaries retreated to the marquee where the champagne was broached anyway. The F.E.2b was wheeled in front of the crowd for their inspection, and Gen Henderson arranged with the CO of the Flying School to stage a flying display with some of their aircraft.

The trouble proved to be a faulty magneto, and 5201 successfully flew the following Monday. On 8 October Pixton delivered it to Farnborough with Stanley Howes as passenger. They flew over the Rose Lane Works on the way, and completed the flight in less than two hours. Stanley Howes was an immediate convert to the joys of flying, and expressed the view that he never wanted to travel by car again.

With the production of the first order proceeding satisfactorily, Gen MacInnis, the Controller of Supply, placed a further order for one hundred F.E.2bs. (6928–7027). During October, to expand production, Boulton & Paul purchased from J J Colman Ltd 14 acres of land on the far side of the River Wensum for £12,000. They immediately began the design of a new factory which was to become known as the Riverside Works. There were new buildings covering 2 acres which cost a total of over £31,500, plus a joinery shop to replace the one at Thorpe Road for a cost of £4,965 and a new steel constructional works costing £5,995. Only the aircraft production was transferred there initially, and the land was drained and the buildings built by the company in only three months, including a power station. The entire move from the Rose Lane Works to the new Riverside Works was completed in one week, when the factory was closed for the Easter holidays in 1916. Production began at the new works on 26 April, 1916.

A drawing of the Aircraft Works, at Riverside, Norwich.

On one of his many visits to Norwich, Gen MacInnis complained to William ffiske that he was having a great deal of difficulty with the supply of propellers. Their manufacture was confined to just two or three companies, and it was felt to be such a skilled job that other companies could not take it on. William ffiske bet him a sovereign that Boulton & Paul were capable of manufacturing propellers, and the General gladly took the bet. The company built 7,835 propellers by the end of the War, and Gen MacInnes paid over the sovereign.

Two more batches of F.E.2bs were ordered from the company (7666–7715 and A5438–A5487), making 250 in all, and then they began the manufacture of the F.E.2d. Apart from 86 F.E.2ds built by the Royal Aircraft Factory, Boulton & Paul were the sole contractors for this model, which was powered by the Rolls-Royce Eagle. Two batches, totalling 300 aircraft were built (A6351–A6600 and B1851–B1900), though A6545 was converted to an F.E.2h by the fitting of a 220 hp BHP engine. This was an attempt to emulate the performance derived from the Rolls-Royce Eagle, which was in very short supply. The conversion was made by Ransomes, Sims and Jefferies of Ipswich, but the performance of the F.E.2h was so inferior to the F.E.2d that the scheme was not proceeded with.

The first three F.E.2ds were delivered in the week ending 20 January, 1917, and the contract was completed by the middle of December, as many as fourteen aircraft being delivered in one week. A small number of F.E.2bs remained to be delivered, though the bulk had been built by the beginning of the year. These were completed towards the end of the year, the Eagle-powered F.E.2d being more urgently required.

Boulton & Paul were requested to assist in bringing other East Anglian manufacturers into aircraft production, helping them take over production of the F.E.2b, while they went over to production of the Sopwith Camel. Richard Garratt & Sons of Leiston built the nacelles for all 300 F.E.2ds, ordered from Boulton & Paul, and then built complete F.E.2bs. In the case of Ransomes, Sims and Jefferies, Boulton & Paul constructed their new aircraft works, and then handed over all their jigs and templates for F.E.2b production.

Boulton & Paul received an initial order for one hundred Sopwith Camels on 2 August, 1917, and then a series of further orders, totalling 1,775. To make way for Camel production a contract awarded to Boulton & Paul for one hundred Handley Page O/400 bombers was cancelled on 20 September, 1917.

The front fuselage of a Sopwith Camel under construction at Riverside.

8

Though 1,775 Camels were ordered from Boulton & Paul, the final batch of 200 was cancelled. The total built by Boulton & Paul was thus 1,575. This total was higher than any other company, except Ruston Proctor, of Lincoln, who also built 1,575. Sopwith only built 553 Camels, their relatively small production facilities being soon entirely turned over to the Sopwith Dolphin.

Over the 57 weeks of Camel production from 15 September, 1917, to 16 November, 1918, Boulton Paul produced an average of 28 a week! The best week's production was that ending 20 July, 1918, when an astonishing total of 70 Camels was delivered, with 55 and 66 in the following two weeks. The company realised that the hold up of any parts, even a single vital nut and bolt, would cause a serious bottleneck. They set out therefore to be entirely self-sufficient, making every part themselves. They installed equipment to make everything, even down to eye-bolts and ball races, and were one of the few companies to install their own oxygen plant. Although this policy seemed at first likely to increase their costs, they soon found the expense was well worth it. Not only were they never held up for want of parts, they were able to supply many of the other manufacturers with aircraft parts, and this became a large business in itself.

In 1918 the company was involved in a programme to fit 150 hp Gnome Monosoupape engines to Camels destined for the US forces, who had ordered these engines before having ordered aircraft in which to fit them. An unusual feature of this engine was the ability to throttle it back with a selector switch which cut off one cylinder at a time. Most rotaries were only able to operate either fully on or fully off. Capt Frank Courtney, had been delegated from the newly formed Royal Air Force to test the Mono Camels. One day he swooped low over Mousehold in one, with the selector switch set for only one cylinder firing. The noise was just like a machine-gun, and it sent everyone on the ground running for cover! He managed to talk his way out of the resulting lynch party, so much so that he was engaged, after the War, as freelance test pilot for the company.

A large number of the Boulton & Paul built Camels were transferred to the United States Air Service. One Boulton & Paul built Camel, F6394, was fitted with a 180 hp Le Rhône, and at least three were converted to two-seaters, B9140, F1346, and F1946. Two Boulton & Paul built Camel fuselages were sent to Sopwith for the T.F.1 Armoured Camel project, Sopwith having by then ceased production of the Camel. One of these was later converted to the parasol monoplane Swallow B9275.

With the expansion of aircraft production further land was purchased at the cavalry ground at Mousehold, and buildings for erecting aircraft constructed. The aerodrome became one of the largest in the country, and in November 1917 No.3 Aircraft Acceptance Park was established there, with aircraft being delivered from all the local manufacturers, including Portholme Aerodrome Company, Mann-Egerton, and Ransomes, Sims & Jefferies. All the extensive extra buildings were built by Boulton & Paul themselves, and the aerodrome was connected to Norwich's tramway system.

During 1917 the management of the company was reorganised. Dawson Paul the elder remained nominally in charge as governing director, but Henry ffiske retired, and actual control of the company was invested in a committee of management, consisting of Capt Dawson Paul (who had served at Gallipoli and on the Western Front), William and Geoffrey ffiske and Stanley Howes. A team of younger men were overseeing the vast changes Boulton & Paul were going through.

The steel construction and woodworking departments were moved to the Riverside Works when the lease on the land where they were located expired. This move had not been completed when the company was asked by the Seaplane Department of the Air Ministry to tender for the construction of wooden flying-boat hulls.

A deputation consisting of William and Geoffrey ffiske, Stanley Howes and the manager of the woodworking department, A Joyce, visited Felixstowe to inspect an F.3 flying-boat hull built there under the supervision of its designer, Commander John Porte. The F.3 was a development of the earlier F.2A and F.2C flying-boats which had performed sterling service. The F.3 had 102 ft span and a length of 49 ft 2 in. The two 345 hp Rolls-Royce Eagle engines were mounted just below the upper wing and it had a top speed of 93 mph at 2,000 ft. The wings were of wooden construction covered with fabric, but the hull was entirely of wood.

The first Felixstowe F.3 flying-boat hull under construction, showing the cross-hatched planking of the hull.

The standard of craftsmanship was excellent, but Joyce ventured the opinion that there was no piece of woodwork which his men could not equal. An initial order for five hulls was offered to each of the contractors being considered for the work, but the directors did not feel it was worth reorganising the workshops for an order of less than 30 hulls. They offered to build 50 hulls and not take a penny in payment if any were rejected.

A naval officer, and former yacht designer, Lieut-Commander Linton Hope, came to inspect Boulton & Paul's woodworking facilities, and subsequently the company was given an order for 30 hulls. The workshop was reorganised so that 10 keels could be laid down at the same time, and the 49 ft long hulls were completed in huge jigs in which they could revolve for ease of access to sides and bottom. Ten hulls were delivered before any other contractor had delivered two, and further orders were soon forthcoming. Boulton & Paul eventually building a total of 70 hulls, consisting of both the F.3 and post-war F.5 which retained virtually the same hull.

The first Felixstowe F.3 hull completed.

The company had to deliver their hulls to Preston, to have the tanks fitted, and then to South Shields for the wings and engines. The completed aircraft then often journeyed back south, still by road with wings folded, for flight trials at Felixtowe! Two lorries with special trailers were purchased for this extraordinary process, quaint forerunners of the Super Guppies transporting Airbus components across Europe in later years.

Boulton & Paul attempted to convince the Air Ministry that Breydon Water or the Norfolk Broads would be perfectly suitable for flight testing, and offered to assemble the complete aircraft, to obviate the need for the aircraft to suffer this arduous journey. The offer was to no avail, and although responsibility for hauling the hulls was later taken away from Boulton & Paul, they were still subject to their long odyssey.

As with many companies, who had been brought into aircraft manufacture by the War with licenced production of other firm's designs, Boulton & Paul soon developed ambitions to produce aircraft of its own design. A design and experimental aircraft facility was created, and to manage it, and to become chief engineer, John Dudley North was recruited. John North was born in London in 1893, and had been educated in Bedford school. He lost his father at an early age, and as his mother wished him to follow his grandfather, who had been a

11

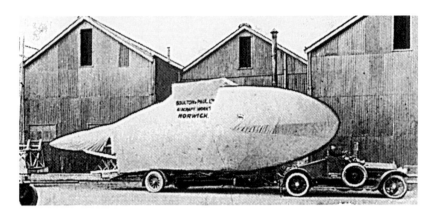

The method of transporting the Felixstowe hulls to Preston.

captain in the merchant marine, he was apprenticed in marine engineering at Harland & Wolff in Belfast. While still an apprentice North won two competitions in the *The Aeroplane*, and the editor, C G Grey, on discovering the winner was only 18 years old, urged him to take up aviation as his career.

With the help of C G Grey, North managed to persuade his mother and grandfather to let him transfer from his marine apprenticeship to a job with the Aeronautical Syndicate Ltd at Hendon. This infant aircraft company had been formed by Horatio Barber in 1909 on Salisbury Plain, but later moved to Hendon where it leased three of the eight hangars belonging to the Blériot company. It became well known for its canard pushers, tail-first monoplanes, built in a number of versions, and given the name Valkyrie. Early in 1912 a more conventional biplane, the Viking appeared, in which the single 50 hp Gnome engine drove two tractor propellers, but shortly afterwards Horatio Barber decided that keeping up with the pace of aeronautical progress was too expensive and wound up his company. John North went to work for the Grahame-White Company next door.

He soon became the chief engineer, and was also in charge of a work force of 70, a not inconsiderable achievement for a young man of 20! The first aircraft he had been asked by Claude Grahame-White to design was a small, easy to build two-seater, which would be cheap to buy and operate. In January 1913 the Type 7 Popular was completed. It was a small pusher, with the seats in tandem, in a flat-sided enclosed nacelle. The upper wings had twice the span of the lower ones, at 28 ft and 14 ft respectively, with 7 ft span ailerons on the upper wings. The prototype was fitted with a 35 hp Anzani three-cylinder engine, but production versions had the 50 hp Gnome rotary. It was priced at £400, less than half the cost of most aircraft of the day, fulfilling Grahame-White's main requirement.

Having served his apprenticeship, as it were, with the Type 7, North also designed the Type 6 Military Biplane in 1913, and it appeared at that year's Olympia Aero Show. It was of similar general layout to the Type 7, which had been finished before the Type 6. There were several fundamental differences however. The wings were of equal 42 ft 6 in span, and the 90 hp Austro-Daimler

12

engine was fitted in the nose of the nacelle, rather than behind the wings. It drove the pusher propeller by an extension shaft and chain, the propeller itself revolving on the upper boom of the triangular structure supporting the tail. This was a feature which had first been evolved by Horatio Barber. The control wires for the tail surfaces passed through the propeller boss inside the boom. The Colt machine-gun which served as the armament was mounted on a pivot on the nose. Guns on movable mountings were to become very important in the career of John North.

A further North design which also appeared at the 1913 Olympia Show was the Type 8. It was a two-seat tractor biplane with twin floats, designed for cheap operation for the private owner, and powered by a 60 hp Anzani or an 80 hp Gnome. Later in 1913 another North design appeared, inspired by the growth in popularity of the joy flights being provided at Hendon Aerodrome. It was the Type 10 Charabanc, and as its name suggests was intended to carry far more paying passengers aloft than was normal. It was once more of the general Farman, pusher layout, but with a span of 62 ft 6 in and powered by a 120 hp Austro-Daimler engine. Normal seating was provided for a pilot in the nose of the enclosed nacelle, with two pairs of wicker seats behind him for normally four passengers, but the aircraft was used to set a world record by lifting first eight, and later ten people. On 6 November the Type 10, fitted temporarily with a 60 hp Green engine, flew 300 miles to win that year's Michelin Cup, and the following year, the first parachute jump from an aeroplane in Britain was made from the Charabanc.

North was responsible for one other aircraft during 1913, the 'Lizzie'. It was not a new design in that it was really just the wings of a Type 7 Popular mated to the fuselage and tail of a Morane tractor monoplane. It was built specifically for

The Grahame-White Type 11 Aerobus designed by John Dudley North (4th from left),
which set a world record, lifting 10 people including the pilot, Louis Noel, in 1913.

aerobatic displays at Hendon, largely in the hands of Reginald Carr and Louis Strange, and was later modified, with almost equal span wings.

John North learned to fly at Hendon, but never took his Aviator's certificate. Despite being such an eminent designer, he could not spare the two guineas fee!

In 1914 North designed the Type 11 Warplane, a two-seat pusher biplane reminiscent of the F.E.2. It had a similar layout, though the pilot sat directly behind the observer, rather than in a raised position as in the F.E.2. The 100 hp Gnome Monosoupape engine drove a four-blade propeller, and the outer wings had slight sweep-back. The Type 11 had longitudinal stability problems and did not go into production.

North's final design for the Grahame-White company was the Type 13 seaplane, and it was very nearly the last aircraft he ever designed. This seaplane was built for use in the 1914 Round-Britain Air Race, and it almost killed him. It was a handsome two-seat tractor biplane, with staggered single-bay wings featuring a very early use of N struts. It was powered by a 100 hp Gnome Monosoupape engine and was also able to operate as a landplane scout. North was flying in it one day with Grahame-White as pilot, they misjudged their height above the Hamble river, because of the mist which was lying above it, and the aircraft crashed heavily into the water. Grahame-White was thrown clear but North was trapped in the wreckage and was underwater for over a minute, struggling to free himself. He finally fought his way to the surface to find Grahame-White clinging to the tail of the crashed seaplane. The two of them had to hang on there for some time, shouting for help in the mist before a boat came out to rescue them. The aircraft was also pulled from the river, but the Circuit of Britain race was cancelled because of the War, and the Type 13 was used as a trainer at Hendon.

In 1915 North joined the Austin Motor Company in Birmingham. Grahame-White had taken on the agency for Morane-Saulnier aircraft and was building those and B.E.2s to Government orders, and so there was little immediate scope for North's talent as a designer. In addition he had fallen out with the works director, and was quite surprised when Grahame-White, in May 1915, accepted his resignation.

Austin, like Boulton & Paul, had been brought into aircraft production by the Government and was just about to start manufacturing the R.E.7. North heard of the opening a few months after leaving Grahame-White and was appointed as superintendent to lay down the production lines, though he was still only 23. He was the seventh man to be appointed to the post, Herbert Austin having sacked the other six in quick succession!

At Austin, too, there was little scope for his creative abilities, though an opportunity did arise to design a scout to the ideas formulated by Albert Ball. In October 1916 Ball had returned a hero from the Western Front, having shot down eleven aircraft, and he had a number of ideas which he thought should be incorporated in an ideal scout. His father was a director of Austin, and took his son's notes and sketches to John North. The only novel aspect of the ideas was the fitting of two upward-firing machine-guns, as Ball had become adept at attacking German aircraft from below pulling the Lewis gun, mounted on the upper wing of his Nieuport Scout, down the Foster rail so that he could fire upwards. North handed the sketches to a member of his staff, C H Brooks, to work on, and by 30 December was able to submit full technical data and estimated performance to the War Office, which would have to sanction prototype construction. This was forthcoming on 21 March, but by the time the first prototype was complete, in June, Albert Ball was dead, and all impetus for continued development of the Austin A.F.B.1, as it was designated, was gone.

With the R.E.7 in full production (A design North later described as the worst he had ever known), shortly to be followed by the R.E.8, there was no outlet for North's creative abilities, and he did not get along with Herbert Austin. The experience of working for such a large company was very invaluable, but when the opportunity arose to once more design aircraft, this time at Boulton & Paul, he willingly accepted the challenge.

The facilities with which he was provided by the Boulton & Paul directors in the experimental and design section at Mousehold were excellent. There was a four-foot wind-tunnel, which showed the directors' foresight, only Handley Page and Airco had their own wind-tunnels during the War, Sopwith never did have one, and Bristol did not obtain one until June 1919. As well as the wind-tunnel, there were chemical and metallurgical laboratories, and equipment to physically test components. The company felt that to prosper in the world of aviation they would have to progress in a systematic way, undertaking fundamental research in order to succeed by innovation and invention. This creed was to become a fundamental facet of the company's future.

Seven sub-departments were created, and suitably qualified experts recruited to head each of them. There were Aerodynamic and Physics Laboratories, a Structures and Testing Section, a Full Scale Testing Section, a Meteorological Section, a Mathematical Section and finally a Records Section. The task of these sections, when not engaged on a specific project, was to accumulate a store of carefully indexed information, which could be drawn on for all future projects. The stressman in the new organisation was Otto Glauert, formerly a maths master, and brother of Herbert Glauert, a Farnborough scientist. M Boudot was appointed as chief designer. He was a Frenchman who had designed a single-seat scout for F G Nestler Ltd, primarily a component manufacturer. The Nestler Scout, powered by a 100 hp Gnome Monosoupape engine, was a highly manoeuvrable single-bay biplane, and was tested by the Air Ministry early in 1917. Unfortunately on 26 March the fabric had ripped from its wings and it crashed into a hanger, killing the pilot. Boudot later moved on to the Grahame-White company, where he was to design the Grahame-White Limousine, the world's first 'executive' aircraft.

The first product to emanate from this new design department was for a Sopwith Camel replacement. A design competition had been instituted against Specification A.1A and North sketched a number of layouts in an attempt to win the order for the replacement for the aircraft that was filling Boulton & Paul's construction shops.

When Bentley developed their 230 hp B.R.2 rotary engine, the Air Ministry immediately saw a requirement for a fighter to take full advantage of it. An alternative engine for the 'Camel replacement' was seen to be the compact ABC Wasp nine-cylinder radial. There were a total of eight contenders, five powered by the B.R.2 and three by the Wasp. The latter three were the Sopwith 8F.1 Snail, Westland Wagtail and BAT F.K.22/2 Bantam, all much more compact fighters than their B.R.2-powered rivals, and destined not to be serious prospects, troubled by the problems of the Wasp engine.

Among the B.R.2 contenders were two who had been brought into licenced production of aircraft having been non-aviation manufacturers before the War. Apart from Boulton & Paul there was also Austin Motors.

Austin's design, for which John North's replacement, John W Kenworthy, and his former subordinate C H Brooks were responsible, was the A.F.T.3 Osprey. It was a triplane, rather surprisingly, so late in the War. Its small size, coupled with the 230 hp of the B.R.2 gave it a good performance, but it had little hope of being preferred to the biplanes offered by other firms.

The frontrunner was the Sopwith 7F.1 Snipe, which appeared late in 1917, powered with a B.R.1 rotary, until a B.R.2 was delivered. It was a single-bay biplane, with a flat-sided fuselage, but this was changed to a two-bay layout with a more rounded fuselage.

Two of John North's designs were initially ordered, the P.5 and the P.3. No details of the P.5 survive, and the three aircraft ordered were cancelled, the serials, C8652–C8654 being re-allocated. It may well have been an ABC Wasp powered fighter, as it seems unlikely that two B.R.2-powered designs would be ordered from the same manufacturer. There are vague indications that all of the first five designs (P.1–P.5) were in fact fighters. It seems that either the P.1 or the P.2 was a single-bay fighter powered by the B.R.2, and might well have born the same relation to the P.3 as the first single-bay Snipe to the subsequent examples. There was also another design referred to as the NF.1 (Night Fighter 1), which had an Eeman gun mounting, three Lewis guns angled upwards at an angle of 45 deg. This may or may not have been redesignated with one of the P numbers.

The P.3 was a two-bay design, with staggered wings, and N struts. The aircraft was initially named the Hawk by the company, but the name was subsequently changed to Boblink, and then Bobolink, an American singing bird. The names of birds of prey had been reserved for aero-engines, and single-seat, single-engined landplanes were to be named after reptiles or land-birds other

The first Boulton & Paul design to be built, the sole P.3 Bobolink on roll-out at Riverside, with the front fuselage still uncovered.

The Bobolink erected at Mousehold, in its original form, without ailerons on the lower wings.

than birds of prey. In addition Boulton & Paul was assigned the initial letters BO.

Three P.3 Bobolinks were originally ordered for evaluation, C8655–C8657, but only one, C8655 was completed. It was delivered to Martlesham Heath for trials alongside the other competitive machines in March 1918 soon after its first flights at Mousehold, after which minor changes were made. These flights were made by Frank Courtney.

Courtney was well known to John North. He had started as a non-paying apprentice with the Grahame-White company in 1913, when he was only 18 years old, after writing to Grahame-White from his post in a bank in Paris. On his first day John North, the chief engineer, had given him a long talk on what his programme as an apprentice would be. In 1914 he had been given the opportunity to learn to fly in the Grahame-White School at Hendon for the discounted sum of £50, which he borrowed from the family lawyer. With special dispensation he had taken his Aviator's ticket after the War had started.

He was refused entry to the Royal Flying Corps as a pilot because of his glasses (he was a little short-sighted), but he enlisted as an Air Mechanic. Because of the general shortage of pilots he was soon put on the list of standby pilots, the only official Air Mechanic 2nd Class pilot in the RFC! He served at Farnborough for a while, and then joined No.3 Squadron on the Western Front, flying Morane Parasol monoplanes. He rose through the ranks and obtained a commission being then posted back to Farnborough as a military test pilot. He did most of the testing work on the F.E.2d, and wangled a transfer back to France to No.20 Squadron, who were flying this aircraft. He moved to No.45 Squadron flying Sopwith 1½ Strutters, and then commanded a flight in No.70 Squadron for a brief time, before moving back to No.45.

He was transferred back to England and was appointed Fighting Instructor to the flying training establishments in the London area. Subsequently he was assigned for military test flying once more, and after the War it was natural that he became a freelance test pilot, working for Armstrong Whitworth, Hawker, Koolhoven, Fairey, and Boulton & Paul amongst others. He became one of the best-known pilots of the time, being dubbed 'The Man with the Golden Hands' by the Press. He was a tall elegant looking man, with dark wavy hair and a clipped moustache. Incongruously, he was in the habit of wearing pince-nez glasses.

The Bobolink had a small all-round performance edge over the Snipe and good flying characteristics, but it was the Snipe which was chosen for production. The reasons given were the Bobolink's narrower track undercarriage, and its more complicated structure, though the latter is debatable. The Snipe's fuselage was a complicated structure of formers and stringers, whereas the Bobolink's was a simple, wire-braced box-girder. Almost certainly the proven record of the Sopwith company weighed heavily in favour of the Snipe, even though the Bobolink might have been a slightly better fighter.

Boulton & Paul were well compensated for not winning the contract however. They were given an immediate order for 400 Snipes beginning with E6137. This order was completed, and they received a further order for one hundred. According to William ffiske's own account of the company's wartime activities written in 1919, only 25 of these were completed before the remainder were cancelled, though some sources suggest that only 15 were delivered. A total of 4,500 Snipes had been ordered from all sources, but because of the end of the War, large numbers of these were cancelled, though production did go on into 1919.

With the more complicated structure of the Snipe, it was a more advanced looking aircraft than Sopwith's previously fairly simple, but practical designs, like the Camel, and the Snipe was therefore a link between those and postwar machines such as the Woodcock and the Gamecock.

Sopwith Snipe assembly at Mousehold. Boulton & Paul built 425 before orders were cancelled.

Completed Snipes in the hangars at Mousehold. Production went on well into 1919.

18

Boulton & Paul built Sopwith Snipe E6430 at Mousehold in February 1919.

The Snipe was the best Allied fighter in service at the end of the War, but of the 264 which had been built by the Armistice, none by Boulton & Paul, only 97 had reached the Western Front, and these never really came into direct conflict with the Fokker D VII, to settle the argument about which was the best fighter of any side in the War. The first Boulton & Paul built Snipe was delivered in mid-November 1918, and production continued well into the second half of 1919. Production never quite reached the rate achieved with the Camel, the second week in January 1919 had the best output, when 26 Snipes were produced. There was not the same urgency as a year before.

The Armistice also brought cancellation of three other orders the company had received, for 150 Vickers Vimy bombers and two batches of Martinsyde F.4 Buzzard fighters totalling 500.

The sole P.6 in postwar guise, but still retaining its wartime special serial X 25. It was used as a company transport after its experimental flying.

19

During the War John North had a little two-seat single-bay biplane built for aerodynamic research. Not counting the fact that virtually every pioneering aircraft in the early days was built for aerodynamic research, in that their designers did not know whether they would fly until they tried, the P.6 was one of the first ever built for this purpose. Special permission had to be obtained from the Air Ministry to build the P.6 as it was forbidden to construct any aircraft which did not have an official order.

In 1918 a revolutionary new engine was being produced, the world's first high-powered radial, the ABC Dragonfly, which promised 340 hp from a 600 lb engine, capable of driving a contemporary designed fighter at 156 mph. It had been designed by Granville Bradshaw who had begun his career in aviation in 1910 as designer of the Star Monoplane and its 40 hp engine, for the Star Car Company of Wolverhampton. Going on to found the All British Engine Company, later reduced to simply ABC, he produced the two-cylinder 45 hp Gnat and then the prototype of a six-cylinder two-row radial, the Mosquito.

The immediate predecessor of the Dragonfly was the seven-cylinder Wasp, which gave 170 hp from 11 litres, and powered the BAT Bantam. The Dragonfly followed the general layout of the Wasp, but was enlarged in both bore and stroke, and had nine cylinders, giving it a capacity of 23 litres. Bradshaw claimed it would give 340 hp at much less weight than a water-cooled engine. It represented a significant improvement over the 230 hp Bentley B.R.2 rotary, which was just coming into service, and the Air Ministry ordered it in huge numbers. A dozen different manufacturers received orders for the Dragonfly, many of them, such as Clyno Cars and Guy Motors of Wolverhampton, being introduced to aero-engine production for the first time. The total involved was

A Napier Lion under test at Mousehold. The Lion was fitted to both the third Bourges, F2905, and the P.8 Atlantic. (*The Boulton Paul Society*)

20

8,580, more than the requirement for the B.R.2 or the American Liberty engine, and nearly twice as many as for the Rolls-Royce Eagle!

In 1918 aircraft manufacturers throughout the country were encouraged to produce designs to take advantage of the power of this engine. John North began working on a twin-engined aircraft which would have the speed and manoeuvrability of a contemporary fighter, but the bomb load of a medium bomber, to the official Specification A.2(b). The resulting design which was designated the P.7 Bourges, was regarded by some as the world's first twin-engined fighter/bomber, such was its performance, and was designated thus on the earliest company sketches.

Three prototypes were ordered but problems with the engines prevented any production orders.

Having produced a design which was clearly outstanding, even with the lower power Bentley rotaries fitted while waiting for the Dragonflies, it was Boulton & Paul's ill luck that the War should end at that time, and that the company would have to change direction and outlook completely, reversing the changes of 1914–15.

The Aftermath of the War

The cancellation of so many orders which followed the Armistice, both in the Aircraft Department, and in other areas of Boulton & Paul's business, necessarily led to major changes in the company. There was a financial re-structuring, reserves were capitalised, there was a further issue of ordinary shares, bringing the issued capital up to a total of £281,138 and the Board of

A drawbench at Riverside, part of the extensive metal-working machinery installed by the company in the early 1920s.

Management, looked on by many as too young and inexperienced, survived a vote of no confidence.

With the new site at Riverside easily able to accommodate all the company's departments, it was foolish to leave many of them scattered all over Norwich. The process of transferring them all to the one site was begun, and Rose Lane Works and all the other scattered sites were disposed of. The wire-weaving business struggled to make a profit against severe foreign competition, the structural steel department was still not making a significant contribution, and even the foundry had to search for new products to make, and ended up casting most of the iron frames for pianos made in Great Britain.

The mainstay of the company's business was once again the woodworking department, which developed a large market in commerical glasshouses and in poultry sheds. There was also a bewildering variety of wooden buildings, houses, sports pavilions, church halls, schools, squash courts, and even complete holiday camps. The company's tradition of diversification still held good.

It was decided to persevere with the Aircraft Department, despite the cancellation of all its production contracts. The production of the Felixtowe flying-boat hulls ran on well after the Armistice, and the production of Sopwith Snipes was not terminated until well into the latter half of 1919. The remaining two Bourges prototypes were completed during 1919, and a great deal of experimental work was done on them. F2903 had its Dragonflies fitted to a mid-gap position, whereas the second prototype, F2904, as well as a gulled

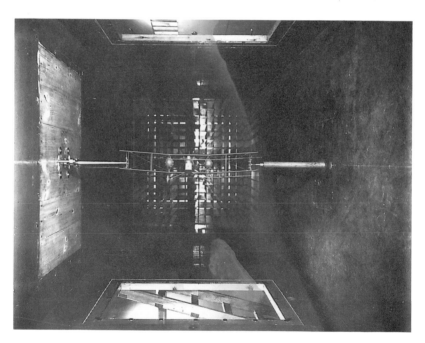

A model of the P.7 Bourges in the Boulton & Paul wind-tunnel.

The P.7 Bourges Mk IIA F2903 in its original form, with the interim Bentley B.R.2 engines. The suffix 'A' denotes the straight-through upper wing.

The second Bourges, the Mark IB F2904 with the ABC Dragonfly engines on the lower wing and the gulled centre section.

centre section also differed in having its Dragonflies mounted on the lower wings.

A planned Mk III version with 290 hp Siddeley Pumas was not built, and the third prototype, F2905, had 450 hp Napier Lions fitted to the lower wings, with the straight upper centre section as on the Mk IA, being thus designated the P.7b. Both versions retained the manoeuvrability of the first prototype, and improved on its performance, the Lions giving it a top speed of 130mph at 10,000 ft, a large increase on the D.H.10 which was in RAF service, having a top speed of only 112½ mph at 10,000ft.

The second P.7 Bourges, after crashing at Mousehold in 1919. The wreckage was used to build the second P.8.

23

With their hopes of British orders foiled by the RAF's decision to retain the D.H.10, Boulton & Paul attempted to sell the Bourges throughout the world, particularly in South America, where they had achieved much export success before the War, but to no avail. There were just too many war-surplus aircraft available at knockdown prices.

Like so many aircraft manufacturers, they hoped that a newly air-minded world would buy civil aircraft in large numbers, and set about designing products to satisfy this hoped-for demand. John North's aim was two-fold, to produce a version of the little P.6 for use as a civil trainer and sporting aircraft, and to produce an airliner based on the Bourges. To publicise the company, something very essential for Boulton & Paul, who had only so far produced five aircraft of their own design and were hardly well-known, they saw the *Daily Mail*'s prize for the first nonstop transatlantic crossing as the ideal vehicle. Many of their competitors were thinking on similar lines.

The first of the two prototypes of the new airliner, the P.8 Atlantic, was therefore built from the outset as a contestant for this prize. The second Bourges prototype, F2904, which had crashed at Mousehold, was actually converted into the first P.8, having basically the same wings, with Napier Lion engines and a new and more commodious fuselage.

Very careful preparations were made for the Atlantic flight but these came to nothing when the P.8 crashed on its first flight. Alcock and Brown achieved success in their Vickers Vimy, and fame and the £10,000 prize eluded Boulton & Paul.

The second P.8 was finally completed as an airliner prototype and test bed but no orders were received for it.

Boulton & Paul had a little more success with their other new product, the

Capt J H Woolner (left), the navigator chosen for the Atlantic flight, and Frank Courtney discussing the flight in April 1919. (*American Heritage Center. University of Wyoming*)

Frank Courtney, and Brown, his engineer, ready to make the first flight of the P.8 Atlantic, in April 1919. (*American Heritage Center. University of Wyoming*)

The P.8 Atlantic after crashing on take off when an engine cut-out, killing all hopes Boulton & Paul had of making the first transatlantic flight.

The first P.9 under construction on 6 May, 1919, against an order from Lieut Long.

P.9, however, even though it too was facing fierce competition from cheap war-surplus aircraft, not least the ubiquitous Avro 504K. The company made their first commercial sale, in 1919, to Lieut A L Long, who ordered a version of the P.6 to take with him to Australia.

The P.9 as it was to become, was slightly larger than the P.6 and in spite of the company's hopes of sales success only eight were built.

One of the eight P.9s built, G-EAPD, was used mostly as a company transport until April 1920 when the registration was cancelled.

If the Bourges was just too late to achieve the success it deserved, the P.9 was just too early. It was a fine little aircraft but after the War there were thousands of surplus aircraft available for very low prices, and no-one had the money or inclination to buy new.

Boulton & Paul was fortunate in that it was a large company with a wide range of products. Its diversification allowed it to survive slumps which destroyed other companies. John North showed his own confidence in the future of his department with an offer he made to the chairman. He wanted the entire Aircraft Department transferred to the buildings at Mousehold, where they could be better organised as a self-contained unit. If this were done he guaranteed to lose no more than £5,000 a year for the next six years. To further reinforce his confidence, North agreed to take only a very small basic pay, to which would be added a percentage of the profits of all designs over the next 14 years. He envisaged the Aircraft Department being a research and development unit, deliberately kept small so as to survive the hard times which had befallen the industry, while maintaining a programme of development which would see the company at the forefront of aviation technology when the upturn came.

They did not stop attempting to secure military orders as new requirements emerged. Specification XXI, issued in May 1919, for a two-seat amphibian which could be operated from land or sea, or from the decks of aircraft carriers, was viewed as a good chance to secure an order. An elaborate mock-up of a Napier Lion powered aircraft was built. It was referred to as the Type XXI on the drawings, and if it was given a P number it could only have been P.11, as the specification which resulted in the P.12 Bodmin was issued the following year. Boulton & Paul's efforts were to no avail as the rival Fairey Pintail was ordered, though only in prototype form.

The following year the P.16 was offered for a requirement for a troop carrier, but it was Vickers and Armstrong Whitworth which received orders for prototypes. Even against this bleak background of few orders John North had already taken the steps which would see the company become pioneers in aircraft construction. The P.9 was not just a milestone in that it was the first

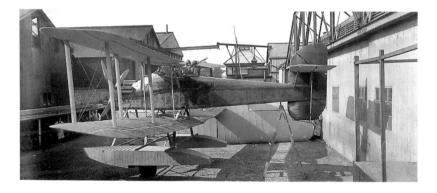

A full-scale mock-up of Boulton & Paul's submission for the RAF Specification Type XXI, for a land and sea reconnaissance aircraft. This was almost certainly designated the P.11.

Boulton & Paul design to achieve production, albeit in limited numbers, it was also the last wooden aircraft they ever built.

The Air Ministry had become very concerned during the War about the shortage of high grade spruce and linen for use in aircraft production, even cypress had been used as a substitute, without very satisfactory results. They were anxious to encourage the exploration of the use of metal in aircraft structures. Metal structures seemed to hold the possibility of greater durability, while retaining or even improving their strength and lightness, when compared to wooden structures. John North was an avid proponent of this theory, and in 1919, encouraged by the Air Ministry's interest, began the design and construction of the first practical all-steel aircraft to be built in this country, the Boulton & Paul P.10.

It was not the first British all-metal aircraft, that honour goes to the Seddon *Mayfly* of 1910, built with 2,000 ft of Accles and Pollock steel tubing, though a number of Howard Wright designs featured metal structural components even before that, but the *Mayfly* never had a hope of flying. It looked more like a piece of modern sculpture than an aeroplane. The P.10 however, was a thoroughly practical two-seat light aeroplane.

The all-metal airframe of the P.10 on display at the Paris Salon d'Aéronautique in 1919. The fuselage panels are Bakelite-Dilecto.

The first postwar air show was held in Paris from 19 December, 1919, to 4 January, 1920. The VIᵉ Exposition Internationale de Locomotion Aérienne, was billed as the greatest ever, which was hardly surprising considering that five years of intensive development of the aeroplane had taken place since the last one. The star of the show, the one aircraft on display which featured any significant advance in aircraft construction, was the P.10.

The entire load bearing structure of the P.10 was of high tensile steel. The Air Ministry would not sanction the use of light alloys, which had been used elsewhere in some aircraft structures, as they were not considered reliable enough at the time. The wings and tail of the P.10 were left uncovered in the Salon, to show off the revolutionary new structure, but the fuselage was largely covered, because it featured a further revolutionary advance in aircraft structures, the use of plastic!

The use of plastics in aircraft structures was put aside, for sixty years or so; the Air Ministry was far too conservative to allow such innovation; but the swinging engine mounting of the P.10 was an innovation which was to feature on Boulton & Paul aircraft for many years.

The Directors had been so disappointed with the venture into civil aircraft construction with the excellent, but unsuccessful P.8 and P.9, and so impressed with North's work on steel structures, they decided the future of Boulton & Paul lay in that area. They scrapped the woodworking plant and re-tooled with metal folding and drawing machinery. A new era was dawning.

Metal Aircraft Construction

Boulton & Paul were soon able to apply their accumulated knowledge in metal aircraft construction in a Government contract for two 'Postal' aircraft to Specification 11/20, emerging as the P.12 Bodmin. The term 'Postal' was used as a public cloak to cover the construction of an experimental aircraft, and did not mean it was intended as a mail carrier. The concept that the contract was to investigate was a multi-engined aircraft with the engines carried within the fuselage, each driving two propellers through extension shafts. One engine drove two tractor propellers, and the other two pusher propellers.

The aim of this layout was to remove asymmetric thrust problems in the event of one engine failing, and to allow the engines to be worked on in flight, within an enclosed 'engine room'. With so much of the fuselage taken up by this engine

The P.12 Bodmin J6910 at Mousehold. The P.9 on the left was the last built, G-EBEQ, which was exported to Switzerland in 1929 where it became CH-259.

room, the layout clearly was not intended for use in a transport aircraft, for carrying mail or passengers, but in a bomber, and drawings of the aircraft show provision for nose and dorsal gun positions. Even the name bestowed on the P.12 shows that it was meant to be a bomber. The Air Ministry had dictated that bombers of less than 11,000 lb gross weight should be named after English inland towns, and Boulton & Paul had been granted the initial letters Bo.

Slowly the company, by a process of experimentation, had become more sophisticated in the construction of metal airframes. A great deal of the credit for this must go to John North's specialist assistant, Harold Pollard. He had been educated at University College, Nottingham, and had previously been with Vickers. He was later to move to the Bristol Aeroplane Company, and had much to do with their conversion to metal structures. The basic problem in the use of steel was that its higher density meant that thinner gauges had to be used than would have been the case with light alloy. A hollow tube bears bending and compression loads better than a solid rod made from the same amount of steel. The greater the diameter of the tube, the higher the load it can bear, but the wall of the tube becomes thinner as diameter increases. There comes a point where compression loads cause the tube to concertina, and only experimention will determine the correct ratio of tube diameter to wall thickness. It was found impossible to get seamless tube in the thin gauges required to a high enough standard, and therefore steel strip was used, which could be obtained to sufficiently high standard.

North still needed to overcome the problems encountered by steel strip being delivered from the makers already hardened and tempered. Because of inconsistences in heat treatment, distortions resulted as the strip passed through the dies or rollers, as it was drawn or rolled to the required section. These had to be straightened, a time-consuming and therefore costly process.

North developed a process of continuous heat treatment of formed sections, which were drawn through electric furnaces at slow speed, and then rapidly cooled for hardening as they passed through water-cooled dies. As the sections were held straight through the heat treatment, they were produced in a very uniform manner.

Before this method was introduced it had been considered impossible to cut high quality alloy steel strip, because to do so created cockling (puckering), bending or tearing of the edge, so that strip could only be rolled at the manufacturer to the required width.

For simplified fuselage construction, a locked joint circular steel tube was developed, to get over the impossibility of obtaining high tensile seamless tube to the required thin gauges. At Boulton & Paul, high quality steel strip was drawn to the required tubular-section with one edge locking round a bead on the other edge, forming a perfectly uniform seam, and therefore enabling fittings to be attached with ease. The tube also left the drawbench perfectly straight. This process allowed tubes of stainless steel to be drawn, not otherwise possible, and thinner sections to result, giving considerable weight saving.

A neat fitting was achieved by a magnesium alloy pad, with flat machined sides, fitting over the end of the longeron, through which bolts could be passed horizontally and vertically. The strut ends were attached to the bolt heads and the bracing wires to wiring plates.

Further experimentation had to be done to produce a corrosion-resistant finish to the steel structure. Shorts were the other British pioneers of metal construction, and had done experimental work that showed duralumin had better anti-corrosive qualities than untreated mild steel, but steel had to be used for the time being. Painting resulted in an unacceptable weight penalty, and required careful use and continuous maintenance. Forty-five different treatments were investigated, and tested for resistance to heat, bending, hot oil, acid and alkaline solutions and even immersion in sea water for six months. Boulton & Paul eventually patented a process of protecting fabricated steel strip from corrosion. It involved coating it with a layer of zinc and then painting with an organic compound.

The first application of this new locked-joint steel tube system was in the P.12 Bodmin. The Air Ministry were convinced by North's arguments that steel could result in a structure up to 10 per cent less weight than an equivalent wooden aircraft, and was better suited to Britain's climate, as well as more easily available than spruce, which was becoming difficult to obtain in the best grades. They even suggested the Postal biplane be constructed with a corrugated metal skin, in the manner of the Junkers aircraft being produced in Germany, but fabric was much lighter.

In building the Bodmin, North learned a great deal about creating a metal girder structure. Every spar, rib, strut and longeron was created in the extensive new metal workshop from high-tensile sheet steel, which was rolled, drawn or stamped to the required section. Everything was joined by solid rivets, and the whole structure involved an enormous amount of detailed work, but North assessed that it finally resulted in a structure 20 per cent lighter than it would have been if made of wood. This was twice the saving he had first estimated, but because of the engine layout of the Bodmin, much of this saving was lost.

Two prototypes were built, the first flying in early 1924. The concept they had been ordered to investigate was not considered worth pursuing, the fuselage 'engine room', involved inherent weight penalties, because of the heavy shafts and gears to transmit power to the propellers. However, building the Bodmin did enable Boulton & Paul to put into practice the steel construction techniques they had evolved. The Bodmin was soon followed with another opportunity to perfect the system.

The all-steel airframe of the P.15 Bolton J6584 the first all-metal aircraft ever delivered to the Royal Air Force.

31

The Air Ministry placed an order for a single prototype of what was in effect a metal version of the Bourges. The P.15 Bolton which resulted, had the same general layout as the Bourges, but featured an all-steel airframe, built of the new Boulton & Paul locked joint system. The system was considered so important at the time that the Air Ministry kept details of it secret.

The solitary Bolton prototype was the first aircraft with an all-metal airframe to be supplied to the RAF, and the Air Ministry was largely convinced that the steel structure of the sort incorporated was essential both because of British conditions and because of its availability. Continuing cash shortages meant no orders beyond the single prototype were forthcoming. The aircraft industry was surviving on what has been described as 'hospital' contracts, the Air Ministry keeping each company ticking over with orders for prototypes, and a few small production batches, so that they were not only able to keep advancing their techniques at the forefront of aviation technology, but were actually able to stay in business, until such time as they would be needed.

These 'hospital' contracts were augmented by spreading the rebuilding and reconditioning of RAF aircraft around all the manufacturers. This was a considerable business, the RAF managed to get through several hundred aircraft each year, one way or the other, and so there was a steady stream of machines to be rebuilt, mostly Bristol Fighters and D.H.9As. Some of these came from RAF stocks, damaged aircraft and those held in store, but many were bought from the Aircraft Disposal Company and needed to be reconditioned. The ADC had obtained 10,000 war-surplus aircraft and was selling them at competitive rates. With the connivance of the AID and Air Ministry inspectors these aircraft were stripped to the last nut and bolt, and absolutely every part was replaced, if the slightest excuse could be found, with the result that virtually new aircraft resulted. In fact many of them may have been better than when they first emerged from an aircraft factory, built under the exigences of war.

The Bolton as completed, in 1922, showing the three crew positions.

The first P.25 Bugle, J6984, in 1923, awaiting roll-out at Mousehold. The man atop the port ladder is Bill Monument who later became a foreman at Wolverhampton, one of many staff to make the move from Norwich in 1936. (*G A Monument*)

Boulton & Paul remained in profit every year except for 1921, when the inevitable slump which followed the postwar boom led to job losses and a cut in salaries and wages of ten per cent. The Aircraft Department was not making any contribution as yet, but the Directors still believed that one day the continued basic research and development would yield results.

In 1922 the first prototypes of a continued development of the Bourges/Bolton theme, the P.25 Bugle, were ordered. Two initial prototypes were built to Specification 30/22, the first flying in June 1923. They followed the general Bourges/Bolton layout, being three-seat, twin-engined medium bombers, powered by 400 hp Bristol Jupiter engines. By now the Air Ministry had relaxed its attitude towards light alloy construction, and allowed minor structural components to be incorporated. Thus, though the Bugle's inner interplane struts were of steel construction, the outer ones were of duralumin.

The following year a third prototype was built, featuring a number of differences to the first two. Jupiter IV engines were used, and it was completed as a four seater. This aircraft was the first Boulton & Paul design to serve with a front-line RAF squadron, when it was used by No.58 Squadron for trials during 1925.

Two further Bugle Is were ordered in January 1924 and then in 1925 two prototypes of the improved Bugle II were built. The Bugle II had Napier Lion engines instead of the Jupiters, and streamlining was improved by transferring the fuel tanks from under the upper wings where they had been located on the Bugle I, and fitting fairings to the bomb carriers.

The second Bugle, J6985, at Mousehold in 1924, one of seven Bugles built.

The Bugle, like the Bourges and Bolton before it, was an outstanding medium bomber for its day. Like the Bourges it had the manoeuvrability of a fighter, and could be looped, spun and rolled, and yet could carry a bomb load approaching that of the RAF's heavy bombers. It was just Boulton & Paul's bad luck, that the type of aircraft they had become specialists in, the high-speed twin-engined medium bomber, was the type in which the RAF had no interest. Most of the major air forces operated twin-engined medium bombers, but Hugh Trenchard's penchant for heavy night bombers, a penchant which became a basic doctrine of the Royal Air Force, meant none of its limited resources were available for medium bombers.

In 1925 Boulton & Paul were in a parlous state, as in fact was most of the industry, with only 400 orders that year to be split between the seventeen approved manufacturers. In fact the Air Ministry was suggesting some of the smaller firms such as Blackburn, de Havilland, Supermarine and Westland should amalgamate either with one another or with one of the bigger firms, Hawker, Bristol or Vickers, and those companies with relatively large orders, including Fairey, Bristol, Gloster and Vickers were urged to spread some of the work amongst their less fortunate competitors. Four companies were even urged to leave the aircraft business altogether, English Electric, Parnall, Saunders, and Boulton & Paul, but only English Electric did so.

Guy ffiske wrote to the Air Ministry complaining that the Boulton & Paul Aircraft Division had been forced to shut down for three months, and would need a year to reach full production again, the workforce being reduced to only 150. Though shutting down was just what they had been urging, his complaint struck a chord in some quarters in the Ministry, anxious not to lose the design capabilities of even one manufacturer, and perhaps knowing that Boulton & Paul's specific expertise in metal aircraft structures was about to be needed. Therefore the contract for the two Bugle IIs was placed to keep the company going.

This trickle of orders for prototypes did allow Boulton & Paul to improve their medium bombers at every stage, and to perfect their locked-joint steel construction system. By now the company was able to produce a catalogue of standard steel sections. Box wing-spars for instance were made in three web-section forms and six flange-section forms, giving eighteen basic spar shapes, each of which could be made in various thicknesses, to give up to 2,000 different spars. Further standardisation was achieved in struts, longerons and other structural members, though the company did begin to use light alloy for some minor components such as ribs, leading and trailing edges, and some lightly loaded struts.

John North hoped to sell his system to other manufacturers, many of whom were hopelessly wedded to wooden construction for a long time, because wood was cheap and it was quick to build prototypes. In the event many of them preferred to invent their own cheaper systems, and only Blackburn and Saunders-Roe took up Boulton & Paul methods. Royalties were sometimes forthcoming for the many patents which the company acquired. For instance Hawker used Boulton & Paul methods for their early steel spars.

An unusual task taken on by the company in 1924 was to redesign a Sunbeam racing car for Malcolm Campbell, for an attack on the World Land Speed Record. The car concerned was fitted with a Sunbeam Manitou 350 hp twin OHC V-12 18 litre engine, and had been successfully raced since 1920 by Sunbeam and then by Campbell himself. Boulton & Paul undertook wind-tunnel tests which resulted in a narrower cowl and a longer tail, together with a general cleaning up of the fairings.

Although Campbell repainted the car blue, it was not named *Bluebird* as were his subsequent cars, and was always referred to as The 350 hp Sunbeam. On its first outing, on Pendine Sands, in September 1924, it broke the World Land Speed Record at 146.16 mph, and on 21 July, 1926, raised it again to 150.86 mph. The car is now in the National Motor Museum at Beaulieu, and a cast aluminium model of the car, made by Boulton & Paul, and presented to Campbell, was auctioned at Christie's in 1983 for over £1,000. While no production contracts were yet forthcoming the company continued with basic research, using their wind tunnel and experimental facilities. They were interested in reducing the interference drag inherent in twin-engined designs of the day, and in producing more streamlined forms. The P.27 project was a twin-Lion powered development of the Bugle, which did not achieve a contract, but this led directly to the P.29 Sidestrand which became the first Boulton & Paul design to go into full production.

Model of Malcolm Campbell's record-breaking Sunbeam car. On 21 July, 1926, Campbell broke the World Land Speed Record in this car on Pendine Sands, at 150.86 mph. (*Mrs L North*)

R101, G-FAAW, at the mooring mast at Cardington.

The R101

By 1925, John North was acknowledged to be the leading authority in Britain on metal aircraft structures, and Boulton & Paul the most advanced manufacturers. This expertise led to them being given the contract for the detail design and construction of the structure of what was to become the largest airship in the world, the R101.

All British airship development had been halted by a Cabinet decision at the end of July 1920. Plans to use existing airships to operate a commercial service to India had been rejected on the grounds of cost, and no immediate need was seen for them in military circles.

At the time the R38 was under construction at Cardington. Begun by Short Bros, R38 was finished as the first project of a newly nationalised industry. The excellent Cardington facility, which included a small town for the workforce, had been built by Shorts in 1917, as the base for their extensive airship work. In April 1919 the Liberal Government had nationalised it with a compulsory purchase order. The compensation paid was £40,000, which Shorts believed was far less than its true worth. Cardington became the Royal Airship Works, and R38 was sold to the United States Navy for £500,000.

On its first flight in US Navy colours, renamed ZR-2, it broke a girder, and finally on 23 August, 1921, it crashed into the Humber, killing some of their country's best airshipmen, as well as a number of US Navy personnel. It had been powered by six 350 hp Sunbeam Cossack engines, and many of the casualties were caused by burning petrol on the surface of the sea.

Despite this crash, and the many others involving rigid airships, there were still ardent protaganists, prepared to argue the merits of the airship. The superior load carrying capability, and range, compared with aeroplanes, was not disputed, and airship enthusiasts made out a strong case for the improved safety features which could be built into modern civil airships. It was argued that the need to fly at high altitude to avoid anti-aircraft fire during warfare had produced airships with structures which were far lighter than they should be. The use of petrol engines, with their better power/weight ratio, was no longer necessary, as diesel engines could be developed, which would be far safer for airship use; with no ignition systems, and heavy fuel oil which was far less volatile than petrol. The heavier weight of compression ignition engines was partially compensated for by their lower fuel consumption.

On 27 March, 1922, Commander Charles Dennistoun Burney, a Conservative MP retained by Vickers as a consultant, put forward a proposal for an Imperial Airship Service to be run on behalf of the Government by a newly-formed subsidiary of Vickers. The new company would take over all existing airships, for experimental work, and the bases at Pulham and Cardington, and would then build six new 5,000,000 cu ft capacity airships, just over twice the capacity of R38, the biggest British airship built to date. He estimated rather optimistically that these ships would be capable of carrying a disposable load of 82 tons, which would include up to 200 passengers and 10 tons of mail, at 80 mph over a range of 3,000 miles. He estimated that on the England–India route an airship service using these larger airships would return revenue of nearly a £1,000,000 a year above costs.

Burney addressed his letter to the Admiralty, with what he thought would be the trump card, suggesting that these ships could be used in the Navy in time of war, the passenger/cargo capacity turned over to extra fuel. In this form they would be capable of flying up to 24,000 miles, or three weeks without refuelling.

Burney's scheme was deemed too expensive by the Treasury, and the Air Ministry raised further objections, as they wished to use Cardington as an RAF base. Nevertheless, on 17 July, 1922, the Government set up a special sub-committee to look into Burney's scheme, and the whole question of rigid airships for civil and military use.

Amazingly, when the committee reported, on 1 August, they accepted Burney's proposal almost in its entirety. However, the report was not acted on before the General Election on 15 November which brought the Conservatives to power under Bonar Law. As is the way with politics, the new Air Minister, Sir Samuel Hoare, set up another committee to study the problem. This was a sub-committee of the first committee to study operational aspects of the proposed service, while the first committee, which was itself a sub-committee of the National and Imperial Defence Committee, studied the finances.

Just as amazingly, Commander Burney was a member of this new committee as an 'independent advocate'. Significantly another member was Brig-Gen Christopher Birdwood Thomson, who was to become the man most associated with the R101.

On 10 July, 1923, this committee also virtually accepted the Burney scheme as first advocated. The Government would contract a new subsidiary of Vickers to build and operate six new large airships on a twice weekly service to India. The Government would pay an annual subsidy of £250,000, and all existing airships would be handed over. The airship stations at Pulham and Cardington would be leased to the new company.

Negotiations began between Vickers and the Treasury, and on 20 November, 1923, the Airship Guarantee Company Ltd was formed, the instrument designated to operate the Imperial Airship Service. The General Election on 6 December brought a halt to the proceedings, and when Ramsay MacDonald's

Labour Government came to power on 22 January, 1924, everything changed once again.

Thomson had stood for the Labour party in the election but had failed to get elected. He was held in such high esteem by Ramsay MacDonald however, and was seen as such a prize asset to the Party that he was offered the post of Secretary of State for Air. In order to become a Cabinet member it was necessary to make him a Peer, so that he could take a seat in the Lords. To show exactly where his thoughts lay, he took the title Lord Thomson of Cardington.

After much discussion and argument on 7 May he was ready to present his revised programme for the future development of British airships. Two new 5,000,000 cu ft airships would be built, one by the Royal Airship Works at Cardington, and one by the private Airship Guarantee Company, now headed by Sir Dennistoun Burney. Expenditure would be £1,400,000 over the next three years to cover the cost of building the airships, new bases in Egypt and

The complete structure of R101, facing towards the nose.

India, and initial test flights. The airships would be completed in 1927, and the experience gained would be used in the construction of further airships.

The programme was approved by Parliament and on 1 July, 1924, Cardington was reactivated for the construction of the Government 'ship, which was designated R101. On 22 October a contract was signed with the Airship Guarantee Company for the construction of R100 for the total fixed sum of £350,000, the chief designer being Barnes Wallis. The following month the Labour Government fell, but the most advanced airship programme in the world had been set in motion.

From the outset R101 was designed with two main guiding principles. It was to be the most advanced airship ever built, with construction only starting after an extensive programme of research and development, and full-scale practical experiments, for which R33 was made available. In this respect R101 was always an experimental ship, whereas R100 was always envisaged as a more pragmatic design, using tried and tested technology wherever possible. The second principle inherent in R101's design, was to be safety. In fact that was the foremost principle, the main criteria against which all details of the design would be tested.

Early in 1925 it was decided that Boulton & Paul would be sub-contracted to complete the detailed design and to build the structure. This was an almost inevitable decision, with Vickers building the other ship, and Shorts unlikely to be interested in helping the Government to build an airship in their former works, a facility for whose loss they considered they had not been justly compensated. Boulton & Paul were the only other company in the country with extensive experience in building metal aircraft structures. John North was appointed as consultant to the Director of Airship Development, with the princely remuneration of £262 a year plus expenses.

The experimental work, which continued into 1925 had determined that R101 would have a streamlined, fat cigar shape, of continuous curvature, rather than the long thin form of earlier ships such as R33. The length to diameter ratio for R101 was 5.5:1, whereas for earlier ships it had been about 10:1. This would lead to far less drag, and therefore less power to achieve the required cruising speed. It also meant that a much larger volume airship could be built within the dimensions of the shed at Cardington.

To achieve as near a circular cross-section as reasonable, the airship would actually take the shape of a thirty sided polygon, increasing to thirty-six sides near the tail to facilitate the fitting of the four tail fins. This shape led to an airship 732 ft long, with a maximum diameter of 132 ft, enclosing a total volume of 5.755 million cu ft, including accommodation and air spaces. To create the thirty sided polygon shape, the structure was to consist of fifteen longitudinal girders around fifteen ring-shaped transverse frames. A further fifteen reefing booms, or intermediate girders, created the necessary thirty sides.

It was estimated that this hull shape would require about 2,000 hp to achieve the design cruising speed of 63 mph, and that therefore at least 4,000 hp should be installed to give a safety margin of 50 per cent on installed engine power. Mainly because of the horrific deaths caused by the petrol fires in the R38, it was decided at an early stage that only compression ignition engines would be considered.

Unfortunately no British manufacturer had yet produced a suitable diesel aircraft engine, and so it was decided to fit the 84 litre 700 hp Beardmore Tornado, eight-cylinder inline which had originally been developed for railcars. Although this engine could be lightened to a certain extent it still weighed 4,700 lb, which was far more than the early calculations had allowed for, and so it was decided to only install five engines instead of the seven originally envisaged, giving just 3,500 hp.

The procedure which was agreed with Boulton & Paul was that Cardington would inform the company of the general arrangement of each structural component and the stresses it was required to sustain. The company's drawing office then designed the component, and when the drawings had been approved, the girder, or whatever piece of the structure it was, would be manufactured, under AID inspection, and delivered to Cardington for assembly.

A large proportion of the structure was to be of high-tensile steel strip, rolled into tubular form in Boulton & Paul's patented locked joint system. Duralumin was used for bracing pieces, but the wire bracing, and gas-bag support wiring

One of the 70 ft long special twisted longitudinal girders for R101 in its assembly jig.

was also of steel. The structure required 27 miles of steel tubing in total, plus 11 miles of bracing wires. The decision to use steel strip, instead of light alloys like duralumin, which was normal airship practice, was largely because of the design input of John North, and the tried and tested experience of the company in its use. It was estimated that the use of steel strip for 65 percent of R101's structure saved 3 tons in structural weight, because steel had a higher specific strength than any light alloy in the thicknesses they were able to specify.

The transverse ring frames were triangular in shape, able to absorb all relevant stresses without bracing pieces. The challenge Boulton & Paul successfully overcame was to produce these triangular girders, up to 45 ft in length, some with both curvature and twist, to a finer tolerance than ever contemplated in an airship structure, plus or minus 0.03 in. A new bolted joint was designed to replace the traditional riveted plates, so that when the parts were delivered to Cardington, they could be just bolted together on simple trestles, and then lifted into place. This greatly reduced the amount of work which had to be accomplished high above the ground. So successful were they at achieving the fine tolerances required that no structural component was returned to Norwich because it would not fit, a remarkable performance considering that there was nearly fifty tons of the main structure.

The Boulton & Paul mathematician to whom the complicated three dimensional geometry of the structure was entrusted was A H Adkins. His task was made more difficult because of the shape of R101. Every transverse ring frame was of different diameter, so that they all had to be separately designed, unlike previous airships of regular cross section, whose transverse frames could be virtually mass produced.

The triangular shape of the girders was also useful in that it provided a handy place within them to install fuel and ballast tanks, and other equipment. The intermediate reefing girders were fitted to telescopic kingposts and screw jacks, so they could push out the fabric outer cover to the required taut cross-section. The rival R100 had a simpler and more conventional way of keeping the outer cover taut, by pulling it in with wires.

The four cantilever tail fins were triangular in shape, and fitted to frames 14 and 15. They had been designed after extensive wind-tunnel research, and the rudders and elevators were fitted with specially designed servos operated by hydraulics driven by a small electric motor. Revealingly Barnes Wallis saw no need to install servos on R100.

Rather extravagantly a complete bay of the structure was ordered from Boulton & Paul solely for test purposes. This money-no-object approach was to be a feature of R101's construction. The first components of this bay were delivered to Cardington in April 1926. First one transverse ring was assembled and tested in both horizontal and vertical positions, with varying loads. Then the complete bay was assembled and loaded to its design limits. When it had proved capable of sustaining the required load, the appropriate gas bag of 500,000 cu ft, was installed, as well as ballast bags, all relevant equipment, and then the outer cover was fitted. Further tests were made, all successfully, and then in December the bay was dismantled, and each component tested to destruction.

This testing revealed that the structure was not just probably the strongest of any airship yet built, but was really too strong. In view of the weight problems which R101 was to run into, hindsight revealed that the safety-first dictums of

The test bay of the R101, complete with its gas-bag, which was eventually tested to destruction.

the Cardington team had worked against themselves. In erring on the side of safety in the strength of the structure they found themselves having to trim weight elsewhere.

In January 1927 manufacture of the components of the actual airship was able to begin. By the end of the year the first ring frame had been delivered from Norwich, bolted together and lifted into place, and by July 1928 frames 4 to 11 were fully assembled at Cardington. By now Boulton & Paul had completed all the detail drawings and they had all been approved by the Royal Airship Works.

By the end of 1928 the bow structure, forward of frame 4 had been delivered and joined up, and much of the outer cover had already been fitted. In March 1929 Boulton & Paul delivered the last of the structure, and the assembly and fitting of the fins began. The basic structure of the ship was complete in June 1929 and the installation of the engines and the final fitting out went ahead.

In June 1929 the Labour Government of Ramsay MacDonald came back to power, and Lord Thomson returned as Secretary of State for Air. Within ten days of taking office he was on the train to Cardington, to see the results of the scheme he had set in motion five years before. He was to find serious problems with R101, and even the enthusiasm of the Royal Airship Works staff could not hide them.

Almost every aircraft ever built exceeds its designer's estimate of empty weight. In the case of airships, this is even more critical than in heavier-than-air machines. Every pound of excess weight means a pound less disposable load. Even the dust lying within such a huge structure can make a significant difference. By June 1929 it was discovered that R101 was in serious trouble because it was 15 tons over the original estimate of 90 tons. This meant that it only had a disposable load of 47 tons, instead of 63 tons, and would only be able to carry 24 passengers and one ton of mail over the route to India with a single stop in Egypt. This was seriously below the original specification. The main structure contributed 5.05 tons to this increase, but 5 tons of this was entirely due to the extra reefing girders not having been included in the original proposal.

There were other serious problems with the ship. It had been intended to use new steel reversible-pitch propellers, for use in mooring, but they had not been able to stand up to the vibration produced by the Tornado engines, and so two-blade wooden fixed-pitch propellers had to be fitted. For mooring one engine had to have a reverse-pitch propeller, so this engine could not be used in normal forward flight, a dead weight of 4,733 lb, which in itself was twice the original estimate for each engine. This also meant that there were now only four engines available for forward flight, and because of the problems with vibration they were experiencing they were having to be run at reduced rpm, giving only 450 hp for cruising.

Worse was to come. When the gas bags were fully filled and the ship brought to equilibrium floating within the shed on 30 September, it was found that the gross weight was 3.3 tons higher than had been estimated, 23.4 tons more than the original design estimate. It was clear that weight reductions would have to be found together with extra lift if possible, if R101 was to be able to operate to India with a reasonable load.

A comprehensive examination of possible weight saving measures, replacing the Triplex windows with Plexiglass, removing twelve sleeping cabins, two lavatories, and two water ballast tanks, and cutting weight in other areas, seemed to indicate that about 2½ tons might be clawed back. If the gas bag restraining wires were let out, they might hold up to another 100,000 cu ft of hydrogen, generating another 3 tons of lift; though some way would have to be found to stop the bags rubbing on the structure. Already the safety first doctrine was being compromised at every turn.

On 12 October, 1929, R101 was walked from the shed for the first time, and secured to the mooring mast. Two days later she made her first flight, a 5 hr 40 min journey to the centre of London and back. On the second flight on 18 October Lord Thomson was aboard, and waxed lyrical to the Press on his return. Everyone who had seen R101's superb passenger accommodation, and had seen her in the air, all agreed what a marvellous flying machine she was. Only the experts knew the truth. She was in deep trouble, weight had to be saved, and more lift secured; maybe even two more mooring masts would have to be built, at Malta and Basra, to enable her to refuel three times on the route to India.

Five more flights were made up to 18 November, and though they were seen with huge enthusiasm by the general populace, they only confirmed the pessimistic indications of the staff at Cardington. On the third flight, on 1 November, R101 flew over East Anglia, and over the Boulton & Paul Works so that the work-force there could admire their handiwork.

There were further problems experienced, including trouble with the engines' steam-cooling system, and an alarming, and continuous leakage of gas, over and above that lost during venting, when climbing, but it was the lack of sufficient disposable load which was putting a large question mark over the entire programme. As things stood, R101 would only be able to lift enough fuel at Karachi, given the local conditions, for 24 hours flying time; and that was with a reduced crew. Even the weight saving programme, and letting out the gas bag restraining wires would not be enough.

By now R100 had completed her lift and trim trials at Howden, and was found to weigh just over 8 tons less than R101 in prepared-for-service form, including crew. Their empty weights, less engines, were almost identical, however, despite the far more lavish passenger accommodation on R101. This seemed to vindicate the highly innovative structural design, for which John North bore a considerable measure of credit. The fact that it had proved to be built too strong, also augured well for the future, the next Cardington airship could be built with a substantially lighter structure.

The weight troubles R101 was experiencing could be laid entirely at the door of the powerplants. The five Tornado diesels in R101 weighed 17.96 tons, whereas six Rolls-Royce Condor petrol engines on R100 only weighed 10.19 tons. There could be no prospect of changing to petrol engines on R101, that was the most fundamental safety dictum in the design. The only answer seemed to be fitting an extra bay.

On 18 December it was announced that an extra bay of 500,000 cu ft capacity would be installed in R101, giving an extra 15.5 tons of lift for only 5 tons installed weight. Boulton & Paul were given the contract to construct the longitudinal girders, but the frame girders would be made in the workshops at Cardington. In addition the restraining wires on the existing bags would be let out to provide another 130,000 cu ft of capacity. Various weight saving measures would also be implemented, including removing the servo motors on the rudders and elevators as they had proved to be entirely unnecessary. By March a way had been found to obviate the need to haul around an engine which was only available for reverse thrust. A simple modification enabled the Tornado to run backwards. With fixed-pitch wooden propellers now fitted on all five engines, enough thrust was available from just one propeller running backwards for mooring purposes.

While waiting for Boulton & Paul and the Cardington workshops to complete the construction and delivery of the new bay, the other modifications were made to R101, including letting out the gas bag restraining wires. Further test flights were made, and the airship flew over the RAF Air Display at Hendon on successive days. These flights revealed further problems. Gas was leaking to an even more alarming degree and it was found that the gas bags were rubbing on the structure and were being holed. In addition severe problems were being experienced with the outer cover, rips were becoming frequent, and much of it was found to be rotten.

A section of R101 under construction at Cardington.

It was discovered that it was not just the holes in the gas bags which were leaking. The Royal Airship Works had decided to design their own side valves for the ship, rather than purchase the normal top valves from Germany, as the pragmatic team at Howden had done for the R100. These valves were designed to remain closed at anything up to a roll of three degrees, but it was discovered that R101 rolled much more than this, and so the valves were continuously leaking.

Even before the gas bag restraining wires were let out it had been discovered when the bags were removed and examined in November 1929, that many holes had appeared, as many as 103 in one bag. Up to 4,000 pieces of padding had been applied to all projecting pieces of the structure, but this was clearly not working well.

The latest test flights over Hendon had produced data which indicated that, because of the gas leakage experienced, R101 would be forced to make a forced landing after only 23 hours at cruising speed. Something drastic had to be done. Lord Thomson wished to fly to India and back during the Commonwealth Conference in the first week in October, and as it stood R101 was not just incapable of making the trip, it was not even airworthy.

Even with the new bay fitted, the extra lift provided by letting out the gas bag restraining wires was still needed. The gas bags would have to be replaced and repaired where appropriate, and reinforced in places most susceptible to damage. New padding would have to be applied, which was both thicker and less likely to slip, as the gas bags rubbed against it, and much if not all of the outer cover would have to be replaced.

After the Hendon flights R101 had been moved into the shed with its stern only 3 ft from the end, so that only the forward part need be moved when the ship was parted at frame 8. This was achieved on 29 July, and by 7 August Boulton & Paul had delivered all the parts for which they were contracted. The new frame (8A), constructed at Cardington, was lifted into place on 14 August and on the 25th the structural work in fitting the new bay was complete. The R101 was now 777 ft long, the largest British airship ever built.

Work continued on fitting the new padding and outer cover. The pressure was still being applied to fly to India in the first week in October, and this would leave time for only one long test flight, but everyone was confident that the schedule could be met.

At 6.30 a.m. on 1 October R101 was removed from its shed and moored to the mast. In the late afternoon she slipped her moorings and flew south for a test flight which was to last 16 hr 51 min. Everything went perfectly, except that the oil cooler in one of the engines failed, so that a full-speed trial with all five engines at maximum revolutions could not be made, to test the outer cover.

The flight to India would start on 4 October with 42 crew and 12 passengers including Lord Thomson. Capt Dawson Paul of Boulton & Paul had tried hard to get a place on the flight, but there was no room. It was to prove one of the luckiest failures he ever experienced.

The first stage of the journey was 2,235 nautical miles to Egypt, which it was hoped to accomplish in 48 hours. The second stage was 2,125 nautical miles, to Karachi, which it was hoped to accomplish in 46 hours. The airship had never been tested in the conditions it was to experience, the heat, and the humidity, it had never been tested at full speed, and its suspect outer cover had never even been tested in conditions other than clear skies with no turbulence. A Certificate of Airworthiness was issued over the head of the Inspector on the spot, and with a verbal assurance that the full-speed trial would be held on the flight to India. If anything was not entirely satisfactory, assurance was given, that R101 would be turned round and flown home.

It was a sign that everyone's confidence and pride in the project had welled up so much, they had washed away all thoughts of caution. It was felt that the new modifications that had been applied would solve all the problems that had dogged the ship.

By 6.20 p.m. on 4 October, 1930, all passengers and crew were aboard R101 and all five engines were running. Sixteen minutes later the airship was free of her mooring and a cheer went up from the watching crowd. The ship slowly slid backwards, and then with the engines at half power slowly turned and climbed away into the gathering darkness, bound for Egypt.

Lord Thomson, and the Labour Government, who had initiated the scheme, had a great deal of political kudos riding on its success, and being socialists it was essential that the Government ship would prove superior to the private-enterprise R100, which had already flown to Canada and back, and was itself having a new bay fitted in the shed which R101 had just vacated. The staff at the Royal Airship Works were convinced that R101 was the finest flying machine ever built, it was certainly the biggest. Many of them had spent six years bringing this moment to fruition, and they all felt that the troubles of R101 were beind her, she was an experimental ship, much had been learned, and things augured well for the future. The next generation of airships were already being planned, the R102 and R103.

R101, showing the streamlined continuously varying cross-section.

Boulton & Paul also had their future hopes riding with R101. It had been an immense job, and had been completed in exemplary fashion. Of all the problems associated with R101, none of any significance had been concerned with the structure. The company had high expectations that a great deal more airship work, over many years would be coming their way.

Studies had begun in the spring of 1929 to decide the size and configuration of the next two airships to be built for the Imperial routes. Data collected from the flights of R100 and R101 caused the ideas of the design department, which consulted extensively with John North, to change several times. In the end it came down to a choice between a 9,500,000 cu ft airship which would achieve all that R101 had originally been intended to, and a more conservative 7,500,000 cu ft design, which would be able to operate the route to India refuelling at two new mooring masts in Malta and Basra.

In the end the vast extra cost of the larger ships, not least in needing to build a much larger shed at Cardington, mitigated against them, and it was decided that R102 and R103 would be of 7,500,000 cu ft capacity. They would be built at Cardington, once more in association with Boulton & Paul, but disappointingly for the company, far less of the work would be sub-contracted to them.

The R101 contract had been worth £202,500 to Boulton & Paul, made up as follows: design £7,000, direct labour £45,000, materials £47,000, overheads £53,000, jigs and tools £13,000, plant and equipment £4,500, delivery £1,000, ex-gratia payment £14,000, profit £18,000. Total £202,500.

The value of the work on the next two airships which was likely to come their way was possibly to be considerably less, but they were bigger ships, and there were to be two of them, and in hard times any work was very welcome. In addition the R104 class of airship was already being pencilled in for construction after the R102 and R103 were in service by 1935. This would be the very large 9,500,000 cu ft class of airship.

All these hopes and plans were to come to nothing of course. In the early hours of 5 October, 1930, R101 crashed at Allone near Beauvais, and shortly afterwards the British airship programme was cancelled, and R100 was broken up in her shed. Of all the factors which led to the crash, none could be laid at the door of Boulton & Paul, it was just their bad luck that they were associated with such a tragic project, a project marred by governmental interference, and over-optimistic and muddled planning by the protaganists of the airship.

The crash was most likely caused by a failure of the outer cover in the nose section of the ship. R101 had suffered very bad weather as it crossed France at low altitude, strong headwinds and turbulence, and also heavy rain which added tons of weight. The suspect cover, which had not been renewed in the nose section, almost certainly failed, causing the gas bags in the immediate area to deflate. When the airship went into a dive, it was the natural reaction of the crew to throttle back the engines, but this caused all dynamic control to be lost, and at low speed the elevators became ineffective, sealing the fate of R101. When it hit the ground calcium flares stored in the control cabin ignited and the airship was burnt out. Of those on board only eight managed to get clear of the burning wreck, but two of these died later of their injuries. Lord Thomson was one of those who died in the crash.

Lying within the storeroom of Boulton & Paul Joinery in the Riverside Works at Norwich is one small girder from the wreck, presented to them after the inquiry, one solitary item from a programme in which the company and country had placed such great store. Many other pieces of the wreck were taken by souvenir hunters, one small piece somehow coming into the possession of my own grandmother in Wolverhampton. A souvenir of the end of a different age.

The P.29 Sidestrand

In 1925 prospects had looked very bleak for Boulton & Paul. They were surviving on only a trickle of prototype orders, justifying John North's plan to maintain the Aircraft Department as a research and development unit, small in size, high in innovation, until such time as the slump conditions changed. Of course they submitted designs for Air Ministry requirements other than their forte, the twin-engined medium bomber, without success however. For instance, the P.17 was a fleet spotter in two versions, the P.20 was a Puma-powered Corps reconnaissance aircraft with an all-steel frame and the P.28 was a single-engined day bomber powered by a Typhoon engine to Specification O/23, but no contracts were forthcoming.

Then in late 1925 they received the contract for the frame of R101, and at the same time were building the prototype of what was to become their first production military aircraft, the P.29 Sidestrand. The protracted development of the medium bomber on which they had expended so much effort, from the Bourges, through the Bolton, Bugle and P.27, now finally paid off.

Specification 9/24 called for a medium bomber powered by two Napier Lion engines. John North chose to install the Jupiter VIa of 450 hp instead, on what was to become the P.29 Sidestrand. The Sidestrand retained the square-cut wings and tail surfaces which had become something of a trademark of Boulton & Paul but was blessed with a streamlined fuselage, with curved upper and lower sections of very pleasing lines.

The prototype Sidestrand, J7938, at Mousehold in 1926.

The extensive investigations into the aerodynamic properties of various combinations of wing, fuselage and engine nacelle, to minimise interference drag were applied to the Sidestrand and led to an aircraft of outstanding performance, which still retained the impressive manoeuvrability of its predecessors.

The first prototype, J7938, flew in 1926, in the hands of Boulton & Paul's new chief test pilot, Sqn Ldr C A Rea AFC. John North had decided it was time that the company had a full-time test pilot on the books, rather than using freelance pilots such as Frank Courtney. Courtney had already been replaced at Armstrong Whitworth by a full-time test pilot, Alan Campbell-Orde, and shortly afterwards left Great Britain for what he saw as greener pastures on the other side of the Atlantic.

Guy ffiske had asked the CO of the MAEE Felixtowe, Grp Capt Maycock, if he knew of a suitable candidate to replace Courtney. Rea was coming to the end of his RAF service, and was a pilot and aeronautical engineer of considerable experience, an ideal company test pilot, also able to put the RAF viewpoint on design matters. He joined the company in July 1926, and the Sidestrand was his first task. The second prototype, J7939, flew later in the year. This aircraft flew with aerodynamic modifications found necessary after flight tests of J7938, then with more powerful Jupiter engines.

Both prototypes went to Martlesham Heath, and for a while, J7939 was operated by No.15 Squadron, the 'shadow' bomber squadron at the A & AEE. An order was placed with Boulton & Paul for eighteen Sidestrands, enough to equip one squadron, which was to be No.101, with reserves.

The prototype J7939 was re-engined with Jupiter XFBs fitted with Townend rings, an invention for which Boulton & Paul had obtained the exploitation rights. In this form it was known as the Mark IIIS, and the changes boosted its performance considerably. Its top speed was 167 mph at 11,000 ft, up from 140 mph for the normal production version, and its ceiling was 30,000 ft rather than 24,000 ft.

The radial engine favoured because of its reliability, suffered from being of larger diameter than the liquid-cooled inline and was hard to streamline. In 1929

49

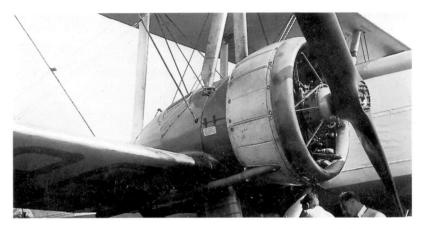

The starboard engine cowling/Townend ring of Sidestrand III J9186.

Dr H C H Townend of the National Physical Laboratory, developed and patented a means of successfully enclosing radial engines, within a close-fitting ring, without impairing the cooling airflow. This system proved a simple means of reducing the drag and increasing the speed of radial-engined aircraft.

It consisted basically of a narrow chord aerofoil-section ring around the engine, either circular or, later on, in a polygon shape corresponding to the number of cylinders. The ring created a 'slot' effect, smoothing out the airflow around the cylinder heads, and thereby reducing the drag. It was found, on the Sidestrand, that fitting Townend rings reduced the drag of the engines by two thirds.

John North quickly appreciated the potentialities of the invention and made an arrangement with the Department of Scientific and Industrial Research for Boulton & Paul to undertake the administration and commerical exploitation of this invention. Numerous forms of the ring were to be evolved, many

A production Sidestrand III, J9186. This was later converted to an Overstrand.

incorporating an exhaust collector, and they saw widespread use. Boulton & Paul issued licences on the basis of a moderate royalty at a flat rate per horse power of the engine fitted. They preferred to issue licences to aero-engine manufacturers, as standard size rings could then be evolved. Licences to build them were taken by a number of major aircraft and aero-engine manufacturers including Pratt & Whitney in the United States. It may have been this which spurred the American National Advisory Committee for Aeronautics to initiate research which led to the development of the long-chord fully-enclosed ring.

Boulton & Paul attempted to seek further orders for the Sidestrand beyond the eighteen ordered for the RAF, but at the time of the worldwide recession no export orders were forthcoming. The basic design was highly streamlined and fitted with a biplane tail unit as the P.57 project for the Irish Free State, but no order resulted. The design was then re-worked with geared Jaguar engines as a photographic aircraft in landplane or seaplane form, for the Royal Canadian Air Force (P.60), again to no avail. The basic wing design of the Sidestrand Mk IIIS with Jupiter XFB engines was offered with a new streamlined fuselage as a mail carrier (P.61), and then a cross between this project and the Sidestrand was offered as a bomber/torpedo carrier (P.62), with a civil transport version (P.62A), powered by either Jupiter XF or Panther engines.

All these attempts to exploit the moderate success of the Sidestrand, excellent aircraft though it was, came to nothing. The only development of the basic design which led to further production orders sprang from the difficulties the 101 Squadron crews experienced in operating such a high-performance aircraft as the Sidestrand. The days of the open cockpit military bomber, with gunners fighting the slipstream to aim their Scarff ring-mounted Lewis guns were drawing to a close, and Boulton & Paul's answer was the P.75 Overstrand, the world's first bomber with a fully-enclosed powered gun turret; but the large gap between the project numbers of these two aircraft P.29 – P.75, indicates that the design department had not been idle in the interim.

Unsuccessful Projects

There was an echo of the past in the first Boulton & Paul design to be built after the P.29 Sidestrand. While at Austin Motors, during the First World War, John North had met Albert Ball, who had developed the technique of attacking aircraft from underneath, pulling the Lewis gun on the upper wing of his

The P.31 Bittern prototype, J7936, with centrally mounted Lynx engines, cantilever outer wings, and twin fixed Vickers guns.

Nieuport down on its Foster rail, so that he could fire upwards into the belly of his (often unsuspecting) victim. The Austin A.F.B.1 Ball Scout had resulted, though it seems never to have been fitted with the upward-firing guns which Albert Ball wanted.

In 1927 Boulton & Paul built the P.31 Bittern, an extraordinarily advanced looking fighter with upward-firing guns, to Specification 27/24. This was one of many official specifications issued between the wars for a so-called 'bomber destroyer'. With the prevailing doctrine of the Royal Air Force being that 'the bomber would always get through', it was inevitable that the Air Ministry would grapple with the problem of how to stop enemy bombers doing just that. The intermittent official specifications which resulted almost always called for large, often unusually armed, fighters, capable of breaking up formations of the sort of large low-performance night bombers which the RAF wielded itself, such as the Vickers Virginia. As it was never envisaged that these creations would ever need to take on enemy fighters, or even high-speed day-bombers, the prototypes which resulted were almost always slow and relatively unmanoeuvrable, and the Bittern was no exception.

It was a twin-engined monoplane, of which two prototypes were built, the second differing significantly in its armament layout to the first, which was conventionally equipped with twin fixed forward-firing Vickers guns. The second aircraft had twin Lewis guns installed in barbettes on each side of the nose which could be tilted upwards to fire into the underside of its intended victim. With two Armstrong Siddeley Lynx engines of only 230 hp, the Bittern was seriously underpowered, with a top speed of only 145 mph, increased by 7 mph when Townend rings were fitted. The Bittern would hardly have been able

The second P.31 Bittern prototype, J7937, with underslung engines encased in Townend rings, outer wing struts and Lewis gun barbettes. (*The Francis K Mason collection*)

Wind-tunnel model of the P.67 interceptor, designed to Specification F.7/30.

to catch its own stablemate, the Sidestrand, though of course it was perfectly able to take-on a Virginia!

Not surprisingly the Bittern was not ordered into production, though the concept of the single-seat twin-engined monoplane fighter was at least ten years ahead of its time. Nevertheless John North did resurrect the layout in 1931 to fit Specification F.7/30. This called for a day/night fighter armed with four Vickers machine-guns, and preferably powered by the steam-cooled Rolls-Royce Goshawk engine.

The P.67 was submitted to meet the specification, but North chose to use two Napier Rapier engines in a low-wing monoplane. Whereas the wing of the Bittern had been shoulder-mounted, and strut-braced, the P.67 had a wire-braced wing of 40 ft span. Many aircraft manufacturers submitted designs to F.7/30, but orders were delayed by problems with the Goshawk, which most of them tried to use. These problems were never resolved satisfactorily, and in the end the requirement was filled, almost accidentally, by the Gloster Gladiator.

That there was official interest in an upward-firing armament layout was illustrated with the issue of the official Specification F.29/27. This called for another 'bomber-destroyer' armed with a Coventry Ordnance Works cannon (COW gun), firing upwards at an oblique angle. The 37 mm COW gun was 8 ft long and fired a shell weighing 1½ lb, at the slow rate of 100 per minute, with a recoil of about 2,000 lb.

Boulton & Paul's submission for F.29/27, the P.35, was a low-wing monoplane powered by a supercharged Rolls-Royce F.IIS engine. The monoplane layout was considered best to give clearance for installation of the COW gun, which was to be loaded in flight by the pilot! The company had already sketched a different layout, however, a design which did not receive a project number, but which just predated the P.35.

This F.29/27 was a compact two-seat biplane powered by a Bristol Jupiter VII engine. The pilot's cockpit was immediately in front of the unstaggered wings, and the COW gun was located behind the wings, firing obliquely upward, with a gunner to load it. It is likely that this layout was discarded in favour of the final P.35 submission. Two prototypes were ordered for F.29/27, a monoplane from

The sole P.33 Partridge prototype, J8459.

Westland similar in concept to the P.35, but with a radial engine, and an extraordinary pusher biplane from Vickers.

A more conventional Boulton & Paul fighter did reach the prototype stage in 1928, the P.33 Partridge. It was submitted to Specification F.9/26 which called for a replacement for the Armstrong Whitworth Siskin and Gloster Gamecock fighters. It faced stiff competition, including most notably the superb Hawker Hawfinch and Bristol Bulldog, and was one of nine prototypes ordered from various manufacturers.

The Partridge used the same construction as the Sidestrand including many of the same components, and the company hoped the economies of standardisation would be a big selling factor. It featured the same design philosophy as the Sidestrand as well, square-cut wings wedded to a highly streamlined fuselage. Unfortunately the position adopted initially for the twin Vickers machine-guns was deemed by the Air Ministry to be too low, and then too high in the second proposal, so that bulges had to be fitted to the fuselage sides to accommodate them, reducing performance.

First flight was in 1928, and the Partridge appeared in the New Types Park at Hendon that year, before going on to Martlesham Heath for flight trials against the other F.9/26 contenders. It had certain shortcomings, and in view of the fact that the Hawfinch and Bulldog were both deemed outstanding designs from the outset, had no chance of securing the production order, which eventually went to the Bulldog.

What was basically the same design, but with the new project number P.34, was also submitted for Naval Specification N.21/26 for a radial-engined fleet fighter to replace the Fairey Flycatcher. Other N.21/26 submissions were the Fairey Flycatcher II (Which had more in common with the Firefly I than the Flycatcher I), the Hawker Hoopoe, the Gloster Gnatsnapper and the Vickers 123/141. None of the contenders for this requirement received production orders, as the appearance of the Hawker Nimrod, conclusively proved the superiority of its inline Kestel engine, and overcame naval prejudices.

A design with a project number before that of the Partridge, but with a longer gestation period, was the P.32 heavy bomber. It was built to Air Ministry Specification B.22/27, which called for a three-engined heavy night bomber. In competition with the very similar de Havilland D.H.72, the P.32 did not arrive at Martlesham Heath until 1931, delayed by prevarication in the choice of engines.

The sole P.32 heavy bomber, J9950. (*The Boulton Paul Society*)

Again Boulton & Paul hoped that standardisation of construction techniques and components with the Sidestrand would weigh heavily in their favour. De Havillands were such novices in metal construction that the D.H.72 was completed by Gloster Aircraft. In the event no orders for this class of bomber were forthcoming. The RAF preferred the lighter Handley Page Heyford which had emanated from a different Specification, B.19/27.

It must have seemed to John North and his design staff that they were stuck with being deemed medium bomber specialists, just the type of aircraft in which the RAF was not interested. Whenever they tried to compete in other areas, as with the Partridge fighter and the P.32 heavy bomber, they found themselves up against experts in those fields, companies such as Bristol and Hawker with long experience of producing superlative fighters, or Handley Page, acknowledged experts in heavy bomber production.

With completion of both Sidestrand production, and the R101 airship contract, Boulton & Paul were not well equipped to deal with the terrible world slump which followed the financial crash of 1929. Their lack of production contracts was not for want of trying. In the years 1929 to 1931 they completed nearly forty design projects, some of which have already been mentioned, and received not one order!

They ranged from a monoplane flying-boat with six Rolls-Royce F.XI Kestrel engines (P.39), to a little four-seater, similar in design to the de Havilland Leopard Moth (P.44). There were derivatives of earlier designs, such as the P.36, a 14-seat airliner based on the P.32 heavy bomber, and the Sidestrand-based projects mentioned earlier. Perhaps the most striking series of projects incorporated design features which had obviously resulted from extensive wind-tunnel experimentation. This series of designs, which were all given the name 'Streamline', began with the P.37, a high-speed sesquiplane day bomber.

It was to be powered by two Rolls-Royce F.XIS engines mounted on an upper wing which was carried on a large pylon over the fuselage, rather like the Catalina, but in the case of the P.37 to cut down on interference drag, rather than to carry the engines clear of the sea. The lower wing was much smaller and of very narrow chord. The fuselage was extremely well streamlined, with a large, all-round vision canopy for two crew members seated in tandem. The most amazing feature of the design was that it had a retractable skid undercarriage!

The same layout was used for the P.47 high-speed mail-carrier, using two Rolls-Royce F engines, and then again in the much smaller P.49 racing aircraft, powered by two Gipsy engines and with the pilot's seat behind the wing rather than in front as in the other projects. The P.56 was another Streamline mail-carrier with the same basic layout but powered by two Armstrong Siddeley Panther engines. This unusual design concept was finally applied to the P.63 high-performance interceptor fighter with two Napier Rapiers, and contemporary with the P.67 F.7/30 project already described.

A project for which the company had high hopes was the P.58 Fleet Spotter. This was designed to Specification S.9/30 which called for a three-seat fleet spotter, with optional wheels or floats. The P.58 was an equal-span biplane powered by a supercharged Panther radial engine, or an inline Rolls-Royce F12 in alternative P.58A form. The company went to the extent of offering a more radical alternative airframe, the P.58B. This bore the hallmark of the P.37

The P.41 Phoenix G-AAIT in its original all-wooden form with ABC Scorpion engine. The Sidestrand behind is J7938. (*The A J Jackson collection*)

project in that it was a sesquiplane with a narrow-chord cranked lower wing. In the wheeled version it was to be fitted with large spats, and it was offered with either engine. The only prototypes emanating from S.9/30 were the Gloster FS.36 and the Fairey submission, which was unusual in its floatplane form in having only a single pontoon float with stabilising wing floats. No production contracts were forthcoming, because Fairey produced a private venture aircraft, the TSR.1 which fulfilled the specification, and was also able to operate as a carrier-based torpedo bomber. Official interest in this led to a further development, the TSR.2 which became the Fairey Swordfish.

The only completed aircraft to emerge from Boulton & Paul in all this period was the P.41 Phoenix. Once more, this was an echo of earlier times. It was intended as a flying test-bed, as the P.6 had been, but with the intention of offering it for sale as a two-seat light aircraft if the concept proved successful, as with the P.9.

It was a strut-braced, parasol-wing monoplane powered by a 40 hp ABC Scorpion, and designed by Capt William Higley Sayers. Capt Sayers had been a designer of naval aircraft at Grain during the War, including the Grain Kitten, powered by a 40 hp ABC engine, and then became Technical Editor of *The Aeroplane*. He had designed a glider, in co-operation with Frank Courtney, in 19 hours for the 1922 *Daily Mail* gliding competition, and it was built by the Central Aircraft Co in 19 days. For the famous 1923 ultra-light aircraft competition he designed a monoplane powered by an ABC Scorpion for Handley Page, but it showed a marked reluctance to leave the ground, and Handley Page began a total redesign.

Sayers left *The Aeroplane* late in 1928 and joined Boulton & Paul as assistant engineer to John North. That he should immediately become involved with designing a light aeroplane powered by a small ABC engine is not surprising, given his previous history, but it is not clear whether the P.41 was started because he had joined the staff, or because the company wanted to build a light

The rebuilt Phoenix with Salmson engine, and oleo undercarriage legs. (*The Boulton Paul Society*)

aeroplane of that type, and therefore engaged Sayers.

The P.41 Phoenix was originally of wooden construction, to test the aerodynamic layout, and proved to have delightful flying characteristics, though it was rather underpowered for a two-seater.

It was exhibited at the 1929 Olympia Show, and offered for sale at only £375. Subsequently it was entirely rebuilt with a new method of steel construction. The frame was spot-welded throughout rather than riveted, and this proved a thoroughly effective, and much cheaper process. It was re-engined with a 40 hp Salmson nine-cylinder radial, and the undercarriage was changed, but when it re-emerged, despite the extensive alterations, it retained its registration, G-AAIT.

In an effort to keep down costs for the private owner, the rudder was interchangeable with each of the elevators. With an all-up weight of 1,089 lb it was still rather underpowered, the de Havilland Moth had already proven the optimum size for a popular light aeroplane, and the lack of sales interest, resulted in it not being put into production. Sqn Ldr Rea used the Phoenix for his personal runabout, replacing the earlier P.9.

The success of the spot-welding process was a valuable result, however. The same technique was used in Blackburn's metal-framed re-design of the Bluebird light aircraft, the Bluebird IV, and then again in the B.2 trainer, with which they were attempting to compete head-to-head with the Moth range. Boulton & Paul manufactured the Bluebird wings under sub-contract to Saunders-Roe, who built 55 Bluebird IVs at Cowes.

When Boulton & Paul exhibited at the 1930 Paris Air Show they displayed a Bluebird wing, without covering, to highlight the new process. They also showed a Bristol Jupiter engine fitted with a polygon Townend ring, and a number of their own spar sections and other structural members.

Boulton & Paul built a strong relationship with Blackburn, which was to last for many years. The Blackburn Ripon of 1933 had many components manufactured by Boulton & Paul, and Sqn Ldr Rea undertook flight trials of various modifications at Mousehold. Being an experienced flying-boat pilot, Rea was also loaned to Blackburn for the early flights of several of their flying-boats, including the Iris and the Sydney. Subsequently Boulton & Paul supplied their tubular steel wing spars for the Blackburn Shark. The company's ties with Saunders-Roe were also strong, and they were to supply the wing structure for the Saro London flying-boat.

In a further attempt to exploit Boulton & Paul's expertise in metal construction, John North sought to co-operate with Armstrong Whitworth and Gloster in the formation of the Metal Construction Pool, to pool each company's patents. An agreement was signed on 29 May, 1931, by John North, S W Hiscocks for Armstrong Whitworth and Hugh Burroughes for Gloster. The resulting company was jointly owned, and took the name Aircraft Technical Services Co, with offices in London. The three parent companies were free to use one another's patents, and the royalties from the substantial number of patents involved, many of which were complimentary, were collected for the benefit of each parent company.

The emerging depression left the other parts of the company in dire straits as well, even the structural steelwork department, which had finally emerged through the twenties as a major cornerstone of the business. Old Dawson Paul had finally retired in 1928, after serving the company for 75 years, since his days in the ironmongery shop in Cockey Lane. Capt Dawson Paul, then in his forties had taken over, with a Board of Directors consisting of William and Geoffrey ffiske, Stanley Howes, and now John North, (Guy ffiske having died on 3 July, 1930, after an operation, aged 41).

After the Crash of 1929 the company recorded losses for three consecutive years, despite considerable cost cutting in all departments. Salaries and wages were cut by ten percent, and any overtime work found to be necessary was unpaid. The only consolation was that relatively few employees were made redundant. During these trying years, both Henry ffiske, and old Dawson Paul died, the latter aged 91.

In 1932 Dawson Paul realised that more drastic measures were needed if the company were to prosper again. Small unprofitable departments, such as the Foundry were closed down, and the business was reorganised into four distinct profit centres, Structural Steel, Woodworking, Wire Weaving and Aircraft, and the last was the weakest of these.

The plethora of civil projects which had been advanced over the previous few years finally resulted in an order for a prototype of a high-speed mail carrier for Imperial Airways. Specification 21/28 had called for a mail carrier capable of carrying 1,000 lb of mail at 150 mph over a stage of 1,000 miles. This performance was to be sustained at half engine power, so that level flight could be maintained should one engine fail.

Boulton & Paul's submission was the P.64, a very clean looking biplane powered by two Bristol Pegasus IM.2 555 hp geared radials mounted on the upper wings. The aircraft featured the same locked-joint steel construction of the medium bombers, with fabric covering throughout, apart from the nose section, which was ply covered for a smooth finish, and the tailplane which was metal covered. The square cut of the wings was a Boulton & Paul hallmark, but the tailplane was of more rounded shape. The mainwheels were contained within large streamlined spats, and the tailwheel was recessed within a fairing.

The two crew were accommodated in a fully-enclosed cockpit just forward of the wings, behind a windscreen which formed a step in the smooth lines of the fuselage. There was a large compartment behind the pilots' cockpit for a radio

The sole P.64 Mail-Carrier, G-ABYK, just before completion at Mousehold. The Sidestrand behind is J9189. (*G A Monument*)

operator or navigator, with the mail hold aft of that.

The first flight of the P.64, G-ABYK, was on 27 March, 1933, at tea-time, so that all the employees could watch. The flight of a new Boulton & Paul prototype was a rare occurrence at that time, and the entire workforce must have hoped that it presaged the start of better times. They might have expected that not only would a large order for the P.64 for Imperial mail routes be shortly forthcoming, but that Boulton & Paul would finally break into the civil airline market, with other designs following: but it was not to be.

Sqn Ldr Rea undertook that first flight with Dawson Paul in the co-pilot's seat. The first flight was entirely successful, but when Rea began the take-off run for another flight a pronounced swing to starboard developed. He closed the throttles and applied the brakes, which proved to be totally ineffective. He could not stop before G-ABYK collided with a fence which surrounded a cricket

The P.64 in revised form with extra rudders.

59

pitch on the aerodrome. Rea must have had mixed feelings about sporting obstacles at Mousehold, having hit a hockey goal-post with the prototype Sidestrand. The mainwheels flattened the wire fence, which then sprang up again, flipping the tail of the aircraft up and the valuable prototype ended up on its back.

This unfortunate beginning was a portent of worse to come. G-ABYK was repaired, and two small fins were added to the tailplane to combat the rudder ineffectiveness which had proved to be the cause of the crash. On 15 June, 1933, G-ABYK was demonstrated to the Press at Mousehold, and the company expounded on their high hopes for the P.64. It was pointed out that it could carry its full load to any country in Europe, except Greece and Turkey, without refuelling, could reach Nigeria in 24 hours, Cape Town in 48 hours and Australia in less than a week.

When it was delivered to Martlesham Heath for testing it was found to have the remarkable top speed for a biplane transport of 185 mph, putting to shame many contemporary fighters. All the high hopes of the company were to come to nothing. On the third flight at Martlesham, on 21 October, 1933, while being flown by Flt Lt G L G Richmond, the P.64 went out of control at a height of 1,200 ft and crashed. Richmond survived with minor injuries, but the aircraft was written off.

No more prototypes were ordered and no production order was forthcoming from Imperial Airways for any dedicated mail-carrier. Whether this crash had any bearing on the decision is doubtful, it seems to have been just a change of policy, and Boulton & Paul were the unfortunate victims.

A development of the mail carrier, the P.65, was offered to AB Aerotransport (Swedish Air Lines) without success, and elements of the design were incorporated in the P.69 bomber/transport to Specification C.26/31. Three prototypes were ordered for this specification, the Armstrong Whitworth A.W.23, the Handley Page H.P.51 and the Bristol Bombay which secured the order. The H.P.51, adapted as a bomber became the Harrow. The P.70 was also based loosely on the P.64, a bomber project to Specification B.9/32, from which the Hampden and Wellington emerged. Finally a straightforward passenger transport version of the P.64, the P.71, was developed into a new airliner for Imperial Airways feeder routes and charter work, the P.71A. This secured Boulton & Paul's first and only order for a civil airliner.

The P.71A Feederliner

Boulton & Paul had made a number of attempts to enter the civil airliner market, beginning with the P.8 Atlantic. They had adapted the P.32 heavy bomber design into a 14-seat three-engined airliner, and on a totally different scale, in October 1929 drew up a design for a four-seat saloon powered by three Hermes engines, the P.43. The following month they offered Imperial Airways slightly larger twin-engined five-seat saloons, the P.45, with alternative Jupiter XIF, Jaguar VI or Lion V engines, and the P.46 with geared Lynx engines.

In February 1930 they offered Imperial Airways the P.48, a four-engined airliner of H.P.42 size, with Jupiter XIF or Jaguar VI engines, and almost as a desperate show of the versatility of the design department, the following month

P.71A feederliner, G-ACOX, before delivery to Imperial Airways.

offered a single-engined six-seat monoplane, with an Armstrong Siddeley Panther geared engine, the P.51.

In May 1930 they again offered Imperial Airways a five-seat saloon, this time a twin-engined biplane, with a biplane tail unit, and Panther engines, the P.54. Later in the year the design department, now almost working on a different project every month, produced the P.59, a three-engined transport with alternative geared Jaguar or Panther M.S. engines.

All this intense activity was to no avail, all these designs remained paper projects. It was desperately hard for a relatively small company such as Boulton & Paul to compete with much larger concerns who were considered experts in producing civil transports, and were well known in airline circles. It must have been a tremendous relief when the order for the P.64 prototype was forthcoming. The production department was surviving on continuing Sidestrand work, and sub-contract orders; to actually cut metal on one of their own designs once more must have seemed long overdue.

When the P.64 did not receive the orders which might have been expected it was an obvious decision to adapt it into a civil airliner, as the P.71. When, in

The second P.71A, G-ACOY. (*The Boulton Paul Society*)

61

May 1933, Imperial Airways notified Boulton & Paul that they required a 6/7-seat high-speed feederliner, the P.71 must have seemed the perfect off-the-shelf basis for a submission.

The aircraft which emerged was similar in general appearance to the P.64 but had a slightly slimmer and longer fuselage. Imperial Airways' requirements were certainly met, and the P.71A had the remarkable top speed, for a biplane airliner, of 195 mph, and yet the take-off run at full load was only 200 yards.

Two P.71As were ordered by Imperial Airways, and both flew in 1934, there being no prototype as such. These were the only P.71As built, the last Boulton & Paul civil aircraft ever to fly, which must have been a grave disappointment to the company. It was perhaps an indication of the unfortunate nature of the decision to offer a biplane to fit Imperial Airways needs rather than a monoplane, that the two Avro 652s ordered at the same time were followed by a grand total of 11,020 Ansons of all Marks.

The Sale of the Aircraft Division

In 1934 there was a major reorganisation of Boulton & Paul Ltd. Hard times still beset the company, and a further loss of £1,854 on a turnover of £468,000 was recorded. It was decided that of the four divisions, the Aircraft Department was the weakest. Apart from sub-contract work for Saunders-Roe and Blackburn, the Aircraft Division was involved in a major re-design of the Sidestrand, including the development of the first power-operated fully-enclosed gun turrets, but it was felt by the Board to be a drain on resources.

Certainly it had never achieved the success other companies had managed, building a total of only 54 aircraft of its own design. This was not an indictment of its management or design staff, a degree of misfortune had simply dogged its efforts. The superlative nature of the Bourges had naturally led to it being considered an expert in the construction of twin-engined high-speed medium bombers, just the category of aircraft the RAF felt it could manage without. Efforts to break out of this mould met with failure because of the fierce competition from larger concerns desperate to win the sparse orders which were forthcoming. The P.9 was a light aircraft which compared well in performance with the de Havilland Moth, an aircraft of similar dimensions and capabilities, but the P.9 was ahead of its time, the Moth arrived just at the right moment. The construction of the R101 was an epic feat, but it was a contract which led nowhere. The demise of the British airship programme, through no fault of Boulton & Paul, left the company nursing its disappointments. It might be that the failure of the P.64 to win a production contract, and the relative failure of the Sidestrand (Compared to heavy bomber orders) were the last straws. Accordingly arrangements were made to sell off the Aircraft Division in its entirety.

The aircraft department was sold to a London financial group, Electric and General Industries Trust Ltd, and a new public company was formed entitled Boulton Paul Aircraft Ltd, with an issue of a million five shilling shares. As from 30 June, 1934, the aircraft business and assets were operated by this new company. Lord Gorell CBE, MC, MA, was chairman, John North and Sam Hiscocks, who had joined the company from Armstrong Whitworth, were joint managing directors, and Viscount Sandon was also a director. The new company continued its work as before, but in premises which were now rented from its former parent.

Changes were made to the old company as well, now reduced to three divisions, steel structures, woodworking and wire netting. New comers arrived on the Board, including C W Hayward, who had assisted with the sale of the Aircraft Division, and J H Tresfon, who became managing director, and eventually became chairman. In 1935 Dawson Paul relinquished the chairmanship, and was to retire finally in 1948, though not before he had become involved in another aircraft company. In 1937 he became a director of British Marine Aircraft Ltd, as part of a package to save the company from extinction. British Marine Aircraft held a licence for Sikorsky flying-boats and built a large factory at Hamble. The unit was later to become Folland Aircraft Ltd.

The new company, Boulton Paul Aircraft Ltd, was already deeply involved in a technological breakthrough which was to form the basis of its prosperity until the present day, the development of the power-operated gun turret, which was to naturally lead in time to the development of power-operated controls, and today's fly-by-wire systems.

On 13 August, 1932, the Air Ministry had asked Boulton & Paul to investigate means of shielding the front gunner of the Sidestrand from the effects of the slipstream. Fraser-Nash received the same request with regard to the rear gunner of the Hawker Demon two-seat fighter. The high speeds being achieved by modern fighters, and the Boulton & Paul Sidestrand, made it very difficult for gunners to aim their Scarff ring-mounted Lewis guns, exposed as they were. Bristol Aircraft had achieved a partial solution with their Type 120. Basically the Type 118 general purpose aircraft, it included a cupola on a light framework enclosing the gunner and his Scarff ring, being turned manually with the gun.

This was not a solution which would work on the Sidestrand. Not only were nose gunners attempting to track attacking fighters while their Lewis guns were being buffeted by the 140 mph slipstream, but frozen fingers could not securely grip magazines to reload, and a number had slipped from gunners' grasps and damaged propellers. Boulton & Paul were already considering the problem, but after two more months of investigation decided that it was not possible to design an adequate windshield for the nose gunner, and asked the Ministry for more detailed requirements.

An Air Ministry official, named Eaton Griffiths visited Norwich to discuss the problem and subsequently, on 28 December, 1932, the Ministry wrote to Boulton & Paul stating that the gunner's field of fire was not to be restricted in any way, but that protection from the slipstream was to be provided in any firing position, while not interfering with the bomb-aimer's position. It was anticipated that this would mean providing some form of totally enclosed cabin of universal movement, under the control of the gunner. This would require the complete redesign of the nose of the Sidestrand, a process which led to the P.75 Overstrand.

The P.75 Overstrand

An initial contract for the new turret (199464/32) included the conversion of a Sidestrand to test whatever design emerged, including the fitting of Pegasus IM3 engines. The problems of designing the new turret were to provide space not only for the gunner and his Lewis gun, but also spare magazines, the bomb-aiming equipment, the gunner's oxygen and heating supply and the intercom. Yet the structure had to fit the relatively narrow fuselage of the Sidestrand, while providing the gunner a safe and swift means of egress in an emergency. The design staff feared for the flying qualities of the aircraft with such a bulky structure added, and it is a tribute to their work that the Overstrand did not suffer greatly in comparison with its forebear.

Once the principle of a fully-enclosed power-operated turret had been decided upon, the design proceeded swiftly under the control of H A 'Pop' Hughes, head of the Armaments Section, and a mock-up was ready for approval by June 1933. It was also submitted as part of Boulton & Paul's P.70 project to Specification B.9/32, which eventually produced the Hampden and Wellington. The P.70 was a cross between the P.64 and the Sidestrand, with both the new power-operated nose turret and a retractable power-operated dorsal turret. This Specification was a forward-looking one, and it is not surprising that the biplane P.70 was rejected in favour of far more advanced monoplanes.

The turret consisted of a glazed cylinder with hemispherical top and bottom. Power was supplied by compressed air, for simplicity of design. A geared

 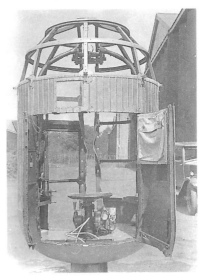

Front view of the Overstrand turret with the Lewis gun stowed at the top, the zip-fastener closed and the bomb-aiming window open.

Rear view of the Overstrand turret showing the entry door.

64

spindle at the turret base was driven by air supplied from storage bottles at 120 lb/sq in. These bottles were recharged by a small compressor attached to one of the engines, and their capacity was good for twenty revolutions of the turret. Speed of revolution was 12/min, which was fast enough to track any target.

The gun barrel protruded through a vertical slot in the turret, which on the prototype was kept closed by fabric and a zip-fastener which opened and closed as the gun was raised and lowered. The turret traversed automatically as the gunner kept his sights on a target. The turret could revolve through 360 degrees, provided the gun was elevated to 70 degrees when pointed to the rear. To save a trainee gunner's blushes, if the turret was revolved with the gun lower than this the gun barrel would not hit the fuselage, because the pressure would then be taken off the plunger valve, the turret merely stopped without damaging anything.

So that the gunner could maintain his sight line along the gun as he raised and lowered the barrel, the gun mounting was connected hydraulically to the gunner's seat, which raised or lowered in unison. This had the added effect of keeping the gunner and the gun mounting balanced. An emergency exit was provided by a quick release lever which removed a number of pins, enabling the entire roof of the turret to fall away.

The Sidestrand used by the company as a test bed, J9186, was converted to take the turret, and Pegasus engines, closely cowled with Townend rings. The comfort of the rest of the crew was not ignored. The rear gunner was protected by a very large windshield behind his back, and the pilot's cockpit was fitted with a fully enclosed, sliding canopy. All crew members benefited from a heating system, drawing heat from one of the engine exhausts.

The outer wings were given a marked degree of sweepback to compensate for the extra weight of the turret in the nose, and the airframe and undercarriage were strengthened to allow for an increased gross weight, and bomb load.

The first flight of the revised aircraft was in 1933 with Sqn Ldr Rea as pilot. One of the technical staff occupied the rear cockpit as an observer. A few moments after the heating system was switched on he seized the rudder cables and yanked them to attract Rea's attention. Dense smoke was pouring from the wing inner sections, and the observer frantically waved his arms and indicated an urgent desire for an immediate landing! It was discovered that the new varnish on the fabric heating ducts was the cause of the smoke.

It was found later, that during construction of the aircraft and during maintenance, care had to be taken not to leave any nuts and bolts or other debris in the heating ducts, or else the next person to switch on the heating system was likely to be hit with a dose of 'Grapeshot' as the parts were blasted out!

While taxi-ing after a subsequent test flight one wheel of J9186, dropped into a hole on the aerodrome, causing the turret support to dig into the ground, and one propeller to be smashed. The occupant of the turret was one of the armament section technical staff, and he was distinctly alarmed. Unsure of what danger he was in, he panicked, and forgot how to operate the emergency release gear. He made desperate signals for the ground staff, who had rushed over, to release him. They were aware that he was in no danger, and were highly amused by the sight of one of the technicians who had helped design the turret, unable to operate it, and trapped in it like a goldfish in a bowl. All he had to do to get out

The turret installed in, J9186, a converted Sidestrand III, which thus became the prototype Overstrand.

was to pull out three pins and push off the whole top of the turret.

The Air Ministry were greatly interested in the new turret, and a party came down to inspect it. One of their members was given the opportunity to try it out himself, after suitable instruction. The air bottles were fully charged, so there was no need to start the engines. The official began to train the gun in various directions while his colleagues watched. He elevated the gun to over 70 degrees and pressed hard to one side, so that the turret began revolving at full speed. Alarmed by the motion he braced himself against the gun, so continuing his revolutions. His colleagues watched his change of expression, and change of colour, with a good deal of amusement, each time he revolved. The turret continued to revolve until the air bottles were exhausted, and the very sickly looking official was helped from the turret.

On 22 February, 1934, J9186 flew to Bircham Newton for trials with No.101

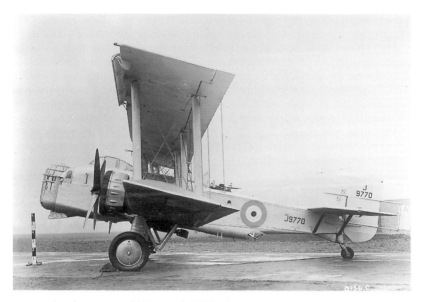

Another converted Sidestrand, J9770, with Handley Page slots extended.

Five Overstrands of No.101 Squadron.

Squadron. The crews there greatly appreciated the new creature comforts of the aircraft, but it was criticised for the cramped nature of the turret, and other minor considerations. Production turrets were therefore built with a slightly larger diameter, which meant widening the forward fuselage of the aircraft.

Such were the changes to the aircraft that, in March 1934, it was given a new name, Overstrand, after another village near Cromer. The Air Ministry ordered the conversion of three more Sidestrands to Overstrands, but powered by Pegasus IIM3 engines of increased power. Finally orders were placed for 24 new Overstrands, which were to re-equip No.101 Squadron, with allowance made for 50 percent wastage. This unit remained for the time being the sole medium bomber squadron in the RAF, and the first Overstrand was delivered in January 1935.

A version of the Overstrand was offered for coastal reconnaissance duties, redesignated P.77, but this requirement was largely fulfilled by the Anson. A substantial further development of the Overstrand was proposed by the company, the P.80 Superstrand. This was to be equipped with Pegasus IV engines and a retractable undercarriage. There was a different nose turret, more reminiscent of the retractable turret offered on the P.70, with only the upper section glazed, and the rear gunner was given a folding transparent hood faired in with the pilot's cockpit canopy. A top speed of 191 mph at 15,000 ft was claimed, with an increased bombload of 1,598 lb. The age of the biplane was rapidly coming to an end however, the new monoplanes were already going into service, and there was no place for the Superstrand.

The first Overstrand, the converted Sidestrand J9186, was built by Boulton & Paul Ltd, but the production aircraft were built by the new company, Boulton Paul Aircraft Ltd, it was thus both the last and the first. All Overstrands were manufactured in Norwich, but the new company was making strenuous efforts to find a site for a new factory.

The Electro-Hydraulic Gun Turret

The pneumatic turret which had been developed for the Overstrand had certain disadvantages, most notably the limited reservoir of power available in the air bottles. A French engineer named de Boysson of the Société d'Applications des Machines Motrices had developed a four-gun electro-hydraulic turret, and had offered it to the French Government, but they were not interested. Knowing of Boulton & Paul's Overstrand turret from mention made of it in the aeronautical press, SAMM approached them with details of their turret, which they considered to be superior.

The turret was hydraulic in operation, but the special feature which made it unique was the electrically-driven hydraulic generator which it contained. Only electric power had to be supplied through a slip ring in the base, otherwise it was completely self-contained. It contained four Darne machine-guns, complete with ammunition boxes and bags to collect the empty cases and links, a major increase of hitting power when compared with the single Lewis gun in the Overstrand turret.

John North immediately saw the potential of this turret and sought the full patent rights. On 23 November, 1935, Boulton Paul Aircraft concluded an agreement with SAMM for the purchase of two turrets for 150,000 francs, with an option to buy the full British patent rights for a period of five months, which was later extended to 25 April, 1937. It seems that one of the major British aircraft manufacturers arrived at SAMM the following day seeking a similar agreement, but found they had been beaten to it. After delivery of the two turrets the option was exercised on 22 April, 1937, and for the sum of 250,000 francs Boulton Paul acquired full licence rights for the manufacture and sale of the de Boysson turret in Britain, its Dominions, Colonies, Protectorates, and Mandated Territories. Boulton Paul also agreed to pay a sum of £50 for each of the first 125 turrets which they built. Payments to SAMM amounted to £8,501 in total, a sum well spent, when considered against the orders that would eventually be received for turrets based on the de Boysson design.

The armament of fighter aircraft was undergoing a revolution during the 1930s. The much higher speeds being achieved by the new aircraft that were appearing seemed to indicate that a greater weight of firepower would be required as each firing pass was so much shorter. The twin Vickers machine-guns which had been the norm for so long, were increased to four guns in the Gladiator and then eight Browning machine-guns in the new Hurricane and Spitfire. This was made possible by the greater reliability of the Browning machine-gun, enabling batteries of them to be mounted in the aircraft wings.

The appearance of the power-operated turret seemed to offer an alternative armament arrangement, as the gunner would be able to maintain his sights on a target for a longer period as he traversed his turret. The Hawker Demon two-seat fighter was becoming obsolescent, and so the turret fighter seemed to

A 20 mm Hispano cannon installed on a de Boysson pedestal mount in the nose of Overstrand K8175. (*John A Chambers*)

be the obvious replacement. Specification F.22/33 had already called for a two-seat turret fighter, but Boulton Paul and the three other manufacturers which had submitted designs, Bristol, Armstrong Whitworth, and Gloster, chose twin-engined layouts which were rejected as being too slow and unmanoeuvrable.

This was Boulton Paul's first turret fighter design, the P.74, and would have been powered by either twin Bristol Pegasus or Napier Rapier engines. The Pegasus-powered version was somewhat larger than the other, but both were otherwise similar in layout, with an Overstrand-like turret fitted in the nose and another turret in the dorsal position. Two different dorsal turrets were offered, one very similar to the nose turret, with a very narrow rear fuselage resulting, and a smaller, half-glazed unit with a wider rear fuselage. In each case the turrets were equipped with just one Lewis gun. In appearance and size they were not unlike the Handley Page Hampden, and not surprisingly had a similar performance. The fastest of the four basic layouts could only manage 232 mph at 15,000 ft.

In June 1935 a new specification was issued, F.9/35, which called for a two-seat turret fighter with a performance approaching that of the new single-seat monoplane fighters. A speed of 298 mph at 15,000 ft was specified (as against 315 mph for Specification F.10/35 which produced the Hurricane and Spitfire), and time to this altitude was to be 5½ minutes. Service ceiling was specified as 33,000 ft and endurance 1½ hours at 253 mph.

Fifteen firms were invited to tender for the specification but only six submitted designs, and of these the one from Supermarine was soon put aside as the company was already fully stretched. Fairey offered a design based on the Battle light bomber, and Armstrong Whitworth redesigned their F.5/33 submission, a twin-engined mid-wing monoplane powered by two Armstrong Whitworth Terriers. At first it had a nose turret, but the final version offered featured the dorsal turret which was the only solution to the field of fire requirements detailed in the specification.

The Bristol submission, the Type 147 was powered by either a Perseus or Hercules radial and had a novel submerged turret which revolved by remote control in response to the gunner moving his reflector sight. The gunner was seated close behind the pilot. The Hercules-powered version was expected to reach a speed of 318 mph at 15,000 ft.

The most favoured design by the Air Ministry was the Hawker Hotspur, based on the single-engined Henley light bomber, both having the outer wings of the Hurricane. The gunner had a similar turret arrangement to Boulton Paul's submission, the P.82.

Hawker's were probably favoured because of their proven reputation as constructors of fine fighter aircraft. Boulton Paul would have been well considered because their turret was clearly more advanced than any other. Seven prototypes were originally ordered on 4 December, 1935, two each from Hawker and Boulton Paul, with two from Fairey as a back-up, and one of the more expensive twins from Armstrong Whitworth.

The Fleet Air Arm also took an interest in the turret fighter, and in 1935 issued Specification O.30/35 calling for a naval equivalent. Boulton Paul revamped their P.82 to produce the P.85, powered by either the Bristol Hercules HE-ISM or Rolls-Royce Merlin. Blackburn submitted a version of their Skua fighter/dive-bomber, which was already going into production.

Boulton Paul pressed on with the construction of the first prototype of the P.82 with some urgency. It was seen as their chance to exploit the obvious qualities of the de Boysson turret and to finally obtain substantial orders for one of their products. It was their first essay into all-metal stressed-skin construction and John North placed great emphasis on simplicity. Reminiscent of the techniques used for the R101, the P.82 was designed to be built in small components which could then be bolted together in a very straightforward manner. A mock-up was finished in February 1936 and the following month metal was cut on the first prototype.

Such was the speed of aeronautical development in the thirties however, and so perilous were the times, that the replacement for the F.9/35 was already being considered. There was a growing belief within the Air Ministry that only cannon armed fighters could possibly counter the new high-speed all-metal bombers which were appearing, and so the P.82 was being considered as a candidate for cancellation before it had even been built.

In the autumn of 1936 the first de Boysson turret finally arrived in Norwich, where the drawings already received had been converted to Imperial dimensions and modifications to the basic design put in hand. The control system for the turret was to be a single control column in a diamond shaped aperture, with the single firing button on top, exactly like the joy-stick provided for current computer games. To overcome the problem of protecting the gunner's own aircraft from the fire of his own guns, with no conscious effort on his part, each gun was fired by a separate solenoid, and an electrical fire interrupter device was fitted to each circuit. Since each pair of guns was spaced quite widely apart, and their line of fire was not in the line of sight of the gunner, each pair had separate interrupter devices.

The Director of Technical Development went to Norwich to inspect the turret, and was very impressed. He was also very impressed with the work already completed on the first prototype P.82, both the state of completion and the techniques being employed. With the move to larger purpose-built premises in Wolverhampton already taking place, the Director expressed the opinion that the P.82 programme had every likelihood of successful progress.

Air Ministry interest in a cannon-turret fighter began to crystallise in Specification F.18/36 for a twin-engined three-seater, with a four-gun turret, to have a top speed of 375 mph at 15,000 ft. Discussions over the ensuing months resulted in numerous changes to the specification as assorted armament combinations were put forward. Eventually on 26 May, 1937, the Air Ministry issued definitive Specification F.11/37 for a three-seat day and night fighter for Home Defence. The gunner was to be in a power-operated turret equipped with four 20 mm Hispano cannon, which either would be able to fire forward, or there would be supplementary fixed forward-firing guns. It was to be capable of at least 370 mph at 15,000 ft, with a service ceiling of 35,000 ft. Six companies tendered for this aircraft, Armstrong Whitworth, Short, Hawker, Bristol, Supermarine and Boulton Paul.

The P.82 had been moved to Wolverhampton in February 1937. The change of site had delayed the prototype's completion and its scheduled delivery date, 4 March, 1937, passed, but the Air Ministry was sufficiently impressed with its progress to place a production order.

The Type A Mk IIR turret newly mounted on the prototype Blackburn Roc.

Decision day for the turret fighters was 28 April, 1937. Fairey's Battle version and the Armstrong Whitworth twin had already been cancelled. Boulton Paul received an order for 87 of its P.82, which was now named Defiant, and Blackburn received an order for 136 of its naval turret fighter, which was to be called the Roc, the first three production aircraft serving as prototypes.

Because Blackburn was fully stretched with the Skua and Botha torpedo-bomber, the Roc order was sub-contracted to Boulton Paul. They undertook the detail design work involved in fitting their own four-gun turret (almost identical to the Defiant turret), to the Skua, and production of all 136 aircraft. Because of their design input, the Roc received the Boulton Paul project number P.93.

As Boulton Paul were to build both turret fighters it seems strange that their P.85, which was basically a navalised Defiant, did not receive the naval order, for production standardisation reasons. It seems the Roc was preferred because of its lower landing speed, and commonality with the Skua already in production. The P.85, had that been ordered, would have been by far the fastest aircraft operated by fleet carriers at the outset of the War, and would have remained so until the Grumman Wildcat appeared. If the naval authorities had not been so conservative, a single-seat version of the P.85, as projected later for the P.82 Defiant, would have given them a conventional single-seat fighter with adequate performance much earlier, without having to resort to stop-gap measures such as the Sea Hurricane. In fact a version of the P.85 with a simple observer's cockpit instead of a turret and forward-firing guns, could have fulfilled the Fulmar's role with a much better performance.

Construction of the Hawker turret fighter, now named Hotspur, was still going ahead, but it was seriously behind the Defiant. Hawker were fully stretched with the development of the Hurricane, and the Henley, while still manufacturing sundry Hart variants. The Hotspur was scheduled to be produced by Avro, but remained on the back-burner, and although the prototype was completed, it remained so far behind the Defiant that it was never ordered into production, freeing Avro for other production.

Boulton & Paul had always been considered a medium bomber specialist. The new company, without the conjunction, now suddenly found itself a specialist in a totally different area, working concurrently on four different turret fighters, the Turret-Demon in production, the P.82 Defiant and the P.93 Roc, ordered for large-scale production, and the next generation P.92 on the drawing board.

Mock-up of the redesigned de Boysson turret to be fitted to the P.82.

Mock-up of a twin-Lewis gun pneumatic tail turret for the P.79 project.

The Move to Wolverhampton

An exhaustive search had been made by the new company for a site for a purpose built factory, with room for the substantial expansion they envisaged in the near future. Among the criteria considered were an abundant local supply of skilled engineering labour, and close proximity to potential suppliers and sub-contractors, both for ease of supply, and close liaison. In both respects Norwich had always been somewhat out on a limb. It was considered essential to have a site adjacent to a suitable aerodrome. Having separate manufacturing and assembly/flight-test facilities, a mile apart as with Riverside Works and Mousehold in Norwich, had always created unnecessary problems.

The secondary considerations were adequate cheap electric and water supplies, good access to road and rail communications, good local housing available for the workforce, and low cost municipal services.

As today, various towns vied to attract new companies, and Wolverhampton was able to offer substantial advantages over the alternatives considered. The town was in the process of building a municipal airport. Sir Alan Cobham had been engaged to select a site, giving such advice being a lucrative sideline for him. For some strange reason he did not choose either of the two fields which he regularly visited with his National Aviation Day Displays, Blackhalve Lane in Wednesfield, or Perton, where an RAF station would later be built, but a site next to Barnhurst sewage works at Pendeford.

This was rather low-lying, and prone to bogginess, bounded on two sides by

Boulton Paul Aircraft's new offices fronting the factory on Wobaston Road, Wolverhampton. (*The Boulton Paul Society*)

canals and on a third by the low hill on which stood Pendeford Farm. The new factory site was slightly round the corner of this hill, right next to the Shropshire Union Canal. The aerodrome only ever had grass runways, but a tarmac taxiway was eventually built round to the factory. The company was given flying rights on the airport for 100 years.

The new factory was built by Wilson Lovatt with all the steelwork coming from Boulton & Paul's structural steel department, with a long row of single storey offices facing the Wobaston Road, and the assembly bays stretching back towards the airport at the rear, with plenty of space for expansion. The move from Norwich began in July 1936, and most of the 800-strong workforce made the transfer.

One who did not was Sqn Ldr Rea, who had no wish to live in the Midlands. He founded a new business of his own, manufacturing aircraft components, and occupied the assembly sheds at Mousehold being vacated by Boulton & Paul. He began by manufacturing aircraft floats, and was later to make Defiant components. The new company chief test pilot was to be Flt Lt Cecil Feather, formerly a specialist armament pilot at the A & AAE, and he was joined a year later by George Skelton. Another who did not make the move was joint managing director, Sam Hiscocks, who resigned and was replaced by Herbert Strickland.

The first aircraft to be manufactured at the new Wolverhampton factory was the Hawker Demon two-seat fighter. In 1931 the high performance of the Hawker Hart single-engine bomber, which exceeded that of contemporary RAF fighters led to the development of a fighter version, which was eventually called the Demon.

The Demon was fitted with a fully supercharged 485 hp Kestrel IIS engine, two front Vickers machine-guns instead of one, and a cut-away gunner's cockpit with a tilted gun-ring to improve the arc of fire for the single Lewis gun. The prototype, a converted Hart, J9933, first flew in 1931, and the parent company built a total of 128 Demons. A contract for a further 59 was then given to the

The new Flight Shed at the rear of the factory, facing towards Pendeford Airport. The Overstrand K8175 with an adapted nose, was being used for turret trials. (*The Boulton Paul Society*)

A Hawker Demon under construction at Pendeford.

new Boulton Paul company at Wolverhampton, (K5683–K5741).

Tooling began at Norwich but it was at Wolverhampton that the first Boulton Paul built Demon flew on 21 August, 1936. Two further orders for Demons were received, for ten (K5898–K5907) and 37 (K8181–K8217) respectively, making a total of 106 in all.

Hawker Demons awaiting delivery at Pendeford.

When fitted with a Mk V Kestrel engine of 584 hp the Demon was capable of 182 mph at 16,400 ft, and it was felt that the gunner needed some sort of protection from the slipstream. Frazer-Nash had been given the job of providing the gunner's protection, and because the gunner was rear facing, found the task easier than Boulton & Paul had with the Sidestrand nose gunner. From October all Boulton Paul Demons were fitted with a Frazer-Nash hydraulic semi-enclosed turret, with a folding shield, which had been tried on the original J9933. The development was known as the Turret-Demon. It is probable that the turrets were fitted elsewhere, as none of the surviving Boulton Paul staff can remember seeing one at Wolverhampton. This version of the Demon was fitted with the 584 hp Kestrel VDR. Production of the Demon by Boulton Paul was completed in December 1937.

The expansion of the new factory was rapid, most of the 800 workforce from Norwich had made the move, the design staff following the production staff in September 1936, and finally the Armament Design Office in November. Further skilled labour was available in the Midlands, not least because of the recent closure of Sunbeam, but more labour had to be recruited in Ulster and Scotland, and a training school was also eventually established in Cannock. Apart from the Demon the factory also initially built Saro London wing structures, 246 Blackburn Shark spars, and tail assemblies for Fairey Seafoxes. The last few Blackburn Bluebird wings were also built at Wolverhampton.

The Saro London flying-boat wings, built using Boulton Paul's locked joint system, were delivered to Saunders-Roe in sets, standing leading edge down, on a low loader. The first set to be sent off made an unexpected reappearance at the factory. The driver made the classic error of driving under a bridge which was too low, and the trailing edge of the wings was severely damaged. After repair, they were sent by a new, carefully researched, route. The wings of the prototype London had been built by Saro, but Boulton Paul supplied the wings for the 48 production aircraft.

One of the de Boysson supplied turrets was tested in 1937 fitted in the nose of

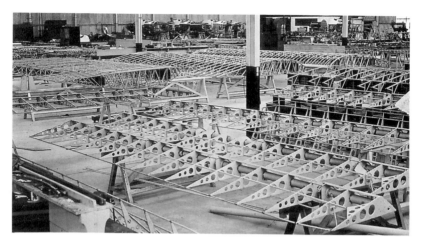

Saro London wings under construction in the new factory, with Hawker Demon fuselages in the background.

Overstrand K8175. A Hawker Hart, K2967, was used as a target aircraft during these experiments which took place at Boscombe Down.

The first prototype Defiant, K8310, made its first flight from Pendeford on 11 August, 1937, in the hands of Cecil Feather. It was flown as a single-seater with no turret, and in this form had an impressive performance, and vice-less handling. Problems were experienced with the undercarriage failing to lock up, and the original Dowty units were replaced with Lockheed supplied ones. The aircraft was flown at the A & AEE during December 1937, and reports were favourable enough for a second production contract for 202 aircraft to be placed in February 1938, when the turret was finally fitted to K8310.

By September 1937 the factory had been increased in size by 80 percent and was eventually extended to cover over three times its orginal area, besides subsidiary factories and stores. The row of offices along the front of the factory were also made two-storey. Development work was continuing on the gun turrets and the second prototype Defiant was taking shape but the aircraft which

Blackburn Rocs under construction at Pendeford. (*John A Chambers*)

followed the Demon onto the production lines was another two-seat fighter, the Blackburn Roc.

The Roc was a low-wing monoplane powered by a 905 hp Bristol Perseus XII nine-cylinder sleeve-valve radial. It was basically a Skua fighter/dive-bomber altered to incorporate a four-gun turret. Changes to the Skua to accommodate the turret were limited to the fuselage centre section, and the increased dihedral applied to the wings.

Boulton Paul did all the detail design work to convert the Skua to take their A turret and gave it the project number P.93. By 5 May, 1938, Boulton Paul were well advanced with setting up the Roc production lines, and envisaged completing the order for 136 by November 1939, though delivery of the first Roc was at the time dependant on modifications being made by Blackburn to the Skua. These had to be incorporated into the Roc in turn. At the same time Boulton Paul forecast being able to complete 450 Defiants by March 1940, at which time the production rate would be fifty a month. As they only had Instructions to Proceed for 289, this number was immediately increased to 450. With all this immense expansion underway Boulton Paul's overdraft was huge, and they asked for financial help from the Air Ministry for the provision of flight sheds at Pendeford. In August it was decided that the Ministry would supply two Bellman-type hangars for this use, on indefinite loan, and these were erected next to the assembly shops.

On 26 October, 1938, the Air Council Committee considered cancelling the Roc altogether. The Fifth Sea Lord did not think the productive effort worthwhile for a machine which would undoubtedly be useless as a fighter. The cancellation was not made because production was well underway with all the jigs and tools made, and it was felt that cancellation would have an adverse effect on the build up of the skilled workforce for Defiant production. It was nevertheless recognised at the time (before the Roc had even flown) that Sea Gladiators would have to be ordered to make up the shortfall in the Fleet Air Arm fighter force by the failure of the Roc, and Boulton Paul were already re-designing the Roc for target towing as early as April 1937.

The first Roc was flown by Blackburn test pilot Flt Lt Hugh Wilson, on its

The prototype Blackburn Roc (Boulton Paul P.93) ready for its first flight on 23 December, 1938. (John A Chambers)

78

initial flight at Pendeford on 23 December, 1938, but Cecil Feather, and his assistants did all subsequent testing.

Top speed was only 196 mph at 6,500 ft, and service ceiling only 15,200 ft, slower and lower than almost any bomber it might have been required to intercept! Not surprisingly it was never a success, though it did serve in fighter squadrons for a short while. It mainly served in Fleet Requirements Units at shore stations at home and abroad. Its stablemate, the Skua, proved a better fighter if anything, at least it had forward-firing guns, so that it did not actually have to overtake its prey before firing.

Production Rocs outside the newly camouflaged factory. (*John A Chambers*)

Two aircraft, L3057 and L3059, were experimentally fitted with floats, L3057 crashing because of directional instability, which was only partially cured on L3059. There had been an operational need for a Roc floatplane, to serve in the Norwegian Campaign, and a Roc floatplane fighter squadron began to form, but after the fall of Norway this development did not go any further. Roc production was completed in August 1940, and there were no further orders.

Continuing Boulton Paul's connections with Blackburn, another Blackburn aircraft, the twin-engined Botha torpedo bomber, was also nearly built at Pendeford. Specification 39/36 was drawn up to allow for production in addition to that by Blackburn themselves. Boulton Paul had submitted their P.83 project to Specification M.15/35 which called for a shore-based twin-Perseus powered torpedo bomber, with an external torpedo. They had also submitted project P.84 to Specification G.24/35 for a shore-based general reconnaissance bomber. Bristol designed an aircraft, the Beaufort, which combined the requirements of these two specifications and so did Blackburn with the Botha. Boulton Paul's answer was their P.86, also built to fulfill both requirements, but the Beaufort and the Botha received the orders.

In the end Botha production, with 442 ordered straight off the drawing board, went to a new Blackburn factory at Dumbarton, not least because of Boulton Paul's rapidly growing order book. It is perhaps fortunate that the seriously underpowered Botha, with its vicious swing, taking off from the relatively short Pendeford grass runways, with the canal and the sewage works representing the overshoot area in the direction of the prevailing wind, would have aged a lot of pilots very quickly!

During the 1930s, as fighter performance struggled to keep ahead of the fast bombers which were emerging, it was deemed likely that interceptors would only manage one firing pass against their target. A heavier weight of armament than the traditional twin Vickers guns was therefore considered essential. This line of thought led on one hand to the eight-gun fighters, equipped with wing-mounted .303 in machine-guns, and on the other to the turret fighters, the Roc and the Defiant.

The Air Staff believed that a cannon-equipped fighter was becoming essential, as bombers became more resistant to the effects of small-calibre machine-guns, even mounted in large numbers. Various lines of thought crystallised into Specification F.37/35 for a single-engined fighter equipped with four cannon. It was to have a top speed 40 mph above that of likely bomber adversaries and a ceiling of 30,000 ft. Speed and fire-power were stressed above climb performance and manoeuvrability, and the pilot was to have a good all round view. It was suggested that there might also be movable guns fitted, to be aimed by the pilot; signs that the turret/fixed-gun argument was still raging. Other features of the design were to be retractable undercarriage, wheel brakes, and an electric starter.

Boulton Paul, Fairey, Hawker, Supermarine, Armstrong Whitworth, Fairey and Westland were invited to tender. There were changes to the specification as work continued. In April 1936, the possibility of movable guns was dropped, and because of the difficulty of finding a powerful-enough engine, a twin-engined design was allowed.

Boulton Paul produced a single-engined design, the P.88, to be powered by the new Rolls-Royce Vulture, which was virtually two Kestrels joined in an X layout. It was hoped that it would produce 2,000 hp. They quoted a price for the first prototype of £20,500, and £17,500 for the second. A Hercules-powered option was also submitted. Another layout, the P.89, a two-seater with two modified Rolls-Royce Kestrel XVI engines, was also offered for Specification F.37/35.

Hawker, fully stretched, merely offered a cannon-armed Hurricane. Super-marine, Bristol and Westland offered twin-engined designs. Of the single-engined designs Boulton Paul's P.88 was considered the best and a provisional order was placed for two prototypes. Supermarine's was considered the best of the twins, with Westland's compact Rolls-Royce Peregrine-engined design a close second, and they both also received orders for prototypes.

The Air Ministry came to the conclusion that a heavy, cannon-armed fighter could not be powered by only one of the available engines, and more powerful engines, like the Vulture were too far in the future. On 11 February, 1937, the Boulton Paul fighter was cancelled, and because of their pressing weight of work with the new Spitfire, so was Supermarine's project. The order for Westland's design, which was to become the Whirlwind, was therefore confirmed.

However, the Boulton Paul project, designated P.92, was chosen for the F.11/37 cannon-turret fighter, and a contract placed in March 1938 for three prototypes. Two were to be powered by Rolls-Royce Vultures and one with the Napier Sabre.

With all this fighter activity, it might be thought that Boulton Paul had abandoned its bomber heritage, but in fact the company submitted designs for all the specifications which produced the major bombers of the Second World War. As already related they offered the P.70 biplane for B.9/32 which produced the Hampden and Wellington. They offered the P.73 for Specification P.27/32 from which the Fairey Battle was eventually ordered, and in 1934 they offered the P.79 for Specification B.3/34, which produced the Whitley.

The P.79 was a low-wing monoplane very reminiscent of the Douglas B-23 Dragon. It had a wing-span of 97 ft, with a chord of 14 ft outboard of the engines, and a length of 61 ft 3 in and was powered by two Bristol Perseus engines. There were gunners in nose, dorsal and tail positions all with Lewis guns in powered turrets, two in the case of the tail gunner, and a mock-up was built of this two-gun tail-turret, showing it to be remarkably compact. The pilot sat behind a swept-in windscreen. The same basic design was re-submitted for Specification B.1/35 which eventually produced the Warwick.

The two specifications which eventually produced the three great four-engined heavy bombers, B.12/36 (Stirling) and P.13/36 (Halifax and Manchester/Lancaster) also received submissions from Boulton Paul. The P.90, to the first of these was a four-engined heavy bomber to be powered by the Kestrel KV26, and the P.91, to the latter, was a twin-Vulture powered bomber. They featured a remarkable design for a tail turret, with four guns mounted in podded pairs on small-articulated winglets. This layout gave the tail gunner a remarkable field of fire, over the whole of the lower and rear hemispheres. Neither of these bombers, of course, progressed beyond the project stage. It is also hard to believe Boulton Paul could have been awarded an order for a heavy bomber, stretched as they were in bringing the Roc and Defiant into production, besides the work being done on the P.92.

Another Boulton Paul project, the P.81, was offered for one of the specifications which led to an aircraft which was in service in large numbers at the beginning of the War, the Westland Lysander. Specification A.39/34 called for an Army Co-operation aircraft, and the Boulton Paul P.81 was a Bristol Pegasus powered monoplane, which again did not progress beyond the project stage.

The company had not made the successful transition from a manufacturer of biplane bombers, to one of monoplane bombers. If any of those bomber projects had been successful the subsequent history of the company would have been very different. It does seem strange however, that John North did not seek to produce one of the many trainer aircraft which were required in the thirties, and which led to large-scale production during the War for so many designs. After the War he was to come to the conclusion that the military trainer represented the best bet for a company of moderate size. For the moment he was a staunch advocate of the power-operated gun turret, and its application in both bomber and fighter aircraft, and there were many within the Air Ministry who agreed wth him.

In fact the company had undergone a sudden metomorphosis, from being a Norwich company specialising in medium bombers to a Wolverhampton company specialising in turret fighters. During 1938 they actually worked on four different turret fighters. There is a film of the Defiant's undercarriage retraction tests, which shows one of the last of the Demons, K8180, in the background, the Demons being replaced by Rocs on the production line, and at the same time the Drawing Office was working on the P.92, the next generation of turret fighter.

The P.82 Defiant

In May 1938, with the Hotspur now cancelled, though Hawker were privately continuing with the prototype's completion, the Defiant was awarded a third production contract, this time for 161 aircraft. Work on the second prototype was proceeding slowly, it was being finished as mostly representative of the production aircraft.

The Defiant represented nearly 80 per cent of all Boulton Paul aeroplanes and its development and Service history is dealt with in full in the aircraft section of this work.

The first production Defiant, serial L6950, flew for the first time on 30 July, 1939. This aircraft was equipped with bomb racks in August 1939, to test the type's suitability for ground attack operations. In many ways the Defiant was an ideal ground attack aircraft, it was rock-solid in a dive, making it a marvellous front-gun platform. L6950 was delivered to Boscombe Down on 19 September, and by the end of the month four more aircraft had been delivered. Comparative trials were undertaken by No.111 Squadron in October 1940, between the Defiant and the Hurricane I. The report indicated that with its huge disadvantage in wing-loading and power-to-weight ratio the Defiant would not have a chance against any competent Hurricane pilot. This certainly did not bode well for the future.

Meanwhile progress was being made with the P.92 cannon fighter. To test the aerodynamics of their design, Boulton Paul built a 2/7th scale model, with a wing span of 17 ft 10 in which was tested in the RAE's wind tunnels between March and October 1939. The results were not encouraging, with the turret and the cannon in certain positions drag increased by a disconcerting amount, and there was a large nose-down pitching movement, and stability was affected.

To further test the aerodynamics of the design Heston Aircraft were contracted to build a half-scale wooden replica, the P.92/2, with a non-retractable undercarriage and powered by two de Havilland 130 hp Gipsy Major engines.

The company did a great deal of development work on the P.92, but on 26 May, 1940, the project was cancelled, when construction of the first prototypes was five per cent complete. The Air Ministry had decided to concentrate on the production and development of existing types, and the concept of the cannon-turret fighter was abandoned. The requirement was filled largely by the Bristol Beaufighter.

It was decided to finish the half-scale P.92/2 however, which was given the serial V3142, and flying trials took place in the spring of 1941. Cecil Feather undertook the first flight at Heston, and shortly afterwards the aircraft was flown to Wolverhampton. After only three hours flying the P.92/2 showed that the aerodynamic layout was totally satisfactory, and had good handling characteristics. V3142 was delivered to Boscombe Down for extensive flight tests. The company's assessment was confirmed, but the measured drag proved to be much higher than the 2/7th scale model predicted, though longitudinal stability was better.

Even had the P.92 programme gone ahead, it is likely that it would have run into trouble with the Vulture engines, as did many other designs, and many within the company were concerned about the radical turret, and the difficulties they might experience in developing it. The extremely large diameter of the ball-bearing turret ring, meant it had to be constructed to intolerable degrees of accuracy. Any distortion at all caused the turret to jam, and the further prospect of even slight wing movement acting on the turret, which was within the wing structure, held the prospect of distortion in flight.

After the programme was abandoned the P.92/2 was kept at Wolverhampton for some time. It was stored in a shed half way down the taxiway from the factory to the aerodrome, but was eventually broken up.

As early as 15 December, 1939, it had been proposed to set up a Bristol Beaufighter Production Group consisting of Bristol factories at Filton and Warwick, plus Fairey, Supermarine and Boulton Paul Aircraft. Boulton Paul's productive labour force at this time was only 2,900 (including 600 on the night shift) plus 1,400 staff. There was no training scheme underway, and there were hardly any women employed except a few on capstan lathes. They were struggling to get the Defiant up to the required production level by bringing in a number of sub-contractors, but were only producing sixteen Rocs and six Defiants a month. Not surprisingly the company was alarmed at the prospect of trying to obtain machine tools for Beaufighter production envisaged at thirty aircraft a month. Even if they could get the machine tools their tool-room was fully occupied with turret production, and skilled toolmakers were becoming as rare as gold dust. They had not yet even received an order for the Beaufighter and on 4 January, 1940, asked for one. On the 17th they received an Instruction to Proceed for 250 Beaufighters with serials in the range W6089–W6410.

On 4 June, 1940, Winston Churchill was to express the officially held satisfaction with the Defiant at that time, when he said in the House of Commons, 'All our types, the Hurricane, the Spitfire, and the new Defiant, and all our pilots, have been vindicated as superior to what they have at present to face'. This was an unfortunate choice of words in the case of the Defiant, whose pilots were very anxious not to be in the position of 'facing' a Bf 109, or indeed almost anything else, as a head-on attack would render them helpless!

In April 1940 King George VI and Queen Elizabeth visited Boulton Paul Aircraft. They saw an aerobatic display by a Defiant flown by Cecil Feather and then toured the factory. They inspected the Defiant production lines and the new aircraft standing on the apron. George Skelton had left the company at the beginning of the year, and his place as Cecil Feather's assistant, was taken by Robin Lindsay Neale and Colin Evans.

With the P.92 cancelled further fighter development was now centred on the Defiant. The original prototype, K8310, was rebuilt during 1940 as a mock-up of a single-seat fighter with four forward-firing guns, as a rapid way of overcoming any shortages of Spitfires and Hurricanes. This scheme was not proceeded with, even though it was estimated that it would have a slightly superior performance to the Hurricane. A prewar scheme for a dual-control trainer was never built, though design work was 80 per cent complete when it was cancelled.

A slightly more advanced proposal was also put forward by the company during 1940, the P.94. This was also a single-seater based on the Defiant, but the changes were more substantial. The armament was to be twelve wing-mounted .303 Browning machine-guns, or four 20 mm cannon and four machine-guns, and the engine a Merlin XX. The profile of the upper rear fuselage was much lower than that of K8310, and the aerial mast was moved to a more conventional upper position. The P.94 might have proved a useful fighter, but offered no real improvement over new versions of the Spitfire which were coming into service, with more advanced aircraft such as the Typhoon not far away. It is interesting to note that a version of the P.94 was offered in which the pilot could depress the wing-mounted cannon for ground attack work. Also during 1940 Boulton Paul offered a dedicated two-seat ground-attack aircraft.

The 20th specification issued in 1940 was for a two-seat close-support bomber. There were conflicting views within the Air Ministry about the value of such an aircraft. The German Junkers Ju 87 had obviously had a startling effect on the armies of Europe, but had proved easy meat over Dunkirk. The nearest British equivalent, the Fairey Battle, had been hopeless, and the much more adequate Hawker Henley was relegated to target-tug duties without even reaching operational squadrons. Hawker submitted a version of the Henley for B.20/40, the P.1006, and Bristol offered their Type 162 project. Boulton Paul's answer was their heavily armed P.95, powered by a Bristol Hercules VI, and having a tricycle undercarriage. It was armed with eight machine-guns or four cannon in the wings, plus two Brownings for the rear gunner. Four 250 lb bombs could be housed internally, two in a fuselage bomb-bay, and one in each wing, with alternative loads of four small-bomb containers, or supply dropping apparatus. There was also provision in the fuselage for an F.24 camera and reconnaissance flare stowage. The concept of B.20/40 was clearly to produce a versatile heavily-armed aircraft which could be used against a German invader, but no prototypes were ordered.

A Defiant cockpit.

The Air Council Committee on Supply was still concerned about Defiant output in September 1940. The company had placed an order with Daimler of Coventry for complete centre sections and fuselages, but without Air Council approval, for which they got rapped over the knuckles. As it happeend Daimler had only just received a complete set of drawings when they were bombed out by the Luftwaffe. They moved to Wolverhampton and took over the empty Courtaulds factory in Henwood Road.

In reply to requests by the Air Supply Board to disperse production, Boulton Paul put forward five possible Dispersal Centres in November 1940, Attwood Garage and Peter Pan Manufacturing in Wolverhampton, C Halldron in Bilston, Shaw Foundry in Willenhall and Pale Meadow Printing Works in Bridgnorth; to which was later added the Training School in Chadsmoor, Cannock.

There is no doubt that the Defiant was not meeting the performance targets which had been expected of it. A suggestion to produce a clipped-wing version had been rejected, so that disruption would not occur to the production lines. Some of the deficiency had been clawed back by fitting de Havilland constant-speed propellers from the 88th production aircraft, the first 87 only having two-speed propellers.

The RAF asked Boulton Paul to try and overcome the deficiencies by giving the Defiant more power. Boulton Paul fitted two Mk I Defiants with Merlin XX engines giving 1,260 hp. The first flew on 20 July, 1940, and the other later in the summer. At the same time changes were made to the cowling and radiator, and a pressurised fuel system adopted, together with extra fuel tankage. With these changes the aircraft was designated Defiant Mk II, and had a top speed of 313 mph at 19,000 ft.

The last order for 280 aircraft was amended to 63 Mk Is and 210 Mk IIs, and the last seven Mk Is were changed to Mk II standard on the production line. Delivery began in January 1941 and ended in February 1942.

By March 1941 the Beaufighter contract had been cancelled because Boulton Paul could not hope to build the proposed thirty a month, and it was now decided that Boulton Paul should build Handley Page Halifaxes in conjunction with Fairey who would undertake final assembly at Manchester, and received an order for 150 aircraft. At the same time Defiant orders were reduced by 330 to a total of 920.

The following month it was decided that Fairey would build the Halifax alone and Boulton Paul would build the Fairey Barracuda, an initial figure of 300 being suggested. On the 28th it was decided to go ahead with the Mk II Defiant, Contract B.34864/39 being amended to 270 Mk Is and 200 Mk IIs, the last 330 being confirmed as cancelled.

Because of the danger of air attack on an easily found site such as Pendeford it was decided to build aircraft blast pens in which to place parked Defiants. Six would be excavated in the hillside between the factory and the hangars, each holding two Defiants in tandem. Work was started on them in November 1940.

The last Defiant was completed in February 1943, and a total of 1,062 had been built. The Defiant was born of an ill-conceived concept, and suffered accordingly. It did what it was designed to do, but a fighter without forward-firing armament was soon found to be an anachronism. Perhaps it is a sign of the unlucky nature of Boulton & Paul that their first design to go in to quantity production, was based on an unfortunate idea.

As an interim night-fighter it achieved a great deal of success, and as a target tug it did important but unglamorous work. It played its part, and is rightly remembered as the best known product of Boulton Paul Aircraft.

John North had been a staunch advocate of the turret fighter at the beginning of the War, and the Defiant was important in that it was the first Boulton Paul design to go into quantity production, but by the end of the War he did not hold it in great affection. In 1945, as a mark of appreciation for Boulton Paul's war effort he was offered a Defiant free of charge by the Air Ministry, to use as a gate guardian at the factory, or for whatever purpose he wished. He declined the offer.

Turret Development

Boulton Paul quickly saw a large market for a whole range of its turrets, based on the original de Boysson design. In July 1937 it proposed the following range of turrets in addition to the A Mk I Defiant turret:

1. A Nose turret with two Brownings and partial rotation.
2. A Tail turret with two Brownings and partial rotation.
3. A 'Centre' turret with two Brownings and complete rotation.
4. A 'Centre' turret with two Brownings and complete rotation and adaptable for retraction.
5. A Ventral turret with two Brownings and complete rotation.
6. A Nose turret with two 'K' guns.

In additon a mounting for a 20 mm Hispano cannon ordered from SAMM along with the de Boysson turret arrived in England in August 1937, and this was tested in the nose of Overstrand K8175 after the de Boysson turret was removed. Cannon turrets represent a separate thread of development, and will therefore be described separately.

Boulton Paul turrets were electro-hydraulic with all the power equipment carried within the turret itself, the electric leads and other services, such as the intercom, coming in through a slip-ring unit on the axis of rotation. Fitting a turret was thus very simple. The whole self-contained unit was just dropped into position, lined up, bolted down, and the central leads connected up.

The main structural parts of the turret were the ball-bearing mounting ring, the support table, the gun plate assembly and gun recoil mountings. The mounting ring was attached to the airframe by twelve retaining bolts. Power for rotation of the turret and elevation/depression of the guns was supplied by a duplex electro-hydraulic generator. The speed of operation was controlled entirely by the amount of displacement of the control handle. Pressure generated in the hydraulic system varied with the resistance to its operation, so that moving the guns against the airstream was no different to moving the other way.

The turret control lever included a 'dead-man's handle', so that no power was consumed should the gunner be incapacitated. There was also provision for manual rotation of the turret in an emergency should the power supply be damaged. The firing button fired all guns at the same time, but there were automatic cut-outs so that the gunner could not shoot-off pieces of his own aircraft. They worked by contact brushes running over a metal cylinder which revolved at the same speed as the turret. A plastic insert in the cylinder corresponded to the shape of the aircraft structure, so that when the contacts ran over that, the guns ceased fire. As there was wide separation between the left and right guns, the cut-outs worked on left and right independently to maximise the field of fire.

The first electro-hydraulic turret manufactured was the A turret, basically the de Boysson four-gun turret with minor improvements such as electric firing, and Browning guns instead of the French Darne guns. This was fitted to the Defiant (A Mk IID) and Roc (A Mk IIR), differing only in the shape of the drum inserts in the interrupter mechanism.

On 28 September, 1937, there was a conference at Boulton Paul to inspect a mock-up of a four-gun tail turret. A representative of Handley Page was called to inspect it. Mr Haynes duly arrived on 4 October and was very complimentary in his report to Handley Page. The following week the mock-up was delivered to Avro in Manchester. At the conference Boulton Paul had been urged to design a full range of turrets for the Specification P.13/36 submissions from Avro and Handley Page, and for Specification B.12/36 submissions from Short and Supermarine. Nash & Thompson, or Frazer-Nash as they became, were doing the same. It seems that the manufacturers preferred the Frazer-Nash turrets because they were lighter, but the Boulton Paul turrets had the advantage of not having long vulnerable hydraulic lines, having their own hydraulic generator.

On 12 July, 1938, the Air Ministry confirmed that the H.P.57 Halifax was to be fitted with the Boulton Paul C Type nose turret, and the E Type tail turret, and orders were placed accordingly. The Stirling and the Lancaster were to have

A Handley Page Halifax fitted with C Mk I nose turret, at Pendeford.

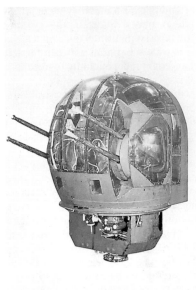

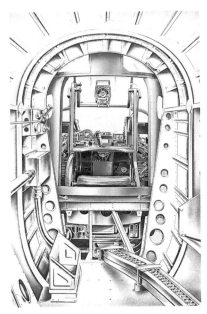

Halifax E Mk I tail turret. (*John A Chambers*)

A drawing of the E Mk I tail turret viewed from within a Halifax fuselage, showing the tracks leading extra ammunition into the turret.

the Frazer-Nash turrets. The C turret was a two-gun turret with 1,000 rounds per gun, rather than the 600 rounds per gun in the A turret. The four-gun E turret was very cramped, and yet it was deemed necessary to provide the tail gunner with more ammunition than the other positions; fighters naturally preferring stern attacks to maximise their firing time and to give a no deflection shot. The 1,750 rounds per gun provided were therefore carried in the rear fuselage, being fed into the turret through its base. The ammunition was held in steel tracks, and fed to the turret with the assistance of small motors.

On 27 October, 1938, the Air Ministry confirmed that the Halifax should also be equipped with a retractable ventral turret with twin guns, and the K Type was ordered accordingly.

Being self-contained units the Boulton Paul turrets were the obvious choice for a number of other applications. When the British Purchasing Commission ordered a military version of the Lockheed 14 airliner in 1938, to be named the Hudson, the C turret was ordered to be adapted for its dorsal position. In the Halifax nose position the master switches and fuse-boxes were fitted to a vertical panel which was also a main structural member, carrying the electrical supply, oxygen lines and intercom leads in from the top of the turret. As it was a structural member, this panel was left on the Hudson dorsal turret version (C Mk II and IIA), so that there was not quite all round vision, and the resulting turret had a marked domed appearance. The electrical and other leads were brought in through the base however, as on the A turret.

The initial order for Hudson turrets was for 208, of which 200 would be fitted

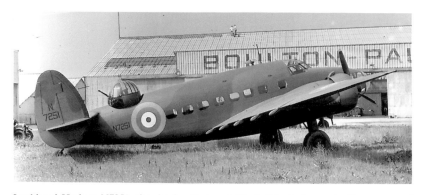

Lockheed Hudson N7251 after having its turret fitted. The factory is in the process of being camouflaged. (*John A Chambers*)

to aircraft and the other eight would be for maintenance and training purposes. The order was worth £208,000 as these turrets cost £1,000 each. A proposal was made on 23 March, 1939, to move turret production to Joseph Lucas in Birmingham. A report on 3 April assessed the requirements for Boulton Paul turrets as 180 per month, whereas Boulton Paul's production capacity was only 110 a month with one shift. For the first time the DGB proposed to transfer turret production elsewhere, especially as it was deemed to be interfering with airframe manufacture at Wolverhampton.

The first Hudson to be fitted, N7208, arrived at Wolverhampton on 2 May, 1939, and its new turret was soon fitted, but most subsequent fittings took place elsewhere. The Hudsons were shipped and later flown over from America and all the turrets fitted in Britain.

Boulton Paul had serious difficulty keeping up with all these developments,

The E Mk I tail turret mounted on a mock-up Halifax rear fuselage.

89

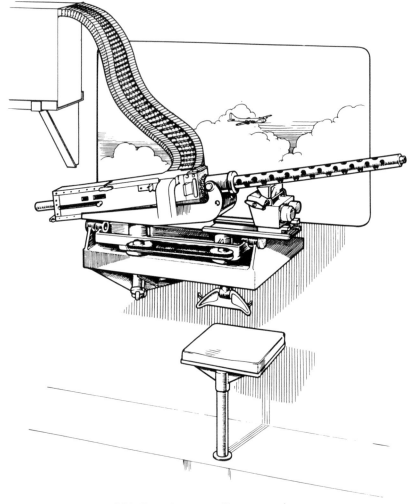

0.5 in Browning powered beam mounting.

not least because the Air Ministry continually changed its requirements and priorities. There was a continuing interest in turrets with 0.5 in machine-guns and 20 mm cannon, but development of these was constantly being delayed by the urgent need to put the .303 in gun turrets into production as quickly as possible, compounded by the ever increasing list of applications for them. The story of heavy-weapon turrets will be presented separately for clarity, but it was in every way contiguous with the small calibre turrets. In 1940 Boulton Paul was ordered to stop all work on cannon turrets for a while.

By April 1939 delays in delivery of Boulton Paul turrets for the Halifax caused the DTD to enter negotiation with Joseph Lucas of Birmingham to take on turret production, even though Boulton Paul were building a new factory at

Pendeford exclusively to manufacture turrets, to cope with the huge numbers which were required.

By 4 October, 1940, the Air Council Committee on Supply was reporting that Boulton Paul's turret capacity was 250 a month with two shifts, and Lucas' was 400 a month, but requirements had again increased with 85 Defiant turrets a month, 378 Halifax turrets (three per aircraft), and now 500 Albermarle turrets (two per aircraft), together with spares giving a total requirement of 1,107 a month. It was proposed to increase Lucas' capacity in Birmingham to 600 a month and to open a new Lucas turret factory in Cwnbran, South Wales, with a capacity of 500 a month. On 29 May, 1940, requirements had again increased to 1,315 a month, and it was therefore proposed to increase productive capacity through overtime working to 1,410 a month.

No sooner was Boulton Paul's new turret factory completed, than the Air Ministry decided, on 14 June, 1940, to transfer all turret production to Lucas, with total orders for 4,242 turrets and 3,982 cupolas. Boulton Paul was to concentrate on building aircraft, though the armament section would continue turret development. Lucas cleared a building in Formans Road, which had previously been used as a store, as a shadow turret factory. Boulton Paul's new turret factory was absorbed into airframe production. Lucas built more than 20,000 Boulton Paul turrets during the War, in Birmingham and Wales, and also made Frazer-Nash turrets.

Many of Boulton Paul's difficulties in producing turrets on time were due to changing official priorities, and the great variety needed. On 31 December, 1941, for instance, the Armament section discovered it had to build 18 different turret prototypes over the following 6–9 months. Delays in turret development were often caused by a lack of machine tools in the armament section, causing many of the parts to be sub-contracted. Naturally enough sub-contractors did not place a high priority on odd parts for new turrets, and so approval was given on 12 December, 1942, for Boulton Paul to receive £15,550-worth of new machine tools just for turret development.

The full set of nose, dorsal and tail turrets were fitted to some marks of the Handley Page Halifax. Aircraft up to the Mk II Series 1 were just fitted with the C Type nose turret and E Type tail turret, but from the Mk I Series 3 a C Type turret was fitted in the dorsal position. This was found to reduce performance too much and coupled with the fact that the nose turret was rarely needed, a clean-up of the airframe took place on the Halifax Mk II Series 1A. The nose was faired over, and the bulky C turret in the dorsal position was replaced by a more compact four-gun A turret, Boulton Paul testing the new installation during July 1942 on Halifax, R9375. The B Mk I turret was also developed for the Halifax dorsal position. It was merely an A turret with 20 deg of depression for the guns and only 65 deg of elevation; and a knock-out exit panel instead of the A turrets' doors.

The two-gun retractable ventral turret (K Mk 1) was also developed for the Halifax, but was rarely fitted as it did not prove to be very effective. Official policy with regard to the ventral position proved to be very mixed, and it was often left to individual squadrons whether guns were fitted there at all. Some Halifaxes, mostly in Canadian squadrons, were fitted with a 0.5 in Browning on a manually-operated Preston-Green mounting, in a low profile blister, others, mostly in Coastal Command, had the Frazer-Nash FN64 ventral turret.

K Mk I Halifax/Albermarle ventral turrets in production.

The three basic turrets, A, C, and E, found their way into other applications. The A Mk III was designed for the Armstrong Whitworth Albermarle, in the dorsal position. Very few aircraft were actually equipped with them, as the aircraft was not employed as a bomber. In its main application as a glider tug the Albermarle was fitted with hand-operated guns in the dorsal position.

Being self-contained the Boulton Paul turrets were the obvious choice to fit to militarised civil aircraft and to equip other American aircraft which followed the Hudson. A further American medium bomber to receive Boulton Paul dorsal turrets was the Martin Baltimore. The Mks I and II did not have a turret, but Boulton Paul four-gun A turrets were fitted to the Mk III. Later marks had a Martin dorsal turret. One Mk III, FA163, managed 103 operations in Tunisia, Sicily and Italy, a record for a medium bomber flying in that Theatre, which is where all the RAF Baltimores were employed.

Another Lockheed product, the Ventura medium bomber was also fitted with a Boulton Paul dorsal turret, which was sited further forward than in the Hudson to improve the field of fire. Early ones were the same two-gun C turret as the Hudson, but later the four-gun A turret was fitted. A total of 394 Venturas were delivered to the RAF.

A United States heavy bomber to be fitted with Boulton Paul turrets was the Consolidated Liberator used mostly by Coastal Command. Both the dorsal and tail positions were usually fitted with Boulton Paul four-gun turrets, to achieve commonality with the RAF's other .303 in machine-gun equipment.

Though the Sunderland flying-boat was equipped with Frazer-Nash turrets, when the RAF decided to militarise five ex-Imperial Airways Short flying-boats, the self-contained Boulton Paul A turret was the obvious choice. Two S.23 C Class boats, *Clio* and *Cordelia*, were equipped with A turrets in tail and dorsal positions, and became AX659 and AX660. The three larger G Class boats, *Golden Hind*, *Golden Fleece* and *Golden Horn*, were equipped with three A turrets, in the tail, above the centre section and over the rear fuselage offset to starboard. These aircraft were then serialled X8273–5. These five boats saw operational service in a stop-gap role until they could be replaced by Sunderlands.

The A turret was also seen as an ideal anti-aircraft weapon for use on small

An armoured mobile anti-aircraft vehicle fitted with a four-gun A turret.

warships. The A Mk II P.B.1 and 2 were fitted to some minesweepers and patrol boats. They were basically the normal Defiant turrets, but with 10 deg of depression, which meant the elevation was reduced by 10 deg to 74 deg, and only partial rotation was available. A prototype four-wheel armoured car was also built, fitted with the A turret, apparently as an aerodrome anti-aircraft weapon for the RAF.

In 1941 the fighter turret-lobby was still strong, and orders were given in April to fit Boulton Paul four-gun turrets in two Beaufighters and two Mosquitos. In the Beaufighter the turret, even with only two nose-mounted cannon remaining, reduced top speed from 335 mph to 302 mph. The Mosquito only flew with the turret in mock-up form, and again performance was affected far too much. The idea was not proceeded with. Boulton Paul suggested a twin 0.5 in machine-gun mount for the Mosquito, sited just behind the cockpit. The guns, with limited degrees of movement would be operated by the navigator kneeling on his seat facing aft, with his head in a blister above the normal canopy line. If this seems far-fetched, it must be remembered that on Intruder Mosquitos the Gee equipment was sited behind the crew seats, and had to be operated by the navigator kneeling on his seat and facing aft, such was the cramped nature of the Mosquito's cockpit.

Heavy-Weapon Turrets

The company had given serious thought to producing cannon-equipped turrets even before the P.92 project. It was clear that foreign fighters at least were increasingly being equipped with cannon, for their greater range and hitting power, and it therefore seemed likely that bombers would also have to be so

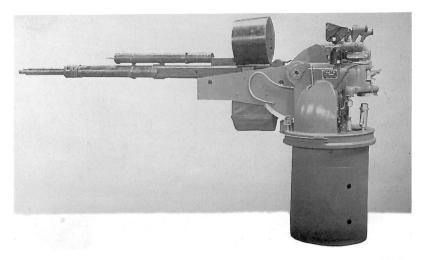

The 20 mm Hispano cannon pillar mounting supplied by SAMM, and later tested in the nose of an Overstrand.

equipped to counteract this trend. Plans were made for both single and multiple cannon turrets.

A 20 mm Hispano cannon was fitted to the nose of Overstrand K8176 on the pillar mount obtained from SAMM, in an open position, to test the effects on the aircraft structure of firing it. The same mounting was also tested on Defiants instead of the turret. A single cannon turret was adapted from the normal A. Mk IID Defiant turret, designated the Type F Mk I, and flown on the second prototype Defiant for the first time on 8 October, 1938.

Multiple cannon turrets were offered for aircraft designed to Specifications B.12/36 and P.13/36, both Boulton Paul's own P.90 and P.91, and competing designs. Further cannon turrets were also offered for flying-boats designed to Specification R.3/38 and bombers to B.1/39.

The low-drag P.92 turret (L Mk I) was even offered in a dual installation in dorsal and ventral positions on the Avro Manchester, and on a version of the Halifax designated H.P.58. A contract was actually placed with Handley Page to convert the prototype Halifax, L7244, as the prototype H.P.58, and a mock-up of the installation was built. Delays with the development of the L turret resulted in the cancellation of the project.

On 5 September, 1939, N E Rowe of the DTD stated that official policy was for a phased introduction of heavier weapons onto the Halifax. The first two stages were with .303 in guns in nose and tail and then additionally in dorsal positions, Stage 3 would add a tail turret with 0.5 in machine-guns (The Boulton Paul D turret), and Stage 4 would replace the dorsal turret with a twin 20 mm cannon turret.

The Air Ministry did actually order twin-cannon turrets for both the Halifax and the Stirling in May 1939. The H turret was to be fitted to the dorsal position, and the R turret to the ventral position, of both aircraft.

On 26 June, 1942, delivery date for the R turret was given as 7 July, though

A D Mk I tail turret with twin 0.5 in machine-guns fitted to a Halifax, at RAF Cosford, 10 February, 1944.

without its drift indicator, but the H Mk I was still in the drawing stage. There is no record of either of these turrets being test flown before being cancelled.

Late in 1940 Boulton Paul were given the go-ahead for the development of turrets with 0.5 in calibre machine-guns, for their greater hitting power, with a view to starting production of them in the United States. The D tail turret with twin 0.5 in guns was revived for the Halifax, with production in this country, and a new series of 0.5 in turrets was designed to comply with American engineering methods and standards. The S, T, U and V turrets were for tail, dorsal, ventral and nose positions respectively, the V nose turret being merely an S tail turret with an underfloor empties-collection box. Only the S and T turrets were actually built, prototypes being shipped to the United States in November 1940 and April 1941 respectively.

Boulton Paul fitted a T turret to Halifax R9436 and it was test flown from Llandwrog by Cecil Feather in June 1942. The emergency door came off it at 250 mph, and there were a few teething problems with pieces of equipment but the turret was successfully tested at the A & AEE in October.

An unusual ventral turret layout was also suggested by the company. The gunner was to recline within the turret as if curled up on a couch, with twin 0.5 in machine-guns alongside him. With his upper body weight supported on one elbow and no support for his head and neck as he sighted the turret, this would seem to be a very uncomfortable way to go to war. The company also designed a powered beam gun mounting for a 0.5 in machine-gun, but this found no applications.

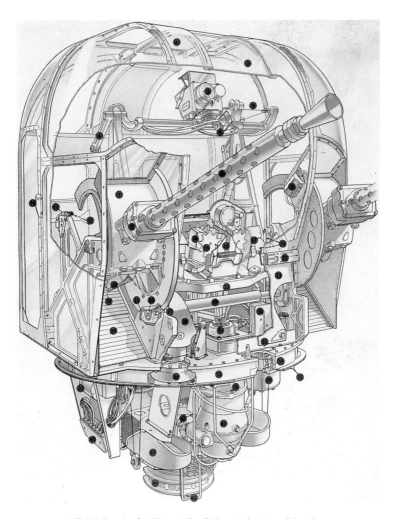

A D Mk I series 2 tail turret for fitting to the Avro Lincoln.

Another powered, non-turret, gun mounting was designed round Boulton Paul's P.97 twin-engined fighter project, and reflected John North's thirty years of interest in mobile gun-mountings. It featured twin 20 mm cannon in slots on either side of the nose able to move only in the vertical plane. Unlike the similar mounting designed for the P.31 Bittern this was primarily for ground-attack, enabling the aircraft to engage ground targets when flying in the horizontal plane, or to bring the guns to bear for longer periods in diving attacks. For the same purpose the wing cannon on the abortive P.94 project had been designed to be depressed by the pilot up to 17 deg. A version of this basic design was eventually to see production for the nose of the Avro Shackleton.

Remote Control and Radar Guided Guns

As early as May 1940 a special 'Cell' was set-up within the Armament Section at the RAE to investigate the 'Remote Control of Guns'. Boulton Paul had already done some work in this area for Specification 24/37, which led to the Barracuda, and there had been talk of testing a system on a Roc, though nothing was done. A mock-up of a Remote Control System was ready at Pendeford in 1939, with standard turret parts being used as much as possible, but little official interest was shown and the mock-up was dismantled during 1940.

In fact little progress was made until August 1942 when it was proposed that the RAE, Boulton Paul and British-Thompson-Houston jointly develop a Remote Control System. A meeting on the 17th at Pendeford agreed the division of responsibility. Boulton Paul would build the barbettes, BTH the electrical link, and the RAE would develop the sighting system and co-ordinate the venture. The advantages of such a system on heavy bombers were i) to get the weight forward on such aircraft, ii) to improve the aerodynamics of the tail, iii) to improve the gunner's comfort, iv) to improve the gunner's view, v) to create room near the gunner for extra equipment, vi) to overcome the problem of gun-flash at night.

On 2 September, 1942, a Halifax, R1009, was taken on charge at Farnborough as a test vehicle for the new system. An E Mk II turret with a Remote Sight was installed in the tail, with the guns in an A Mk II turret in the dorsal position. This installation was to prove the techniques. A completely new defensive system was ordered for testing on the Lancaster. This consisted of remotely controlled cannon barbettes in dorsal and ventral positions with the gunner located in the tail; the barbettes being electrically operated. Design was complete by February 1943 and a Lancaster B.I. LL780/G, was allocated to test the system, tests beginning at Farnborough in January 1944. No production of this system was to take place, despite the high priority given to it at various times during the War.

The official view was that there would be no requirement for a Remote Control System on the Lancaster, but that the new bomber to Specification B.3/42 would have to have it. In the same way the new Boeing B-29 in the USA was emerging with a complete Fire-Control System, and this was studied by the RAE. All this work came to nothing of course, but another technical development did make progress.

Late in 1942 the twin Browning 0.5 in machine-gun turret was ordered for the tail position of the Halifax (D Mk I). This was to be radar guided, for night and bad weather operation. The radar system was termed AGLT (Airborne Gun Laying for Turrets) and was introduced in 1944 under the code name 'Village Inn'. The system was also fitted to Frazer-Nash turrets on Lancasters. Handling trials with a mock-up of the installation on an E turret were undertaken on Halifax W1008. The first D turret with AGLT was tested at the A & AEE in May 1943 on Halifax HX238 but there were prolonged delays because of teething troubles. Sets were in short supply so it could not be introduced at Gunnery Schools. Gunners had to learn how to operate it in service, and it did not prove a great success. It was eventually ordered for the Halifax Mk X, and the Lancaster Mk V which was to be re-named the Lincoln.

To assess the system, and to train gunners in its use, it was necessary to operate it by daylight, so that results could be compared with cine film. After the war attempts were made to provide shields so that the gunner operating the system could not actually see his target, but these proved ineffective, there remained the possibility of the gunner cheating by peering round the screen. By early 1946 it had been decided that screening within the turret was impossible and that an external screen had to be provided. A canvas cover was tried at first, on the Boulton Paul tail turret on Lincoln B 2, RF389, but it was impossible to prevent it ripping against the effects of the slipstream. Finally a grey protective solution called Spraylat was used. It was found that by adding black dye an opaque cover could be sprayed onto the turret, which was easily removed when required. Thus it was that menacing all-black tail turrets appeared on some Lincolns.

A new turret was also designed for the nose position of the Lincoln, the F mounting. The turret contained two 0.5 in machine-guns, installed very close together. The gunner sat beneath the revolving portion of the turret in the fixed bomb-aimer's position, operating the turret by remote-control through a periscope sight. The twin cannon dorsal turret on the Lincoln was not made by Boulton Paul but was a Bristol turret.

Turret development by all companies was hampered throughout the War by official prevarication and muddled thinking. Almost all bombers continued in operation with small-calibre defensive weapons, hopelessly out-ranged and out-gunned by cannon-equipped German fighters. Even when evidence abounded that German night fighters were equipped with the Schräge Musik upward-firing cannon installation, the fitting of ventral guns was not officially pursued, and was left to prudent commanders in the field.

At an Air Ministry conference on 22 November, 1944, Air Vice Marshall Harris stated that Bomber Command had wanted 0.5 in machine-gun turrets but

A D tail turret with AGL(T) (Airborne Gun-laying radar).

there had been unnecessary delays. Bomber Command had gone so far as to arrange for the development of the Rose Turret itself. He pressed for the Boulton Paul D turret on all of the new Lincolns, with any surplus going to the Halifax, and the new FN.82 turret for the Lancaster.

The company built 1,597 turrets itself, during the War plus the equivalent of 207 more for testing and training purposes; apart from the 20,000 plus built by Joseph Lucas. It created a turret school for the training of RAF fitter/armourers and electricians, 2,285 personnel passing through this establishment. The company's electro-hydraulic system was shown to be the most successful one used for gun turrets during the War. An analysis of the operational records of the Halifax, with electro-hydraulic turrets and the Lancaster, with Frazer-Nash all-hydraulic turrets (driven by the aircraft's hydraulic system) showed that the Frazer-Nash system could be four to five times more likely to be damaged, due to the greater vulnerability of the hydraulic lines.

Sadly, the man who had pioneered the electro-hydraulic gun turret for Boulton Paul, as chief armament designer, H A 'Pop' Hughes, was killed during the War. On returning from a trip to America to impart the company's knowledge of gun turrets, his ship was torpedoed and sunk. John North was on the same trip, but luckily for him he returned by air.

Norwich Resumes Production

Back in Norwich history repeated itself. Because of their woodworking skills, Boulton & Paul were asked to return to aircraft production. They became part of the group of companies building the Airspeed Oxford which was of course built of wood. They built the fuselage sides and cabin doors for Airspeed, but not for the three other companies producing the aircraft (de Havilland, Percival, and Standard Motors). They also made the gun turret mounting for the Armstrong Whitworth gun turret which was fitted to a relatively small number of Oxfords.

They later became part of a consortium building Airspeed Horsa gliders. The Horsa was probably the most completely wooden aircraft ever built, even the cockpit controls were made of wood. It was manufactured in thirty sections, and Boulton & Paul were responsible for the nose, which was the most complicated, as it included the cockpit, controls and instruments (which were among the few non-wooden parts in the aircraft). Their first Horsa nose had just been completed when Norwich suffered from the attentions of the Luftwaffe. An air raid destroyed the assembly shop at the Riverside Works which had been the Aircraft Department, and now housed part of the woodworking department.

Production of the Horsa and Oxford were moved to the Midland Woodworking Company at Melton Mowbray. This was part of the Boulton & Paul Group, and many charge-hands and foremen moved from Norwich to oversee production. A number of them had worked on F.E.2, Camel and Snipe production in the First World War, and though Horsa noses were less glamourous in comparison, they were no less important.

The Boulton Paul factory at Pendeford also suffered an air attack during the War. As it was an obvious target, isolated from other buildings and Wolverhampton in general, it was heavily camouflaged and the aerodrome was

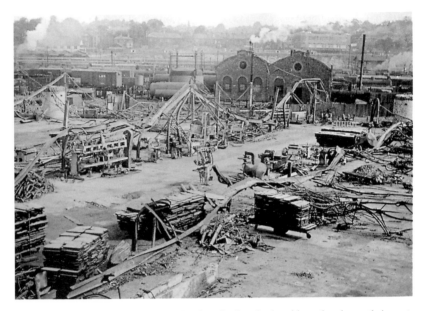

The Boulton & Paul Works, Norwich, after the fourth air raid on the city on 1 August, 1940. A Ju 88 hit the paint-shop, drawing office, canteen and joinery department with two high explosive bombs and many incendaries, causing an inferno, and killing nine employees. (*Alan Hague*)

painted with dummy hedgerows to disguise it. As a further precaution a dummy factory was built further along the Shropshire Union canal, complete with dummy aircraft, standing on the dummy aerodrome. However, this did not fool the crew of a sole Ju 88 on 29 September, 1940. At about 6.45 pm on a quiet Sunday evening it emerged from cloud, dived over the factory and then swung back. It dropped four or five bombs, which exploded on the sewage beds at Barnhurst, half a mile from the factory. The anti-aircraft gunners on the factory roof must have been half asleep, because they did not open fire until the bombs had exploded. The Ju 88 must have been hit however because it crashed in the Nuneaton area.

A system was instituted during the War for British aircraft manufacturers to become 'Sister' firms for US aircraft operated by the RAF and Fleet Air Arm. This work involved adapting the aircraft concerned to British operational standards, and the design and trial of the numerous modifications that were found necessary, and the installation of sundry pieces of new equipment, without the need to refer back to the original manufacturer in the United States. Boulton Paul became the 'Sister' firm for the Boston/Havoc light bomber/night fighter, and the Harvard trainer. Similar work was also done on these aircraft by Helliwells Ltd at Walsall, and both companies used nearby RAF Perton for most of their flight testing, as the respective grass aerodromes at Walsall and Pendeford were not really large enough for Bostons. The aircraft would be flown into Perton, which had paved runways, have all movable equipment taken out, and then be flown to Pendeford to have whatever modifications were necessary. These could be fairly major or very minor indeed. One of the latter was a message transportation system, in the event of intercom failure. There was no way for the pilot and rear gunner to communicate should the intercom fail, and so a line was rigged so that written messages could be pulled from one to the other!

A more extensive modification was the redesign of the Boston III/IIIA for glider towing. Boulton Paul did the stressing and design work, but Helliwell undertook the trial conversion of two aircraft, BZ292 and BZ311, with their test pilot, Peter Clifford undertaking the test flights.

The technical department took on a number of other tasks during the War including the design of the 170 gal ferry tank for the Spitfire, under Vickers sub-contract B.6833. A Mk Vc, BR202, was modified to take the new tank, and test flown with it for the first time on 4 May, 1942; Colin Evans being the pilot. The same aircraft was also fitted with a Vickers-designed 27 gal rear fuselage tank, with other equipment being relocated to accommodate it.

Boulton Paul also redesigned the Hampden T.B.1 to carry the American 22.4 in torpedo, and ASV radar. These and other modifications were undertaken at Pendeford on Hampden, P4369.

Another important contribution to the war effort, was the servicing of Boulton Paul's products. Apart from building the equivalent of 395 complete aircraft in the form of spare parts for Rocs and Defiants, they also made repairs to 355 Defiants at Pendeford, and sent out working parties for the local repair of both aircraft and turrets.

There were a number of changes to the Board during the War, with N R Adshead and J Kissane joining it in 1941, the former replacing Herbert Strickland, who resigned as joint managing director, due to ill-health, in November 1942. Both Lord Gorell and Viscount Sandon resigned from the Board during 1942 and R G Simpson became chairman in February. An appointment which rather put John North's nose out of joint was that of R G Beasley, formerly of Armstrong Whitworth Aircraft as general manager to oversee Barracuda production. The appointment was made by the Ministry of Aircraft Production, and there was little North could do about it, though he believed his authority was being diluted.

Further Fighter Projects

For a night-fighter to replace the Defiant, Blenheim and the Beaufighter Specification F.18/40, issued in August 1940, called for a two-seat aircraft armed with six 20 mm cannon. It was to have a speed of 400 mph at 20,000 ft, a three-hour patrol endurance, and a ceiling of 35,000 ft. An alternative armament could be four cannon and six machine-guns.

Boulton Paul offered their P.96 in a plethora of different versions for this requirement, with different engines and armament layouts. Three engines were offered, the Napier Sabre, the Rolls-Royce Griffon, and the Bristol Centaurus, for all armament layouts. In one form the P.96 featured both the A turret of the Defiant, as well as fixed forward-firing guns—an important departure from the original 'pure' concept of the turret fighter. In another form no turret was fitted,

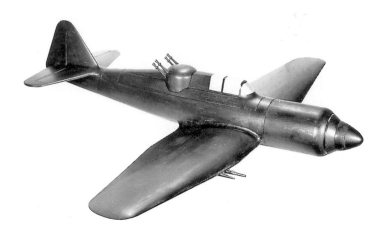

The potential Defiant replacement, the P.96 in this version with Bristol Centaurus engine, fixed forward cannon, and the A turret.

and the aircraft was strictly a conventional fighter with six wing-mounted cannon.

With a Griffon a speed of 367 mph at 21,000 ft, was hoped for, or 389 mph if a turret were not fitted. With a Sabre NS6SM, high-altitude engine, top speed rose to 392 mph and 415 mph at 34,000 ft respectively. It was decided by the Air Ministry that no single-engined fighter could meet the Specification.

Boulton Paul now put forward a twin-Sabre design, the P.97, with a twin-boom layout, again both with and without a turret, but the Ministry of Aircraft Production decided that it was too radical, rather conservatively as just such a twin-boom turret fighter was at that moment being built by Northrop in California, the P.61 Black Widow. On 23 September, 1940, further submissions were invited.

Gloster Aircraft were told that their F.9/37 twin-Taurus single-seater could well meet the Specification if enlarged to include a radar-operator, and

Alternative design for a Defiant replacement the P.97, in this form with Napier Sabre engines, fixed forward cannon and A turret.

re-engined with Merlins. On 13 October a go-ahead was given for a mock-up of the proposed layout, with Boulton Paul's design department aiding Gloster. Only four cannon would fit the nose of the aircraft, and these were to be supplemented with wing-mounted machine-guns. The mock-up was ready by 24 October, and the aircraft, with twin Merlin XXs, was given the name Reaper. The emergence of the de Havilland Mosquito, with its phenomenal performance, meant there was no need for the Reaper, and it was cancelled on 1 May, 1941.

This was not the only association between Boulton Paul and Gloster during the War. Gloster suffered from an overstretched design department while Boulton Paul usually had surplus capacity. It was for this reason that detail design of the wings for the Gloster E.28/39 (Britain's first jet aircraft) was undertaken at Boulton Paul. A similar arrangement was almost made with the Meteor. Gloster did not have the design capacity, or the production capacity to build the jigs and tools for their order for Meteors which amounted to 80 a month. The Ministry of Aircraft Production undertook to find suitable sub-contractors for what was a priority project. On 5 March, 1941, Gloster were able to confirm that Boulton Paul had the design and productive capacity to undertake the detail design of the Meteor wings, and to produce twelve pre-production wings followed by production of 80 a month. However, Boulton Paul did not become involved in the Meteor programme.

During the War the fighter became steadily heavier as more power meant heavier engines, and heavier airframes to carry them, and all the other equipment, including heavier armament, which was being built into new requirements. The Hurricane grew from a loaded weight of 6,600 lb for the Mk I to 8,510 lb for the Mk V, and its intended replacement, the Typhoon, had a loaded weight of 11,250 lb, even without any underwing armament. Extra weight was inevitably detrimental to performance in the climb, and manoeuvrability.

In August 1942 consideration was given to developing a new fighter which would excel in just these two aspects. It would need to climb at 4,500 ft/min up to 20,000 ft, which was seen as its optimum fighting altitude, as it was expected that the new jet fighters would rule at higher altitude. It was essential that it should have excellent manoeuvrability, with a fast rate of roll, and the high rate of climb would be coupled with rapid acceleration. Manoeuvrability was stressed before speed, but it was expected to have a top speed of 450 mph. Looking to the future, it was also felt desirable that it had sufficient range for Far East operations.

The Specification issued was F.6/42, and the Air Ministry was anxious that companies which were already fully committed to other projects should not have their attention diverted, and anyway felt that the main two fighter manufacturers, Hawker and Supermarine, would only try to adapt their existing designs to fit the new requirement. Companies such as Westland, Folland, Airspeed and Boulton Paul were canvassed, though inevitably Hawker and Supermarine also took an interest.

Boulton Paul was anxious for success with another of its own designs after the disappointment of the Defiant, and the cancellation of the P.92. It put forward a number of possible projects, not all of them directly tailored to the requirements of F.6/42.

Boulton Paul were concerned that existing engines in conventional layouts could not provide the necessary performance, and put forward their P.98 project, which was for a Griffon-powered aircraft in a tail-first layout, with the engine driving contra-rotating pusher propellers. Further versions were offered with the Sabre and the Centaurus. The all-up weight of the Sabre version was estimated to be 9,892 lb, hopefully giving a wing loading which would match the Fw 190. Its top speed at 20,000 ft was estimated to be 446 mph. The MAP considered it to be 800 lb overweight and so Boulton Paul submitted a conventional design.

The P.101 was a highly unorthodox layout being a staggered biplane, with cantilever wings! It was powered by a single Centaurus 12SM (Modified), driving a single tractor propeller. If this was not radical enough the aircraft also had a non-retractable undercarriage with the cannon armament housed within the very large wheel spats! Not surprisingly the Ministry were not too keen on the P.101, and the submissions from Miles and Airspeed were considered still too slow. Boulton Paul then put forward two more unconventional layouts.

The P.99 was a Griffon-powered aircraft with a twin-boom layout. The engine was a pusher driving contra-rotating propellers, leaving the nose free for the armament. The pilot sat right in the nose of the fuselage with a bubble canopy, giving him an excellent all-round view, compared with conventional fighters of the day.

The P.100 was another tail-first design, with the pilot once more seated right in the nose, just in front of the shoulder-mounted canard foreplanes. The swept wing was mounted on the lower rear fuselage with the vertical tail surfaces and rudders on the tips. A tricycle undercarriage layout had to be adopted because of the tail-first layout.

In mid-September the RAE compared all the submissions for the Specification, which were many and varied in number. Folland's was preferred, though the company was not thought capable of producing it. Hawker's submission came second, and they were thought most likely to receive an order, if one was forthcoming, with their vast experience and design capacity, allied to that of Gloster. Airspeed's was thought the next best design, then those from Vickers and Westland. Boulton Paul's submissions were all considered too futuristic. In the end no production orders were made for this Specification, and versions of existing aircraft had to fulfil the requirement.

Boulton Paul offered one more design during the War for a land-based fighter, the P.107. This was a two-seat long-range escort fighter, powered by a single Bristol Centaurus CE12SM, but it received little official interest.

It is hard to escape the conclusion that the Defiant had stained the company's credibility. They had produced a fighter which had proved a failure, because it was built to a flawed concept. They had been ardent advocates of the concept it is true, but that was only to be expected as they were the licence holders for the electro-hydraulic turret. They had produced as good a design as could be expected, but the Defiant had never been tested in the role for which it was designed, a daylight destroyer of unescorted bombers. It was not the only flawed concept to be advocated and implemented during the War, the Turbinlite Havoc was another, but in terms of orders placed and resources consumed, it was one of the most glaring. It is impossible not to wonder if this did not affect judgements when further Boulton Paul proposals were received, in competition with such as Hawker's, Bristol's or Supermarine's. Of the seventeen major aircraft manufacturers before the War, Boulton Paul was the only one which received orders for just one of its designs.

Naval Aircraft

When Defiant production came to an end it was replaced in the factory by licenced production of the Fairey Barracuda. This aircraft was a result of Specification S.24/37, issued in November 1937, for a Naval dive-bomber/ torpedo bomber/reconnaissance aircraft. Fairey won the contract in January 1940.

The Barracuda was an unusual-looking high-wing monoplane with a high-set tail. Its sheer ugliness was due to the varied roles the designers had had to try to incorporate. The high wing was to give the crew downward visibility for the reconnaissance role, and this meant an immensely long and strong undercarriage was needed, made even longer by the fact that room for a torpedo under the fuselage was also required. One of the more repeatable nicknames bestowed upon it was 'the pregnant stork'. The wing was so high, special handles had to be fitted beneath the tips so that deck crew could reach them to manoeuvre the Barracuda on the ground.

The tail had to be in its high, strut-braced position because the dive-brakes affected the airflow over the prototype's more normal low-set tail. Even the

Fairey Barracuda production line at Pendeford on 21 August, 1942.

105

dive-brakes were rather strange. They were Fairey-Youngman invertable flaps, which when horizontal provided lift.

The Mk I was powered by a Rolls-Royce Merlin 30 giving 1,300 hp, which was not enough for such a large aircraft, and only thirty were manufactured by Fairey. The Mk II was fitted with a Merlin 32 of 1,640 hp, and orders were placed beginning in 1941 for 1,688 aircraft, with licenced production by Blackburn, Westland, and Boulton Paul. Fairey built 675, Blackburn 695, Westland only 18 and Boulton Paul 300.

The first Boulton Paul built example to fly was DP855. Unfortunately someone forgot to remove the pins preventing undercarriage retraction, and so the flight was made with the undercarriage down! This aircraft was later converted to become the Mk III prototype. The Barracuda saw widespread service with the Royal Navy. Its most famous action was the first carrier-launched dive-bombing attack on the German battleship *Tirpitz*, in a Norwegian fjord. The ship was severely crippled from fifteen hits from 500 and 1,000 lb bombs. Two more attacks on the *Tirpitz* were unsuccessful.

The Barracuda Mk III was an anti-submarine reconnaissance version with an ASV Mk X scanner in a radome under the rear fuselage. The prototype was converted from DP855, which was the first Boulton Paul built Barracuda. Production orders for 600 Mk IIIs were received by Boulton Paul, of which 392 were built. The last 208 were cancelled at the end of the War.

By 1943, though the factory was busy producing the Barracuda, the design staff was running out of modification work on the Defiant and Havoc/Boston. New tasks were being forseen for aircraft to operate in the Pacific. Perhaps because of his involvement with the Barracuda, John North became interested in the design of naval aircraft.

Sir Stafford Cripps (centre) inspecting a completed Barracuda, with J D North (left) and R Beesley (right).

In his usual analytical way he tried to express the problems of carrier conflict in a mathematical way. He hoped to create the parameters for a new generation of naval aircraft. He laid out his thoughts in a treatise in 1943 entitled *Note on carrier borne aircraft*. In it he examined the problems of naval warfare in the context of the large distances of the South Pacific. He expressed the problems in a single mathematical expression $K(R - D)n$, where R was the range of the aircraft and D the distance from land. The co-efficient n was a complex factor which altered for land or carrier-based aircraft.

He gathered as much data as possible about existing carrier aircraft, so that he could test this expression against them. Then an opportunity arose to apply his theories, Specification N.7/43 for a high-performance single-seat naval fighter to be based around an existing design but fitted with a radial engine, though an inline could be offered as an alternative. Boulton Paul succeeded in getting the requirement changed to a design study to be fitted with a Griffon engine, and to be submitted by 24 April, 1943.

Boulton Paul's submission was based on the Defiant, the P.103A with a Griffon RG5SM, and the alternative P.103B with a Centaurus CE12SM. A more radical submission was also offered to fit the same specification, the P.104, which was a tail-first pusher with the Griffon engine.

By May the Naval Staff had reacted favourably to a suggestion from Hawker that their lightweight Tempest project to F.2/43 (which was to become the Hawker Fury) would be easily amended to fit N.7/43, by navalising it and fitting a more powerful Centaurus XII engine. Work on the P.103 and P.104 was abandoned but the company was compensated to some degree because Hawker's design staff was so stretched that Boulton Paul were awarded the contract to navalise the Fury. Later in the year a new Specification, N.22/43, was issued to cover production aircraft. In April 1944 a contract was placed with Hawker for 200 Furies and 200 Sea Furies, half the naval aircraft to be built by Boulton Paul.

Many of the features of Boulton Paul's N.7/43 submissions were of such interest that a Defiant was ordered with some of them built in, for testing purposes. This 'Special Features' Defiant was to have a Griffon engine with a Rotol contra-rotating propeller, and an undercarriage which extended in length when lowered, to give the propeller sufficient clearance. There were to be automatic electric trim tabs on the elevator, and a 'dive-brake' propeller, with automatic undercarriage door opening to simulate bomb doors. There would also be automatic closure of the undercarriage doors. A Defiant, TT.1, DR895, was used to test the electric trim tabs, but the Special Features Defiant was not built.

Many of these features were intended for another Boulton Paul naval project, the P.105, which was a multi-purpose attack aircraft powered by a Bristol Centaurus CE12SM. It was designed so that it could be converted aboard a carrier from single- to multi-seat configurations, depending on the role to be undertaken. The design, interesting, though it was, and echoed in later years by the Douglas Skyraider, failed to gain a contract.

Late in the War the company received a request from the Naval Staff to convert an existing naval strike aircraft to take a jet engine as a 'power egg' in the rear fuselage. No type was specified, so John North naturally chose the Barracuda, as it was being produced in the factory. The Air Ministry then decided that they preferred the Fairey Firefly to be the basis of the conversion, but in the end relented and let the Barracuda jet project proceed, as the Boulton Paul P.102.

The company chose the Barracuda II and redesigned it to take a Whittle W.2B/37 engine. The Air Ministry decided they would prefer the Barracuda V, and so the company re-drew the project on that basis. Once more the scheme was rejected as, by now, the more powerful Whittle W.2/700 was available, offering better performance. Before this engine could be substituted, the Air Ministry had lost interest, and the Jet Barracuda was abandoned.

The first Boulton Paul built Sea Fury, VB857, was nearing completion as the end of the War approached. The Boulton Paul contract for one hundred Sea Furies was then cancelled, and VB857 was transported to Hawker's for completion. It first flew on 31 January, 1946, powered by a Centaurus XV. With the cancellation of the last 208 Barracudas as well, the company suddenly found itself without an aircraft to build.

The company also suffered the reduction of another order for a naval craft, a collapsible two-man canoe. Designed during the War and made of sheet metal, these interesting canoes were powered, and capable of a speed of 8 knots, with a range of 35 miles. They featured catamaran outriggers on each side, filled with table-tennis balls. They were capable of being ejected through a standard 21 in torpedo tube, and an order for 200 had been placed with Boulton Paul, but this was reduced to 25 at the War's end.

The Balliol

The end of the War left Boulton Paul in a parlous state, production contracts for the Barracuda and Sea Fury having been cancelled. The work-force had expanded during the War from 1,200 to over 4,800, and work had to be found to occupy them. Turret production was moved back from Joseph Lucas of course, but production contracts for turrets had also been severely curtailed.

On 15 January, 1946, the company was lucky enough to secure a contract to convert redundant Wellington bombers to T.10 standard for Flying Training Command. A total of 270 were converted between January 1946 and November 1950, filling an important gap on the production lines. The Wellingtons, often arriving at Pendeford in a very poor condition, with fabric hanging off, were stripped completely on arrival, totally overhauled and then re-assembled and re-covered.

Though a Cirrus Major powered three-seat light aircraft, the P.110, had been projected and then abandoned, John North decided that military training aircraft held the best prospects for a company of Boulton Paul's size. The P.106 project had already been submitted for Specification T.23/43 which called for the definite replacement for the RAF's elementary trainers, the Tiger Moth and Magister. Unusually the specification called for a three-seat aircraft, with the third seat behind the normal side-by-side pupil and instructor, for a second pupil to gain extra experience by watching his colleague. An example of 'peer pressure' being put to some use. Boulton Paul submitted a design powered by either the Gipsy III or the Gipsy Queen II, in both three-seat form (P.106A) and

Model of the P.106 three-seat elementary trainer to Specification T.23/43, in March 1944.
The contract was awarded to the Percival Prentice.

more normal two-seat tandem form (P.106B), but Percival received the contract for their Prentice, which was to go into service in 1947.

Specification T.7/45 was issued for a complimentary advanced trainer to replace the Harvard and Master. It also was to be a three-seat aircraft, and was to be powered by a 1,000 hp propeller-turbine, either the Rolls-Royce Dart or the Armstrong Siddeley Mamba, with an alternative of the improved Bristol Perseus. It was to be designed from the outset for easy conversion to a carrier deck-landing trainer, with folding wings, provision for arrester gear and a strong enough undercarriage.

The one ray of hope for the British aircraft industry as a whole in 1945 was the jet engine. Advanced though they were, all the piston-engined aircraft that had been built during the War could be rendered obsolete overnight by turbo-jet and propeller-turbine powered aircraft, and with the destruction of the German aircraft industry it was Britain which led the world in this new technology.

There were two main contenders for Specification T.7/45, the Avro Athena T.1 and the Boulton Paul P.108 Balliol both of which were designed to be powered by the Rolls-Royce Dart. Boulton Paul's alternative, with Bristol's improved Perseuis engine, was designated P.109, but this version was abandoned very quickly. By August 1945 a contract was drawn up for the supply of four P.108 prototypes, with the Dart engine.

Delays with the Dart engine led to the consideration of other engine choices. By the end of August 1946 a further contract was placed for twenty pre-production Balliols, and Boulton Paul decided to fit ten with the Dart and ten plus the four prototypes with the Armstrong Siddeley Mamba. The Mamba was a scaled-down Armstrong Siddeley Python with a straight-through gas flow, rated at 1,320 hp.

The first prototype Balliol, VL892, had to be fitted with a Bristol Mercury 820 hp piston engine, as a temporary measure, so that flight trials could get under way, as the Mamba was not ready. The first test Mamba did not achieve its design shaft power until December 1946, when 1,013 hp was recorded, and it was not until May 1947 that the reduction gear could be made to run

The Armstrong Siddeley Mamba powered second prototype P.108 Balliol, VL917, the world's first single-engined propeller-turbine powered aeroplane.

satisfactorily, but further small difficulties still remained, the greatest being the development of a combustion system which would survive long enough to complete a 150 hour type test without attention. The first flight of the Mercury-powered Balliol took place on 30 May, 1947, in the hands of Robert Lindsay Neale, who had taken over from Cecil Feather as Boulton Paul's chief test pilot.

Lindsay Neale had learned to fly in 1931 and in 1935 set up his own aviation consultancy business under the title Lindsay Neale Aviation. He was also a director and test pilot for Dart Aircraft Ltd, which produced the little single-seat Dart Kitten. He suffered a motor-cycle accident which left him with a plate in his leg. This may be why, though he joined the RAF at the outbreak of the War, he was released for service as a test pilot with Boulton Paul in 1940. When test flying Defiants rather than take ballast he would often ask anyone on the apron whether they would like a short flight. Those that accepted often discovered that what he had in mind was more than a simple circuit, and emerged from the turret looking rather green. When Cecil Feather retired because of ill-health in 1945, Lindsay Neale therefore took over as chief test pilot.

On 28 June, 1947, Lindsay Neale performed a remarkable feat of airmanship. When flying with his family on holiday in the South of France in a Miles Messenger the engine fell off. A wooden propeller blade had broken off, and the huge out-of-balance forces tore the engine, complete with its mountings and cowlings right off the aircraft. By getting his family and all their luggage piled as near the windscreen as they could, and with the stick hard forward, he managed to retain enough control to glide down for a landing in a field. This was a testament both to his flying skill and the slow-flying qualities of the Messenger. Miles later presented him with a model of the aircraft in its 'glider' mode, as a momento of an occasion which gave new meaning to the nautical expression 'Finished with engine'.

In August 1947 Peter Tishaw was employed as a second test pilot. He had joined the RAF in 1941, and learned to fly in America. After serving as a flight instructor, he left the RAF in January 1947, took his 'B' Licence and his Navigator's Licence and joined Boulton Paul in August.

Within two weeks of the Balliol's first flight the decision was made to change the production engine to the Rolls-Royce Merlin 35. Delays in development of the Mamba, which did not complete its 150 hour type-test until February 1948, and its expense, had led to a change of view by the Air Ministry. There were large numbers of war-surplus Merlin engines and spares, and in 1947 Specification T.14/47 was issued for a Merlin 35 powered two-seat advanced trainer, for which both the Balliol and the Athena were redesigned. The testing of the Mamba-powered version was still to go ahead however and it was the second prototype, VL917, which became the world's first single-engined propeller-turbine powered aircraft when it took to the air from Wolverhampton on 24 March, 1948, flown by Lindsay Neale, followed by the third prototype, VL935, on 27 May from Bitteswell. The rival Mamba-powered Avro Athena did not fly until 12 June, 1948.

Problems occurred with the first Mamba-powered aircraft, VL917. It suffered engine troubles, on a test flight at Wolverhampton, and in an attempt to land at Pendeford clipped the boundary fence and crashed. Lindsay Neale, who was flying it, suffered a broken leg. Testing of VL935 was moved to Bitteswell, near Coventry, which had longer runways, and was suitably near Armstrong Siddeley's factory.

Once more it was the Balliol Merlin-powered prototype, VW897, which was first in the air on 10 July, 1948, flown by Peter Tishaw, followed by the first Merlin-powered Athena on 1 August. Three more Merlin-powered Balliol prototypes, redesignated T.2 were also constructed, and then a contract was placed for seventeen pre-production aircraft for service trials, replacing the

Balliol VL917 after clipping the fence at Pendeford while Lindsay Neale was attempting an emergency landing without power.

Three Balliols all with different engines (right to left). VL892, the first prototype with interim Bristol Mercury, VL935, the third prototype with the Mamba, and VW897 the Merlin-engined prototype T.2.

earlier order for twenty turbine-powered aircraft. With Lindsay Neale still recovering from his broken leg, it was Peter Tishaw who demonstrated the Balliol T.2 at Farnborough in 1948, putting in a spirited performance, which contrasted strongly with that of the more sedate Mercury-powered prototype the previous year at Radlett.

Boulton Paul tendered for two more trainer specifications. The Prentice had proved less than satisfactory in service, being under-powered and clumsy. As early as August 1948 OR.257 was issued for a two-seat replacement, and this was followed by Specification T.16/48 for which the company submitted two designs, the P.112 with the Alvis Leonides engine, and the P.113 with the Pratt & Whitney R-1340 Wasp, both aircraft being reminiscent of the Balliol. An elaborate mock-up of the P.112 was built but prototypes were ordered from Handley Page and Percival, and it was the Percival Provost which replaced the unloved Prentice.

Mock-up of the P.112, an Alvis Leonides powered elementary trainer project.

Although the Prentice had been originally ordered to replace the Tiger Moth, this type had been retained in service for the first primary part of the flying training syllabus, and so Specification T.8/48 was issued for a true replacement for the Tiger Moth. Boulton Paul again submitted two designs, the P.115 with the Gipsy Queen 71 engine, and the P.116 with the Gipsy Queen 50. Choice finally fell between the Fairey Primer and the de Havilland Chipmunk, and the latter received the production orders.

Disaster struck the Merlin-powered Balliol prototype on 3 February, 1949. Lindsay Neale had found elevator reversal occurred on the Balliol at around 320 mph. With Peter Tishaw as co-pilot he set out to dive VW897 at over 400 mph to check the control responses. Unfortunately the windscreen disintegrated and the aircraft dived into the ground killing both men.

Flt Lt A E Gunn, who had been testing the Balliol at Boscombe Down, took over the test programme, and became Boulton Paul's chief test pilot. Alexander Ewen Gunn, known to most people as 'Ben' was born in Glasgow in 1923. From 1942 to 1943 he attended the RAF College, Cranwell, and then served with No.501 Squadron, flying Spitfires and No.274 Squadron, flying Tempest Vs. On VE Day he took up a post test flying at the A & AEE, Boscombe Down in 'A' Fighter Test Squadron. In 1948 he attended Course No.7 at the Empire Test Pilots School. Over the whole of his career he was to fly 175 different types of aircraft from gliders to V Bombers.

A E 'Ben' Gunn, Boulton Paul Aircraft's last chief test pilot.

A pre-production Balliol T.2, VR596.

At Boscombe Down, to prove that the Balliol was safe to spin he had taken it through 25 turns from 27,000 ft, but its spinning characteristics remained a little strange. Those of the Athena were even stranger, however.

Two of the pre-production Balliols, from the Central Flying School gave a display of aerobatics at the 1950 RAF Display at Farnborough.

The control reversal problems were solved by altering the tailplane incidence, and strengthening it. The 1,245 hp Merlin 35 gave the Balliol T.2 a top speed of 288 mph at 9,000 ft and a ceiling of 32,500 ft. It was armed with a single .303

The Balliol production lines at Pendeford.

Browning machine-gun in the port wing and provision for two 60 lb rockets under each wing. Fully loaded it weighed 8,410 lb.

With the end of the Wellington conversion programme, the factory floor space at Pendeford was able to be totally cleared ready for mass-production of the Balliol, for which the RAF had a requirement for several hundred, as the basic trainer for the Prentice/Balliol flying training programme. Contracts for a total of 418 aircraft were placed for the Balliol T.2, and Blackburn Aircraft were brought into the programme by the Air Ministry, in a reversal of previous associations between the two companies, setting up a second production line to build 120 more Balliols. Once more Boulton Paul's bad luck intervened and the Air Ministry had a further change of plans. It was decided it was more appropriate to have a jet aircraft as an advanced trainer, and the Vampire T.11 was ordered for this role. Balliol contracts were substantially reduced. Boulton Paul were to build only 132 T.2s at Wolverhampton, and Blackburn only 30.

Extensive efforts were made to sell the Balliol abroad. In 1950, VR597 was

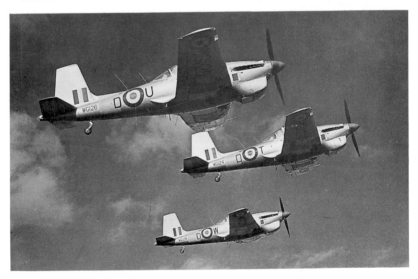

Three Balliol T.2s (WG126, 124 and 128) of No.7 Flying Training School at Cottesmore.

taken on a sales tour of the Middle East, through Egypt, Iraq, Syria and the Lebanon. Operation in hot and dry conditions proved to be acceptable, but no orders were forthcoming. For a time there seemed an excellent prospect of large sales to India, but with the RAF receiving delivery priority, the order went elsewhere.

The Royal Navy had a requirement for a deck-landing trainer, and the Balliol had been designed from the outset with this in mind. The prototype fully-navalised Balliol was a converted pre-production Balliol T.2, VR599, which flew in October 1952 and a total of 30 were ordered, designated Sea Balliol T.21s. R B (Dickie) Mancus, was employed as Ben Gunn's assistant in June 1953, and a year later George Dunworth also joined the flying staff.

The last Sea Balliol was delivered on 7 December, 1954. The Sea Balliol equipped HMS *Triumph* Ship's Flight, No.702 Squadron, Junior Officers Training Course at Ford, which became No.781 Squadron, No.796 Squadron,

Richard 'Dickie' Mancus, Ben Gunn's assistant test pilot during the early fifties, sitting in the last production Balliol immediately after painting.

Sea Balliol T.21 WL718 landing on HMS *Triumph*.

The Balliol company demonstrator, G-ANSF.

Observer and Air Signals School at Culdrose, and later on No.727 Dartmouth Cadet Air Training Squadron.

Boulton Paul operated their own Balliol demonstrator, an ex-RAF machine, with civil registration G-ANSF, which flew for the first time on 23 August, 1954, and was demonstrated at Farnborough that year. Only one further order for the Balliol was forthcoming however. The Ceylon Air Force ordered twelve, the first being delivered in April 1955 and the last in August 1957.

Further Trainer Projects

In 1951, with Balliol production under way, Boulton Paul announced a private venture jet conversion trainer, the P.119. With RAF pilots going from the Merlin-powered Balliol straight to the jet fighters of the day, the company felt there was a need for a relatively high performance jet trainer, which could also be used for weapons training, with a secondary counter-insurgency role, though that term was not then current.

Although not built to an official requirement, great hopes were invested in this project. An elaborate full-scale mock-up was built, of what was a very

Mock-up of the P.119 applied jet trainer, with Derwent or Nene engine.

116

attractive swept-wing design. The P.119 was designed to take the Derwent or the Nene engine with unusual cheek-mounted NACA intakes. Intakes of this type were more normally used for small air vents, though similar intakes were tested on the Sabre in the United States. With the Derwent the top speed was estimated to be 475 mph at 22,500 ft, and with the Nene 555 mph at 10,000 ft.

In the same manner as the Balliol, the P.119 was designed from the outset to be very easily maintained. The most startling feature of this was that the whole of the rear fuselage and tail assembly could be removed in one piece, leaving the engine totally revealed, attached just behind the rear spar. To some extent this was a reminder of the swinging engine mount which John North pioneered on the P.10 in 1919.

RAF and Fleet Air Arm members inspecting the P.119 mock-up.

Side-by-side seating was fitted, and there was provision for two 20 mm cannon in the lower forward fuselage with wing hard-points for rockets and bombs. Allowance was made for the construction of a deck-landing version, with provision for wing-folding and arrester gear.

Another trainer was also subsequently offered, the P.131, to O.R.AIR/37, with a Bristol Orpheus engine. In this aircraft the intakes were in the wing roots. Neither of these projects drew any official interest, and the introduction of the Vampire trainer to the syllabus, instead of the Balliol, eliminated the need. In the same way that Balliol export hopes had been destroyed by the availability of cheap Harvards, export hopes for the P.119/P.131 were slim, against the keen competition of the Lockheed T-33 and the Vampire.

When the RAF decided to change to an all-jet training syllabus, Boulton Paul offered their P.124 as a replacement for the Provost. Once more it was an attractive design with a moderately swept wing, powered by an Armstrong Siddeley Viper engine. A simple conversion of the Balliol powered by a Derwent, the P.125, was also projected. The Provost was eventually replaced by

117

the Jet Provost and none of the Boulton Paul jet trainers were built. If any of them had secured an order the future of the company would have been very different. The jet trainer projects were the last serious throw of the dice for Boulton Paul's aircraft production hopes. Further aircraft were projected for different roles, but they were all far more ambitious, and beyond the scope of such a moderately sized company. The British aircraft industry was about to contract into two and finally one large grouping, and there was little scope for a small unit such as Boulton Paul, at least in the production of full-size aircraft.

Experimental Aircraft

At the end of the War a large amount of German experimental data about delta-wing aircraft came into British hands. This wing form offered many advantages, most notably the elimination of the weight and drag of the conventional tail, but there was still much to be discovered, particularly in the areas of stability and control. The Government decided to fund a large research programme, and as part of this issued Specification E.27/46 for the construction of jet-powered delta-wing aircraft dedicated to research. Boulton Paul was awarded the contract to design and build this aircraft, which became the P.111, and work began on its construction in 1947.

The design certificate for this aircraft was to be signed by the new chief engineer at Boulton Paul, Dr S C Redshaw. N R Adshead had died in 1948 and John North became sole managing director, Dr Redshaw being appointed to the

Dr S C Redshaw, chief designer of Boulton Paul Aircraft when the last complete aircraft, the P.111 and P.120, were built.

118

Dr S C Redshaw (left) and 'Ben' Gunn in front of the P.111.

Board as chief engineer, along with G C Haynes as company secretary.

The P.111 had a 5,100 lb static thrust Nene, with an elliptical nose intake. The delta wing had 45 deg leading edge sweep, and had detachable tips to investigate both blunt and pointed versions. Control was by powered elevons and a rudder set in the triangular fin. It was capable of a very high rate of roll. An anti-spin parachute was incorporated in a fairing on the starboard side of the rear fuselage.

After completion and taxi-ing trials at Wolverhampton, which included deploying the anti-spin parachute in a braking role, the P.111 was dismantled and taken to Boscombe Down. Its first flight was undertaken there on 10 October, 1950, by Sqn Ldr Smyth, the CO of the Aero Flight. It was found to be pleasant to fly but at higher speeds it was tricky to handle because of the very sensitive controls. It was clear that a better system of 'feel' had to be imparted from the powered controls to the pilot. Other problems arose with the undercarriage, and the unframed windscreen. A minimum of 7,000 rpm was needed from the Nene to keep the generators running, and this resulted in quite fast flat approaches. As it was such a clean design pilots experienced difficulty slowing the aircraft enough for landing.

After 28 flying hours a new framed windscreen was fitted, and a new 'feel' system fitted to the controls. The P.111 appeared at the Farnborough Show of 1951. Between October 1951 and 29 August, 1952, three landing accidents were experienced, the last one quite serious. The aircraft was returned to the company for repair, but to everyone's embarrassment the removal of the Flight Sheds had meant the aircraft would no longer go through the main doors. As the management tried to figure out a solution, a young apprentice named Brian Holmes suggested running one mainwheel on to a ramp, so that the wing just squeezed through the door at an angle, and this was successful. While repairs

119

The P.111 VT935 over Boscombe Down.

The P.111A, in new all-yellow paintwork, wth air-brakes extended.

were being made, the opportunity was taken to make more fundamental modifications.

A long pitot head was fitted to the intake splitter plate, the undercarriage doors were modified, and most important of all, four petal air-brakes were fitted around the centre fuselage. The most striking change was the all-yellow paint scheme, which soon gained the P.111A, as it was now redesignated, the sobriquet *Yellow Peril.*

After being taken by road back to Boscombe Down the P.111A made its first flight on 2 July, 1953. After 40 flights undertaken by Boulton Paul to test their modifications it rejoined the Aero Flight and began an extensive research programme at the A & AEE, Bedford, which finished in June 1958. It was capable of Mach 0.93 (650 mph) in level flight at 35,000 ft. With the improved 'feel' of the controls the P.111A was pleasant to fly throughout the speed range.

Once its flying days were over it was used as an instructional airframe at the College of Aeronautics, Cranwell, for many years, before moving nearer home to the Midland Air Museum at Coventry Airport. Displayed in the open, the Museum has found it so well constructed that it suffers far less from the elements than other contemporary airframes. It was completely repainted during 1992, still in its *Yellow Peril* scheme.

A further development of the P.111A, the P.120, was built to Specification E.27/49. It was designed to continue the programme of basic research into the delta wing. It featured a swept fin and rudder, unlike the triangular unit of the P.111, and had a horizontal tail surface set near the top of the fin. In addition it had provision for movable wingtips.

It first flew on 6 August, 1952, piloted by Ben Gunn. On its first flight it consumed an alarming amount of Boscombe Down's runway before getting into the air. The problem was the tailplane setting, but once in the air it proved quite pleasant to handle. On its first flights it was left unpainted apart from RAF roundels and serial, but in preparation for the Farnborough Show of 1952 it was given an all-black scheme, which immediately earned it the nick-name *Black Widowmaker*, which was to be almost prophetic. The powered controls had no feedback system, and on 28 August, after only 11 hours of flying the P.120 crashed because of this.

As he was flying along the south coast at about 5,000 ft Gunn heard a loud

The P.120 VT951 at Pendeford, in its original unpainted condition.

The P.120 newly painted all-black, at Boscombe Down.

121

buzz, and then there was a heart-stopping bang. The P.120 began a series of rolls to port, which he was only able to correct with full opposite rudder and stick. He pulled out of the resulting dive using the tailplane trimmer. An intense flutter had developed in the port elevon, unknown to Gunn, and a hinge had eventually failed.

He fought for half an hour using the remaining elevon, and the trimming tailplane, to control the aircraft, steering it towards the long runway at Boscombe Down, but it became obvious that even a wheels-up landing would be impossible. When he jettisoned the canopy the P.120 went into a roll, and though he tried to eject immediately, the aircraft was upside down when he did so. By mistake he pulled the parachute ripcord before jettisoning the seat, and this saved his life as he crashed through some trees just as the canopy opened. He had the dubious distinction of being the first pilot to eject from a delta-wing aircraft. The P.120 ploughed into Salisbury Plain.

The P.111/P.111A came too late to affect the design of the two main aircraft to emanate from the delta-wing programme, the Gloster Javelin and the Avro Vulcan, but it did serve to confirm much of the data which was accumulated elsewhere. Because of its short existence, the P.120 contributed little or nothing in the way of extra knowledge, but did hasten the introduction of automatic ejection seats!

Apart from these two little deltas Boulton Paul was engaged in a great deal of other basic experimental work through the 1950s. The Gust Alleviation Lancaster was the most substantial physical example of this.

The company hoped to alleviate the problems of turbulence on aircraft structures (and passengers) by a system it devised for gust alleviation. The system was tested using a modified Lancaster. A long probe in the nose of the aircraft containing an electro-manometric transducer detected the vertical

The Gust Alleviation Lancaster outside the factory, showing the long nose probe designed to detect sudden gusts, and to take automatic corrections with the ailerons.

122

components of gusts and caused the ailerons to operate symmetrically, to counteract the effect. There was a built in delay to allow for the distance of the probe in front of the wing, and the speed of the aircraft, a delay in the order of $\frac{1}{10}$th of a second. The ailerons were operated by Boulton Paul electro-hydraulic power control units. The only addition to the normal controls of the aircraft was a lever which operated through a gate in Manual, Power, and Gust modes. The Lancaster with its long nose probe, was a familiar sight for some time operating from Pendeford, usually flown by Ben Gunn.

Further Boulton Paul experimental work tended to result in groups of projects, some of them involving basic research, and some of them applied research with commercial aspirations. There were a number of studies in high-speed design, including the P.113 and P.114, supersonic designs with one and two Avon engines respectively, and the P.118 for a highly swept-wing aircraft powered by a Rolls-Royce Nene. One project in this area, for which a great deal of work was done was the P.126 Very Thin Wing Project.

Production of a very thin wing, as part of the P.126 Very Thin Wing Project.

Because airspeeds at low altitude resulted in very high airframe temperatures, and low angles of attack prevail at supersonic speed, the immensely stiff wings which were being designed in the mid-1950s to overcome this problem, led to wings which were very thin. The wings of the F.104 Starfighter being an obvious example. Boulton Paul devised a process for creating such wings from solid light alloy. The wing was built up of a series of 'I' section strips, created in an extrusion process, each being a small part of the upper and lower wing surface. These were locked together and the final machining done on the finished wing, which was very rigid as a result. The whole project was centred on a tentative design project for a single-seat twin-engined fighter not unlike the Bristol Type 188 in layout.

This aircraft, along with a number of other fighters with unusual layouts was never built. There was the P.121 single-seat supersonic fighter to ER.110T with a Rolls-Royce Avon RA.8 engine, the P.122 rocket-powered interceptor with an Armstrong Siddeley Screamer engine and the P.127 interceptor which evolved from the Thin Wing Project. The P.128 was a twin-Sapphire powered research aircraft for Mach 2 flight and the P.129 was a research aircraft with a Viper jet engine for cruising flight augmented with a Screamer rocket, very similar in layout and concept to the French Sud-Ouest 9050 Trident II.

Another project outside the general flow of high-speed fighter and trainer designs on which the design department were working through the early fifties was the P.123 short-range expendable bomber. This project to Specification UB.109T, was laid out in two basic versions, and was broadly reminiscent of the US Martin Matador. It was basically a radio-controlled unmanned bomber powered by two Rolls-Royce RB.93 1,750 lb st low-cost expendable turbojets, with a simple aerodynamic layout of swept wings and a V tail. It was to be available in interchangeable versions, one being a straightforward cruise missile containing 4,000 lb of high explosive, and the other, more interestingly, a multi-bomb version containing eight 500 lb bombs.

The device would be of the simplest and cheapest design, with no undercarriage, being launched from an inclined trolley with rocket assistance, and would have a 400 miles range. It was proposed that a piloted version be built to test the flight characteristics, but no order for the P.123 was forthcoming.

Engine test house at Pendeford with a working lift-fan under test.

In the late 1950s there were a whole series of projects, twenty-six in number, devoted to VTOL aircraft, for both civil and military applications. Most of them incorporated fan lift, for which much research work was done using an engine testing facility at the rear of the factory. The fan lift principle emanated from General Electric in the USA in the mid-fifties, who suggested that the hot gases from a jet aircraft's propulsion engines could be diverted to drive large-diameter fans buried in the wings and fuselage. Because the fans dealt with a much larger mass-flow than a basic jet engine, they would be better at producing thrust at low speeds, and could thus enable quite low-powered aircraft to achieve VTOL. There was an element of support for the principle within the Air Ministry, who saw the advantages of the system's reduced downwash, and therefore ground erosion, reduced fuel consumption in the VTOL mode and the economy of tailoring the thrust of the propulsion engines to the aircraft's cruise requirements, rather than its take-off performance.

The disadvantages from the airframe manufacturers' point of view were the large, weight and drag-inducing cut-outs in the aircraft's structure required to accommodate the large diameter fans, which also demanded wings of very wide chord if fans were to be sited there.

124

In the United States the lift-fan principle was turned into hardware with the construction of the Ryan XV-5A Vertifan, an aircraft designed to investigate the principle while being tailored as a two-seat battlefield surveillance aircraft. It was powered by two GE J85 2,650 lb st turbojets and was equipped with three lift fans. It first flew in May 1964, but never led to a production aircraft.

The Boulton Paul projects incorporating fan-lift included a number of basic research designs to test various layouts and applied designs ranging from a delta-wing fighter with four Vipers and fan-lift (P.132) to a number of transports, including the P.143, a 46/52-seat airliner with an amazing total of ten RB.144 engines and forty Rolls-Royce 28.5 in diameter fans.

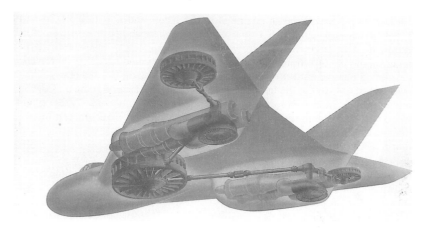

The powerplant/lift-fan layout for the P.132, one of a clutch of VTOL projects in the late fifties.

A small number of VTOL projects were laid out with direct thrust dedicated lift engines. Perhaps the most ambitious was the P.146, a 96-seat VTOL airliner with eighteen RB.154 lift engines and three modified RB.163 propulsion engines.

Given that most of the work was funded by the Air Ministry, it is hard to see why a company as small as Boulton Paul was working on such large projects. Even if such an airliner as the P.146 had been a practical proposition, it is hard to see how Boulton Paul could have produced it. Handley Page, a much larger company was unable to find the resources to put the Jetstream into production, basically a quite straightforward feederliner with a great deal of potential.

The future of Boulton Paul had already been assured, and it was not in the production of complete aircraft, the company was just too small for that. Its future lay in contract work for other companies, and its own pioneering work in powered flying controls. The P.120 remained the last of its designs to fly, though the P.108 Sea Balliol T.21, WP333, was the last Boulton Paul aircraft ever built.

Sub-Contract Work

After the Wellington T.10 conversion programme Boulton Paul obtained a variety of other sub-contract work, both for the Air Ministry and other manufacturers. The de Havilland Hornet and then a Vampire were converted to take a variety of target-towing equipment, and an icing rig was fitted to a Fairey Spearfish.

In November 1949 Boulton Paul were awarded a contract to redesign and modify the intakes of the Vampire F.1 which had been re-engined with a Rolls-Royce Nene. When first installed the Nene, despite its 2,000 lb extra thrust, drove the Vampire F.1 at a slightly slower top speed than the Goblin it replaced. The aircraft flew into Pendeford, despite its grass runways, and received the modifications before flying out for continued tests elsewhere. They developed neat wing-root intakes reminiscent of those on the Sea Hawk, which were at last able to use the full power of the Nene, level speed going up from 548 mph to 576 mph, and climb rate from 4,800 ft/min to 7,090 ft/min. Nene-powered Vampires with the Boulton Paul intake were ordered in large numbers by France and Switzerland. Another Vampire, VX985, had a survey unit fitted, again flying into Pendeford's grass runways.

Pendeford, with its short grass runways was not really suitable for jet aircraft, and there was no possibility of Wolverhampton Council providing paved runways against local objections, so another flight-test facility was needed. The former RAF aerodrome at Seighford, just west of Stafford, was used for a short while, and then flight-testing was shifted to the Royal Radar Establishment's aerodrome at Defford. When the RRE moved, soon afterwards, to Pershore, Defford was no longer available, and so the company decided to take over

Vickers-Armstrongs Wellington NA843 newly converted to T.10 configuration.

The Nene-powered Vampire TG276 at Pendeford, where it was fitted with new intakes.

126

Supermarine Swift wings in production at Pendeford.

The Gloster Meteor T.7 WL377 at Defford, after fitment of Window dispensing apparatus.

Seighford itself. The main runway was extended and repaved, and extra hangarage was provided for a full modification and overhaul facility.

Boulton Paul used this Seighford facility for development and overhaul work on a number of aircraft. Following installation of a 'Window' ejection apparatus on a Meteor T.7 at Defford, there was further work on Gloster aircraft. For instance a Javelin F.(AW) Mk 1, XA562, from the first production batch was used as a trials aircraft with a Rolls-Royce Avon RA.24 installation.

With English Electric fully stretched with the manufacture of their Canberra bomber through the 1950s, and Short, Avro, and Handley Page also engaged in its production, Boulton Paul became the prime contractor for the development and flight-testing of a whole series of Canberra variants and modifications. These varied from the simple installation of the odd 'black box' to major conversions to new Mark numbers, and the preparation of prototypes of export Canberras for different countries. Although other companies, such as Marshalls of Cambridge, were also engaged on such modifications, Boulton Paul was the contract leader on all such work.

Amongst the most notable were the camera installation on the PR.3 and PR.7s, the modification of the B.15 to carry Nord AS-30 missiles, and nine Canberra B.2s converted to T.11s. The T.11 was a Target Interception Trainer, and had a lengthened nose to carry the radar. A Boulton Paul designed and built

English Electric Canberra B.2 WK161 at Seighford, after fitment of DX3 anti-radar material and infra-red suppression exhausts.

four-cannon pack was fitted to interdiction Canberras. The 14 ft long boat-shaped pack fitted into the rear of the bomb-bay and contained four 20 mm Hispano cannon, and a total of 2,320 rounds. It was heated and quickly detachable.

An interesting programme involving a Canberra was the development of stealth technology for the Radio Dept, RAE Farnborough, over the years 1957–63. The programme began with a Balliol being covered with radar-absorbing tiles, which proved unsatisfactory as they tended to come off in flight. The Balliol was then covered with DX3 material and radar-reflection measurements taken. The Balliol could not have been much of a 'stealth' aircraft with that large propeller revolving up front, and the experiments were extended to include Canberra B.2 WK161. Selected parts of the aircraft were covered with DX3 material in four stages, and further measurements taken. The thick rubber-like DX3 material found many other uses in the works, and was particularly popular for re-soling shoes!

Ben Gunn's call sign during test flying was Husky One, Dickie Mancus was Husky Two, George Dunworth, Husky Three and John Powers, Husky Four. Dickie Mancus was only allowed to fly early Canberra T.4s, as they had no ejection seats. His thigh length was too long for safe ejection. The flying was not without its unpleasant moments. In 1957 Ben Gunn was taking off from Culdrose in a mine-laying Canberra B.6, XA567, (rotating bomb-bay), when a seagull was sucked into the port engine, which failed. He aborted the landing but crashed into the arrester gear alongside the runway, coming to rest overhanging the road, and giving a bus-driver quite a fright!

On New Year's Day 1959, he was taking off from Seighford in WH779, a

Canberra B.2 fuselage transported from Seighford to Pendeford for modification work.
(*John A Chambers*)

128

Boulton Paul designed and built four-cannon bomb-bay pack for interdiction Canberras.

Canberra B.15 WH967 at Seighford, with the Boulton Paul designed and fitted Nord AS.30 missile system.

Canberra PR.7, but on selecting undercarriage up experienced hydraulic failure, with the mainwheels half way up and the nosewheel fully up. He circled Seighford for some time to reduce the fuel load and then tried a landing on the half-up wheels, with no flaps. All went well until he crashed into a tree stump on the overrun area. He had a very near miss on another occasion, in a Canberra over Wales. He had a double engine failure at 42,000 ft, and did not manage to relight one until he was down to 5,000 ft. Ben did not attract all such incidents however, George Dunworth had a runaway tailplane on Canberra B.2 WK128 in 1955. Boulton Paul solved this problem, saving the Canberra in service.

Similar modification work was begun on the Lightning in 1961, most notably the conversion of a number of F.1 pre-production aircraft to F.3 standard. Boulton Paul's pilots did not fly the Lightnings however, as they were collected and delivered by English Electric pilots, who did all the requisite test flying at Warton. The cancellation of TSR.2 caused the British Aircraft Corporation to withdraw the modification contracts which were re-distributed within its own divisions to make up for the sudden reduction in their workload. All the Canberra drawings were passed on to Marshalls for minor Canberra modifications, and Seighford was then soon closed, the Flight Test Department having been shut down with the delivery of the last Canberra T.4 to Farnborough on 23 December, 1965.

In the 1960s the company became a sub-contractor for Beagle Aircraft and built the wings and nacelles for the Beagle 206 light twin, known as the Basset in RAF service, and undertook the structural testing of its fuselage.

It was perhaps unsurprising that when Ben Gunn left Boulton Paul on the closure of the Flight Test Department he became chief test pilot at Rover Gas

English Electric Lightning XG310 at Seighford, during conversion as the F.3 prototype.

Beagle 206 wing/nacelles in production at Pendeford. (*John A Chambers*)

Turbines, testing the Rover-powered Chipmunk and Auster – he had after all flown the world's first single propeller-turbine type, the Balliol T.1. In 1967 he became marketing director for Beagle Aircraft in Africa and the Middle East, as well as their experimental test pilot, and in 1971 he became manager of Shoreham Airport.

Throughout the period from the War Boulton Paul has been the sub-contractor for various structural parts of a whole variety of aircraft. This continues right up to the present day, providing parts for the BAe 146 amongst others, but the one area in which the company has slowly specialised, leading directly from its development of the electro-hydraulic gun turret, is the powered flying controls which dominate its business today.

Powered Flying Controls

After the end of the War the development and production of powered gun turrets continued, most notably with the Lincoln nose and tail turrets, but the short era of the gun turret was coming to an end as bomber speeds increased and missiles became the main armament of interceptors. Both the United States and the Soviet Union saw some value in retaining gun turrets in their jet bombers, but the British Canberras and V-bombers were designed without defensive armament. The final such installation completed by Boulton Paul was the nose turret for the Shackleton, and that was not really a turret.

In its initial form as fitted to the first Shackleton Mk 1 prototype, VW126, the two 20 mm cannon were installed in blisters on either side of the nose. They only moved in the vertical plane, and were basically the mounting designed speculatively for the P.97. This installation was called the 'L' mounting, and the first Shackleton also had a Boulton Paul D turret in the tail with twin 0.5 in machine-guns, and a Bristol mid-upper turret.

In production MR.1s there were no nose and tail guns, but when the Shackleton MR.2 was developed the mid-upper turret was abandoned, the radar was moved from beneath the nose to a ventral position and the twin cannon were restored to the nose in a revised mounting.

The 'N' Mounting as it was known, was also not able to revolve, the guns moving only in the vertical plane. The two 20 mm cannon were remotely controlled by the gunner who sat above the mounting in a much cleaned up nose. Its use was not defensive at all, but strictly offensive, against surface targets, in particular ships, and submarines on the surface. There was no need for the mounting to revolve, because the pilot would aim the aircraft to overfly the target, and the vertical movement would give the gunner extra time on target. This, the last such Boulton Paul installation, echoed the first one, the revolving barbettes on the nose of the P.31 Bittern twenty years before. It was fitted to all production Shackleton MR.2s and MR.3s.

Though the era of the turret had come to an end, with the knowledge gained in building these electro-hydraulic systems it was only natural that Boulton Paul would become involved in the production of electro-hydraulic powered flying controls. The coming of the jet aircraft had meant that powered flying controls were needed, as pilots could not manually operate controls against the huge forces involved. With their knowledge gained in designing and building electro-hydraulic turrets, John North, and Boulton Paul became pioneers of powered control systems.

The first Boulton Paul powered flying control systems were installed in the Saunders-Roe Princess, the last of the very big flying-boats. The system was actually designed by Saro, who had recognised that such a large boat would need powered controls to assist the pilots. They had built a rack-and-pinion based system for the Shetland, which had been less than satisfactory, and so they turned to Boulton Paul for help in building an electro-hydraulic system for the even bigger Princess.

A team of twelve in Saro's design department produced the specifications and Boulton Paul built the units. There were three virtually identical units, one in

Twin 20 mm cannon, L gun mounting on Shackleton MR.1 prototype.

the top of the hull for the ailerons, and two in the stern for rudder and elevators. They were linked by cables to the pilots' controls, and consisted basically of two torque converters, 120 volt DC motors rated at 7½ hp, driving through a differential gearbox. This was a fail-safe provision, as the failure of either converter merely halved the output of the unit. The motors ran continuously but normally the pump stroke was zero, so the hydraulics remained dormant. A control input started the pump working at a rate relative to the demand. The output was by large lengths of spinning shafts linked by numerous bearings to change-speed gearboxes, right-angled boxes and universal joints to the control surface.

The whole system was tested on a rig, and then flown on a Sunderland. It

Standard twin-cannon N mounting on Shackleton MR.3, the last Boulton Paul 'turret'.

The Tay-Viscount VX217, the first aircraft in the world with electronic signalling on all controls, landing at Seighford. (*John A Chambers*)

worked well, and to overcome the problem of 'feel', a 'Feel generator' was inserted in the system at the flight deck. Plans were also afoot to design an electronic signalling system, but the demise of the Princess put an end to that.

The Ministry of Defence then granted Boulton Paul a contract to design and install an electronic-signalling system, or fly-by-wire as it is now known, for the Tay-Viscount, a Vickers Viscount re-engined with two Tay turbojets. Dickie Mancus played a large part in the development of this system, being learned in the field of electronics, and was to make the first two flights of the aircraft in 1956, before being stricken by multiple-sclerosis. Duplex DC signalled electrical channels were fitted to all three control surfaces, the first aircraft in the world so equipped. Ben Gunn continued the flight trials, with the aircraft being operated from Seighford, making the first complete fly-by-wire flight on all three surfaces. In 1958 many flights were made by invited test pilots and airline pilots, with Gunn monitoring. The aircraft suffered a hydraulic fire in a wheel bay late in 1958 which burnt through the main spar, putting an end to its use.

ACT Jaguar, XX765, fitted by Dowty Boulton Paul with the world's first all-digital quadruplex flight control system, with no mechanical back-up.

This work was followed by the design of an AC signalled quintuplex (five-lane) unit for experimental testing, and then quadruplex actuator packs were fitted to an RAE Hawker Hunter T.12. Commercial electronic signalling installations were obtained for the spoilers on the Short Belfast, and most significantly on Concorde, which was fitted with fly-by-wire elevon, rudder and relay-powered flying control units.

Boulton Paul designed many power-control systems based on the packaged unit concept, in which an electrically-driven hydraulic pump, hydraulic actuator, servo valves and control mechanism accept electrical and back-up mechanical signals. This is basically the system which operated the gun turrets and was first used for control surfaces in the P.111. The system was fitted commercially on a number of aircraft including the Valiant and Vulcan bombers, and the VC10 airliner. A great deal of test work was done with different systems, especially in trying to give pilots the same sort of 'feel' as a simple mechanical control used to give.

In parallel the Valve-Ram power control unit, which received hydraulic power from hydraulic pumps normally driven from the main engine accessory gear box drives, was installed on such aircraft as the Bristol Type 188. BAC One-Eleven, Buccaneer, Hindustan HF.24, and the Aeritalia G.222.

The Merger with Dowty

It was also natural that Boulton Paul should diversify into industrial hydraulics and such areas as pressing body panels for the motor industry. In 1961 John North, now chairman of the company, proposed a merger with the Dowty Group of Companies, and this went ahead.

George Dowty had been a pioneer in the 1930s, in building aircraft systems. In 1931 he felt the time was right for a company that would specialise in high-quality aircraft components, and left his job on the Gloster Aircraft design

The Dowty Boulton Paul offices on Wobaston Road, Wolverhampton, as they are today.

staff and set up a company called the Aircraft Components Company.

He attempted to sell his unique design for a streamlined lightweight shock-absorbing undercarriage leg, but it was another of his inventions, the internally sprung aircraft wheel, which set his company on the road to success. The time was right, and the company went on to produce hydraulic units, undercarriage legs and propellers, and by 1961 had become one of the world leaders in the manufacture of aircraft components. It was perhaps inevitable, in an era of aircraft industry rationalisation, that Boulton Paul should combine with Dowty to produce a strengthened competitor on the world market, but perhaps it was slightly sad when the word 'Aircraft' was dropped from the company name, to more closely reflect its new products, and then perhaps inevitably in the unsentimental world of business in 1991 the name Boulton Paul also disappeared, and the company is now trading as Dowty Aerospace, Wolverhampton.

This was a move which John North would never have allowed, he saw the merger with Dowty as strictly a partnership, but he was no longer there to guide the company. He died suddenly at his home on 11 January, 1968, and was cremated four days later in Shrewsbury with a private service. On 1 March there was a memorial service in St Peter's Church Wolverhampton, and among those attending were his old friend Lord King's Norton and the Minister of Aviation, John Stonehouse.

John North ranks with all the great pioneers of British aviation, such as Geoffrey de Havilland, A V Roe, Frederick Handley Page and the Short brothers, and yet for obvious reasons, his is not a household name. Unlike the others he did not found the company with which he was mostly associated and so it did not bear his name, and yet as much as any of the others, he was the guiding light and controlling influence of one of this country's main aircraft manufacturers. In fact he wielded a greater influence over a longer period on the affairs of the company than many of the others.

He has been criticized for keeping Boulton Paul so small, in order to be able to more closely control it himself, and to a certain extent this is true, he did avoid chances to take over other companies. In many ways this policy kept Boulton Paul in existence, when so many other aircraft companies have disappeared.

John Dudley North CBE, FRAeS, MIMechE, 1893–1968, guiding light of Boulton Paul Aircraft from 1917 until his death.

The great passion throughout his life was the systematic solving of technical problems, and to this end he employed over the years some of the country's top mathematicians. Their role was solely to help him produce solutions to problems in which he had an interest. He saw the main function of management as thinking, and his thoughts took him into pioneering work in many spheres, and yet he had no technical education at all, he was self-taught in everything he did.

Man-management was not his forte, he paid his workforce to do a job and he expected it done. He never became the popular father figure that many did, and yet there is no doubt that he earned the great respect of everyone who worked for him. His dealings with the Air Ministry were very mixed. He did not suffer fools gladly, and earned enemies that way, perhaps that is why he never received the knighthood he deserved.

He was awarded a CBE and an Honorary Doctorate of Science at Birmingham University, and was also made an Honorary Fellow of the Royal Aeronautical Society and a Freeman of the City of London. His real memorial was to leave the company he served so long as a prosperous aeronautical engineering concern of the highest quality.

It is now one of the world's leading companies in the design and production of hydraulic systems, and in particular it has been at the forefront of innovation in fly-by-wire systems. In 1977 a Jaguar was fitted with Dowty Boulton Paul flight control actuators for the taileron, rudder and spoilers, a digital quadruplex system made to production standard. It was the first aircraft in the world to fly solely by digital fly-by-wire with no mechanical back-up.

Dowty Boulton Paul systems are currently to be found on the Tornado, Airbus, BAe 146, Agusta A129 Mongoose, Aeritalia/Aermacchi/Embraer AMX, Soko Galeb and Jurom, BAe ATP, Fokker 100, Bell-Boeing V-22 Osprey, and the BAe Experimental Aircraft Programme, which is leading to the European Fighter Aircraft. As an example the Airbus A300–600 series has ten spoiler speedbrake actuators, four inner speedbrake actuators and two aileron droop-signal actuators.

In 1984 Dowty Boulton Paul helped fund the development of a revolutionary aircraft recovery system for small ships, Skyhook. Created with British Aerospace, British Robotic Systems and the crane manufacturers Stothert & Pitt, the Skyhook was basically just a crane mounted on a small ship, which hooks onto a BAe Harrier hovering alongside, and swings it on board. For take-off the reverse process would be undertaken, a system enabling relatively small ships to operate fixed-wing aircraft without any major modifications.

In 1987 a major reorganisation of the company was undertaken by the newly appointed managing director, Frank Nugent. The heavy machine tools were concentrated in one area of the factory, the work-force was slimmed, and the product design and production engineering staff were concentrated in one large office, with each computer terminal linked to a central data network. A redundant building was turned, at a cost of £3 million into a Space Facility which makes Dowty Boulton Paul the only European manufacturer of propellant tanks and control valves.

From wooden propellers to propellant tanks for space rockets, Boulton Paul has come a long way, but yet it is still engaged in the same basic business, the manufacture of high quality components for the aircraft industry. Along the way it has built some innovatory and advanced aircraft, and only by a combination of bad luck and bad timing did only one become a household name, the Defiant.

Even by stretching the meaning of the word to its limit, only six aircraft of Boulton Paul design ever went into production, and only two of them, the Defiant and the Balliol, in any numbers. The catologue of bad luck is extraordinary. The Bourges would have been one of the great aircraft of the First World War, if only it had lasted another year, but its very excellence led Boulton & Paul into becoming specialists in the design of twin-engined medium bombers, the one category of aircraft in which the RAF had no interest.

As did many companies, Boulton & Paul tried to cater for an expected boom in private flying at the end of the War, with the P.9, but good aircraft though it was it could not compete with the many thousands of cheap war-surplus aircraft that were available. The P.9 was just too early. Six years later de Havilland's produced their Moth at just the right time.

The P.8 Atlantic was probably the outstanding design of all those being prepared for the *Daily Mail* transatlantic flight, and yet on its first flight it suffered an engine failure, no fault of the airframe, and crashed. Before the second aircraft could be finished Alcock and Brown and their Vickers Vimy had gained lasting fame, and the £10,000 prize.

Twin-engined medium bombers became the company's forte, with a series of outstanding designs, the Bourges, Bolton, Bugle, Sidestrand and Overstrand, and yet for a long time the Royal Air Force did not order any and did not have any, unlike the air forces of many other countries. Apart from the prototypes the sole production orders for these outstanding aircraft were just one squadron of Sidestrands and one squadron of Overstrands.

Yet when they tried to branch into other areas, as with the P.33 Partridge fighter, or the P.32 heavy bomber, they found themselves competing with manufacturers who had become specialists in such areas.

To have built the frame of the R101 was a remarkable achievement, and yet any company associated with that ill-planned, and tragic project, was tarred with the brush of others' incompetence, no matter how little they deserved it.

When a Boulton Paul design finally got into quantity production, the Defiant, it was for a specification which was doomed to failure from the start. Again it was no fault of the company, they produced an aircraft which performed remarkably well, given the parameters they were forced to work to; but it is hard to escape the conclusion that the Defiant stained Boulton & Paul's credibility as constructors of viable combat aircraft.

The last aircraft they built, the Balliol, was produced in the expectation of large orders as the standard advanced trainer of the Royal Air Force. In the event, orders were cut back drastically because the Air Ministry changed its plans and decided they needed a jet advanced trainer.

Given all this bad luck, it is a shining testament to the standards of the company that it has survived for over seventy-five years.

The P.3 Bobolink when first rolled out at Riverside in December 1917, with Lewis gun fitted to the upper wing.

P.3 Bobolink

With Boulton & Paul producing large numbers of Sopwith Camels, it was logical that John North should take an immediate interest in producing a Camel replacement, for which the Air Ministry had issued the official Specification A.1A. North began to urgently consider several layouts. The engine designated by the Air Ministry for use in the A.1A contenders was the 230 hp Bentley B.R.2 rotary, which was only 93 lb heavier than the 150 hp B.R.1. A second clutch of designs was built around the compact 170 hp ABC Wasp radial, the Sopwith 8F.1 Snail, the Westland Wagtail and the BAT FK.22/2 Bantam.

Sopwith's entry in the design competition was the Snipe, which was some way ahead of its competitors, first flying late in 1917, powered by a B.R.1, as the larger engine was not yet available. It began life as a single-bay design, with a slab-sided fuselage, with two prototypes of slightly differing layouts being evaluated in December 1917. The third prototype was converted to a two-bay layout with a rounded fuselage, being delivered to Martlesham Heath fitted with one of the first B.R.2s in February 1918.

Although the Snipe represented the main competition, there were also two other important contenders for the Camel-replacement order, the Austin A.F.T.3 Osprey triplane, designed by North's successor at Austin, John Kenworthy, along with C H Brooks; and the Nieuport BN.1, Henry Folland's first design for the British Nieuport company, and owing much to his earlier design, the S.E.5A.

Boulton & Paul were awarded orders on 1 December, 1918, for two of their layouts, the P.3 and the P.5. Three prototypes were ordered for each design, the earlier set of serials, C8652–C8654, going to the P.5, and the later ones, C8655–C8657, to the P.3. The company bestowed the name Hawk on the P.5, though it may well have also been used for the P.3, but were forced to change it because of an Air Ministry nomenclature system which came into effect in 1918.

The names of birds of prey were reserved for aero-engines, (the Hawk being a Rolls-Royce engine), and single-seat single-engined landplanes were to be named after land-birds, other than birds of prey, or reptiles. In addition Boulton & Paul were awarded the initial letters BO. (Sopwith were awarded the initial letters SO, SA and SN—hence the name Snipe, and Austin were awarded AU, AS or OS—hence Osprey.) Boulton & Paul chose to rename their entry Boblink, later to be changed to Bobolink, which is a North American bird.

The P.5 was abandoned at an early stage and the serial numbers were re-allocated to other aircraft, but construction of the first P.3 went ahead with some urgency, to ready it for trials against the other three contenders at Martlesham Heath. Availability of the B.R.2 was as much a constraining factor as construction of the aircraft, and the first P.3 Bobolink, C8655, was eventually fitted with only the fourth B.R.2 built.

Like the revised Snipe it was a two-bay design with equal-span wings with 2 ft 3½ in stagger. They featured N struts, which were still an unusual feature, though they had been used by North before the War on the Grahame-White Type 13. Their advantage was that they simplified rigging. The structure was a conventional wooden one, with fabric covering. The wings were very light, the lower ones, without their fabric covering weighed only 29 lb, a tribute to North's design, and Boulton & Paul craftsmanship. To begin with ailerons were only fitted on the upper wings, but a lack of manoeuvrability shown in early trials at Mousehold caused strut-linked ailerons to be fitted to the lower wings. There was a large rectangular cut-out in the upper wing to give the pilot excellent upper hemisphere vision.

Of necessity the front fuselage was of circular section to accommodate the rotary engine, but the aft fuselage was flat-sided, made up of a simple wire-braced box-girder, with a curved upper section behind the pilot's head. One feature displayed the clever thinking and careful design which were to become associated with North. These were the two fuel tanks, of 34 and 6 gal, placed behind the pilot, with an armour plate between them, so that one bullet would have little chance of damaging both. In case they caught fire, both tanks could be jettisoned in flight so that the pilot could glide safely to a landing, saving the rest of his aircraft. In the days when pilots were still not being allowed

The Bobolink at Mousehold on 19 February, 1918, with different propeller, no Lewis gun, but still with ailerons on upper wing only.

to wear parachutes in highly inflammable wood and fabric aircraft, this was a very clever idea.

The tail had a sharply-swept leading edge running to a curved fin. Overall length of the aircraft was 20 ft, span was 29 ft, and the height was 8 ft 4 in.. In comparison the third prototype Snipe had 2 ft 1 in greater span, 1 ft 2 in more height, but was 9 in shorter.

Two Vickers machine-guns were fitted on the forward fuselage, firing through the 9 ft diameter arc of the two-blade propeller, and provision was made for a Lewis gun on a rail on the upper wing. When C8655 was rolled out of Riverside Works in December 1917, complete except for the front fuselage covering, this rail and Lewis gun were actually fitted, as well as the twin Vickers guns. Before delivery for evaluation the Lewis mounting was removed however. As might be expected the engine mounts and Vickers installation were very similar to those of the Camel.

Capt Frank Courtney undertook the company's initial flight trials at Mousehold. He had been transferred from training to RFC experimental flying and was engaged in the programme to fit 150 hp Monosoupape engines to Sopwith Camels for the Americans. Flight testing for this programme was undertaken at Mousehold on Boulton & Paul-built Camels, so it was natural that, as an experienced test pilot, he should give the Bobolink its first flights.

As well as finding fault with its manoeuvrability, which caused the ailerons to be fitted to the lower wings, Courtney also criticised the Bobolink for the narrow track of its undercarriage, which made taxi-ing difficult, though he felt it was not so serious a fault as to warrant any immediate change. The propeller fitted when the aircraft was first rolled out at Riverside had markedly square-cut tips, but all later pictures of it show conventionally rounded tips, probably the Snipe propeller with which it was fitted at Martlesham.

Delivery of C8655 to Martlesham Heath was made in the week ending 9 March, 1918, where it joined the Snipe. The Nieuport BN.1 and Austin Osprey were delivered in the same week, and flying evaluations were undertaken as a matter of urgency. As a final test a number of Service pilots, including Capt James McCudden were invited to evaluate the four aircraft in a day's trials at Sutton's Farm.

Each of the machines was tested with a Snipe propeller and a full specification load *ie* 40 gal of fuel, 8 gal of oil, 150 lb of Vickers guns and ammunition, 50 lb of Lewis gun and ammunition and 25 lb of electrical clothing and oxygen. Because of a breakage of its cowling no reliable performance trials could be made on the Nieuport.

The Osprey with its 23 ft wingspan was easily the most manoeuvrable, followed by the Nieuport, with the Bobolink the least favoured because of heavy handling and slow lateral reaction. The Osprey was clearly the slowest of the four; the short era of the triplane was really over. It had not in fact been granted an official order, but was built as a private venture, with special permission from the Air Ministry under Licence No.17, and awarded the serial X.15 in a special series reserved for such private-venture aircraft. The BN.1 was a two-bay design like the Bobolink and Snipe, but featured revolutionary I struts, which were looked on with suspicion. It was the fastest of the four aircraft, with a very promising all-round performance, but on 10 March it suffered an unfortunate accident, catching fire in the air, and was completely destroyed, ruling it out of

The Bobolink, at Martlesham Heath, fitted with strut-connected ailerons on lower wings.

the contest, as a second prototype was not immediately available.

The view from the pilot's seat was best in the Snipe, followed by the Nieuport and the Bobolink, though with small alterations all three would be very similar in this respect. The Osprey was very much poorer, and there was no easy way to improve the pilot's view. As far as accessibility to engines and accessories were concerned, the Osprey was clearly the best, followed by the Snipe and the Bobolink, which were much on a par. The Nieuport was much the worst of the four, though alterations could improve to the standard of the other two biplanes.

The Vickers guns were equally well sited on the biplanes, but the crank handles were difficult to reach on the Osprey. The Lewis gun was difficult to use on the Bobolink and Snipe, as the pilot sat too near the rear spar, the Nieuport being much better in this respect. The Lewis gun was impossible to fit on the Osprey, except in a fixed vertical mounting.

The Applied Design Branch submitted a report on the ease of production and maintenance of the four aircraft. The Osprey and Nieuport were considered the best, though the design of the Nieuport's wings was criticised. The Bobolink was described as very bad from the production and maintenance point of view. This view does seem strange as the Bobolink had such a simple rectangular box-girder fuselage, whereas the Snipe for instance had a complicated rounded fuselage made up of formers and stringers.

There was little to choose between the four aircraft, though the greater experience of the Sopwith company, and the fact that the Snipe had been flying for some time, and had already had fundamental changes to its design, weighed heavily in its favour. Although its top speed was disappointing, (121 mph at 10,000 ft, 4 mph slower than the Bobolink), its rate of climb was magnificent, and its handling at altitude was excellent, feeling like a well-behaved Camel in the air.

Taking all factors into account the following order of merit was arrived at, 1. Snipe, 2. Nieuport, 3. Osprey, 4. Bobolink.

Perhaps inevitably the Snipe was chosen, even though the Bobolink displayed

The Bobolink at Mousehold in June 1918. This is the only known picture of it fitted with horn-balanced rudder and cable-connected ailerons. (*J M Bruce*)

a fractional edge in overall performance. Some of the other criticisms of the Bobolink were the narrow track of its undercarriage, and, though this could presumably have been cured, the poor access to the cockpit, which was set well within the cut-out of the upper wing.

The Bobolink was later fitted with a larger horn-balanced rudder to try to cure the ground-handling difficulties, the horn balance being unshielded, looking rather incongruous above the unchanged fin. The strut connection of the ailerons was also changed, being replaced by cable links. The Snipe too required a larger rudder, increasing its length to 19 ft 10 in.

Another B.R.2 powered fighter appeared later in the year, the Armstrong Whitworth Armadillo. By the time it flew there was no chance of it being ordered, but its details are included in the following comparison of the various contenders for completeness.

Performance and Dimensional Comparisons

	Bobolink	Snipe	Osprey	Nieuport BN.1	Armadillo
Speed at 10,000 ft	125 mph	121 mph	118½ mph	127 mph	113 mph
Climb to 6,500 ft	5min 20 sec	4 min 55 sec	5 min 30 sec	n/a	6 min 30 sec
Climb to 10,000 ft	9 min 20 sec	8 min 50 sec	10 min 20 sec	n/a	n/a
Climb to 15,000 ft	18 min	17 min 40 sec	21 min 20 sec	16 min	n/a
Service Ceiling	19,500 ft	19,500 ft	19,000 ft	26,000 ft	24,000 ft
Endurance	3¼ hr	2¼ hr	3 hr	3 hr	2¾ hr
Span	29 ft	31 ft 1in	23 ft	28 ft	27 ft 9 in
Length	20 ft	19 ft 3 in	17 ft 7 in	18 ft 6 in	18 ft 10 in
Height	8 ft 4 in	9 ft 6 in	10 ft 8 in	9 ft	7 ft 10 in
Loaded Weight	1,992 lb	1,964 lb	1,888 lb	2,030 lb	1,860 lb

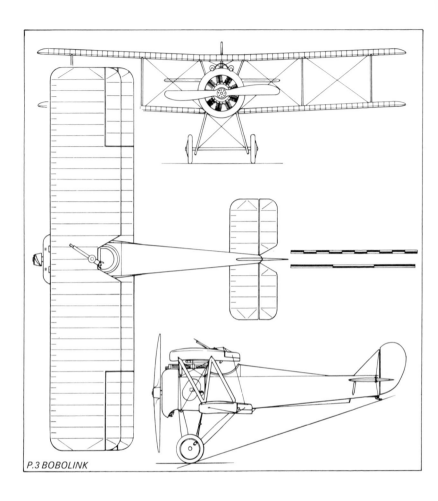

P.3 BOBOLINK

The Snipe was ordered in large numbers, including an initial 400 from Boulton & Paul, which must have been a bitter pill for John North to swallow. The other two Bobolink prototypes, C8656 and C8657 were cancelled on 9 April, though the fact that the serials were not re-issued may indicate that the construction of these two aircraft was well advanced.

The sole Bobolink was delivered to RNAS Hendon on 18 June, for assessment as a shipboard fighter, though it was sent to Norwich the following day, for three days, possibly for modifications. It returned to Hendon on the 21st, and then returned to Norwich on 22 July, where presumably it ended its days.

P.3 Bobolink

230 hp Bentley B.R.2.
Span 29 ft; length 20 ft; height 8 ft 4in; wing area 266 sq ft.
Empty weight 1,226 lb; loaded weight 1,992 lb.

144

Maximum speed 125 mph at 15,000 ft; climb to 6,500 ft 5min 20 sec, to 10,000 ft 9 min 20 sec, to 15,000 ft 18 min; service ceiling 19,500 ft; endurance 3¼ hr at 15,000 ft.
Armament: two forward-firing Vickers machine-guns; provision for Lewis gun on universal joint mounting on upper wing.

P.6

John North (centre) with the P.6, at Mousehold, in original colour scheme. (*Boulton Paul Society*)

Immediately after the Bobolink was cancelled Boulton & Paul's design department began work on a full-scale experimental aircraft, drawings for the wings for example being dated 14 April, 1918. Building such an aircraft was quite an unusual step at the time, given that most pioneering aircraft could be considered full-scale experimental machines, as their designers/builders did not really know if they would fly, or how well, until they tried. That John North should consider it, shows the meticulous way he intended to go about improving the company's design potential.

Because the Defence Regulations introduced in 1917 made it illegal to build an aircraft without official sanction, permission had to be obtained for construction of the P.6. It was registered in a special 'X' series reserved for such aircraft, and given the serial X.25, the last of this special series to be awarded.

The P.6 was a conventional wood and fabric two-seat biplane, the main purpose of which was to examine different aerofoil sections, as part of Boulton & Paul's basic systematic research programme. Having a full-size aircraft was useful for eliminating the errors of scale found in wind-tunnel data.

The wings were single-bay, unstaggered, and equal-span with a basic RAF 15 section. The chord was 5 ft and there was a relatively wide gap also of 5 ft compared with the span of only 25 ft, the forward cockpit being beneath the centre section of the upper wing. The wings were built of spruce spars and ribs,

145

Mrs Dawson Paul about to take her first ever flight, in the P.6.

with a spruce leading edge, and an ash trailing edge. The 7½ sq ft area ailerons were identical on upper and lower wings.

The fuselage contained a large number of Sopwith Camel parts, and was a similar box-section design, with slightly curved upper surface. The use of Camel parts was only to be expected as the company were still producing an average of 29 Camels a week. The engine cowling was metal, and left unpainted. The very rounded horn-balanced rudder was of 9 sq ft area compared with only 2½ sq ft for the fixed fin.

The P.6 was powered by the RAF 1a air-cooled V-8 of 90 hp driving a four-blade propeller of 9 ft 3 in diameter. This gave it a speed of 103 mph at 1,000 ft and the 20.1 gal fuel tank gave an endurance of 2 hr 20 min.

The date of the P.6's first flight is unknown, but it is likely to have been late in 1918, the use of Camel parts suggesting construction of the P.6 before Camel

The P.6 with Boulton & Paul Ltd painted on the fuselage, as used to make the first business flight in the United Kingdom, 1 May, 1919.

146

production gave way to Snipe production in November. It is probable that Frank Courtney made the first flight, he certainly flew the aircraft on several occasions, and gave Mrs Dawson Paul her first flight in it in March 1919.

Whether interchangeable mainplanes were actually fitted to the aircraft at any time is not recorded, but considerable experimental data was collected from its operation. The P.6 was a handy light aircraft, apart from its experimental usefulness, and after the War was actually offered for sale for £600, though the company built a slightly larger version, the P.9, as their main offering for the civil flying boom which they hoped would follow.

The P.6 was put to practical use as transport for the company's general sales manager, being registered K-120/G-EACJ on 20 May, 1919; though there is some doubt that the aircraft ever wore these markings, retaining its X.25 serial and RAF roundels in all surviving photographs. It was painted with the large letters Boulton & Paul Ltd, Sales Dept, on the fuselage sides in an early form of aerial advertising, and so became one of the first corporate aircraft, and is credited with making the first business flight, on 1 May, 1919, from Norwich to Bury St Edmunds.

P.6

90 hp RAF 1a.
Span 25 ft; length 19 ft; height 8 ft; wing area 235 sq ft.
Empty weight 1,100 lb; loaded weight 1,725 lb.
Maximum speed 103 mph at 1,000 ft; climb to 5,000 ft 9min; endurance 2 hr 20 min.

P.7 Bourges

Bourges F2903, as first flown with Bentley B.R.2 rotaries in lieu of ABC Dragonflies, and designated Mk IB in this form.

During 1918 John North began work on a twin-engined day-bomber to the official Specification A.2(b) which called for a twin-engined reconnaissance bomber. The design received the project number P.7. With the formation of the RAF a new list of specifications was issued, and the P.7 was aimed at three of them, No.IV, (Long-distance photographic-reconnaissance fighter), No.VI (Short-distance day bomber), and No.VIII, (Long-distance day bomber). The company referred to it as a Fighter-Bomber, however.

Three prototypes were ordered, each of which was to differ in some details.

They were each three-seat, three-bay aircraft with unstaggered wings, and a spruce frame. They were fabric covered with the standard PC10 khaki-green finish on upper and side surfaces, with clear-varnished linen on the underside. The P.7 was in competition with the Avro Type 533 Manchester, a development of the earlier Types 523 Pike and 529, and the Sopwith Cobham triplane.

The Air Ministry had decided that all twin-engined landplanes with an all-up weight of less than 11,000 lb were to be named after inland towns of England and Wales (Seaplanes being named after coastal towns); and Boulton & Paul also still had to use the initial letters BO. For some reason the company chose a French town, Bourges, as the name for the P.7, but this was in keeping with Airco, who chose Amiens for their D.H.10, and Vickers who chose the name Vimy. The name did not find favour with the workforce who tended to call it the 'Burgess' or the 'Boanerges'.

The crew consisted of two gunners in nose and dorsal positions, and a pilot seated in front of the wings. The pilot's position was slightly raised compared with that of the nose gunner, and he was provided with a large windscreen. The nose gunner's Scarff ring was canted forward and fitted with a trunnion device to carry two .303 in Lewis guns. There was transparent panelling in the nose and a sliding panel beneath the nose for bomb aiming. The front gunner acted as bomb-aimer, being equipped with a bombsight, and release gear. The pilot was also able to release the bombs in an emergency. The dorsal gun position was also equipped with twin guns, and the Scarff ring was recessed below the fuselage top-line.

To fulfil the aircraft's role as a reconnaissance bomber, a large camera position was located just in front of the dorsal gunner's position, the gunner operating the camera, with provision for a case of spare plates. Provision was also made for fitting a transmitting/receiving radio.

The first Bourges, F2903, was supposed to be fitted with ABC Dragonfly

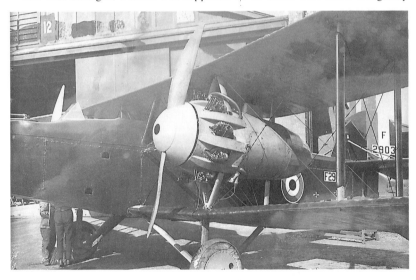

A close up of the ABC Dragonfly installation on Bourges F2903. (*Boulton Paul Society*)

engines, and as such was designated the Mk IA. The Dragonfly engines were late in coming, and they suffered horrendous development problems. Designed by Granville Bradshaw they were the first high-power radial engines. Unfortunately they suffered from tremendous vibration and especially cooling problems, the cylinders running a dull red after a few minutes. Their normal power was 320 hp, but this fell away considerably after a little running time. The Bourges was one of many aircraft to suffer from having been designed to take them, another being the rival Avro Manchester.

To enable flight trials to start Bentley B.R.2 rotary engines of 230 hp were fitted to F2903, and it was redesignated Bourges Mk IIA in this form. The letter 'A' denoted the fact that the upper wing was carried straight above the fuselage on conventional struts, the letter 'B' being reserved for a different layout with the upper wing inboard of the engines being of gull configuration, sloping down to join the fuselage, to give all crew members a better all-round view, and the dorsal gunner a better field of fire.

The fuselage was a straightforward wire-braced box-section, with slab sides. The horizontal tail was built into the upper surface of the rear fuselage, and was supported by two struts above each side, connected to the fin, which possessed pleasingly curved lines.

Bourges F2903 at Mousehold with newly fitted horn-balanced ailerons.

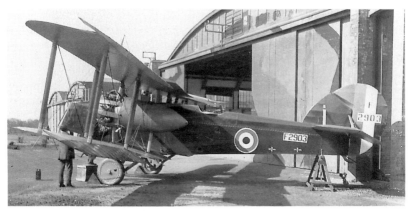

Bourges F2903 with engines at mid-gap.

149

The B.R.2s were set midway between the wings at the inner bay struts, and were eventually replaced by Dragonflies in a closely-cowled arrangement with large spinners and two-blade propellers. The cooling problems of the Dragonfly led to the spinners soon being discarded and the cowlings redesigned with a curved frontal section. Early flight trials had also led to the introduction of large horn balances on the four cable-connected ailerons, which increased the span from 54 ft to 57 ft 4 in.

The undercarriage had a very wide-track, the single mainwheels being carried on V struts directly beneath the engines with a bracing strut running to the underside of the fuselage.

The all-up weight was 6,300 lb, with a fuel capacity of 190 gallons and an internal bombload of 900 lb. The bomb-bay was between the lower spars and the shutter-opening bomb doors were operated by a system of laths and tensioned cords.

Rare air to air view of Bourges F2903 flown by Frank Courtney. (*The Boulton Paul Society*)

Top speed was 124 mph at 10,000 ft, and that height could be reached in only 11 minutes. The landing speed was only 50 mph. The Bourges proved to be capable of being rolled, spun and looped with ease, and in the hands of the usual Boulton & Paul test pilot, Frank Courtney, it astonished the crowds at its first public outing at Hendon in 1919, at the reception for Commander Read and the transatlantic NC-4 flying-boat.

The handling of the Bourges was delightful, and by shutting down one engine, Courtney was able to emulate the gyroscopic effect of the rotary in the Sopwith Camel, making up for the larger dimensions and greater inertia of the Bourges. Charlie Brown, the mechanic on the Bourges was quite happy to lean casually out of the front gunner's cockpit of the aircraft while Courtney was rolling or looping it!

Despite the excellent performance of the Bourges no production orders were forthcoming. They were under discussion at the end of the War, but the Armistice brought an end to them, and the RAF used the D.H.10 which was just coming into service. But for the delays caused by the Dragonfly engines, the Bourges might have secured large contracts before the War's end. After the end of the War Boulton & Paul made strenuous attempts to sell the aircraft around the world, but were not helped by the attitude of the Air Ministry. The company wanted to display the Bourges at the Amsterdam Aviation Exhibition and the Paris Air Show of 1919, but were refused permission to do so by the Air Ministry. The situation must have been very frustrating for John North and the board of directors, though in truth it is unlikely that any sales would have been forthcoming.

The rival Avro Manchester also only flew in prototype form, initially with Siddeley Pumas instead of the Dragonflies, and it was not before December 1919 that the Manchester received its Dragonflies. Because of its larger dimensions the Manchester had a slightly inferior performance to the Bourges, and was not nearly so manoeuvrable.

The other competing aircraft the Sopwith Cobham triplane was unique in being the only Sopwith/Hawker twin-engined aircraft ever built. Like the others it was designed for the ABC engine, but it first flew with Pumas, until the Dragonflies finally arrived. Its development made leisurely progress after the end of the War and it did not even go through its trials until the spring of 1920.

The second prototype Bourges, F2904, was the Mk IB, and apart from differing because of the sloping inboard upper-wing sections, also had the Dragonflies installed on the lower wing, rather than at mid-gap. Work at Farnborough with a D.H.10 in which the engine positions were varied had shown, against all expectations, that placing the engines in the mid-gap position caused higher drag than if they were placed on the lower wing. Work on the first Bourges had been too advanced to change the engine arrangement, but the opportunity was taken to do so with the second prototype.

The engines were mounted inboard of the inner wing-struts, so that the undercarriage struts had to be slightly lengthened, to give the propellers the necessary clearance. The tail also differed, the rudder being increased in area, and the fin reduced, and a large dihedral angle was given to the tailplane to match the angle of the sloping section of the wing.

A new bomb-release system was also introduced. Stowage for three bomb supporting beams was arranged between vertical guides and supported by quick-pitch screws geared to a common horizontal shaft. When this was free to rotate each bomb came in turn to the discharge position, then left the screws and moved down laterally between oblique guides, and out of the way of the next beam and bomb. There were three bomb cells with shutter doors.

Bourges Mk IB, F2904, with gulled centre section and Dragonflies on lower wings instead of at mid-gap.

151

Bourges P.7B F2905 with Napier Lion engines.

A complete bomb-loading system was also devised for the Bourges. The bomb cell was hoisted into position by gear attached to the upper longerons and could be removed before flight.

The third and last Bourges, F2905, was designated P.7B, and first flew in December 1920. It had the straight upper wing of the Mk IA, but was fitted with 450 hp water-cooled Napier Lion engines on the lower wing. The mainwheels were moved slightly outboard of the engines. The engines had frontal radiators and drove four-blade propellers, giving the aircraft a top speed of 130 mph at 10,000 ft, up from 124 mph with the Dragonflies. This was a very high speed for a bomber, and coupled with the exceptional manoeuvrability of the aircraft, meant it was sometimes categorised as a fighter/bomber, and was claimed to be the fastest twin-engined aircraft in the world.

On this aircraft revised gun mountings, designed for lightness, were fitted. They could take one or two Lewis guns and had padded stocks to help prevent the gunners receiving bruises as they pressed against them with their shoulders to help traversing.

With a relatively short wing-span and small overall dimensions, the light wing-loading of only 8 lb/sq ft, gave the Bourges almost single-seat fighter-like agility, and yet it had an endurance of 9¼ hours, and could carry a significant

Bourges P.7B F2905 at Mousehold. (*The Boulton Paul Society*)

bomb-load. A projected Mk III version of the Bourges, fitted with 290 hp Siddeley Puma engines was never built.

F2905 was delivered to Martlesham Heath in March 1921 with 3 hr 49 min flying time. A further 5 hr were flown, most of them involving its full range of aerobatic manoeuvres, then serious failures occurred to some of the wing fittings. The top rear centre section strut was badly bent, the fitting plate attaching it to the rear spar with bolts being distorted. The front spar fittings were also deflected, but not as much. Several other fittings in adjoining bays of the top plane also showed signs of deflections. It was considered that the upper wing was moving back during a loop.

As the aircraft was due to fly at the RAF Pageant urgent modifications were made. Oblique struts were fitted from the top longerons to the rear spar of the centre section, and further oblique struts in the bay comprising the gunner's cockpit.

After a further 1 hr and 20 min flying which included aerobatics in practice for the Pageant and the actual display itself, further failures occurred, but not as badly as before. It was considered that the entire wing system was moving relative to the fuselage during violent manoeuvres. These failures show that the impressive aerobatic performance of the Bourges was undertaken right on the edge of the limits of the aircraft's stressing. After the second failures further strengthening was instituted to the plates, and the anti-drag wires were doubled.

As late as 1923 F2905, by then entered on the civil register as G-EAWS, was still thrilling the crowds at the RAF Pageant at Hendon. In the hands of Frank Courtney it undertook a mock dogfight with a pair of Nieuport Nighthawk fighters performing its full reportoire of loops, rolls and spins, completed with speed and accuracy. F2903 had also entered the civil register, as G-EACE, but was scrapped in May 1920. F2904 crashed at Mousehold early in 1919, and

F2904 after its crash at Mousehold. The wreckage was rebuilt as the second P.8 Atlantic.

ended upside down with severe damage. The remains were obtained from the Air Ministry by the company and were totally rebuilt as the P.8 Atlantic, for an attempt on the nonstop transatlantic flight.

The Armistice had meant the Bourges, outstanding aircraft though it was, never went into production. The Bourges was the first twin-engined combat aircraft which was fully manoeuvrable, an outstanding advertisement for the design skills of John North and the Boulton & Paul company, but it came just too late.

Frank Courtney later stated that of the many aircraft that he flew in his career, the Bourges was one of his four favourites. The other three were the Camel, the Bristol Fighter and the Siskin; exhalted company indeed!

The Air Ministry and RAF were also impressed, even though they no longer had the money to place production orders, and awarded Boulton & Paul a contract to build a version of the Bourges with an all-steel airframe, the P.15 Bolton.

P.7 Bourges

Mk IA and IB: two 320 hp ABC Dragonfly 1; Mk IIA: two 230 hp Bentley B.R.2; P.7B: two 450 hp Napier Lion.

Span 54 ft (57 ft 4 in with horn-balanced ailerons); length 37 ft; height 12 ft; wing area 738 sq ft.

Mk IA and IB: Empty weight 3,820 lb; Mk I: loaded weight 6,326 lb; P.7B: loaded weight 6,800 lb.

Mk IA and IB: Maximum speed 123.5 mph at 6,500 ft, 121 mph at 10,000 ft, 112.5 mph at 15,000 ft; P.7B: 130 mph at 10,000 ft. Mk IA and IB: Climb to 6,500 ft 7 min 40 sec, to 10,000 ft 13 min 35 sec, to 15,000 ft 25 min 25 sec; service ceiling 20,000 ft; endurance 9¼ hr.

Armament: one or two Lewis machine-guns on Scarff rings in nose and dorsal positions. 900 lb bombs.

P.8 Atlantic

At the end of the War there were two dozen aircraft manufacturers in the United Kingdom with their own design departments. All of them were faced with the fact that their only products were no longer wanted. The RAF had thousands of surplus aircraft on strength, and hundreds more were being built each week until contracts were cancelled. There was no prospect of military orders in the immediate future, but most companies hoped for a boom in civil flying, and set about converting whatever designs they had for their most suitable civil use, or drawing new purpose-built machines.

Although they had only built three aircraft of their own design at the end of the War, a Bobolink, a P.6, and the first Bourges, with two more Bourges nearly completed, Boulton & Paul had some advantages over many manufacturers. The P.6, though basically experimental, was really just a two-seat light aircraft, ready for promotion as a private aeroplane with very little modification, and the Bourges was an outstanding twin-engined bomber, once the Dragonflies were abandoned in favour of Napier Lions, and offered a very advanced basis for the design of an airliner.

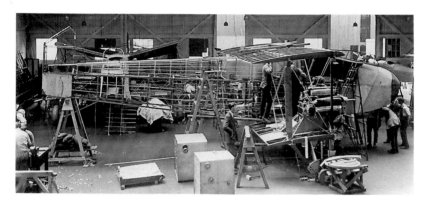

The first P.8 Atlantic under construction, with the Bourges Mk 1B, being cannibalised in the background. (*Miss L North*)

The company suffered from one grave disadvantage, however. Although they had built over 2,000 aircraft during the War, because so few were of their own design, their name was not in the forefront of aviation circles. There was, however, one very good chance to place their name in the limelight and to promote a new airliner based on the Bourges at the same time. The *Daily Mail* £10,000 prize for the first nonstop flight across the Atlantic had been held in abeyance since before the War.

Of course many of the other manufacturers joined the immediate race to win this prize, and to promote their own products. Each attempted to maintain the utmost secrecy so as to try and steal a march on their rivals. Quickest off the mark were Sopwith with their single-engine Atlantic, based largely on their wartime B.1 with many Cuckoo components for speed of construction, and Martinsyde with a much enlarged version of the F.4 Buzzard renamed The Raymor. Frederick Handley Page saw his four-engined V/1500 as the ideal aircraft for the job, and Vickers entered with their twin-engined Vimy. Shorts saw the excellent range of the Shirl torpedo bomber as a basis for a machine capable of flying the Atlantic east to west, unlike all the others who preferred to fly in the other direction with the prevailing winds. Fairey made preparations to convert their Fairey III seaplane for an attempt and the Alliance Aircraft Company built a special aircraft for the task, their P.2 Seabird, powered by a single Napier Lion. Finally Boulton & Paul began the preparation of what would be one of the most thoughtfully conceived designs to be prepared to contest the *Daily Mail* prize, the P.8 Atlantic.

Two prototypes were to be built, and from the outset the first was designed and built purely for the Atlantic attempt. The second Bourges prototype, F2904, having been heavily damaged in a crash at Mousehold, was obtained from the Air Ministry and dismantled. The remains of its structure formed the basis for the first prototype, the sloping upper wing centre section, and the Dragonfly engines being dispensed with entirely.

The wings of the P.8 were of increased span, to 60 ft 4 in, but were the same basic Bourges three-bay unstaggered units with the straight-through centre section on the upper wing which had 8 ft chord and the lower 6 ft 6 in. There

The first P.8 Atlantic at Mousehold.

were horn-balanced ailerons on all four wings. Standard wooden construction was used but the spar fittings were very substantial, with all the struts pin-jointed and backed by metal fish-plates at every junction.

Though John North had already decided that the future of aircraft construction lay in metal structures the use of wood was continued in the P.8 for convenience, and above all for speed of construction. That did not prevent him introducing certain improved techniques. For the securing of metal fittings to the wooden fuselage longerons, tubular rivets were introduced instead of bolts. The rivet was inserted through metal fishplates on each side and the ends flattened with rivetting tools which were developed especially for the job, resulting in just a splayed mouth on each side instead of a projecting bolt. This resulted in a joint which was much lighter and compact and they were much quicker to fit, though they took longer to replace than conventional bolts.

Although the major visual change in the P.8 from its predecessor was the fact that the fuselage filled the 6 ft 6 in gap between the wings, the fuselage actually retained the basic Bourges structure. The upper part was merely a fairing of bridges and runners, this, too, was to speed completion, to prepare the aircraft for the Atlantic attempt before its rivals. The fuselage had four longerons braced and cross-strutted with tie-rods. The upper longerons being dead straight when the aircraft was in the flying position, and therefore very useful for bracing purposes. The gunner's position in the nose was replaced by a rounded construction covered with plywood and fabric.

The pilot's cockpit was situated just in front of the wings, as in the Bourges, but it was given a fully-enclosed canopy, a very advanced feature for the day. It was faired into the fuselage upper surface, so that rear view was restricted, but the view forward, sideways and down was excellent, better than any airliner extant, and not equalled until the D.H. Dragon appeared. For conservative pilots who liked to feel the wind around their ears, an upper skylight was provided, which could be opened. In the first prototype, for the Atlantic attempt, provision was made for a relief pilot and a radio operator who was provided with two sets, one for communications and one for direction finding. In the event of ditching in the Atlantic, a small balloon and hydrogen bottle were provided, to carry the radio aerial aloft for emergency signals. The radio operator and navigator were accommodated in a cabin just behind the cockpit, illuminated by large rectangular windows on each side.

Behind the crew compartment the whole of the cabin space was taken up with six fuel tanks. They were fitted with jettison valves, so that the entire fuel load could be dumped in 1¼ minutes, and were so situated that once empty they would keep the aircraft afloat the right way up. The fuel capacity was sufficient for a flight of 3,850 miles, and the performance of the aircraft was such (its cruising speed of 116 mph was much higher than any potential competitor), that it could maintain height on only one engine after only two hours' fuel had been consumed. More importantly, of course, this meant that the aircraft could maintain height at only half throttle, thus putting little strain on the engines.

Close up of the Napier Lion installation in the P.8.

The engines were 450 hp Napier Lions, with aluminium cowlings, carried on the lower wings inside the inner interplane struts. The frontal radiators fitted to each engine on the Bourges P.7b were dispensed with, and replaced by one retractable fuselage mounted radiator. This was connected to a header tank above each engine with two cut-off valves each side so that the system could be closed off should a leak develop on either side. The oil tanks, each of 6 gal capacity were fitted behind each engine, alongside self-starting magnetos. The engines drove four-blade propellers of 9 ft 6 in diameter, and were braced by steel tubing to the fuselage longerons, forming a strong triangulation with the bracing wires.

The fin and horn-balanced rudder were circular in profile, but the tailplane was square-cut like the wings, and the elevators had no horn balance. Because the rudder was insufficient to maintain heading on asymmetric power two small fins were fitted, projecting above and below the tailplane. These could be locked at an angle in the airstream in the event of one engine failing.

The P.8 was so stable it could virtually be flown hands off when fully trimmed, and it was possible, by moving a single lever, to lock the elevators and ailerons

157

and transfer rudder control to the wheel. This was unusual in that such a device would normally have operated the ailerons only, since on most aircraft steering on rudder only produces the effect of tightening into a dive. On the P.8 a slight touch of rudder was enough to return it to the required heading with no loss of height. This device was also useful for steering the aircraft on the ground using hands only instead of feet, as long as the pilot remembered to unlock the controls before taking off!

To the left of the pilot was the wheel for lowering and raising the radiator, to his right were two wheels, one to set the angle of the auxiliary fins on the tailplane, to overcome asymmetric thrust, and the other for controlling the angle of tailplane incidence.

The undercarriage was probably the most advanced feature of the aircraft. The units were V-shaped, with the legs attached at the inner interplane struts, giving a very wide track, and the split-axles hinged at the bottom fuselage longerons. One very large Palmer aircraft wheel and tyre was fitted on each side. The technological advance was in the springing, which was not the normal simple rubber bungee, but also contained an oleo-pneumatic leg to take landing shocks. This combination springing was even more advanced in concept that the pure oleo-pneumatic undercarriages which were soon to appear. The early oleo-pneumatic systems could take landing shocks very well, but were less able to absorb the frequent vertical jolts caused by taxi-ing over rough grass aerodromes.

The crew chosen for the Atlantic flight was, Maj K S Savory as first pilot, Capt A L Howarth as second pilot and radio operator, and Capt J H Woolner as navigator. Boulton & Paul's managing director, Maj Guy ffiske went to Newfoundland and chose a suitable take-off field, and the weather conditions over the North Atlantic were studied in great detail for several months.

The race for the prize was developing publicly. After test flights in February 1919 the Sopwith was shipped, and on 19 March the *Daily Mail* was officially notified of its entry for the prize. The entries of the Short Shamrock as the modified Shirl had been named in honour of its proposed take-off point at the Curragh, the Martinsyde Raymor, and the Fairey III seaplane were to follow in quick succession.

The Sopwith Atlantic arrived in Newfoundland on 29 March, and shortly afterwards the Martinsyde had a 24 hr ground test, followed by its Rolls-Royce Falcon engine being stripped down and examined. At Vickers the modifications to the 13th Vimy off their production lines were nearing completion and both the pilot, John Alcock and the navigator, Arthur Whitten Brown had been chosen.

Preparations by Boulton & Paul were severely delayed when the still unregistered P.8 crashed. In the haste to get the P.8 ready for the Atlantic flight, Frank Courtney ran up each of the engines separately before the first flight in April 1919, thereby failing to discover that there was a fault in the fuel system which did not give an adequate supply to both at once. One of the Lions cut out just after take off, the aircraft yawed into wind and a wingtip struck the ground, virtually writing it off. The entire nose section broke free, with Courtney within it, and he was unhurt.

The second P.8 was being built, and preparations were put in place to use this on the Atlantic flight. On 11 April the Sopwith Atlantic had been test flown in

The first P.8 Atlantic after crashing on take-off for its first flight. (*American Heritage Center, University of Wyoming*)

Newfoundland, but was soon grounded because of rain and thick mist. The Martinsyde had just arrived in Newfoundland and four days later the Handley Page V/1500 was shipped.

On 18 April the Vickers Vimy was test flown at Brooklands, and on the same day the Short Shamrock, which was basically a Shirl with the wing extended to three bays and a huge droppable cylindrical fuel tank bringing the total fuel load to 435 gal, took off from Eastchurch for Ireland. Piloted by Maj J C P Wood with Capt C C Wyllie as navigator, it was refuelled at Holyhead, and then took off for the Curragh, which was considered the only place in Ireland with a long enough take-off run for the fully-laden machine. Twelve miles out across the Irish Sea the engine stopped and Wood had to ditch. The Shamrock remained afloat, though upside down, and was towed into Holyhead harbour, and Wood announced his intention of remaining in the contest.

Although not in competition for the *Daily Mail* prize, the Americans were mounting an official government attempt to be the first across the Atlantic, albeit in stages via the Azores. Three Curtis NC flying-boats would fly in formation via Newfoundland and the Azores to Lisbon, along a route which would be marked by a line of 68 destroyers stationed at intervals of 50 miles, with five battleships stationed at distances of 500 miles. Every fourth destroyer would act as a meteorological station. Just in case the flying-boats failed to make it, despite this massive support, a four-man airship was moved to Newfoundland to make the attempt. On 8 May the three NCs took off from Rockaway, New York, on the first leg to Newfoundland, though it took five days for them all to get there.

The threat of the Americans being first spurred the small private British teams into action. Both the Sopwith and Martinsyde crews made hasty preparations, but the Americans took off first. On 16 May the three NCs lifted off from Trepassey Bay and headed for the Azores, but only one was to arrive, NC-4 at 9.25 am on 17 May.

Though news of the Americans' arrival in the Azores reached Newfoundland, there was still a chance that the British could be first across. On 18 May the Sopwith Atlantic took off from Newfoundland, piloted by Harry Hawker, with Lieut Cdr MacKenzie-Grieve as navigator. It was eight days before anything

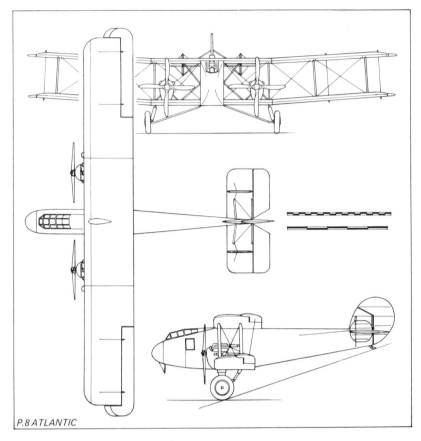

P.8 ATLANTIC

more was heard from them. They had ditched in the ocean, and were luckily picked up by a ship, though they were over 100 miles off course after flying 800 miles on dead reckoning. Their failure justified safety measures built into the Boulton & Paul P.8, the single-engined performance, and the direction-finding radio in particular.

The Sopwith aircraft actually passed over the heads of the Martinsyde crew as they were making frantic attempts to get the Raymor ready. Attempting to take off 20 min after the Sopwith had disappeared the undercarriage of the overloaded Raymor collapsed, and the aircraft was heavily damaged.

On 27 May the NC-4, commanded by Lieut Commander Read left the Azores and reached Lisbon the same day, the first aircraft to fly the Atlantic. The honour of making the first nonstop flight, and with it the £10,000 prize still remained to be captured however.

Meanwhile the Handley Page V/1500 and Alcock and Brown's Vickers Vimy had arrived in Newfoundland. The Handley Page was found to be damaged, and repairs were put in hand. It was to have a four-man crew, Maj H G Brackley, pilot, Admiral Mark Kerr, second pilot, Tryggve Gran, navigator and third pilot and F Wyatt, wireless operator. After the repairs had been completed, a trial

160

flight could not be made until 10 June because of bad weather conditions. Trial flights revealed that the engines had an alarming tendency to overheat, and new radiators were sent for from England, but were not to arrive before the 18th.

Repairs were also instituted to the Martinsyde Raymor, but before a second attempt could be made and before the second Boulton & Paul P.8 could be finished John Alcock and Arthur Whitten Brown made the first nonstop transatlantic flight in their Vickers Vimy, taking off on 14 June.

The Boulton & Paul project was abandoned, but the Martinsyde crew did make a second attempt, only for the undercarriage to collapse again on take off. The Handley Page was sent instead on a publicity flight to Long Island, where many demonstrations took place.

The second P.8 was completed and was flown for some time as both the prototype airliner and as a flying aerodynamic test-bed, registered G-EAPE. It was never converted to airliner configuration but the company did build a fuselage mock-up of the proposed layout, and artist's impressions of the finished product were prepared by Geoffrey Watson.

Although the layout of the passenger/cargo accommodation and fuel tankage

The second P.8 Atlantic, G-EAPE, at Mousehold.

The second Atlantic.

161

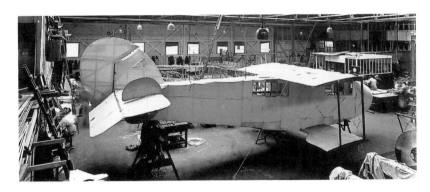

Mock-up of the airliner version of the Atlantic.

was kept fluid to suit any airline requirements, the basic version offered was with 100 gal of fuel and seven passengers. The main tank was sited within the fuselage, just beneath the upper wing, so the engines could be gravity fed. Forward of that was a cabin for three passengers, and behind it another cabin for four passengers. Passengers entered through separate doors to each cabin. To improve the head-room on entry, a portion of the roof over each compartment could be slid aside. The forward door was rather high off the ground being just behind the cockpit, and necessitated climbing a 10 ft high set of steps to gain entry. Even the door sill of the rear cabin was about 6 ft off the ground. Both cabins were heated, and great play was made in the brochure that passengers would not have to be wrapped up in warm clothing, an inconvenience on many of the makeshift airliners being put into service at the time. Both cabins had large picture windows on each side.

A mail box, capable of carrying up to 500 lb of mail could be loaded by special loading gear patented by Boulton & Paul, and directly related to the bomb cell hoist developed for the Bourges. The full disposable load of the aircraft, not including fuel was 1,870 lb. The top speed was a remarkable 149 mph at sea level, and 143 mph at 10,000 ft, and even its cruising speed of 116 mph was faster than the top speed of all contemporary airliners being offered for sale. The P.8 was in fact claimed to be the fastest twin-engined aircraft in the world.

With a wing loading not much above that of the Bourges, at 10¼ lb/sq ft, the P.8 also retained much of its forebear's agility. To placate the conservative nature of most pilots of the day, the airliner version was also offered with either the enclosed canopy, or an open cockpit with a simple windscreen.

There is little doubt that the P.8 was the most advanced and competent design to be prepared for the Atlantic flight, but fate decreed that lasting fame was not to come Boulton & Paul's way. The company's attempts to market the P.8 as an airliner, were also without success. The power which gave it such an outstanding performance and made it safe to fly on one engine, meant it could not compete economically with some of its competitors, and with the desperate economics of some of the early airline operations, this counted more than safety and passenger comfort.

A total of 900 hp and only seven passengers compared unfavourably with the D.H.18, which first flew in March 1920. This lifted a pilot and eight passengers

An artist's impression of the airliner version of the P.8 showing the passenger cabins, fore and aft of the wings. Other artist's impressions show an enclosed pilot's cabin like the transatlantic version.

on just one Napier Lion. The fact that it had only a single engine, a top speed of only 121 mph and an abysmal view for the pilot, sited as he was behind the passenger cabin, nearer the tail than the nose, were of less importance than the economics. Even Handley Page's conversions of their O/400 bomber, though twin-engined, were totally unable to maintain height on the power of only one, and only their very low landing speed prevented the many emergency landings becoming crashes.

If only that first P.8 had not crashed, and the Atlantic prize had been won, the kudos which would have resulted might have caused potential airline passengers to clamour to fly on the aircraft which was safe enough to fly the Atlantic.

P.8 Atlantic

Two 450 hp Napier Lion.
Span 60 ft 4in; length 40 ft; height 12 ft 4 in; wing area 770 sq ft.
Empty weight 5,170 lb; loaded weight 7,880 lb.
Maximum speed 149 mph at sea level, 143 mph at 10,000 ft, 138 mph at 15,000 ft; climb to 10,000 ft 8 min, to 15,000 ft 15 min; service ceiling 25,000 ft.

P.9

As related Boulton & Paul offered the experimental P.6 for the postwar civil market for £600 in unchanged form. They sold none but received an order for a slightly larger version from Lieut A L Long, who wished to take it to Australia for use on sheep stations. The revised aircraft which became the first P.9 had the same 90 hp RAF 1a engine as the P.6 but wedded to larger dimensions.

The fuselage was lengthened by 6 ft to 25 ft and the span increased by 2½ ft to 27 ft 6 in, but the wings remained single-bay. They were built in five sections, three for the upper and two for the lower which were attached directly to the lower fuselage longerons. The upper wing was carried on wooden N interplane struts and the centre section was supported above the fuselage by two struts each side. Ailerons were fitted on both top and bottom wings. The undercarriage was a conventional V-type with an elastic-sprung tubular axle.

The first P.9 at Mousehold. It was never registered in the United Kingdom or Australia.

The same tail unit and centre fuselage section were used, but both the wing chord and gap were increased by 6 inches to 5 ft 6 in each. The fuselage was a simple wire-braced box-girder but the top longerons were not horizontal. They sloped up 10 deg so that the tailplane was above the line of thrust. The fuel tankage was increased by nearly 4 gal to 24 gal, giving an increased endurance of 3 hr at full throttle at sea level. The engine, driving a 9 ft 3 in diameter four-blade propeller, was mounted directly on the upper longerons, and was partially enclosed by a cowling cum air-scoop. Long exhaust pipes discharged behind the rear cockpit. The changes also resulted in an increase in disposable load from 400 lb to 526 lb, with little change in overall performance. The first flight date of the aircraft is not recorded, but construction was nearing completion on 6 May, 1919.

Lieut. Long (inset) and his P.9 ready to make the first aerial delivery of newspapers in the Commonwealth, from Elwick to Launceston, Tasmania.

It is not clear whether the changes were made because of Long's require-ments, or because the design department had already decided that they represented a better layout for a two-seat light aircraft, but they formed the basis for the aircraft which Boulton & Paul now promoted as a commercial or sporting machine, available for £700.

Long used his P.9 for newspaper and mail flights within Tasmania. His first flight from Elwick to Launceston stopping at intervening towns was claimed to be the first delivery of a newspaper by air in the Commonwealth. Then on 17 December, 1919, he made the first northbound crossing of the Bass Strait, inaugurating the Hobart–Melbourne mail service. Amongst his cargo were letters from the Governor of Tasmania and the Mayors of Hobart and Launceston to their mainland counterparts. He took off from Launceston at 6.30 a.m, and landed at Carey's Aerodrome, Melbourne, 6¼ hr later. Extra tankage was fitted to give sufficient range, and a simple release was improvised so that the oil supply could be replenished in flight. Unfortunately this broke, necessating a landing in a field at Torquay, just after crossing the coast of the mainland. Without stopping the engine, Long jumped out, released the oil cock, and then took off again. On 27 November, 1926, a memorial was unveiled at Torquay by the Historical Society of Victoria, commemorating this flight. Long's P.9 was never registered and bore no markings at all except red white and blue stripes on the rudder.

Lieut Long and his P.9 on the occasion of the first aerial crossing of the Bass Strait on 17 December, 1919.

Seven more P.9s were built by Boulton & Paul who hoped that a developing market for light aircraft would appear after the War. These definitive production P.9s had slight changes to Long's aircraft, which never received a constructor's number. The rudder horn-balance and the tail incidence gear were both altered. The tailplane incidence could be altered by means of a lug with three holes, one or other of which received a bolt attaching it to a bracket on the rear spar. Extra centre-section struts were installed, the centre section being supported above the fuselage on metal tube N struts, the vertical members having streamlined fairings. In a typical piece of John North ingenuity a luggage space was created behind the two seats, and two hemispherical suitcases were specially made to fit the resulting compartment, which was covered by a metal

The use of the two inbuilt suitcases being demonstrated on P.9 G-EAPD. (*The Boulton Paul Society*)

cowling with quick release catches. The fabric covering of the fuselage could easily be removed by undoing the lacing by which it was fixed. The cockpit decking and engine section were covered in three-ply.

Full dual controls were fitted so that the aircraft could be used as a trainer, the control column in the front cockpit being removable. Instruments and engine controls were provided in both cockpits, except for the engine revolution indicator which was mounted in a streamlined casing outside the forward fuselage on the port side where it was visible from both cockpits. Wicker-work seats were provided in both cockpits, which were comfortable and roomy. The P.9 was also promoted for every possible commercial and sporting use, including 'Exploring uncharted territory, fighting forest fires, carrying mails to distant mines and police purposes.'

The first two built after Long's machine were registered G-EAPD and G-EASJ in April 1920, the first being used by Boulton & Paul as a company transport until November 1920 when the registration was cancelled, and the second being sold to Brig J G Weir.

First true production P.9, G-EAPD, showing the extra strut supporting the centre section.

166

108 year-old Henry Moore being given his first flight in P.9 G-AUCP on 26 February, 1926. The suitcase installation can be seen behind the cockpit.

After the high-profile success of Long's aircraft, the next three P.9s went to Australia where they were registered G-AUBT, 'UCP, and 'UCT, in June 1921.

G-AUCP, owned by Howard Jolley, was flown to victory in the Herald Cup Race at Essendon in 1923, by E W Percival. On 26 February, 1926, G-AUCP was used to give a 108-year old man, Henry Moore, his first flight as a birthday treat. Born in Jamaica in 1816, and moving to Australia in 1847, Moore was believed to have been the oldest person in the world to fly. The aircraft, still owned by Jolley, was piloted over Melbourne by P H Moody. This aircraft crashed in 1927 at Willaura, when owned by A T Tilt.

One of the other Australian P.9s, G-AUCT, piloted by F S Briggs, established two inter-city records. He flew the 550 miles from Mildura to Sydney in 6 hr 10 min and Sydney to Melbourne in 6½ hr. Unfortunately, on his return to Sydney the aircraft crashed. Apparently the remains were later converted into a monoplane by Aviation Ltd.

Two more P.9s were built, G-EAWS, which was retained by the company, and G-EBEQ, which was used by Boulton & Paul for a while, after being built for another Australian order which was subsequently cancelled. It was later sold to Flg Off F O Soden in 1926. In 1927 G-EBEQ was sold to Lieut H Kennedy, who flew it extensively from Stag Lane. In October 1928 he flew it from Croydon to Switzerland via Paris. The aircraft sank through the ice while trying to take off from a frozen lake near St Moritz on 9 February, 1929. It was recovered and registered in Dübendorf in September 1930 as CH-259 to Gerber and Greiner. Its registration was cancelled in January 1932.

In April 1922 Frank Courtney bought G-EASJ from Brig Weir, and based it at Croydon using it to fly to his various freelance test-flying assignments and air races. In September 1922 C T Holmes flew G-EASJ in the round Britain King's Cup Air Race, in which one of his fellow competitor's was G-EAWS, flown by Lieut Col J L Tennant, both acquitting themselves well. G-EASJ was 6th away and finished 11th, averaging 69 mph on the outward journey to Glasgow, via Birmingham and Newcastle, and 85 mph on the return via Manchester and Bristol. G-EAWS was 8th away, averaged 68 mph out and 88 mph back,

P.9 G-EAWS which was used by Sqn Ldr Rea, Boulton & Paul's test pilot, as his personal aircraft.

finishing a creditable 9th. The event was won by a D.H.4A with a Martinsyde F.6 second and a D.H.9B third.

Sqn Ldr F L Robinson flew G-EAWS in the 1923 King's Cup, which started at Hendon, but was otherwise the same course as the previous year. The event was won by Frank Courtney flying a Siskin, with Alan Cobham second in a D.H.9. The same year the eighth and last Aerial Derby was flown around London and G-EBEQ raced in it flown by Flt Lt J W Woodhouse. The race started at Croydon and was over two laps of the 99.5 miles course. The overall winner was L L Carter in the Gloucestershire Gloster I, but the P.9 came third in the Handicap section, averaging 91.25 mph behind an Avro 552 and a D.H.9A.

In January 1928 the Henderson School of Flying bought G-EASJ and then took it to South Africa for a joy-flying tour. It was subsequently sold to John Wilkinson of Cape Town and based at Young's Field, being re-registered G-UAAM.

Courtney's successor as Boulton & Paul test pilot, C A Rea, used G-EAWS as his personal aircraft, and flew it successfully in the Bournemouth Air Races of 4/5 June, 1927, with two firsts and a second, and being disqualified from first place in another race for cutting a pylon to avoid another competitor. He was later presented with an inscribed gold cigarette case by a well-known bookmaker who had made a lot of money at the meeting because the 'Dark horse' P.9 had done so well!

When the chairman of the Board, Capt J Dawson-Paul and his son Frank Dawson decided to learn to fly they enrolled with the Norfolk and Norwich Aero Club, but received further tuition from Rea in the P.9, both obtaining their pilot's licences. Rea had also found that many members of the design staff had never flown, and he obtained permission from John North to give them short flights in G-EAWS when opportunities arose.

Rea thought that the P.9 was a useful lightplane, and that it was a pity it had not been developed further. It just appeared ahead of its time, and like so many other manufacturers Boulton & Paul could not successfully market a brand-new

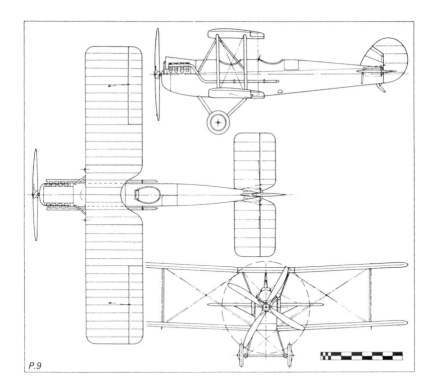

P.9

lightplane against the competition of cheap surplus Avro 504Ks. Rea found the P.9 easy to fly and even the old RAF engine was quite reliable provided it was not run at full throttle for too long. This was exactly how G-EAWS met its fate. Another pilot borrowed the aircraft for the Lympne flying meeting on the Easter weekend of 1929. The engine was run flat-out for too long and shed a cylinder. The aircraft crashed in the resulting forced landing, and was written off.

The P.9 was important from two standpoints, it was the first Boulton & Paul aircraft to go into production, even though only eight were built, and it represented the last attempt by the company to sell a wooden aircraft. Although one more wooden aircraft would be built after the P.9, the P.41 Phoenix, it was only as a full-scale experimental lightplane. When the company came to market the P.41 it was totally rebuilt with an all-metal airframe.

P.9

90 hp RAF 1a.
Span 27 ft 6in; length 25 ft; height 10 ft; wing area 323 sq ft.
Empty weight 1,244 lb; loaded weight 1,770 lb.
Maximum speed 104 mph at 1,000 ft; cruising speed 85 mph; climb to 5,000 ft 8½ min;
    ceiling 14,000 ft; range 300 miles; endurance 3 hr at full throttle.

The P.10 on display at the Paris Salon d'Aéronautique in 1919, uncovered to show the all-metal structure.

P.10

John North became convinced that aircraft structures were better made of metal, both for lightness and strength, and also for durability. Despite the history of Boulton & Paul as woodworking manufacturers, the reason they had been brought into the aircraft business in the first place, he now turned to metal construction as the basis for the whole future of the company.

The logical first step in the move to all-metal construction, after a period of research and experimentation, was to rebuild the P.9 with a metal airframe, but though the P.10 was a two-seat light aircraft of the same layout as the P.9 it was a fundamentally different design.

It was slightly larger than the P.9, and did not resemble it in the slightest. Every part of the airframe structure was made of steel, the only wood used was for the four-blade propeller of 7 ft 6¼ in diameter. The engine was a Cosmos Lucifer three-cylinder radial. The Lucifer was a curious engine, being really one third of a nine-cylinder Jupiter, but with only a 6.25 in stroke. With only three cylinders producing 100 hp at 1,700 rpm, every firing stroke was noticeable! The most prominent feature of the Lucifer was the large doughnut-like exhaust-collector ring.

Displaying the ingenuity which was to be a feature of most John North aircraft, the engine was fitted to a clever hinged mounting, so that the rear of the engine could be worked on without disturbing any of the control lines. The

170

engine mounting consisted of two long hinge bolts, and by withdrawing one, the engine could be swung on the other to provide access to the magneto and carburettor at its rear. All the piping was arranged so that it did not need any disconnection. The Lucifer was enclosed in a close-fitting conical cowling from which the three cylinders protruded. A 26 gal fuel tank was fitted, which was thought would give the P.10 a duration of 5 hours at 90 mph at 3,000 ft.

The airframe was made entirely of steel treated and varnished to prevent corrosion. Rolled sections of high-tensile steel were formed into tubes, strips and angles for every part of the structure. Rolled steel sections had been extensively tested to destruction so that the full weight/strength advantages of steel over wood could be used. John North maintained that the P.10 was thus lighter and stronger than if it had been built of wood, and far more durable, especially for hot and humid climates. A further advantage of using steel was its consistency compared with wood, much of which had to be thrown away in the construction process because of irregularities of grain.

The unstaggered single-bay wings were of 30 ft span, rather more than the P.9 but with the same 5 ft 6 in chord and 5 ft 6 in gap. The spars were of I section built up of a box of four thin rolled sides. The flanges were corrugated for extra strength and rivetted to the webs, which had lightening holes at intervals, connected by horizontal lengths of tube, which were flanged over the webs to prevent them bending.

Ailerons were fitted to all four wings and connected by cables. The entire wing structure was covered with fabric. The interplane struts were of ordinary streamlined tube connected to the compression struts inside the spars. Further V struts supported the wing centre section on each side of the fuselage, with an additional strut angled forward to the engine bulkhead.

The forward fuselage consisted of four tubular longerons and the rear fuselage was a monocoque of oval formers of channel section placed back to back with double S-section longitudinal stringers. The fuselage covering was probably the most remarkable feature of the P.10, it featured the first ever use of plastic in an

The P.10 at Paris. The fuselage panels were of Bakelite-Dilecto.

171

aircraft structure. Sheets of Bakelite-Dilecto, a cellulose-formaldehyde based plastic, were rivetted to the metal parts. This material, devised by Boulton & Paul, was claimed to be unaffected by heat and humidity, and both fire and insect proof.

Full dual controls were fitted to the two cockpits, and both had large windscreens. The front cockpit was beneath the leading edge of the upper wing, and the rear cockpit was just behind the trailing edge. With the close cowling of the engine, and its oval shape the fuselage was very streamlined and torpedo-like, the effect being slightly marred by the unstaggered wings. The P.10 was both 2 ft longer and taller than the P.9 at 26 ft and 12 ft respectively.

The fin and horn-balanced rudder were of tear-drop shape, and the tailplane was braced by two struts on each side, connected to the fin. The undercarriage was carried by V-struts of streamlined steel tube with rubber shock absorbers. It was stated that oleo struts would be fitted at a later date.

The P.10 was displayed at the Paris Salon d'Aéronautique of 1919 with the wings, tail and part of the fuselage left uncovered so that the structure could be examined. Representing, as it did, the first practical British aircraft with an all-steel structure, and the first use of plastics in aircraft construction, it caused a sensation. It was described as 'The only real advance in aeronautics on show'. *Flight's* technical editor reviewed it with the words 'The Boulton & Paul all-metal machine, the P.10, is the machine of the show, from a constructional point of view.'

Strangely the P.10 was not displayed at the Olympia Aero Show of 1920, making the Short Silver Streak the only British metal aircraft on show. It has been said that the P.10 was damaged when the engine failed, which does seem a likely reason for not exhibiting an aircraft which had caused such a sensation at Paris, but there is no record of it ever having flown or even being finished; so how it came to be damaged is not clear.

As the expected boom in civil flying had failed to materialise John North was by then of the opinion that the future for the company lay in seeking military contracts. He regarded the P.10 as an experiment in constructional techniques, and though sales brochures were produced for it, no price was quoted. With so few willing to pay £700 for a P.9, it was clear that there would be little civil

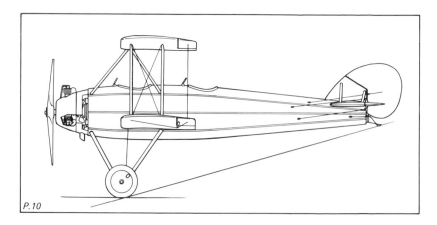

P.10

market for an aircraft with all the complications of steel construction.

With no market for it, and no real need to examine its qualities, given that it was an exercise in construction rather than aerodynamics, the P.10 quietly disappeared. I am also sure the AID and Air Ministry would have viewed the use of plastic covering with extreme scepticism—Shorts were making little headway in getting them to accept duralumin in aircraft structures.

The P.10 was not the first British aircraft with an all-metal structure, that honour goes to the Seddon Mayfly of 1910, though the Mayfly had no prospect of flying. It was however the first practical British aircraft with an all-steel structure, and set Boulton & Paul on the road to becoming the leading pioneers in steel aircraft structures. Amazingly the tail, and a wing of the P.10 still survive, in the Bridewell Museum in Norwich. They are the oldest pieces of British metal aircraft structure in existence.

The P.10 wing on loan from the Bridewell Museum, Norwich, at a Boulton Paul Society exhibition at the Aerospace Museum, Cosford, in 1993. This is the oldest British metal aircraft wing in existence.

P.10

100 hp Cosmos Lucifer.
Span 30 ft; length 26 ft; height 12 ft; wing area 309 sq ft.
Empty weight 1,104 lb; loaded weight 1,700 lb.
Estimated performance: maximum speed 104 mph at 1,000 ft; climb to 5,000 ft 8 min; service ceiling 14,000 ft; endurance 3½ hr at 100 mph at 3,000 ft, 5 hr at 90 mph at 3,000 ft.

The first P.12 Bodmin, J6910, at Mousehold in 1923.

P.12 Bodmin

Air Ministry purchasing policy involved a specification being issued to major firms and their submissions being assessed by the Department of Research after the Contracts Department had rendered them anonymous, as far as they could with most designers having clearly recognisable traits. The best two designs would receive contracts for the production of prototypes.

In this way, in 1922, Boulton & Paul built two prototypes for a proposed 'Postal' aircraft, which was Air Ministry shorthand for an experimental aircraft. The concept being investigated in this case was the construction of a multi-engined aircraft with the engines buried in the fuselage, driving propellers on the wings.

The concept had originated at Bristols, where Frank Barnwell had suggested building a version of their huge Braemar triplane powered by two 1,500 hp turbine engines contained in a fuselage engine room. The expense of developing such a revolutionary idea was too high, but the Air Ministry were interested in the 'engine room' concept, as a means of making long-distance flying safer, and suggested a design with four Armstrong Siddeley Pumas in the fuselage.

Specification 1/20 was drawn up for a so-called 'Spares Carrier', another Air Ministry euphemism, and a prototype contract was given for the resulting Bristol Tramp, a triplane with four Pumas in its engine room. A separate Specification, 9/20, was issued for the 'Postal' aircraft, which was to be smaller than the Tramp. Two designs won orders for this specification, the single-engined Parnall Possum, and the rival twin-engined Boulton & Paul Bodmin.

The Bodmin was a biplane, very reminiscent of the Bourges, as far as the concept allowed, with two Napier Lions driving four propellers, two tractor, and two pusher. The airframe was of all-steel construction. The larger Tramp was ordered against a tender price of £23,000, whereas the tender price of the Bodmin was only £20,000.

Much of the credit for developing the steel spars and structure has to go to Harold John Pollard, who had previously been at Vickers, after having trained at University College, Nottingham. He had been employed by North as his

The P.12 Bodmin centre section, showing the 'engine room', and aerofoil section containing the radiators, fuel tanks and transmission shafts.

specialist assistant in the development of metal structures, and was later to move on to Bristols to undertake similar work. The 'engine room' concept was an ideal opportunity for John North to demonstrate the inherent advantages of all-metal construction, and in particular its weight-saving potential.

The airframe was entirely made of high-tensile sheet steel rolled, drawn or stamped to the required section, with most of the tubing being constructed by the new Boulton & Paul locked-joint system. The covering remained fabric throughout, though the Air Ministry, convinced by North's argument that building the Bodmin in steel would result in a structure 10 per cent lighter than wood, had also suggested that it should be skinned in currugated steel sheet, as developed by Junkers in Germany.

The transmissions, connecting shafts, and the structure supporting them, which had to be independent of the wing structure for rigging reasons, were all added weight. Not only that but because the location of the engines placed a larger load on the wings than in a conventional layout, they had to be built stronger, and therefore heavier.

The aim of the layout was to produce a safer aircraft. A mechanic could work on the Napier Lions within the engine room, which was lit both by its windows and by electric light. All the engine instruments were located in the engine room, the revolution counters, temperature and oil pressure gauges, as well as the necessary controls. Moreover each engine could be shut down without exerting any asymmetric thrust. The forward engine drove the two tractor propellers, and the rear engine the two pushers, with the propellers being opposite handed so there was no torque-induced swing. The aircraft was able to fly level on the power of only one engine.

The mainwheels were fitted with oleo-pneumatic legs for shock absorption.

Their design was quite novel, in keeping with the rest of the aircraft. The oil pressure in the legs was allowed to rise freely to a certain limit, and was then released by the opening of spring-loaded valves in the piston and cylinder head.

The nose and centre section of the Bodmin being transported from Riverside to Mousehold. The circular gun position in the nose belies the 'Postal' designation of the aircraft. (*Alan Hague*)

The engine bay of the P.12 Bodmin, looking aft.

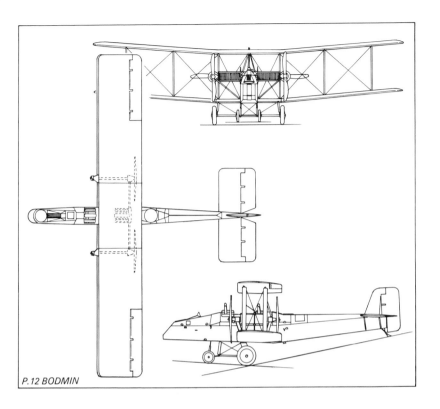

P.12 BODMIN

The aircraft was supported when at rest, not by springs, but by air pumped into the cylinder by an ordinary tyre pump, to a pressure of 60 lb/sq in, which was thought to be enough to cushion the taxi-ing shocks, and to extend the leg after take off to the landing position. Forward of the mainwheels were two smaller wheels to prevent nosing over on landing.

There were further safety features built into the design. There were six fuel tanks, each of which could be closed off from the system should it become damaged. The radiators were built in six sections, each of which could be shut off in the event of a leak. The radiators were sited so that they faired in the extension shafts and fuel tanks, forming an enclosed integrated structure between the wings. The engine exhausts were fitted with specially-designed flame guards to protect the rear gunner, provision for which was made directly behind the engine compartment, showing that this so-called Postal aircraft was in fact a prototype bomber. Its long nose, and auxiliary nosewheels may also have been designed for the later provision of a heavy calibre weapon in the nose, but there was a faired-over nose station for a normal Scarff ring.

The unstaggered wings were a three-bay layout of 70 ft span, with markedly square-cut tips. They were of relatively high aspect ratio, and this was largely due to Otto Glauert, Boulton & Paul's mathematician. Prof Prandtl of Göttingen had confirmed mathematically Lanchester's work from before the War, which showed that the resistance of a wing comprised not only drag due to

177

the shape of its profile, but an additional proportion depending on its aspect ratio. Glauert's brother worked on the same theory at Farnborough, and he converted John North to its benefits, flight tests with the Bourges having already confirmed them.

The aircraft was over 53 ft long, much of which was the elongated nose, shaped rather like the bow of an inverted boat. The pilot had an open cockpit well forward of the wings. The tailplane was square-cut like the wings, and the fin and rudder were far more angular than previous John North designs.

Frank Courtney was to be responsible for the first flight of the first Bodmin prototype, J6910, early in 1924, and because it was designated a 'Postal' aircraft, there were no military restrictions on Press interest. He was plied with questions about the possible failure of the complicated drive-shafts, gears and clutches, and what they would do to the airframe if they disintegrated and flew apart. After the first flight went off without a hitch, followed by a couple more, the newsmen took Courtney to lunch in Norwich, probably disappointed that stories about the first flight of so 'hazardous' an aircraft had not proved sensational. The reporters did get a story of sorts in the end, however. As Courtney was leaving the restaurant he was knocked to the ground by a messenger boy on a bicycle and his glasses were broken, cutting his face. The line they took was that he was safer in the air, in the 'dangerous' Bodmin, than on the ground.

The Bodmin actually flew very well, though it was plagued with cooling and transmission difficulties. The engine room was noisy and stuffy, but it did have one advantage for the engineer. In this hot enclosed little world he was often oblivious to the problems facing the poor pilot in his open cockpit in the nose. Courtney wrote of one test flight, 'I have vivid memories of Martin, the Inspector, busily tending the mechanisms in the engine room of the Bodmin whilst, low on fuel, I was trying to get back to Mousehold in a thunderstorm.'

The novel undercarriage system suffered a failure on 11 February, 1924. Whilst taxi-ing at about 6–10 mph across Mousehold to a take-off position, the aircraft went over a hillock as it was turning to port, and the starboard side collapsed. It was found that the available travel on the oleo struts was insufficient to cope with such hillocks, except at very slow speed, or indeed at a much higher speed. The only possible rectification seemed to be ensuring that the struts were fully filled with oil before each flight – and to level off all such hillocks at Mousehold.

Two prototype Bodmins were built, J6910 and J6911. Speed at sea-level was 116 mph, a disappointing figure when compared with the contemporary Boulton & Paul P.15 Bolton, and the ceiling was 16,000 ft, also inferior to what might be expected from a conventional aircraft.

It was thought the disadvantages of the layout, that is the excess weight, exceeded the advantages, which were mainly the safety features. The Bodmin was able to lift a useful operational load only because the extra weight of the engine transmissions was offset by the lower weight Boulton & Paul had managed to achieve with all-steel construction, compared with wood, North calculating that 20 per cent had been saved rather than his initial estimate of 10 per cent.

The operation had been a success, but the concept died. Boulton & Paul learned a great deal about the manufacture of steel structures in the process however, which was to stand it in good stead in the future.

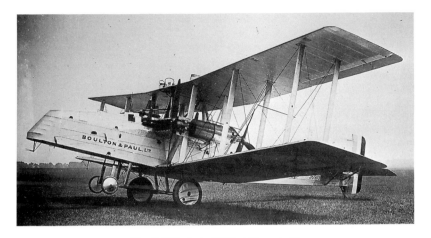

The P.12 Bodmin J6910 at Mousehold.

P.12 Bodmin

Two 450 hp Napier Lion.
Span 70 ft; length 53 ft 4½ in; wing area 1,204 sq ft.
Empty weight 7,920 lb; loaded weight 11,000 lb.
Maximum speed 116 mph at sea level; climb to 6,500 ft 8 min 9 sec; service ceiling 16,000 ft.
Armament: provision for nose and dorsal Scarff ring mounted Lewis machine-guns.

P.15 Bolton

The sole Bolton, J6584, at Mousehold in 1923.

The Air Ministry was largely convinced that the steel structure of the type incorporated in the P.10 and under development by Boulton & Paul's research department was essential both for British conditions and because of its

179

A close up of the P.15 Bolton's centre fuselage uncovered, showing the fuel tanks within the metal structure.

availability, the wartime difficulties of obtaining high grade spruce being still fresh in the memory. To aid the company in the further development of their steel techniques Specification 4/20 was issued in 1920 for a steel-framed version of the Bourges. One prototype was ordered, J6584, and the aircraft was named Bolton by the company. Though the Bolton was given a later project number by Boulton & Paul than the Bodmin, the aircraft was actually built first, and was to be the first all-metal aircraft delivered to the RAF.

Though the Bolton was essentially a Bourges with a high-tensile steel frame, the two aircraft differed significantly in appearance. The span of the three-bay unstaggered wings were increased beyond that of the Bourges to 62 ft 6 in. The spars were similar in design to those used on the P.10, with four corrugated strips forming a box, the webs being joined at intervals by tubes of carbon steel cut to length and flanged at the ends. The broad interplane struts basically consisted of two triangular sections joined by a lattice of channel-sectioned members, and the whole structure being faired over with fabric.

The Napier Lion engines were carried, between the inner wing struts and the fuselage, in an unusual way. They were fitted to the lower wing as on the P.7b Bourges, but integral with a slightly raised section, in front of which were the radiators. The upper part of the engines were not enclosed, so that smaller radiators than normal could be fitted; the engines were in effect both air- and water-cooled. The metal panels fairing the lower part of the engines were corrugated for greater strength.

The 450 hp Lions were fitted with four-blade propellers. The exhaust silencers were a patented Boulton & Paul design with aluminium manifolds terminating in steel pipes in which saw cuts were made. This arrangement meant the exhausts were very efficiently cooled. The engines were fitted on special

The uncovered nose of the Bolton, revealing the front gunner/bomb-aimer's position.

anti-vibration mountings, and were started by handle at the rear of the nacelle. This was a boon for mechanics who did not have to clamber on the wing to crank the engine, risking damage to the aircraft and injury to themselves. The fuel tanks were all in the fuselage, with two main tanks and an upper feeder tank, at sufficient height to gravity feed the engines. Fuel was continuously pumped to the feeder tank by two windmill-driven fuel pumps.

The inner section of the upper wing was carried on oblique struts straight over the fuselage as on the Bourges Mk 1A. The flat-sided fuselage had a triangular upper frame to give a pointed top surface, allowing the dorsal gunner to aim his

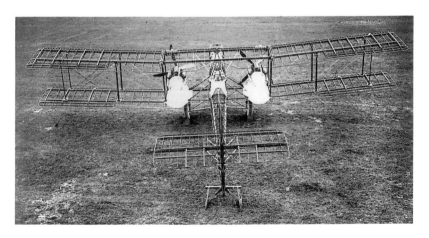

The Bolton complete but uncovered to show the all-steel structure.

181

Lewis gun down at quite a steep angle. The under surface was flat and jutted out further than the upper surface at the front, giving the nose something of the impression of the upturned stern of a ship, and very similar in appearance to the nose of the Bodmin.

The longerons were of tubular section built up of two pieces, one piece forming three-quarters of the circle, stiffened with flanged rings and the ends turned outwards, and the other piece filling the gap. They were designed in this manner so that the one quarter piece increased the resistance of the longeron to secondary torsional stresses. The one quarter piece was cut away to attach the longeron struts with an L-shaped bracket.

The main undercarriage included oleo-pneumatic legs, especially developed by Boulton & Paul, and very different in design to those used on the P.8. A nosewheel was fitted to prevent the aircraft nosing over on the ground. This wheel was connected to both the fuselage, and the mainwheels in a tricycle arrangement, both clumsy in appearance, and giving a much narrower track than the Bourges, which had been excellent in this respect.

Further evidence of North's ingenuity was displayed by the smaller vertical surface hinged to the upper leading-edge of the fin, which acted as a trimmer, controlled by a pilot-operated wheel. The fin and rudder projected well below the fuselage underside, and were rectangular in shape, with rounded corners. There was a large horn-balance for the rudder projecting forward of the upper fin. The horizontal tail, also rectangular, was carried across the rear fuselage top surface, bisecting the fin.

The crew arrangement was the same as the Bourges, with nose and dorsal gunners, equipped with single Lewis guns on Scarff rings plus the pilot's open cockpit situated just ahead of the wings. The front gunner acted as bomb aimer, and there were two windows in the nose through which to operate the bomb-sight. Provision was made for a camera operated by the dorsal gunner.

Frank Courtney undertook the first flight of the Bolton in September 1922. The secrecy imposed by the Air Ministry at the time, in contrast to the almost contemporary Bodmin, has resulted in the performance figures not being recorded for posterity.

The solitary Bolton, J6584, was the very first aircraft with an all-metal airframe to be supplied to the RAF. The Air Ministry though convinced of the

View of J6584 showing the very narrow track of the undercarriage compared to that of the Bourges.

value of all-metal aircraft, was faced with continuing cash shortages and this meant no orders were forthcoming beyond, the single prototype, but the following year the first prototypes of a continued development of the Bourges/Bolton theme, the P.25 Bugle, were ordered.

P.15 Bolton

Two 450 hp Napier Lion.
Span 62 ft 6 in; length 48 ft.
Loaded weight 9,500 lb.
Estimated maximum speed 130 mph at 10,000 ft.
Armament: single Lewis machine-guns on Scarff rings in nose and dorsal positions.

P.25 Bugle

The prototype P.25 Bugle, J6984, at Mousehold. Its first flight was on 25 July, 1923, piloted by Capt Frank Courtney.

Boulton & Paul received another opportunity to further develop their steel structure and medium-bomber design with an order for another twin-engined type to Air Ministry Specification 30/22. The resulting P.25 Bugle was an aircraft which retained the basic Bourges layout which had been continued with the Bolton. Two prototypes were ordered initially, J6984 and J6985, each powered by two 400 hp Bristol Jupiter II/III nine-cylinder air-cooled radials.

The wing-span was larger than the Bolton at 65 ft 0½ in and the four ailerons were connected by struts, rather than cables as on the earlier designs, with self-aligning bearings introduced to eradicate stiffness of the ailerons due to in-flight wing distortion. The unstaggered wings were again three-bay with 7 ft gap, and the engines mounted mid-gap at the inner struts. The engines had the Boulton & Paul patented hinged mountings pioneered on the P.10, so that the Jupiters could be swung aside for access to their rear for servicing. The engines were fitted with two-blade propellers and were enclosed in streamlined nacelles. The semi-circular fuel tanks were slung beneath the upper wings in the inner bay. This was because there was an Air Ministry dictum in force, preventing fuel tanks being sited within the fuselage.

The Bugle was built of Boulton & Paul's now standard steel construction with box spars of corrugated steel strip, and steel ribs. The aircraft was fabric covered, as before. A patented interplane strut design was used, load bearing structure of the inner struts being of steel and the outer ones of duralumin, but the fairings were of wood which could be removed for inspection during overhaul or repairs. The use of light alloy indicates the Air Ministry's relaxing attitude to its appearance in secondary structural members. The attachment of the interplane struts also differed from previous designs. They were fixed to plates which straddled the spars.

The fuselage was a rectangular frame of four longerons built up of two drawn sections so that by cutting out one of the sections a bearing was afforded for an angle plate. Struts and bracing wires were attached to this angle plate. The upper fuselage behind the dorsal gun position was of triangular shape to afford the gunner the maximum field of fire in a downward direction.

Both the main undercarriage and the tailskid were fitted with oleo-pneumatic shock-absorbing legs, the mainwheels being of the Bourges layout, without the nosewheels of the Bolton and Bodmin. This layout allowed the return to a wide track, of 16 ft 11 in, overcoming one shortcoming of the Bolton, and returning to the stability of the Bourges when taxi-ing. The main undercarriage had two

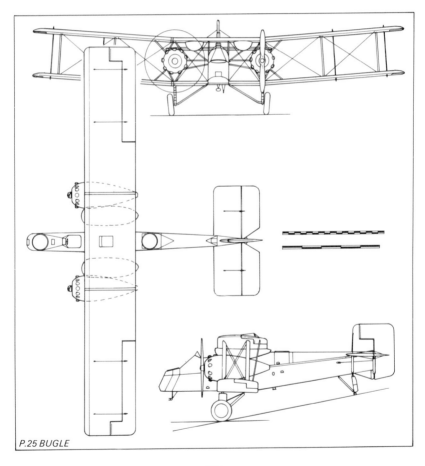

P.25 BUGLE

further tubes added with coil springs, which provided additional damping when taxi-ing.

The ailerons and rudder had inset horn-balances and were of large area to retain the sort of manoeuvrability which was now a standard feature of North's twins. The wings and tail surfaces had the markedly rectangular appearance which, by now was becoming a Boulton & Paul trademark. The trimming tail differed from that of the Bolton in having a very large balance area set into the fin, which was inoperative at normal flight angles, being sheltered from the airflow, but if the power was reduced on one side, it could adequately cope with the swinging moment. Locking devices allowed the rudder to be set to one side to cope with asymmetric thrust, while retaining full movement.

The crew positions were as in the Bolton and Bourges, the pilot's cockpit being just in front of the wings. The gunners were supplied with Lewis guns on Scarff rings in nose and dorsal positions. The Scarff ring in the nose was canted forward to afford a better field of fire in a downward direction. The gunners position was set much lower than the pilot's cockpit to give the pilot a much improved forward view. The bomb load was all carried externally, with two bomb rails under the lower longerons and two under the inner wings. As before, the nose gunner acted as bomb-aimer and was provided with a small handwheel coupled to a friction clutch and a push and pull rod, to make small adjustments to the rudder independently of the pilot while on the bombing run. There was a small window in the nose of the aircraft, with a sliding panel beneath it, the gunner being prone to use the bomb-sight. His seat folded to one side for this purpose.

The second prototype Bugle, J6985, showing its greater similarity to the Bourges than the earlier P.15 Bolton. (*The Boulton Paul Society*)

The first Bugle I, J6984, first flew on 30 June, 1923, in the hands of Frank Courtney, after taxi-ing trials the previous day. The second prototype, J6985, was also built and flown in the same year. The following year a modified version appeared, J7235. It was completed as a four-seater, and with 436 hp Jupiter IV engines replacing the earlier ones. The span was reduced to 62 ft 6 in and the fuel capacity was increased.

This aircraft joined No.58 Squadron at Worthy Down in 1925 for Service trials, and comparisons with the Vickers Virginia which had been in use since December 1924. Sqn Ldr Longton, the CO, arranged to fly the aircraft at the 1925 Hendon Display in a mock-fight with two Gloster Grebes, flown by two instructors from the CFS, Flt Lt H A Hamersley and Flg Off J Boothman. They practised the display for some time over Upavon, with Longton putting the Bugle through violent aerobatic manoeuvres. Pilot Off C Clarkson, who flew as observer in the Bugle had the job of manually maintaining the pressure in its fuel tanks. The combination of this arduous task and the violent manoeuvres so disconcerted him that upon landing he temporarily forgot that he was not in a Virginia. He walked straight into the turning propeller, was hit luckily by the flat of the blade, and hurled backwards. Boothman grabbed him and just prevented him rebounding back into the propeller.

At the Hendon display, Longton gave an astonishing display of aerobatics in his mock dog-fight with the two Grebes. He indulged in loops and spins, and even flew inverted. He must have greatly enjoyed the change, after flying the stately Virginias. As well as featuring excellent manoeuvrability, the Bugle I had a sprightly top speed of 120 mph at sea level, and could climb to 10,000 ft in 15½ min. In comparison the Virginias could only manage 98½ mph at sea level.

In 1924 two further Jupiter-powered Bugles were built, J7259 and J7260, broadly similar to J7235. One of them, J7260, was demonstrated at Mousehold on 25 February, 1927, flown by Flt Lt W N Plenderleith, in an air display

The third Bugle, J7235, with horn-balanced ailerons, Jupiter IV engines, and a crew of four. (*Crown Copyright A & AEE*)

The first of two P.25a Bugle IIs, J7266, with Napier Lion engines on the lower wing, and the fuel tanks moved from beneath the upper wing to the fuselage. (*The Boulton Paul Society*)

186

celebrating the formation of the Norwich and Norfolk Flying Club. This allowed the workforce to see the results of their work, though many might have been dissuaded from coming as it was pouring with rain.

In 1925 another version of the aircraft was built. The P.25a Bugle II had 450 hp Napier Lion engines mounted on the lower wings instead of the Jupiters, the fuel tanks being transferred from under the upper wings to the fuselage. Streamlining was further improved by fitting light fairings to the ventral bomb-carriers. The changes increased all-up weight from 8,760 lb for the Bugle I to 8,914 lb.

Bugle J7235. Two further prototypes were built broadly similar to this aircraft, J7259 and J7260. (*Crown Copyright A & AEE*)

Two Bugle Mk IIs were built, J7266 and J7267, making seven Bugles in all. All the Bugles were finished in the standard aluminium dope of the 1920s.

Despite the excellent performance and exceptional manoeuvrability of the aircraft, cash shortages prevented any more being built, but at least by continuing its policy of ordering more and more advanced prototypes from Boulton & Paul, and other manufacturers, the Air Ministry kept the industry ticking over, and developments to be made, until such time as national emergency required all-out production.

P.25 Bugle

Bugle I: two 400 hp Bristol Jupiter II/III or 435 hp Jupiter IV.
Bugle II: two 450 hp Napier Lion.
Span 65 ft 0½ in (Bugle I J6984–5), 62 ft 6 in (all others); length 39 ft 9 in; height 15 ft 8 in; wing area 932 sq ft (J6984–5), 924.7 sq ft (all others).
J6984–5 empty weight 5,079 lb; loaded weight 8,110 lb; other Bugle Is loaded weight 8,760 lb; Bugle II loaded weight 8,914 lb.
J6984–5 maximum speed 120 mph at sea level; Bugle II maximum speed 112 mph at sea level; J6984–5 climb to 10,000 ft 15½ min.
Armament: single Lewis machine-gun on Scarff ring mounting in nose and dorsal positions; external bombs.

The prototype P.29 Sidestrand, J7938, at Mousehold before its first flight. (*Miss L North*)

P.29 Sidestrand

The Specification 9/24 for a twin-engined day bomber powered by Napier Lions allowed the company to refine the Bourges/Bolton/Bugle theme even further, and to create an aircraft which would reap the benefit of the extensive aerodynamic research they had undertaken. The aerodynamics of various wing/fuselage/engine nacelle combinations had been investigated, in order to find the layout with the minimum interference effects. The culmination of these experiments, and the lessons learned with the previous medium bombers was the P.29 Sidestrand Mk I, named after a village near Cromer.

It retained the same three-bay square-cut wings of the earlier designs, but the rectangular shape of the fuselage was altered by curved upper and lower sections. This, and the graceful curve of the nose, marred only slightly by the forward gunner's position, gave the Sidestrand a much more attractive appearance than its angular predecessors.

The structure was the, by now, standard Boulton & Paul steel construction, based on the locked-joint circular tubes with pads fitted over them for the fitment of struts to longerons, bolts passing through the pads vertically and horizontally, and bracing wires being attached to wiring plates. Three metals were used in the structure, nickel-chrome steel for the heavily loaded members, duralumin for lightly loaded struts and aluminium-silicon alloy for die-cast strut end fittings.

The fuselage was built in three basic sections, the front being a monocoque of duralumin consisting of flanged horizontal channels and U-shaped frames connected by stainless steel fittings. Over this a covering of plywood sheet was fitted, strengthened by V-shaped strips on the inside. The front section stretched as far back as the front spar attachments. The front part of the nose section was hinged so that it could be swung aside for access to the rear of the pilot's instrument panel as well as the nose gunner's position.

The remainder of the structure was mostly fabric-covered, plywood with spruce only being used for the cockpit, bomb-bay and ventral gun position fairings. Bracing wires within the fuselage were so fitted as to be adjustable in flight, by a crew member crawling back through the fuselage. Bracing wires had

188

The front fuselage of the P.29 Sidestrand under construction, showing nose gunner's, pilot's, and optional fourth crew member's cockpits.

a tendency to slacken during violent manoeuvres or in extreme turbulence, and this was considered a useful safety feature.

The centre bay was of high-tensile steel tube, using unusually, shear bushes instead of rivets to join thin-walled members, saving time of construction and weight. The centre section carried the wing-fittings, centre section struts and the bomb racks, and inside was the main fuel tank. The 190 gal main tank had a 30 gal reserve tank inside it, and occupied most of the upper portion of the centre section, the top of the tank being curved to the fuselage shape. There was also a saddle-shaped service tank, or second reserve tank of 30 gal.

The rear fuselage was of locked-joint high-tensile steel tube, the top longeron having a liner to strengthen it in the first two bays, where the dorsal gunner's cockpit was located. This area was further strengthened by cross bracing, the braces allowing sufficient room for the gunner to descend to the ventral gun position as required.

The high aspect ratio wings were of B.P.10 section, a modified Joukowsky profile, and were of equal 71 ft 11 in span, with more discernible wing-stagger than the earlier designs. The outer wing sections had a slight sweep-back. The four plain ailerons were once more connected by wire. The wings were built in seven sections, the four outer wings, the top centre section and the inner sections of the lower wings. The spar sections were of the common series developed over the previous seven years in 26 or 28 gauge high-tensile steel strip. The compression members or drag-struts were also of steel with light alloy sockets. Most of the ribs and the control surfaces were of duralumin, though the elevators had tubular steel spars. Wooden fairings were used on the interplane struts, as in the Bugle, with the outer ones being made of duralumin, and the inner ones of steel.

Like the wings the vertical and horizontal tail surfaces were also markedly square-cut, the horizontal surfaces being braced by two struts on each side. The structure was the same as for the wings, but of lighter gauge metal.

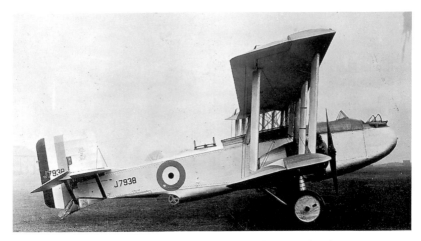

The prototype Sidestrand before the fitment of the three Lewis guns.

The company chose not to install the Napier Lions which had been specified, but fitted two ungeared 425 hp Bristol Jupiter VIs on the lower wings at the inner wing-struts, the forward struts being an inverted V. The engines were fitted with Boulton & Paul's special hinged steel mountings, so that they could be swung aside for ease of maintenance. No hand-cranking gear was fitted to the engines, they were started by RAE Mk II gas starters, and two-blade propellers were fitted. The engines were gravity fed from the fuselage fuel tanks. The 16 gal oil tanks mounted above each engine were only totally filled when the reserve fuel tank was in use, more normally they only contained 11½ gal.

There were two mainwheels, with oleo-pneumatic legs, but no smaller wheels to prevent nosing over. The swivelling, self-tracking tailskid was rubber-sprung, and capable of being lifted on the standard tail trolley for towing. Its vertical movement was limited to 4½ in by the compression strut.

There were three gun positions, the usual Scarff rings in nose and dorsal positions, plus one for an extra Lewis gun in a special plywood ventral tunnel, covering the area below the tail. The rear gunner was to operate either the dorsal or ventral gun, but strangely, it was not intended that both guns should be carried at the same time. Likewise, though provision was made for six spare drums of ammunition in each gun position, spare drums would only be carried in dorsal or ventral position depending on the gun fitted. It was considered that for operational sorties the Sidestrands would fly in a close formation, the gunners giving complimentary protection, and the choice of ventral or dorsal gun would be made before take-off, depending on where in the formation the aircraft would fly. Obvioiusly it was not considered likely that such a formation would be broken up, the individual aircraft having to protect themselves.

The narrow nose of the aircraft not only improved the pilot's view it also allowed the gunner to point his gun down at quite a steep angle. The gunner had a firing step, and a tip-up leather-upholstered seat attached to the starboard side. Beneath the nose was a glazed panel covered by a sliding plywood panel, where the front gunner lay prone for bomb-aiming using a Mk 2H (High Speed)

190

course-setting bomb-sight. A small cushion was provided for the gunner to use when lying prone, being clipped to one side when not in use. There were two small boards alongside the bomb-sight with altimeter and air-speed indicator, and the bomb-aimer had a speaking tube to talk to the pilot.

The pilot's open cockpit was situated well forward of the wings, slightly in front of the propellers. The pilot's position was slightly higher than the nose gunner's, for better visibility, but not so markedly as in the Bugle.

A second cockpit was positioned just behind the pilot for another optional crew member, to act as navigator, or relief pilot on long flights. A second set of flying controls could be fitted for this, and also for pilot training. The radio and navigational instruments were fitted here, and could be reached by either the rear gunner or the nose gunner crawling through a passage below the pilot's seat, when only three crew members were carried. The navigation table to the rear of this cockpit was actually the top of the bomb cell, and this table served as a seat when the wireless was being used. The wireless was a continuous wave transmitter/receiver.

A cushion was provided for the rear gunner to use in the ventral tunnel, being clipped to the fuselage side when not in use. The gun was fitted to a cross tube

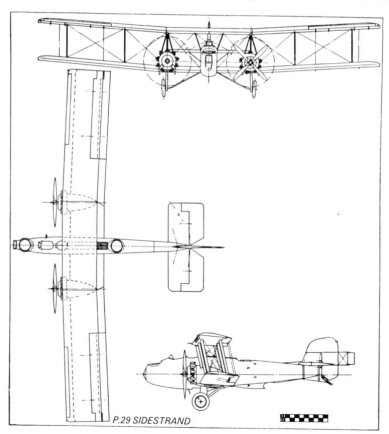

P.29 SIDESTRAND

191

mounted on bearings so it could be moved radially and vertically. The gun was fitted to a shock-absorber cord so that it could be raised and lowered without effort by the gunner. When not in use the gun was swung up and clipped in a padded channel in the fairing. The ventral position was further aft than the dorsal position, which was just behind the wings.

The bomb load totalled 1,050 lb, made up of two 220 or 250 lb bombs plus a single 520 or 550 lb bomb or four 112 lb bombs. The bombs were carried in a recessed and faired open bay, under the lower longerons and lower wing. Two bomb carriers were fitted in the bomb-bay and also on further carriers under the inner wing roots. A fully enclosed bomb-bay could not be included because the fuel tanks occupied so much of the central fuselage, as in the Bugle II. The alternative would have been to sling the fuel tanks under the upper wings as in the Bugle I, thus defeating the advantages in lower drag gained by having an enclosed bomb-bay. The front carrier in the bomb cell was of Boulton & Paul's own design and could carry two 230 lb or 250 lb bombs, a single 550 lb or 520 lb bomb, four 112 lb bombs, or a light series carrier for practice bombs. Provision was made for the pilot to jettison the bomb-load in an emergency. A P.7 or F.8 camera could also be fitted, to be operated by the rear gunner.

The prototype Sidestrand, J7938, first flew in 1926 from Mousehold, the first new type to be flown by Boulton & Paul's new chief test pilot, Sqn Ldr C A Rea, who joined the firm in July of that year. Feeling there was insufficient upward travel on the elevator he had discussed the problem with John North, who gave orders to re-check the elevator movement. When told that all was as it should be, Rea as a newcomer to the company felt unable to insist any further, but he made the first flight with no-one in the nose and a passenger in the dorsal gunner's position, to move the centre of gravity to the rear.

Even with this precaution he found he had to land at a very high speed to prevent the nose dropping and had to practically fly the aircraft onto the ground at 90 mph. He only just stopped before hitting the boundary fence, but the wingtip clipped a hockey goal-post. The problem was discovered to be a mathematical error in calculating the elevator's upward movement, and this was rectified before delivery to Martlesham Heath early in 1927 for further trials.

Lateral control was found to be very heavy, applying rudder without bank required a very strong leg, and with one engine out trim was impossible, unless the aircraft was flown with side-slip. The solution was to fit a servo rudder, a small surface on struts behind the main rudder, and Frise-type aerodynamically-balanced ailerons. Manoeuvrability was further improved by fitting Handley Page slots, and though the Sidestrand could be rolled, looped and spun like Boulton & Paul's earlier twins, it did so with a certain degree of stateliness, springing from the rock-like stability it exhibited.

With these improvements the handling of the Sidestrand was highly praised as well as its sprightly performance, taking 10½ min to climb to 10,000 ft where its top speed was 129 mph, and reaching a service ceiling of 21,500 ft. In addition it could maintain height and even climb, on only one engine, a not entirely usual attribute in the twin-engined aircraft of the day.

A second prototype, J7939, flew later in the year, fitted with new vertical tail surfaces, and later fitted with Jupiter VIIF engines. Both prototypes went to Martlesham Heath, and for a while, J7939 was operated by No.15 Squadron, the 'shadow' bomber squadron at the A & AEE. This aircraft was later used by

Production Sidestrand Mk III, J9186, with geared Jupiter VIIIF engines enclosed in Townend rings. At Mousehold in September 1929, before delivery.

Boulton & Paul as a flying test-bed, Sidestrand development being covered by Specification 25/27.

On the basis of these trials in July 1927 the Air Ministry ordered six production aircraft, designated P.29a Sidestrand IIs, still fitted with the Jupiter VI engines. One of these, J9176, was later modified to Specification B.10/29, with 460 hp geared Jupiter VIIIF engines. In this form, re-designated the Sidestrand III, twelve further aircraft were ordered to a new Specification 10/29, enough to equip just one squadron, No.101, which was to be based not far from Norwich, at Bircham Newton. The first five production Sidestrand IIIs were ordered in April 1928, the next four in November 1929, and the final three were ordered much later as replacement aircraft.

Apart from the Jupiter VIIIF engines there were further changes to the Mk III Sidestrands. The prone bomb-aiming position was abandoned in favour of a seated position behind a large nose window. The front window opened to admit the bomb-sight, and the gunner used a tip-up seat fixed to the port side with the release controls on the starboard side. The fuel tank layout was altered, the front service tank being above the main tank with the other service tank behind the main tank. Telephone intercommunication was fitted between the crew positions instead of speaking tubes. The increased power of the Mk III gave it an improved top speed of 140 mph at 10,000 ft, and an improved ceiling of 24,000 ft.

Some confusion has sometimes arisen because of Boulton & Paul's policy of giving prototypes the first Mk number, making the first production aircraft the Mk II. Most companies made their first production specimens the Mk I. It has been said that Sidestrand Mk IIs were sometimes fitted with Jupiter VIIIs and then VIIIFs, but this is not so. Where these engines were fitted it was done so in service, and they were not fitted as standard. Some Mk IIs were later brought up to Mk III standard by Boulton & Paul, and this has further confused matters.

The Sidestrand III prototype, J9176, was exhibited at the Olympia Aero Show of 1929. It was shown high up with one side uncovered to display the metal structure to best effect. It achieved further fame in a more public arena, the annual Hendon Displays, and more locally in the Grand Aerial Display at Mousehold on Whit Sunday and Monday 1929, Sqn Ldr Rea gave a display of a Sidestrand, which included loops.

The second prototype, J7939, was used by John North in trials of different vertical tail surfaces, exhaust-collector rings and engine cowlings. It was also

193

The second prototype Sidestrand, J7939, was used extensively for various trials of modifications, in this case with Bristol Pegasus engines with four-blade propellers, and the new window in the nose for the seated bomb-aimer's position.

fitted with different engines, first supercharged Jupiter XFBs and then 555 hp Bristol Pegasus I.M.3s, and in this form was redesignated a Sidestrand IIIS. With the Jupiter XFBs it achieved a top speed of 167 mph at 11,000 ft, taking only 8 min 30 sec to climb to this altitude. Service ceiling in this form was 30,000 ft. Each engine installation was also tested with different Townend rings, both circular and nine-sided, the latter proving the most efficient.

In addition to these tests a Sidestrand III, J9186, was also used to test various exhaust collectors and was then re-engined with 555 hp Bristol Pegasus I.M.3s. The aircraft was tested at Martlesham Heath with the standard Bristol circular rings and also the nine-sided rings. The latter were heavier but gave the aircraft a better rate of climb, taking one minute less to reach 16,500 ft and 1 minute 26 seconds less to reach 18,000 ft, and a 5–6 mph higher top speed at all heights up to 15,000 ft. The service ceiling was also reckoned to be about 500 ft higher with the polygon rings at 20,800 ft, though they required more maintenance, and the engines ran at slightly higher temperatures.

The Sidestrand in No.101 Squadron Service

No.101 Squadron was one of four new squadrons formed in 1928 as part of the RAF's slow expansion. When its new commander, Sqn Ldr J C P Wood arrived at Bircham Newton on 28 March, he found just 23 airmen and no aircraft. The first two Flying Officers, J W Duggan and J G Elton arrived shortly afterwards, and they were immediately dispatched to Martlesham Heath for a short course on the Sidestrand using J7938.

By 25 January, 1929, No.101 still had only one Sidestrand, the prototype J7938, though its complement of men had risen to 13 officers and 117 airmen. It acquired a couple of Avro 504s to keep the pilots' hands in, and towards the end of 1928, No.39 Squadron, which was leaving Bircham Newton for India, had donated a few D.H.9As. The first production Sidestrand II was delivered in March 1929, and the Squadron's complement of just two Flights slowly built up.

Equipped with its new Sidestrands No.101 was the first true medium bomber squadron since the D.H.10 had been withdrawn, though the single-engine Hawker Horsley had been designated a medium bomber by the RAF. It was

The second production Sidestrand Mk II, J9177, 'C' of No.101 Squadron. (*Crown Copyright, A & AEE*)

looked on by the Air Ministry as a full-scale experiment in the use of twin-engined day-bombers, which is why it only ever operated two Flights of Sidestrands, whereas other day bomber squadrons normally had three Flights.

The first two production orders totalling eleven aircraft had envisaged a Squadron complement of eight aircraft in two Flights with three aircraft in reserve. It was normal policy to operate day bomber squadrons with three Flights of three aircraft, so they could fly in the standard formation of three 'vics', to give defensive covering fire. As twin-engined day bombers were such a novelty it was envisaged that No.101 would discover in practice the best method of operating them. Three alternatives were considered, two Flights of four or five aircraft, or three Flights of three. As only seven Sidestrands were available by the end of 1929, it was to be 1930 before such assessments could be made. In the event they were operated mainly in vics of three, though the two-Flight system was retained for administrative purposes.

There were considerable comparison tests done between the Sidestrand and the Fairey Fox, and later the Hawker Hart, to determine whether twin- or single-engined day bombers were preferable. They were flown against 'attacking' Bristol Bulldogs and Hawker Furies, and their gunnery and bombing results were closely compared. The results and conclusions drawn were mixed.

It was normal policy to carry both rear guns, though only one would normally be manned. This was because if the aircraft became detached from the formation, it was felt preferable that the gunner should operate the dorsal gun. The lower gun mounting was criticised in service, and a Fairey Fox gun

No.101 Squadron Sidestrands on manoeuvres in France. (*Alan Hague*)

195

mounting was tested by the Squadron, installed upside down. It was found to be preferable to the Boulton & Paul mounting.

As day bombers the Sidestrands were flown in the standard silver finish of the day, that is the metal areas were painted light grey and the fabric areas were finished in aluminium dope. Because such a large area of silver, reflecting sunlight, could prove very tiring on the eyes of the crew, certain areas were painted matt green. The upper decking from just in front of the fin, curving around the nose and along the underside (because of the ventral gun position) was all matt green, tending to emphasise the pleasing lines of the fuselage. The engine nacelles were also matt green, which also helped to hide oil stains from the engines.

No.101 Squadron operated two Flights of four aircraft each. The aircraft featured the individual aircraft letter on the side of the aircraft nose and the number 101 on the fuselage side, painted in red for 'A' Flight and yellow for 'B' Flight.

The Squadron soon began showing what a superb bombing platform the Sidestrand was, achieving better results than any other aircraft had ever managed, and soon holding all RAF bombing records. At the practice camp at Catfoss in September 1930 the combined results of the two Flights were Bombing 84 yards and Gunnery 33 per cent, which was better than all the other day bomber squadrons. In fact on the 29th a Sidestrand with Flt Lt Collins as pilot and Corporal Thrussell as bomb-aimer broke the record for Catfoss with an error of just 21 yards from 6,000 ft.

The Sidestrand put the RAF's heavy bombers to shame, carrying the same bomb-load over a similar range, but possessing the speed and manoeuvrability of a single-engined light bomber. The pilots regarded it as a joy to fly, though it did require a lot of muscle-power. One Flying Officer took things too far on 17 July, 1929, and indulged himself in some low flying at Hunstanton. He was severely reprimanded at his Court Martial in September.

As with previous Boulton & Paul bombers, the Sidestrand's manoeuvrability was displayed at Hendon with 101 Squadron aircraft performing admirably in mock-fights with the latest fighters from 1929 to 1933. In 1932 this display featured a Sidestrand flown by Sgt W Methven, being 'attacked' by three Bristol Bulldogs of No.41 Squadron. In the mock dog-fight which followed, Methven looped, spun and rolled his Sidestrand just as Frank Courtney had with the Bourges years before. He and his crew apparently succeeded in 'shooting' down two of the Bulldogs, before limping away, pouring smoke, seemingly to crash behind a clump of trees.

This may have fooled the public into thinking it was Royal Air Force policy for its medium bombers to dog-fight their way out of trouble when attacked by fighters, but nothing could be further from the truth. As the alternative rear gun positions indicate, it was intended that 101 Squadron's Sidestrands should provide mutual protection for one another in close formation, not to be heroically flung around the sky in single combat.

Two small problems kept re-occurring with the Sidestrands. First the snapping of fuselage bracing wires, which could happen at any altitude, but was particularly prevalent towards the aircraft's ceiling. This only became really worrying to a crew when two wires on the same side snapped. The other nasty habit was leaking oleo legs. The Boulton & Paul patented design had the oil

Four Sidestrand Mk IIs of No.101 Squadron.

chamber above an air chamber, sealed by a diaphragm, and leaking oil was not uncommon, though not serious.

The first Sidestrand accident was on 25 April, 1929, when J9178 crashed on take off. The aircraft was rebuilt as a Mk III. On 20 August J9181 crashed while landing, and was written off. In October 1929 the Squadron moved to Andover in Hampshire, where it was the only day bomber unit in the Wessex Bombing Area, and where three more aircraft were lost. On 22 November, 1929, J9176 crashed at Gosport, on 5 May, 1930, J9180 hit a tree at Catfoss and on 5 March, 1933, J9768 crashed while on an endurance test.

There were Fighter Affiliation exercises from 28 July to 4 August, 1930, with No.111 Squadron's Siskins, and the fighters had difficulty planning effective attacks against the Sidestrands. From 12 to 15 August, 1930, No.101 was part of Blueland's forces in the annual Air Exercises, and made an effective raid on Redland's HQ at Cranwell. Another raid was made to Catfoss in a 60 mph gale, a flight taking 5¾ hours. They were highly praised for their performance in the exercises, but it is interesting to note that observers at the time stated that it would be more normal policy in wartime to send solitary Sidestrands on raids, as they would be more difficult to detect than formations, and would be well able to take care of themselves. This is diametrically opposed to the views expressed in the aircraft's manual about the disposition of the defensive guns, and the mutual protection they would provide for a formation. It is also naïve in the extreme to think a solitary medium bomber could protect itself against determined fighter attack.

Sqn Ldr Coleman took over from Wood as CO of the Squadron and on 8 April, 1931, they took part in bombing trials against HMS *Centurion*, an old battleship stripped and armoured as a target ship. For this purpose the

Sidestrands were modified at Boulton & Paul with tail drift sights, gyrorectors, Mk VIIA vector bomb-sights, electric bomb-releases, and had electric intercom retro-fitted to those aircraft without them. New Jupiter VIII engines with four-blade propellers were also fitted, together with Mk II starters. All this work was completed within three weeks. The Sidestrands bombed from 5,000 ft against a zig-zagging ship and achieved a remarkable 80 per cent hit rate.

In March 1932 the Squadron undertook its first night flying practice, but it remained essentially a day bomber squadron. At the Catfoss Camp of 1932 a revolutionary bombing tactic was tried out. The Sidestrands were glided down from an altitude of 10,000 ft to 2,000 ft at a speed of 135 mph and then dropped their bombs, this process then being repeated. This tactic was obviously to give the attacking aircraft an element of surprise (and to make the bombing more accurate from the lower altitudes), but it seems strange that a second attack should then be made in the same way, as the defenders would by then be fully alert.

In 1933 the Prince of Wales visited Mousehold and Sqn Ldr Coleman and members of No.101 Squadron were presented to him. On 21 December, 1933, Sqn Ldr E B C Betts took over as CO of No.101, and in November 1934 the Squadron moved to Bicester in Oxfordshire as part of the Central Region of the Air Defence of Great Britain Command, with re-equipment soon to come.

Boulton & Paul attempted to seek further orders for the Sidestrand, beyond the eighteen ordered for the RAF, but at the time of the world-wide recession no export orders were forthcoming. Further versions of the basic design were offered as a bomber for the Irish Free State (P.57), a photographic aircraft for Canada (P.60), a streamlined mail-carrier (P.61) and a bomber/torpedo carrier (P.62), all to no avail. The only development of the Sidestrand which was to achieve further sales was in providing its own replacement.

The high speed (140 mph) of the Sidestrand made it very difficult for the front gunner to train his gun, not least because of frozen fingers, which also made changing the ammunition drums on the Lewis gun very difficult at times—a number of propellers were damaged by being struck by weighty 97 round Lewis gun drums. The Air Ministry and John North thought the time had come to consider some form of protection from the slipstream. The only acceptable way of doing this, without reducing the field of fire, was to design a fully-enclosed power-operated turret.

The re-engined J9186 was rebuilt with a nose turret and other modifications to improve crew comfort. The airframe was strengthened to take a greater all-up weight, and a number of other modifications were undertaken. The aircraft was initially designated a Sidestrand V, but in view of the extensive nature of the changes it was eventually given a new type number and name, and became the prototype P.75 Overstrand, named after another village near Cromer.

P.29 Sidestrand

Mk I/II: two 425 hp Bristol Jupiter VI.
Mk III: two 460 hp Bristol Jupiter VIII or VIIIF.
Mk IIIS: two 530 hp Bristol Jupieter XFB.
Span 71 ft 11in; length 40 ft 8 in (46 ft including servo rudder); height 14 ft 10 in; wing area 979.5 sq ft.
Empty weight 6,010 lb; loaded weight 10,200 lb.

Mk I/II: maximum speed 130 mph at 5,000 ft, 129 mph at 10,000 ft, 122 mph at 15,000 ft, 106 mph at 20,000 ft.
Mk III: maxium speed 144 mph at 5,000 ft, 140 mph at 10,000 ft.
Mk IIIS: maximum speed 167 mph at 11,000 ft.
Mk I/II: climb to 5,000 ft 5 min, to 10,000 ft 10½ mm, to 15,000 ft 19 mins, to 20,000 ft 35½ min; service ceiling 21,500 ft. Mk III: service ceiling 24,000 ft; Mk IIIS: service ceiling 30,000 ft.
Armament: Lewis guns in nose and alternative dorsal and ventral positions. Bomb load 1,050 lb.

P.31 Bittern

The first prototype P.31 Bittern, J7936, with twin fixed forward-firing Vickers machine-guns, cantilever outer wings and the Lynx engines set centrally on the wings.

The basic philosophy of the Royal Air Force between the Wars, was that the bomber would always get through, a philosophy which continued until the crews of Wellingtons, Hampdens and Whitleys received a very rude shock during the Second World War. It followed then, that a counter had to be found to stop enemy bombers hitting targets in Great Britain, and throughout the inter-war period the Air Ministry toyed with various ideas for fighter aircraft capable of breaking up formations of heavy bombers. Many of these ideas featured novel armament layouts, and often included heavy weapons, but none of them reached production until the Defiant, with its armament concentrated in a power-operated turret, finally came to fruition.

None of the operational specifications written for these 'bomber destroyers', foresaw that they would have to be capable of defending themselves against traditional fighters, and therefore performance and manoeuvrability were not seen as an important part of the requirement. The aircraft produced were just weapons platforms, and the idea of them having to face fighters escorting the incoming bombers was not even considered.

Specification 27/24 outlined a requirement for a fighter to break up formations of heavy bombers. To meet it, at a time when fighters were almost exclusively single-engine biplanes, John North took a step ten years into the future. He produced a single-seat twin-engined monoplane night fighter, the

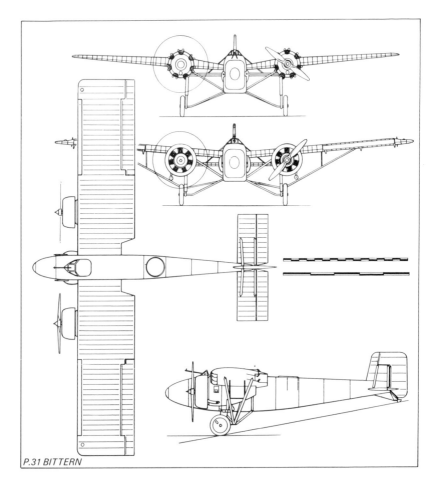

P.31 BITTERN

P.31 Bittern. Apart from its overall layout, its most startling feature was its armament.

North was noted for being very thoughtful in his design of the armament for his aircraft, and in the Bittern he designed revolving barbettes fitted on either side of the nose each containing a single .303 in Lewis machine-gun. They could be elevated by the pilot from straight ahead to an upward angle of 45 deg so that bombers could be attacked from below. The ring and bead sight elevated with them on a special frame.

It is possible that his inspiration came from the work North did at Austin with the First World War ace, Albert Ball. Ball liked to begin his attacks from below, pulling down the Lewis gun on the upper wing of his Nieuport Scout on its curved Foster rail, and firing upwards. The vulnerable spot of most bombers was below the tail, and this method of attack exploited that. Ball later took his ideas to Austin Motors, where his father was a director and North was the chief engineer, and the A.F.B.1 Scout was initiated featuring such upward firing guns. The first aircraft North designed at Boulton & Paul, the P.3 Bobolink, also featured a Lewis gun on a rail, initially; like Ball's Nieuport.

Two Bitterns were built, J7936 and J7937, each powered by two 230 hp Armstrong Siddeley Lynx seven-cylinder radials, the Lynx being virtually half a Jaguar. The two aircraft differed and the first, J7936, was a shoulder-wing monoplane with strut-braced inner wings and tail. The outer wings were cantilevered, deep at the root and tapering to a very shallow tip section. There was a very-wide-track non retractable undercarriage, which was believed to be essential for night landings. The pilot sat in an open cockpit just ahead of the wings, where he had a fine view each side of the sharply rounded nose. The wings were very square-cut in plan, a continuing North trademark, and aft of the cockpit the fuselage sides were flat. The engines were very closely cowled with the cylinder heads exposed in the slipstream.

The first prototype did not have the revolving barbettes, but was equipped conventionally with two fixed Vickers machine-guns on the fuselage sides, firing forward in the normal way, and with a conventional ring and bead sight. Only the second aircraft, J7937, was equipped with the barbettes. Both had provision to carry a rack of flares beneath the fuselage to aid night landings. The first Bittern on its initial flight, in February 1927, in the hands of Rea, was found to suffer from a lack of lateral control. The ailerons had adequate movement, and there was no lost motion when they were tested on the ground. Various adjustments were made, but there was no improvement. Rea felt he could solve

The steps in the rear fuselage of Bittern J7936 show the pilot's method of entry along the upper fuselage. The tail shows a marked similarity to that of the Sidestrand. (*The Boulton Paul Society*)

The second Bittern, J7937, with twin Lewis guns in revolving barbettes on the fuselage sides, the Lynx engines underslung and fitted with Townend rings, and extra struts supporting the outer wings. (*Francis K Mason collection*)

201

the problem if he could see the aileron in flight, but the outer wings were shielded from view by the engine nacelles, even with the seat adjusted to its highest position. Rea added cushions to the seat, bringing his head uncomfortably high above the windscreen. Despite the battering slipstream, he was just able to see that the outer wings were flexing so much in flight that the control effect of the ailerons was being neutralised by an opposite wing twist!

A ground test was undertaken with ailerons and wings loaded to produce the effects of aerodynamic forces, and it was found that the flexing was positively dangerous. On the second Bittern, strut bracing was fitted to the outer wings, to solve the problem. The wing span was also increased by 5 ft and leading-edge slots were fitted. The aircraft also differed in the fitting of Townend rings to the engines, and the lowering of the engines from being centrally placed on the front spar, to being slightly underslung.

The under-fuselage flare racks, for night landings can just be seen in this view of J7937. (*Francis K Mason Collection*)

It is hard to understand why North chose engines of such low power for such a heavy aircraft (loaded weight 4,500 lb), when it would have been just as easy to install engines of twice the power. The top speed of the first prototype was only 145 mph, though this was increased by 7 mph with the Townend rings fitted. It was only intended that the Bittern should attack slow heavy bombers, over which the Bittern had a 30–40 mph advantage, but lighter bombers such as the Fairey Fox and even Boulton & Paul's own Sidestrand were just as fast, and so the Bittern would have been incapable of intercepting them. The Bittern had little chance of being ordered, as it offered little advantage as a bomber destroyer over the existing biplane fighters, and was far inferior in performance to the Bristol Bulldog, which was about to be ordered as the next generation of RAF fighter. The fate of the Bitterns is not recorded but the front spar was still being tested in various forms in October 1931.

The Bittern concept of the single-seat twin-engined heavy fighter was at least ten years ahead of its time, too far ahead for it to gain acceptance. The concept of upward-firing guns to attack heavy bombers at night was revived by the Luftwaffe in the Second World War. Given the code name Schräge Musik (literally sloping music, the German for Jazz) the German night fighters had great success with upward-firing cannon, though they were usually fixed installations.

202

P.31 Bittern

Two 230 hp Armstrong Siddeley Lynx.
Span 41 ft; length 32 ft.
Loaded weight 4,500 lb.
Maximum speed 145 mph (J7936), 152 mph (J7937).
Armament: two fixed forward-firing Vickers machine-guns (J7936), two .303 in Lewis
machine-guns in revolving nose barbettes (J7937).

P.32

The sole P.32, J9950, showing the unusual engine layout and four-wheel main
undercarriage.

In 1927 the Air Ministry issued Specification B.22/27 for a three-engined
long-range night bomber. It was to be metal framed, have four seats and the
nose was to be left free for a gunner/bomb-aimer. Two prototypes were ordered,
the de Havilland D.H.72 and the Boulton & Paul P.32.

Sometimes when two designers set out to solve the same problem they arrive
at startlingly different conclusions, but often they produce remarkably similar
products, as was the case this time. De Havilland were unused to working in
metal and set about enlarging the successful D.H.66 Hercules to fit the
specification. The result was a three-bay biplane with two engines on the lower
wings and the third on the upper centre section. It had four mainwheels on two
axles and twin fins and rudders. This was exactly the layout John North
produced for the P.32.

Though the broad layouts were the same the ancestry of the two designs could
still be seen. Details of the D.H.66 and the Sidestrand, influenced their
designers. The shape of the P.32's fuselage and the square-cut of its 100 ft span
wings were clearly descended from the Boulton & Paul twins. The all-metal
construction was largely similar to that of the Sidestrand.

Boulton & Paul quoted a price of £33,000 for one prototype to be delivered on
31 March, 1929, but by the time of the first mock-up conference, held at
Mousehold on 8 August, 1928, delivery was re-scheduled for January 1930, for
comparative trials with the D.H.72 in early 1930, but development was to be
slow. Delays were caused by Air Ministry requested modifications and late
arrival of the intended Bristol Mercury engines. The final design conference did

not take place until 26 November, 1930, and delivery was then being projected for February 1931.

The sole P.32 was given the serial J9950. It was a 5/6-seat aircraft, the optional sixth crew member being an instructor or relief pilot for long flights. The pilot's cockpit was originally placed ahead of the wings on the starboard side of the fuselage, but the first of the modifications was to move it to port, with the second pilot position just behind it. The nose gunner also acted as bomb-aimer and navigator. He was equipped with a single Lewis gun on a Scarff ring, and had a swivel seat, to operate the Mk VI Course Setting bomb sight when facing forward, and to use the chart table and navigation instruments when facing aft. There was a hatch in the floor of his compartment for a parachute exit, and a door led to the access walkway alongside the pilot's cockpit, in the floor of which was a hatch for another parachute exit.

A door at the rear of this walkway led into the wireless and camera compartment. The wireless operator was provided with a padded seat, with a headrest, facing forward. At the port rear corner of this compartment was the P.7 or P.8 camera. From here another door led to a further walkway which ran alongside the petrol tanks which encompassed the full chord of the wings. There were three main tanks and three header tanks. The bomb racks were beneath the floor in this area. The walkway led aft to the tail gunner's position.

The P.32 was originally projected with dorsal and ventral (prone) gun positions, as in the Sidestrand, but one of the early modifications requested at the second August Mock-up Conference, was to delete the ventral position in favour of a tail gunner. The dorsal gunner, sited roughly half way between wings and tail, was equipped with the usual single Lewis gun on a Scarff ring, and also acted as the wireless operator. The tail gunner, also with a Scarff ring-mounted Lewis gun, was sited behind the twin rudders and was to some extent protected from the slipstream by a screen behind his back. As in the Sidestrand the rear gunner was supposed to use either the dorsal or tail guns, which seems extraordinary, but is confirmed by the decision taken at the conference on 13 March, 1929, when the mock-up of the new tail position was examined. A request was made for an extra parachute to be stowed in the tail so that the gunner did not have to go to his other position to get out in an emergency. Thus there was one more parachute carried than crew members. At another conference six days later it was decided to fit a light in the rear walkway and to give the tail position a folding seat so that the occupant could stand or sit to fire his gun. The rear navigation lamp was sited at the base of the tail-gunner's position.

A toilet was fitted, and to keep this as light and simple as possible, it amounted to nothing more than an aluminium funnel discharging into the slipstream through a 3 in orifice. Entry to the aircraft was through a sliding door opening on to the walkway on the starboard side, just in front of the dorsal gunner's station.

The bomb-load was four 520 lb or 550 lb bombs, or six 250 lb bombs in a recessed but not fully-enclosed bomb-bay beneath the fuselage, and six 120 lb bombs beneath the inner wings. Provision was also made to carry a single 1,000 lb bomb.

The structure was the now standard Boulton & Paul locked-joint steel for major members, with duralumin lightly loaded members and die-cast light alloy fittings. The unstaggered wings with the square-cut tips which were now a standard Boulton & Paul feature, could be folded to a width of 47 ft 6 in. The upper wing was straight but the lower was given anhedral. The pairs of mainwheels on each side were given very long axles, the outer wheels being outboard of the engines and the inner wheels being almost beneath the fuselage sides.

The major cause of delays was in deciding the engines to be used. The Bristol Mercury V had been the originally specified engine, with provision for fitting the Bristol Pegasus when that became available, but when even the Mercury was not available in time, the choice fell on the Bristol Jupiter XF with three-blade propellers, and even this was not ready so there were further delays, especially with technical problems experienced with the centre engine. Located as it was above the upper wing, very high off the ground, there were problems even

The special hoist, which attached to the aircraft structure, was designed for the removal of the inaccessible centre engine.

servicing it. A special engine hoist was designed which was attached to the aircraft structure to facilitate engine changes.

The Jupiter XFs were later changed for the 575 hp medium supercharged Jupiter XFBM, fitted with Townend rings incorporating exhaust collectors, and four-blade propellers. If the aircraft had gone into production it would have been with the Mercury V engines.

With the Jupiters there was only a 9 in clearance between the tips of the propellers and the pilot instructor's head, and so a guard had to be fitted. Moving his seat forward only cramped his legs – by giving his head a clearance of 14 in from the propeller left him with only 6 in of rudder-bar travel, but gave him a little more piece of mind when he was signalling with his arm to the ground crew. Having the instructor's position proved to be pointless because communication with the pilot was impossible due to the intensely high noise level of the three engines and propeller arcs so near his ears.

The fuselage resembled in construction and appearance, an enlarged Sidestrand's, rather marred by the drooping tail-gunner's position, though the upper fuselage was flatter and did not have the triangular shape of the smaller bomber. The main fuel tanks were in the fuselage centre section.

Each of the twin horn-balanced rudders was fitted with a servo surface on struts to the rear, and the elevators were also fitted with servos. Originally there were two coupled tailskids beneath the rudders, but this was later changed to a single tailwheel. The gross weight of this very large aircraft was 22,700 lb.

At the final conference on 28 November, 1930, a total of 41 further modifications was requested, plus eight more to be included in any further aircraft. Because of the delays with the Jupiter engines, delivery had been put back to 1 March, 1931, but ground runs revealed further problems, and so delivery was put back even further, to 9 July. More problems, including a failure of the port engine in September meant that Rea did not make the first flight from Mousehold until 23 October, 1931, with a further two flights on the 26th, one on the 27th and two on the 30th. There were further problems with the non-standard port engine which had been installed, the reduction gear having to be replaced, and the new reduction gear was not received until 16 November.

View of the P.32 showing the nose, dorsal and tail gun positions.

206

The P.32 was finally delivered to Martlesham Heath in November along with the D.H.72 which had been experiencing similar problems. In fact the D.H.72 was largely built by Gloster Aircraft because de Havilland had so little experience with metal structures. It had suffered from directional control problems, and took five days to make the flight to Martlesham, with a number of forced landings on the way because of various problems, mostly related to the engines.

A total of £5,135 had been added to the P.32's price because of all the modifications which had been undertaken. By now the Ministry had largely lost interest in the concept of a three-engined bomber, if they ever had much enthusiasm in the first place.

The P.32 was displayed for the first time publicly in 1932 at Hendon. The aircraft was finished in the standard night-bomber scheme of dull green overall, with the white deleted from the roundels. In early 1933 it suffered a tailwheel collapse while being taxied into a hangar. The swivelling movement was restricted to 50 deg, and it was recommended, in the resulting report, that this be increased to 180 deg. The aircraft ended its days at Martlesham.

The Air Ministry did not order any of this class of bomber, concentrating instead on the lighter twin-engined bombers built to Specification B.19/27 as replacements for the Vickers Virginia and Handley Page Hinaidi. It is perhaps significant that two companies inexperienced in the world of heavy bombers, Boulton & Paul and de Havilland had won the orders for Specification B.22/27 prototypes, whereas the heavy bomber experts, Vickers and Handley Page won the contract for Specification B.19/27 prototypes, with Handley Page obtaining the eventual order for its Heyford, the last of the RAF's biplane heavy bombers.

P.32

Three 575 hp Bristol Jupiter XFBM.
Span 100 ft (47 ft 6 in folded); length 69 ft; height 21 ft.
Loaded weight 22,700 lb.
No performance figures known.
Armament: single Lewis gun in nose, dorsal and tail positions. Bomb load four 520/550 lb
    or six 250 lb plus six 120 lb bombs.

P.33 Partridge

Boulton & Paul's second single-engined fighter to be built was the P.33 Partridge, the first being the P.3 Bobolink. The Air Ministry issued Specification F.9/26 in April 1926 for a fighter to replace the Armstrong Whitworth Siskin and the Gloster Gamecock, which equipped thirteen RAF squadrons between them. Not surprisingly most companies in the industry hoped to win what promised to be a substantial order for those times, and the Ministry, mindful of the importance of the new fighter in the RAF's immediate future, encouraged the construction of nine prototypes. Among those in addition to the Partridge were the Armstrong Whitworth Starling, Avro Avenger, Blackburn Turcock, Bristol Bulldog, Hawker Hawfinch, Vickers 141, and Westland Wizard.

The sole P.33 Partridge, J8459, at Mousehold.

John North originally laid out a design powered by the well-proven Bristol Jupiter engine, but when details of the Specification became known this was changed to the new Bristol Mercury. In the event, teething troubles were experienced with the Mercury, and the prototype Partridge, J8459, first flew with a 440 hp geared Jupiter VII, supercharged to 10,000 ft. It was intended to install the Mercury in the Partridge Mk III, but this was never built.

The Partridge displayed the sophisticated degree to which Boulton & Paul's metal construction techniques had reached. Many of the components of the structure were standard Sidestrand parts, which would have resulted in cheap and rapid production. It was hoped that commonality with the Sidestrand, from a maintenance point of view, would be a significant factor in the Partridge's favour.

The staggered single-bay wings were made in four sections, the upper ones joined in the centre, and though Frise ailerons were only installed on the upper wings at first, they were added, before delivery to Martlesham Heath for evaluation, to the lower ones, with interplane connecting rods. The upper wings had a span of 35 ft and the lower of 31 ft. The upper-wing chord was 5 ft 6 in, and that of the lower was a foot less.

The square-cut of the wings and tail showed a family likeness to the

Partridge J8459.

208

View showing the shorter span and marked dihedral of the lower wing.

Sidestrand. The wing-spars were, as usual built up of corrugated flanges and webs of high-tensile steel, strengthened by tubular stiffeners. The mainplane ribs were constructed with U-section flanges braced by tubular diagonals. As on the Sidestrand the interplane struts were duralumin with removable wooden fairings. They were splayed outwards, the struts supporting the centre section even more so, and with the marked 4 deg dihedral of the lower wings gave the Partridge an angular appearance when viewed from ahead, which contrasted with the slim, streamlined lines of the fuselage.

The fuselage was of oval section, curving with attractive lines from spinner to tail. The fuselage frame was basically a rectangular frame in two parts, with wooden formers creating the oval section. In the front part of the fuselage, containing the engine, fuel tank, wing-mountings and cockpit, the frame was built of Boulton & Paul's high-tensile solid-drawn steel tubes. To the rear of the pilot's seat the fuselage was made of the locked-joint steel tube longerons, with steel and duralumin struts. The bay around the pilot's seat was built of larger-diameter tube for crash-resistance. The fairing behind the pilot's head was of three-ply mounted on wooden formers. The cockpit was just behind the upper wing, in which there was a small cut-out to improve visibility. The pilot's seat was adjustable in height, rubber springs counter-balancing the pilot's weight, in the single-lever operation. Two gun-sights were fitted, a ring and bead to port and an Aldis to starboard. There was provision to carry four 20 lb bombs under the wings.

Like the Sidestrand, the Partridge had a reserve fuel tank within the main tank, with total capacity being 62 gal. The inner tank served as a baffle for the main tank, and its supporting structure braced the fuselage bay in which it was contained rather than just the tank walls. The inner tank was filled automatically when the outer tank reached a certain level (One sixth from the top).

The Jupiter, driving an 8 ft 9 in diameter two-blade propeller, was closely cowled to maintain the fuselage streamlining, but there was provision to fit a Townend ring. The fuselage lines were ruined, however, by the bulges for the twin Vickers machine-guns. The originally proposed position for these had to be altered because the Air Ministry insisted they were too low, and then the second proposal was considered to be too high, as they had to be accessible to the pilot in flight to clear stoppages. They were then set on the fuselage sides within bulges, which was found a better way of preserving the streamlining than widening the oval section of the fuselage to accommodate them. These bulges still affected the performance however.

The undercarriage was mounted on V struts, with oleo-pneumatic legs, and had 5 ft 6 in track. The tailskid was sited behind a small fairing beneath the fin and was fitted with rubber shock-absorbers.

The Partridge first flew early in 1928, and was shown in the New Types Park at Hendon that year, as New Type No.2. Competitive trials were undertaken early in January 1928 at Martlesham, between all the types vying for Specification 9/26.

The Partridge was found to have deficiences in several respects. Although lateral control was light and effective at all speeds the aircraft was longitudinally unstable at all speeds and control was very heavy unless trim was first obtained using the tail adjusting gear, which in itself was found to be unsatisfactory. It was later modified by Boulton & Paul so that it became quite rigid. Directional control was effective, though there was a tendency to hunt at top speed, which was 167 mph at 10,000 ft. In aerobatics, control was only fair and longitudinally it was considered to be very bad. Considerable force had to be used to pull the Partridge out of a steep dive. With the tailplane wound right back, when the engine was idling, and then opened out, it was found to be almost impossible to control the aircraft longitudinally by the elevators alone.

The taxi-ing qualities of the Partridge were also criticised. The undercarriage was thought to be too spongy and the track too narrow. A cross-wind take-off

A rare flying view of the Partridge. The square-cut wings and the shape of the tail show a considerable family resemblance to the Sidestrand.

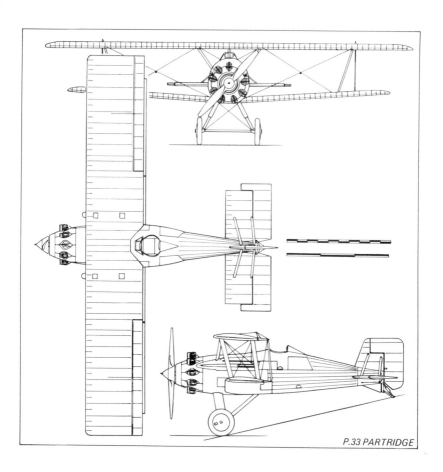

P.33 PARTRIDGE

was very difficult, and in only a slight cross-wind full rudder was required. The view was good in landing and level flight, but otherwise it was considered only fair. Though the cockpit was found to be comfortable and warm, it was initially criticised for being too small for the pilot to easily bale-out, and was enlarged by Boulton & Paul. This and other modifications led to the aircraft being re-designated Mk II.

Fault was even found with the construction of the Partridge, which the company had hoped would be a good selling point; because it used their standard parts, also to be found in the Sidestrand. It was thought to be too complicated, and expensive to construct and maintain, and probably seemed so in comparison with the simple system used by Hawker for their Hawfinch.

The Hawfinch and the Bristol Bulldog were the front runners in the competition from the outset. They were so well liked by all that flew them, for their delightful handling qualities, that any slight shortfall in some areas of their performance could be overlooked. The Partridge had a better climbing ability than the Hawfinch, and a better service ceiling than both. The Bulldog was the fastest of the three, with 174 mph at 10,000 ft, 3 mph more than the Hawfinch,

211

and 7 mph more than the Partridge. The Partridge was unofficially placed third in the contest, not good enough to attract further development, and it ended its days at the RAE Farnborough.

Against manufacturers with long experience of fighter production such as Bristol, and Hawkers, Boulton & Paul would always have been struggling to win the order. Their expertise lay in building superlative twin-engined medium bombers.

A naval version of the Partridge, the P.34, was submitted for Specification N.21/26, but no aircraft met this requirement, which eventually led to an order for the Hawker Nimrod.

P.33 Partridge

One 440 hp Bristol Jupiter VII.
Span 35 ft (upper), 31 ft (lower); length 23 ft 1 in; height 11 ft; wing area 311 sq ft.
Empty weight 2,021 lb; loaded weight 3,097 lb.
Maximum speed 167 mph at 10,000 ft, 164 mph at 20,000 ft, 152.5 mph at 26,000 ft; climb to 10,000 ft 6 min 30 sec, to 20,000 ft 15 min 4 sec, to 26,000 ft 26 min 19 sec; service ceiling 28,950 ft.
Armament: two fixed forward-firing Vickers machine-guns. Four 20 lb bombs.

P.41 Phoenix

The P.41 Phoenix in its original form with the ABC Scorpion engine. The pilot is Capt Dawson Paul, the chairman of Boulton & Paul. (*The A J Jackson collection*)

In 1929 Boulton & Paul once more built a lightplane, the P.41 Phoenix. They had been justifiably disappointed with the impact of the P.9 immediately after the War. It was a useful light aircraft which compared favourably with the de Havilland Moth, but was marketed just too early, the Moth appeared at exactly the right moment for the boom in private flying. It is possible that the impetus for Boulton & Paul re-entering the light aircraft sphere may have been the chairman, Dawson-Paul. Having recently learned to fly with the Norfolk and

212

Norwich Aero Club he may well have been imbued with sufficient enthusiasm to see his own company competing in the light aircraft market.

Producing a straightforward competitor for the Moth was a non-starter by 1929, so many others having already appeared, with the Avro Avian, Blackburn Bluebird, Westland Widgeon and others. The decision was taken to produce a two-seater which undercut those aircraft both on first cost and on running costs and the P.41 Phoenix resulted.

The first prototype was intended primarily as an aerodynamic flying test-bed, but with the intention of eventually offering it for sale as a light-weight two-seater, much as the P.6 had led to the P.9. It was designed by Capt William Higley Sayers, former technical editor of *The Aeroplane*. He left *The Aeroplane* in 1928 and joined Boulton & Paul as assistant engineer to John North. It is not clear whether the P.41 was designed because Sayers had joined the company, or he was recruited because the company wished to build an aircraft of this type. In the War he had served on the Isle of Grain and was largely responsible for the little Grain Kitten, powered by a 40 hp ABC engine. In 1922 he had designed, in 19 hours, a glider for a *Daily Mail* competition, which the Central Aircraft Company had built in 19 days. The following year this was fitted with an ABC engine by Handley Page for that year's Light Aircraft Competition, but it failed to take-off.

The Phoenix was a strut-braced parasol-wing monoplane powered by a two cylinder 40 hp ABC Scorpion, with which Sayers was clearly familiar. It was of wooden construction, to test the aerodynamic layout, the first wooden aircraft Boulton & Paul had built since the P.9, and the last they ever built.

The wings were supported above the fuselage on two main struts which ran to the lower fuselage, and several smaller struts at the centre section. The wings could be folded for easy stowage in a small hangar. The all-moving vertical fin was identical to each half of the tailplane to reduce the number of spares required. The rubber sprung undercarriage was carried on very short legs beneath the fuselage, so that the Phoenix sat very low on the ground. The forward cockpit was beneath the wing, and the rear cockpit was just behind the wing.

The Phoenix was registered G-AAIT to Boulton & Paul on 11 June, 1929, and was exhibited at the International Aeronautical Exhibition at Olympia the following month, being offered for sale at only £375. The first flight took place on 7 July in the hands of Sqn Ldr Rea, but lasted for only one circuit, as the engine revolutions fell away considerably after taking off.

A mechanic from ABC was called in to tune the engine and three more flights were then made on the 9th, with more satisfactory results, the engine running steadily throughout, and the slow running being much improved. With only one pilot, but with a parachute and full tanks, take off was in about 100 yards and best climbing speed was around 50 mph. Top speed was 70 mph, and the best gliding speed was 60 mph, though it was thought this could be reduced to about 55 mph if Frise-type ailerons were fitted, because of the greater control they gave. The controls were generally good but lateral control was slow, especially when climbing in bumpy weather. The view was good except for the blind spot upward and forward, and this even though the pilot was sitting on a parachute. Taxi-ing seemed easy and stable, and the undercarriage robust.

The first flights were followed by a deliberate policy of giving flights to a large

The P.41, showing the poor upward view. (*The A J Jackson collection*)

number of mostly amateur pilots. Many of them had only accumulated a few hours since obtaining their 'A' licences, and the idea was to obtain the opinions of the sort of people who would be likely to buy the Phoenix.

The general opinion was unanimous that the Phoenix was easy to fly, easy to land, and easy to handle on the ground. In the course of these flights in the hands of inexperienced pilots, the aircraft was obviously subjected to some heavy landings, and the structure stood up to such rigours very well. The main cause for criticism was the engine. Few pilots were willing to trust a two-cylinder engine out of sight of an aerodrome, and most people wanted better performance than the Scorpion's low power could provide.

With these encouraging results the decision was made to entirely rebuild the Phoenix with a totally new fuselage and undercarriage incorporating a new method of steel construction. The frame was spot-welded throughout rather than riveted, and this proved a thoroughly effective, and much cheaper process. The wooden wing and tail remained unchanged, but the search for a more suitable engine was a difficult one, and one which had frustrated many designers trying to find a reliable engine of lower power than the Cirrus or Gipsy. In the end it was re-engined with a 40 hp Salmson nine-cylinder radial, weighing 191¾ lbs including the propeller.

The undercarriage was completely changed, being fitted with large oleo-pneumatic legs, which looked rather out of place, stretching vertically down from the parasol wing, with the wheels set lower than on the first version of the Phoenix, giving the underside of the fuselage greater ground clearance. The number of struts, coupled with these large undercarriage legs, rather wasted the aerodynamic benefits of the monoplane configuration. When the aircraft re-emerged, early in 1930, despite the extensive alterations, which made it

214

The rebuilt P.41 with Salmson engine, oleo undercarriage legs and all-metal fuselage.

virtually a new machine, and certainly visually entirely different from its initial layout, it retained its registration, G-AAIT.

The increased power raised the top speed to 86 mph at sea level, or 80 mph at 5,000 ft with a maximum rate of climb of 470 ft/min at sea level. The first flight was on 12 June, 1930, after a little trouble with the engine, which had a 'flat spot' at small throttle openings. The flight was undertaken with a 10 per cent Benzole mixture, but subsequent flights were tried with straight aviation spirit and other mixtures.

The same testing programme as with the initial version, using mostly amateur pilots, was undertaken in the second half of 1930 with a view to putting the Phoenix on sale later in the year. Emphasis was placed on its low first cost, excellent all-round performance for its size, and low oil and fuel consumption, reflected in a fuel tank capacity of only 7 gal, and an oil capacity of just one gallon. Unfortunately, with an all-up weight of 1,089 lb it was still rather underpowered. The de Havilland Moth had already proved the optimum size for a popular lightplane, the lack of sales interest, resulted in it not being put into production. Rea then used the Phoenix as his personal runabout, replacing the earlier P.9, until the registration was cancelled in November 1935.

The success of the spot-welding process was a valuable result, however. The same process was used in the B.2 and the metal-framed Bluebird IV, with which Blackburn were attempting to compete head to head with the Moth range. Boulton Paul built the Bluebird wings under sub-contract, and so had a substantial interest in the private market after all.

P.41 Phoenix

One 40 hp ABC Scorpion (Phoenix I), one 40 hp Salmson (Phoenix II).
Span 30 ft.
Empty weight 646 lb (Phoenix II), loaded weight 1,089 lb (Phoenix II).
Phoenix I: maximum speed 70 mph at sea level; best climbing speed 50–52 mph.
Phoenix II: maximum speed 86 mph at sea level, 80 mph at 5,000 ft; maximum rate of climb 470 ft/min at sea level, 280 ft/min at 5,000 ft.

The P.64 in its early form.

P.64 Mail-Carrier

In 1928 the Air Ministry's Directorate of Technical Development issued Specification 21/28 for a high-speed mail-carrier for use on Imperial routes. There had been much criticism of Imperial Airways' air mail service. The passenger aircraft on which the mails were carried, operated at such a leisurely rate, flying for a minimal number of hours before having to stop, as the next oasis of civilisation was often out of their reach before darkness fell, that the air mail was calculated to cover the ground at an average of only 30 mph.

The answer was seen to be a designated high-speed mail-carrier which could cover greater distances, in conditions it was thought passengers would be unlikely to endure. It was to be able to carry 1,000 lb of mail at 150 mph with a range of 1,000 miles. This performance was to be achieved on half engine power, and level flight was to be maintained on one engine without the necessity to run it at full power.

Around twenty designs were submitted for this requirement, some companies submitting more than one, but late in 1931 the project was postponed for financial reasons. It was resurrected in 1932, when resources had been found for the construction of one prototype, and Boulton & Paul's design received the contract, in February 1932.

Boulton & Paul's submission, the P.64 was a very clean-looking biplane. Great attention was paid to every item of the airframe to reduce the overall drag and empty weight to a minimum to meet the exacting specification. It proved capable of 185 mph, faster than the RAF's standard fighter of the day, the Bristol Bulldog, and yet was able to lift a disposable load of over 60 per cent of its empty weight. To some extent this was achieved by giving it a span of only 54 ft, and therefore a wing loading at gross weight of 14.9 lb/sq ft, for which a landing speed of 60 mph proved necessary. This was possible because the excellent single-engined performance which was inherent in the specification, meant forced landings because of engine failure were less likely. The days of scheduled airliners putting down in a field because of engine failure en route were about to come to an end.

The P.64 had equal-span wings with very little stagger, and 7 ft chord. They had square-cut tips, and two bays, the centre section having no dihedral, the outer sections having slight dihedral. The ailerons, on both upper and lower wings, were aerodynamically-balanced, in the manner designed by Leslie Frise at Bristol. The connecting rods for the ailerons ran inside the outer interplane struts, where they were protected from damage, and did not add extra drag. Handley Page automatic slats were fitted to the upper wings. These were operated by rack and pinion and torque rods, so that drag-inducing external brackets could be dispensed with.

While the centre section of the lower wing was in two parts fitted to the bottom longerons on each side of the fuselage, the upper centre section was in one piece, faired into the upper surface of the fuselage. The engines were mounted on the upper wings, slightly underslung, above the N-struts at the outer edges of the centre section. Mounting the engines on the upper wings rather than the lower ones gave adequate clearance for the propeller and yet allowed an undercarriage of minimum length, and therefore drag, to be fitted. The wings were wire-braced supported by a further set of parallel interplane struts.

The wings were of standard Boulton & Paul construction, but of slightly more advanced design than the Sidestrand. They had dual high-tensile steel spars, but the front spar was made up of two tubes joined by a sheet metal web, while the rear spar was a 'Double Eight' section, two pieces joined at top and bottom by the locked joint principle. The ribs were of duralumin with tubular bracing sections. The wing was entirely fabric covered, and had markedly square tips.

The engines were Bristol Pegasus I.M.2 geared and supercharged nine-cylinder radials giving 555 hp and driving two-blade propellers. They were fitted with close-fitting nine-sided Townend rings incorporating exhaust collectors, backed by cone-like wood and fabric streamlined fairings. The engines were started by an RAE Mk II gas-starter with the starting panel in the fuselage.

The P.64 with the added rudder surfaces.

217

There were five fuel tanks in the wings, four main ones of 74 gal each in the upper outer wings and a collector tank of 29 gal in the starboard upper centre section. All tanks were fitted with jettison valves. There was a 15 gal oil tank above and behind each engine.

The decision to fit spatted mainwheels rather than a retracting undercarriage was made when wind-tunnel tests suggested only 2 mph would be added to the performance, with all the extra weight and complications, a retracting mechanism would entail. The mainwheels were each fitted with two Boulton & Paul oleo-pneumatic legs and Dunlop pneumatic brakes. They were enclosed in large wooden spats, which were able to rise and fall with the wheel, the front part being attached to the wheel axle, the rear part being hinged below the rear spar. Thus on the ground the spats were well above the streamlined position they adopted in flight, when the oleos were at their fullest extent.

The spats were fitted to the lower wings at the inner interplane struts, giving the aircraft a wide track. The castoring tailwheel, fitted with a low pressure tyre, was set within a streamlined fairing, the rear part forming the base of the rudder. No oleo-pneumatic strut was fitted to the tailwheel, rubber springing being used, and it was able to turn through 360 deg for ease of handling on the ground.

The tailplane was tapered and had rounded tips unlike the wing, and the large rudder had an angular pointed shape. The structure was different to that of the wing. Instead of two spars, two channel members were joined by corrugated sections to form a box. The tailplane had a duralumin skin and the leading edge was a separate aluminium structure; the fin and rudder, however were fabric covered. Both rudder and elevators were fitted were servos flaps, and the rudder was fitted with a horn-balance.

The fuselage was basically rectangular in section with smooth rounded corners giving it a very attractive shape. The two pilots were accommodated in a fully enclosed cabin forward of the wings, with dual-controls provided. Their side-by-side seats were fully adjustable both in height, and fore and aft. The pilots sat shoulder to shoulder in the narrow fuselage, with no gap between the seats, access to the seats being eased by sliding them backwards. There was a large compartment behind the pilots for a radio operator or navigator, with no partition behind the cockpit. It contained a chart table and rack, instrument locker, radio, and stowage for food and drinking water. The engine starting panel, fully independent of ground facilities was on the forward part of the upper spar. The overall cockpit was a spacious 7 ft long, 7 ft high and 4 ft 4 in wide.

Behind the cockpit was the mail cabin. It was 10 ft 3 in in length, had an average height of 5 ft 2 in, and average width of 3 ft 4 in, giving it 175 cu ft in volume. The standard mail bags were hung on a row of hooks on each side of the compartment, which was lined with nets. The compartment had a central walkway to allow any mail bag to be reached, and a trap-door through which bags could be dropped by parachute over their destination. There was also provision to pick up bags in flight through this same trap-door.

Great attention was paid to the shape of the forward fuselage, in particular, to achieve the optimum aerodynamic shape. The step formed by the windscreen was carefully investigated in the wind tunnel, the angle of the windscreen was found to alter the drag quite considerably. The nose consisted of a plywood shell, to give the necessary smooth finish, pulled over the internal metal structure and clipped only lightly into place; as it bore no aerodynamic stresses. The shell took the form of a many-sided polygon built up on light wooden frames. Interestingly, in the manufacture of the mahogany plywood, Bakelite was used instead of glue, to give a totally waterproof finish. The rest of the fuselage was fabric covered.

The fuselage structure was made up of three steel and duralumin rigid sections, forming an overall rectangular girder. The longerons were the usual closed joint steel Boulton & Paul patented system. Most of the vertical and horizontal struts were duralumin, only a few in the region of the wing were of steel.

The P.64 landing at Mousehold.

The crew door was on the starboard side over the wing leading-edge, and was fitted with a small circular window. The cargo door was on the rear port side. There was another circular window on the port side, between the wings, providing light for the cargo hold. A chemical toilet was fitted.

Construction of the P.64 began in August 1932, with a tight schedule to have it ready for the contracted first flight date of 22 March, 1933. By 3 February, 1933, the schedule had become so tight that an emergency programme was instituted to make sure the first flight date was met. There were two shifts and overtime and weekend work was authorised. In addition a bonus of 10 per cent of hours clocked-on was promised if the P.64 achieved its first flight on 22 March, with an extra 2½ per cent for every day before that. In the event the P.64 was ready for taxi-ing trials on 22 March, 1933, but the first flight of G-ABYK, as it had been registered, was on 23 March at tea-time so that all employees could watch.

The handling seemed pleasant but on the third flight, on 30 March, with Dawson Paul in the co-pilot's seat, Rea was unable to correct a pronounced swing to the right during take off in a cross-wind. He had to cut the throttles and apply the brakes, which proved to be all but useless at high speed. He could not stop before colliding with the wire boundary fence around a cricket pitch. The mainwheels flattened the fence, but it sprang up again after they had passed over it, and caught the tail, pushing it up and flipping the aircraft onto its back. Some damage to the nose and engines resulted, delaying further flights for several weeks.

It was found the brake effectiveness had been reduced in agreement with Ministry officials, and that the rudder was blanketed at small angles. It had only been tested in the wind tunnel at neutral, maximum and minimum angles, and not at the small angles normally used in flight. The solution was to fit two small fins to the tailplane, both above and below it, and the aircraft was flying again by June, thanks to sterling efforts by the works manager, Sam Hiscocks.

On testing at Martlesham in October 1933 the P.64 was found to have the remarkable top-speed, for a biplane transport, of 185 mph, a cruising speed of 160 mph, and a ceiling of 19,500 ft. For its handling trial flight the P.64 was loaded to its maximum permissible weight of 11,300 lb, with only one pilot aboard. In the 35-minute flight he found the elevators and ailerons light and effective, but the rudder, though effective was heavy for initial movements, becoming lighter as the angular movement increased. When gliding, if the pilot took his feet off the rudder bar with the rudder fully displaced, it remained in that position.

The P.64 was reasonably stable fore and aft in normal flight, but directional stability was poor. Firm use of the rudder was required to maintain control if bumps were encountered during turns. As soon as sideslips developed the nose tended to rise violently, and quick use of the rudder was needed to maintain the gliding angle, and at 20–30 deg full bottom rudder was needed to keep the nose down.

On one engine the aircraft behaved normally and straight flight could be maintained at 115 mph. At 110 mph, the aircraft turned gently towards the idling engine. Speeds of less than this were not attempted. A long take-off run was needed, but the rate of climb was good. The approach speed was high at 90 mph, and at least 100 mph was needed if steep gliding turns were to be made.

The P.64 in an impressive climb.

220

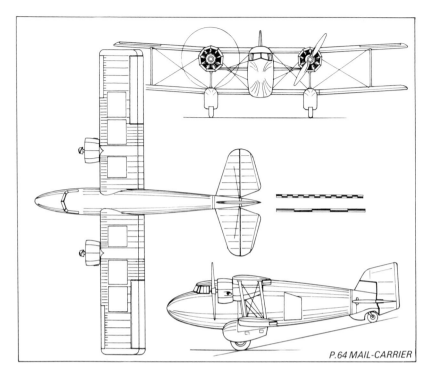

P.64 MAIL-CARRIER

One stall was attempted, and it occurred at about 68 mph. In general the testing pilot found the cockpit comfortable, the view good and all controls well-placed and accessible.

Unfortunately on the third flight at Martlesham Heath, on 21 October, while being flown by Flt Lt G L G Richmond, the aircraft went out of control in a turn and crashed. At 1,200 ft it had gone into a sudden dive, probably caused by an inadvertant stall, recovered, but then dived again. The aircraft was destroyed but the pilot escaped with only minor injuries. It is likely the lack of lateral control had not been improved enough with the provision of extra fins, something indicated by the report on the brief handling flight.

A re-design was initiated with triple fins and a longer fuselage but no further P.64s were built, and the concept of a dedicated mail-carrier seems to have been abandoned. It was thought that the use of air mail by the public was becoming so commonplace that they would soon object to the high premium placed upon it, thus making the costs of a special mail aircraft far too high, even though Boulton & Paul took steps to offer the P.64 at a lower price.

Redesignated P.65, the design was offered to AB Aerotransport (Swedish Air Lines) as a cargo floatplane, with Jupiter XFAMs, Jupiter XFAs or Panther M.5s. It was redesigned with an upper fuselage cargo hatch, but no order was forthcoming. The design of the P.64 was taken as the basis for Boulton & Paul's submission for Specification C.26/31 for a bomber/transport, the P.69. It featured nose and tail gunners' positions, equipped with single Lewis guns on Scarff rings, two Pegasus engines, and a biplane tail with twin fins and rudders.

221

No order was forthcoming for this version either, for which the Bristol Bombay secured the eventual order.

The basic design was further amended for Specification B.9/32 which called for a twin-engined day-bomber. Boulton & Paul's project, the P.70, featured the first new application of their power-operated turret technology, with both nose and retractable dorsal turrets. This Specification eventually led to the production of the Handley Page Hampden, and the P.70 received no contract.

A straightforward passenger version of the P.64 with Pegasus II.M3s or Double Mongoose engines was designated P.71, and this design was to form the basis for the next Boulton & Paul civil transport to be built, the P.71A airliner.

P.64

Two 555 hp Bristol Pegasus I.M.2.
Span 54 ft; length 42 ft 6 in; height 13 ft; wing area 756 sq ft.
Empty weight 7,008 lb; loaded weight 11,267 lb.
Maximum speed 185 mph at 5,000 ft; rate of climb 1,400 ft/min; service ceiling 22,500 ft; range 1,000 miles.

P.71A

The first P.71A, G-ACOX, having its engines run up at Mousehold.

In May 1933 Imperial Airways notified Boulton & Paul and Avro that they had a requirement for a high-performance 6/7-seat airliner for use primarily on charter flights but also on low-volume feeder routes. Avro produced the Type 652 monoplane, which eventually led to the Anson, but Boulton & Paul redesigned the passenger version of the P.64 Mail-Carrier, the P.71, as the P.71A to fit the requirement. Imperial Airways ordered two of each design. The P.71 had been a straightforward passenger version of the P.64, powered by two 580 hp Pegasus II.M.3s or two Double Mongoose engines, but this did not entirely fit the requirement, not least in being overpowered, so more substantial changes had to be made, including increasing the cabin volume.

The P.71A was approximately the same size as the P.64 but there was 37½ sq ft less wing area, despite the span being increased by 1½ inches. This was because of the introduction of rounded wingtips, something of a radical depature for the Boulton & Paul design team. As with the P.64 the centre section of the upper wing was in one piece, carried through the upper fuselage, and the lower centre sections were two-pieces attached to the lower fuselage sides. The outer sections were slightly swept back and with slight dihedral.

The fuselage was slightly slimmer, but also a little longer, and the tail was totally revised with a large fixed central fin and two balanced rudders inboard of the tailplane tips and both above and below it. This was to give an abundance of lateral control at low speeds, especially with one engine shut down, to overcome the problems which had been experienced with the P.64. The tail had 16 ft 8 in span and was entirely metal-framed with fabric covering.

The structure was generally similar to the P.64 except for the fuselage centre section incorporating the passenger compartment, which was built up of light alloy members covered with corrugated light alloy sheeting, with four square windows on each side.

The flight deck had two side-by-side seats, but dual controls were not fitted. A radio operator or navigator would be the normal occupant of the starboard seat. There was a sliding roof hatch above the pilots' seats.

The passenger cabin was fitted out by L A Rumbold & Co, who specialised in such work. The inner walls were luxuriously appointed in blue leather, walnut veneer and beige cloth, with extensive heat and noise insulation in the wide gap between the inner and outer walls. There were six fixed tubular-framed seats, three on each side, but slightly staggered rather than side by side. In addition there was a seventh seat which folded into a recess in the centre of the rear bulkhead. Each seat had a controllable fresh-air outlet. Hot air was taken from the engine exhausts, and cold air from a scoop, the two being mixed in a chamber in the rear fuselage, used air being exhausted from the front of the cabin. A hat rack was provided for each passenger, and they were spring-loaded, so they could be folded out of the way when not in use.

This view of one of the P.71As at Mousehold, shows the streamlined form, for a biplane. (*Alan Hague*)

223

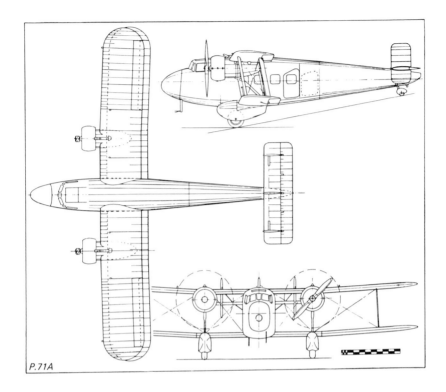

P.71A

At the front of the cabin there was a toilet on the starboard side, which was provided with a small circular window. Alongside the toilet, on the port side was a door to the pilot's cockpit. There were two baggage compartments with external doors in nose and tail. The capacity of the nose compartment was 28½ cu ft and the rear fuselage compartment was 55 cu ft.

The engines were 490 hp Armstrong Siddeley Jaguar VIA fourteen-cylinder double-row radials enclosed in circular cowlings, driving two-blade wooden propellers. As with the P.64 they were mounted on the upper wing at the inner N interplane struts, and were slightly underslung. There were four fuel tanks in the wings, two of 65 gal in the upper centre section and two of 30 gal in the outer sections. The oil tanks formed the leading edge of the wing in front of the main fuel tanks, and acted as surface oil coolers.

Both aircraft ordered by Imperial Airways flew in 1934, the first, G-ACOX, in the hands of Rea, and the second, G-ACOY, by the forthcoming chief test pilot, Flt Lt Cecil Feather. They had a top speed of 195 mph, which was faster than anything else in Imperial Airways service, and a cruising speed at 4,500 ft of 145 mph. This altitude could be maintained on one engine. With a full load of fuel, maximum range was 600 miles. Full load normally included six passengers, 186 gal of fuel, 13½ gal of oil and 30 lb luggage. With all seven seats occupied the fuel load had to be reduced. The take-off run at a full load of 9,500 lb and no wind was only 248 yards (656 yards to reach a height of 128 ft) and the landing run was 270 yards with brakes, or 560 yards without.

The aircraft's Certificate of Airworthiness trials were undertaken in October 1934. It was noted that the elevators and ailerons were light and effective and quick in response, but that the rudder was slightly heavier initially becoming lighter as the aircraft responded. With one engine throttled back the aircraft could be turned against the port engine, but only just against the starboard engine. In fact the P.71A was directionally unstable, with a marked tendency to turn to starboard. The inspectors thought it tiring to fly for a long period on only one engine, though in this condition the aircraft could maintain 1,600 ft at 85 mph at a full load of 9,500 lb.

The view from the cockpit was considered good in downward, forward and sideways directions when in normal flying attitude, but bad when gliding, especially to the rear. Entry to and exit from the cockpit was criticised for being difficult.

G-ACOX *Boadicea* in Imperial Airways service. (*Alan Hague*)

The P.71As were delivered to Imperial Airways in January and February 1935 and named *Boadicea* (G-ACOX) and *Britomart* (G-ACOY). The P.71As did not have a great deal of use. *Britomart* crashed on landing at Evère Airport, Brussels, on 25 October, 1935, after a flight from Croydon. It undershot the runway and was badly damaged, two of the seven passengers being injured. *Boadicea* then served on the Croydon–Brussels route along with a D.H.86. It too was lost, but on a cargo flight. With Capt A C Thomas at the controls, and a radio operator, it disappeared over the Channel on 25 September, 1936. There was an extensive search by aircraft and lifeboats, but nothing was found. The pilot's body was later washed ashore, along with some wreckage, but that of the radio operator was never found.

No further orders for the P.71A were forthcoming even though Boulton & Paul offered them in different layouts. There was an ambulance, and a cargo version with an extra roof hatch, through which to lower the cargo. This system was being used on Junkers aircraft flying cargo into the goldfields of New Guinea. In the cargo version the toilet was dispensed with, giving 410 cu ft available for cargo, plus 28 cu ft in the forward baggage hold. The P.71A was also offered as a 13-seat feederliner. To provide the available room for 13 seats, the toilet and rear baggage hold were removed, which would seem to inconvenience potential passengers on two counts. Six single seats were arranged down the starboard side, and five to port with a double seat against the

The second P.71A, G-ACOY *Britomart.* in Imperial Airways service.

rear bulkhead. A folding fourteenth seat could be fitted by the exit door, if safety considerations were to be ignored.

Swedish interest had centred on the possibility of a floatplane version with the upper freight-loading door. A great deal of work was done to satisfy this requirement, including mooring and unloading aspects, but the interest came to nothing.

The company's venture into the airliner business amounted to a total of only three aircraft. At a time when, across the Atlantic, the Boeing 247 and the Douglas DC-2 were showing the way that the airliner was to go, Boulton & Paul had chosen to adapt their well proven biplane technology to suit the rather staid requirements of Imperial Airways. Many years later the VC10 and the Trident were again to show the foolhardiness of tying airliner specifications to the unrepresentative requirements of the national airline. To Boulton & Paul's defence it has to be said it was logical for them to develop the airliner version of the already flown P.64 Mail-Carrier to fit the requirement, an aircraft which had been designed well back in the biplane era, but which had been delayed for official reasons for so long. It had finally appeared well after the monoplane era was underway. Avro, starting with a blank drawing board, had chosen to

G-ACOY after undershooting at Evère Airport, Brussels, on 25 October, 1935.
(*Alan Hague*)

226

produce a monoplane to fit the requirement, though of conservative construction, and over 11,000 of the resulting Anson were eventually produced, as opposed to just two P.71As.

P.71A

Two 490 hp Armstrong Siddeley Jaguar VIA.
Span 54 ft 1½ in; length 44 ft 2 in; height 15 ft 2 in; wing area 718 sq ft.
Empty weight (unfurnished) 6,700 lb; loaded weight 9,500 lb.
Maximum speed 195 mph; cruising speed 145–150 mph at 4,500 ft; climb to 4,500 ft 4½ min; service ceiling (one engine shut down) 4,500 ft; full tanks range 600 miles.

P.75 Overstrand

The prototype Overstrand, J9186, a converted Sidestrand III.

The Boulton Paul Overstrand achieved distinction on two counts. It was the last of the RAF's biplane bombers to enter service, and it was the first aircraft in the world to carry a fully-enclosed power-operated gun turret.

Boulton Paul's first gun turret, for which much of the credit goes to H A 'Pop' Hughes, Boulton Paul's chief armament designer, emerged as a Perspex-glazed, metal-framed cylinder with domed top and bottom. There was a vertical slot for the single .303 in Lewis gun, closed by a large zip fastener in a canvas strip, the movement of the gun opening and closing the zip. Elevation of the gun was manual. The turret was turned by pneumatic power from a set of air-bottles, maintained under pressure at 200 lb/sq in by an engine driven air-compressor, and fed through a reducing valve at 40 lb/sq in to the turret. The turret air-supply was common to the engine gas-starter system, and the compressor also supplied air for the brakes, which was stored in a separate bottle. The port engine could not be swung on its gate because of the flexible drive-shaft to the compressor unless this was disconnected. Access to the compressor was only possible by removing the cowling.

The turret rested on a ball-bearing system on a bracket attached to the extended bottom longeron. The top longerons ended in a circular track which engaged rollers on the top of the turret, holding it in position and absorbing side stresses. The air motor drove the geared spindle at the base of the turret.

The turret revolved through its normal travel of 240 deg in less than 3½ seconds, and the air in the bottles was enough for twenty such turns. It was possible to turn the turret through 360 deg if the gun was raised to an angle of 70 deg to avoid it striking the fuselage. The area covered by the turret was about two-thirds of a sphere, the largest ever achieved by a powered gun turret.

So that the gunner could concentrate on aiming his weapon, revolving the turret was accomplished by the pressure of the gun on plungers at each side. As he maintained his sights on a moving target the turret turned automatically. Should a gunner attempt to revolve the turret to the rear with the gun lower than 70 deg, the gun touching the fuselage simply took the pressure off the plunger valve and the turret stopped. The gunner's seat and the gun mounting were connected hydraulically so that they remained balanced, as the gunner pointed the gun down, his seat rose so that he maintained his eyeline on the sights, thus balancing the gunner and his weapon. There was a foot-control valve for the seat/gun connection which enabled adjustment of the system for different weights of gunner.

View of J9186 showing the nine-sided Townend rings.

The nose gunner still acted as the bomb-aimer, the bomb panel being contained within the turret, offset to port. There were four glazed panels in the bomb-aiming window, the upper two opening outwards. The bomb-sight had to be removed and stowed when the turret was being used, as the gun fouled it. During normal flight the gun arm was fully elevated and the gun was stowed in the top of the turret, by a quick-release strap through the spade grip. During bomb-aiming the turret was locked in its forward position. The bomb controls were duplicated in the cockpit. The two doors of the turret entrance were in the lower fairing behind the turret. The emergency exit for the nose gunner was through the top of the turret. This was held in place by three pins, two by the slot and one at the rear. They were secured by slip pins with finger rings. All the gunner had to do was pull out the pins and push the top of the turret off.

The turret was also submitted as part of the P.70 project for Specification B.9/32. This was a bomber version of the P.64 mail-carrier, with Sidestrand components and both the power-operated nose turret and a retractable power-operated dorsal turret. The retracting dorsal turret was not used on the

Overstrand, there was not enough fuselage depth to accommodate it. The dorsal gun position was fitted with a conventional Scarff ring and a single Lewis gun as in the Sidestrand, and there was provision for six drums of ammunition. The gunner was only protected by a large windscreen behind his back. The ventral position was also fitted with a single Lewis, with a prone position for the gunner, and provision for six drums of ammunition, just as before. An F.8 camera was fitted as standard, and was operated by the rear gunner, who also operated the wireless equipment. A T.1083 transmitter, and an R.1082 receiver were fitted to production Overstrands, with a T.R.11 transmitter/receiver, but on Sidestrands converted to Overstrands the T.73 transmitter and R.74 receiver were retained. There was a telephone communication system between the crew positions as in the later Sidestrands.

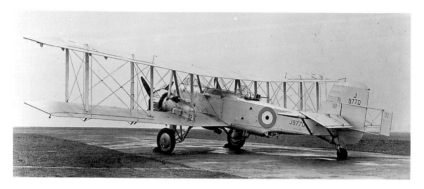

The second Sidestrand converted to an Overstrand, J9770, with a slightly wider turret and front fuselage, and other minor changes. (*Crown Copyright, A & AEE*)

For testing, the turret was installed in Sidestrand Mk III J9186 which had already been experimentally fitted with 555 hp Bristol Pegasus I.M.3 engines, close cowled with special nine-sided Townend rings. The nacelles each contained a 17 gal oil tank, hand-starting magnetos, priming pumps and a Type A gas starter.

The pilot was given a fully-enclosed cockpit canopy, with a sliding hood, with slightly-tinted anti-glare Perspex. An autopilot, as introduced on the Sidestrand, was fitted as standard. All three crew members enjoyed heating taken from muffs on the inboard side of the exhaust system of each Pegasus, an arrangement made possible by the Townend rings and close cowlings.

The airframe was strengthened, allowing an increase in gross weight to 12,000 lb, and an increased bomb load of 1,500 lb. Two 500 lb bombs could be carried in the recessed bomb cell plus two 250 lb bombs on external carriers. Two light series carriers could be fitted, one forward and one aft of the fuselage carriers, each carrying four 20 lb bombs, or two 20 lb bombs and two reconnaissance flares. A new levered main undercarriage was fitted with larger wheels, and a 9 in by 5 in tailwheel replaced the tailskid of the Sidestrand. The outer sections of the wings were given a marked degree of sweepback (1 ft 1.6 in on the upper wing, 1 ft 0.7 in on the lower wing), to compensate for the extra weight in the nose.

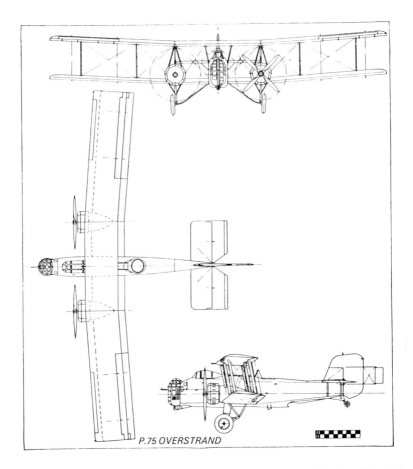

P.75 OVERSTRAND

The first flight of the modified aircraft was in 1933 in the hands of Sqn Ldr Rea. To begin with it was known as the Sidestrand Mk V, but such were the changes it was later renamed the Overstrand, after another village near to Cromer.

The aircraft was delivered to Andover on 22 February, 1934, for No.101 Squadron trials alongside its standard Sidestrands. In an A & AAE report fault was found in the cramped nature of the turret. There was also criticism of the longitudinal controls and the engine vibration which was experienced. As well as the increased gross weight, the Overstrand achieved higher speeds than its predecessor, up to 153 mph at 6500 ft, but retained its manoeuvrability. The crew warmed to the extra creature comforts, quite literally, and especially because of the time of the year. The aircraft was returned to Mousehold on 19 March for changes to overcome the problems experienced.

Another Sidestrand, J9770, was also converted to an Overstrand, incorporating the changes which resulted from the criticisms. A larger diameter turret was fitted, with a slightly wider front fuselage to accommodate it. The zip fastener was deleted when the aircraft went into service, the slot in the turret being

230

closed by a canvas strip held by clips when the gun was not in use. Slight changes were made to the fin section, the autopilot aileron controls, and the horn-balance on the elevators. In addition the connections to the rear of the swinging engine mount were simplified and a platform was provided for servicing the compressor. In addition Bristol Pegasus II.M.3 engines of 580 hp were substituted for the earlier ones, and fitted with two-piece four-blade propellers to try to cure the engine vibration problems.

The top speed was 148 mph at 6,500 ft, and 146 mph at 10,000 ft to which height it took 9.3 min. The ceiling was 21,300 ft. During high-speed diving tests with the two-piece propeller vibration and yawing oscillations were experienced and in one the forward attachment fitting of the fin failed. A strengthened fin and forward fitting were provided but the vibration and oscillation were still present. In later tests with K4546, one of the new-build aircraft, there were similar results, but the vibration and oscillation was not nearly so bad.

A production Overstrand, K4560, with a Sidestrand III in the background.

The Air Ministry ordered the conversion of two more Sidestrands to Overstrands, J9179 and J9185, also equipped with 580 hp Pegasus II.M.3s. Finally an order for nineteen new Overstrands, K4546–K4564, was placed to Specification 23/34, to replace the Sidestrands of No.101 Squadron and to increase the Squadron strength to three Flights, with provision for spare aircraft.

One Overstrand, J9770, was experimentally fitted with Pegasus IV giving 720 hp, the intention being to eventually take advantage of the increased power by fitting a retractable undercarriage. This development was to be designated P.80 Superstrand, but it was never built. The age of the monoplane had arrived.

This view shows to advantage the clean lines of the Overstrand.

231

Five more new Overstrands, K8173–K8177, were ordered in 1935, as further replacements, making a total of twenty-four built, plus the four converted Sidestrands.

The de Boysson four-gun turret was experimentally fitted in the nose of K8175 in 1937, and trials were flown using Hawker Hart K2967 as the target aircraft. A single 20 mm cannon on a pedestal mount was fitted to the nose of another Overstrand, K8176.

The Overstrand in RAF Service

The first Overstrand, one of the converted Sidestrands, J9185, was delivered to No.101 Squadron on 24 January, 1935, and new aircraft began arriving in October of the same year; deliveries continuing to July 1936. No.101 Squadron, thus re-equipped, remained the sole RAF medium-bomber unit. To commemorate the fact that it was the first RAF squadron to operate a bomber with a power-operated turret, the unofficial crest which had been adopted at Bircham Newton was now changed and made official. It featured a lion rampant on a turret of a more medieval nature, with the motto Mens Agitat Molem (Mind over Matter), but more usually said by airmen to mean 'They don't mind and I don't matter'.

The first four Overstrands delivered formed a third 'C' Flight, which featured green squadron lettering. Subsequently each Overstrand replaced a Sidestrand in 'A' and then 'B' Flights, still featuring red and yellow squadron lettering respectively. The Overstrands wore the standard silver finish, but in squadron service, unlike the Sidestrands, did not have any matt green areas (apart from the prototype J9186, which had the upper and lower surfaces and an even larger proportion of the nose painted green). The nose gunner, in his turret was not affected by any reflective surfaces and the pilot was protected by the anti-glare Perspex of his hood.

The improved creature comforts of the Overstrand made it a more popular aircraft with the crews than even the Sidestrand had been. As well as being just as good a bombing platform, the nose gunners were now able to increase their efficiency from as low as 15 per cent hits to 85 per cent, a remarkable testament to John North's foresight in developing the turret.

The Overstrand made its first appearance at the Hendon Air Display in 1933, J9186 taking part in the 'Parade and Fly Past of Experimental Types'. The following year a No.101 Squadron Overstrand resumed the usual role which Boulton & Paul medium bombers took at Hendon displays, when 'attacked' by three Hawker Furies of No.1 Squadron, a rather more unequal 'contest' than those suffered by some of its predecessors. In the last Hendon Air Display in 1937 the Overstrand featured in a flight-refuelling demonstration, being refuelled in the air by a Vickers Virginia tanker. Also a No.101 Squadron aircraft this time took on three No.604 Squadron Hawker Demons. Coincidentally Boulton Paul were at the time building Hawker Demons under licence, so the company's products could be said to have finally 'won' one of these Hendon battles, which had begun with three Nieuport Nighthawks versus a P.7 Bourges.

On 21–23 May, 1935, the Squadron gave a demonstration of salvo bombing to students of the Imperial Defence College, with a 200 yard by 30 yard target representing a bridge. All three salvoes hit the target, which greatly impressed the students, but not those wise enough to recognise the difference of attacking a large immobile undefended target in good weather with the realities which would ensue in wartime.

On 6 July, 1935, No.101 Squadron moved its two Flights to Mildenhall, and took part in the King's Jubilee Air Review. HM King George VI inspected the ranks of aircraft lined up for the purpose. He stopped at Sgt J L Thrussell's Overstrand, K9185, and he was presented as the best bomb-aimer of 1935. The King climbed aboard the aircraft, which represented the very latest bomber in the Air Force and inspected the new turret.

In the same year a No.101 Squadron Overstrand won the Sassoon Trophy for photographic reconnaissance. The pilot was PO Williams, the observer, AC1 Goad and the camera was operated by LAC Gregory. Their score was 89.5 per cent, the highest achieved up to the time.

No.101 Squadron lost its first Overstrand on 9 September, 1935, when J9185 crashed on the North Coates range. Three more crashed the following year, J9179 lost an engine on take-off and it crashed on the aerodrome perimeter, and the other two crashed in landing accidents. K4562 experienced brake seizure and ended up on its nose, and K4556 force landed on boggy ground by a Bicester hangar, piloted by a Flight Commander, and also ended up on its nose.

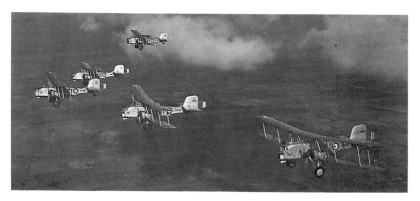

Five Overstrands of No.101 Squadron.

In 1937 a modification notice was issued to strengthen the front fuselage covering to reduce vibration in flight. At the same time the opening in the cockpit canopy was enlarged to facilitate ingress and egress.

In January 1937 No.144 Squadron formed alongside No.101 Squadron as part of the RAF's general expansion, and used four of 101's Overstrands for a month until it obtained equipment of its own. In January 1937 K4564 flew into the ground in thick fog at Swanbourne, Buckinghamshire, when returning to Bicester from Mildenhall, killing the crew. In June 1937 another Overstrand crashed on landing at Bicester after a practice flight. On 27 August, 1938, No.101 Squadron began receiving Bristol Blenheim bombers. By the end of the summer of 1938 the last Overstrand had been removed from front-line service, but they were to continue in use for testing purposes and as gunnery trainers.

Surviving Overstrands were allocated to the Armament Training Camps, which were re-named Armament Training Schools in 1938, and subsequently Air Observer Schools. Five Overstrands were concentrated at No.2 AOS at Dumfries, which later became No.10 Bombing and Gunnery School. No.1 Air Armament School at Manby, in Lincolnshire, operated K4552 until it was relegated to a Ground Instructional Airframe in December 1939. On 28 April, 1940, it was badly damaged when hit by an overshooting Gauntlet. In July 1940 K8173 broke up in the air over the Chesil Bank ranges, killing the crew members, and the remaining Overstrands were relegated to ground instruction only.

Two Overstrands continued to fly for a few months, however. The Special Duty Flight at Christchurch used K8176 and the Balloon Development Unit at Cardington had K4559 to provide a slipstream for barrage balloons, in the testing of balloon cables for fatigue. The aircraft being struck off charge in April 1941. K8176 was transferred to the Army Co-operation Development Unit, where it was probably the last Overstrand to fly. The type finally being declared obsolete in mid-1941.

Overstrand production was completed at Norwich, but two Overstrands, K4559 and K8176, did appear at Wolverhampton for turret development work. The latter was written off when being flown by a new Boulton Paul test pilot, Robert Lindsay Neale, in mid-1941. On a flight to Edinburgh in bad weather, the aircraft was forced out over the sea, and in attempting to land at Blackpool undershot the runway and crashed. This aircraft had been camouflaged the day before and the paint was still wet when it took off. The Overstrand represented the last link with the old era in two respects, as a Sidestrand development, (with four Sidestrands being converted to Overstrands) they could be said to be the last of the Boulton & Paul designs to fly, and yet they were manufactured by the new company, Boulton Paul Aircraft, and are therefore regarded as the first of the new company's designs.

They were also the last of the company's biplanes, and the last aircraft to be completed at Norwich. The first Boulton Paul Aircraft design, at the new factory in Wolverhampton, would be one of the new high-speed monoplanes, the Defiant, but the Overstrand did represent the first step in the future of the new company. The turret was the first of their many power-turrets, which would lead the company almost inevitably into power controls, and the work it still does to this day, but before the new era was represented on the production lines, they obtained an order to build another biplane, the Hawker Demon.

P.75 Overstrand

Two 580 hp Bristol Pegasus II.M.3.

Span 71 ft 11.3 in; length 46 ft 1.8 in; height 15 ft 9 in; wing area 979.5 sq ft.

Empty weight 8,004 lb; loaded weight 11,932 lb.

Maximum speed 153 mph at 6,500 ft; rate of climb at 5,000 ft 1,110 ft/min; service ceiling 21,300 ft.

Armament: One .303 in Lewis machine-gun in power-operated nose turret and one .303 in Lewis gun in dorsal and ventral positions. Bomb load 1,500 lb.

The prototype P.82 Defiant without turret at Pendeford. It has hinged lower wheel flaps.

P.82 Defiant

The Defiant is rightly remembered as the most famous product of Boulton Paul Aircraft. It did, after all, represent over 79 per cent of all Boulton Paul designed aircraft built by the company. (77.4 per cent when including the P.92/2 built by Heston Aircraft and the thirty Balliols built by Blackburn). There were 1,062 Defiants eventually built, out of a total of 1,341 Boulton Paul aircraft (plus the 31 by other manufacturers). It was the company's greatest success, and their greatest disappointment. It was seen as a failure by many, and yet it was never tested in the role for which the concept of the turret fighter was first envisaged, as a destroyer of unescorted bomber formations.

During the 1930s the bomber went through a metamorphosis of startling proportions. From being little changed from the fabric-covered biplane bombers of the First World War (except perhaps in having a metal airframe instead of wood), and with very little increase in performance, they became all-metal stressed-skin monoplanes with double the top speed, very often winning the performance race with their fighter counterparts. At these higher speeds traditional fighter armament of twin machine-guns was hopelessly inadequate. Firing passes were going to be shorter, bombers were likely to be able to withstand heavier punishment, and, as many were being armed with power-operated multi-gun turrets, they were likely to be able to give as good as they got.

That any attacking bombers might be escorted by fighters seems to have been completely discounted, which in a sense was totally logical, because this had never happened. The only major uses of strategic bombers had involved unescorted Gothas and Handley Page O/400s, and as the most likely threat to this country in the 1930s was Germany, well out of the range of any front-line fighter, the so-called bomber-destroyers did not appear to need the ability to defend themselves against single-seat fighters.

It was the revised threat of improved bombers which troubled military planners and, in Great Britain, led to two distinct concepts for the fighter needed to deal with it. The development of the reliable Browning machine-gun made possible the fitment of batteries of up to four of them in each wing of the new monoplanes, giving immense hitting power during a short firing pass. On the other hand, the development of the power-operated gun turret, so ably pioneered on the Overstrand, made possible the construction of a two-seat fighter armed with one of these new turrets, which could prolong the length of the firing pass, thereby delivering an equal or greater weight of bullets.

The two-seat turret fighter thus created was seen as the obvious replacement for the Hawker Demon, which was rapidly becoming obsolescent. The Demon had been born almost by accident, being evolved because the Hart day bomber was so much faster than contemporary RAF fighters. As soon as the Hawker Fury and the Gloster Gauntlet entered service, the stop-gap Demon no longer had a sensible role to play, and yet no-one seemed to question the need to replace it with another two-seat fighter.

As early as 1933 the Air Ministry issued Specification F.5/33 for a two-seat monoplane fighter equipped with a power-operated turret as a Demon replacement. Boulton & Paul submitted their P.76, with either two Napier Rapier or two Bristol Pegasus engines, Bristol their Type 140, Armstrong Whitworth their A.W.34 and Gloster another monoplane. All these submissions were deemed too large and slow, and further discussions were held in an attempt to evolve a more realistic replacement for the Demon.

The prototype Defiant, K8310, with its turret fitted, the hinged wheel flaps removed and stub exhausts fitted.

Although a two-gun turret had been envisaged for F.5/33, the weight penalty involved led to the belief that the greater hitting power of a four-gun turret would be needed to compensate. In 1934 the Air Ministry knew of the existence of the de Boysson turret, equipped with four Darne machine-guns. John North, had been invited to view it by its manufacturers, the Société d'Application des Machine Motrices (SAMM), and seeing its potential immediately had urged the Ministry to buy the turret. When they had demurred, preferring to seek a British-built alternative, on 23 November, 1935, North had bought the rights to SAMM's turret, and ordered two examples. This decision immediately placed Boulton Paul in a good position when the Air Ministry's revised specification for a turret fighter was issued on 26 June, 1935, to the fifteen major manufacturers.

In its final form Specification F.9/35 called for a two-seat fighter in which all

236

the armament was to be concentrated in a power-operated turret, thus discarding the versatility of the Demon and the Bristol Fighter before it, with their combination of fixed forward-firing, and movable rear guns. The turret was to be able to fire over the entire upper hemisphere, and the guns were to be capable of being depressed to some extent at the side.

Up to eight 20 lb fragmentation bombs would be carried for army co-operation sorties. Fuel for 1½ hours cruising at 15,000 ft and a top speed of 298 mph at 15,000 ft were required, and climb to that altitude was to be 5½ minutes. The service ceiling was to be at least 33,000 ft.

Of the fifteen firms which were invited to tender, just six offered submissions. At the Design Conference in September 1935 these six were discussed. Hawker's Hotspur was based on their Henley light bomber, which itself used the Hurricane wings, and because of their experience, and proven track record, they quickly became favourites for the order. Boulton Paul's P.82 was also looked on with favour mainly because of the de Boysson turret, which was clearly the company's ace. Fairey offered a version of their Battle light bomber, and Armstrong Whitworth a version of their Specification F.5/33 submission, which differed from the other five in being a twin-engined design. Bristol offered their Type 147, a version of their Type 146 single-seat fighter, fitted with remotely-controlled turret, and either their Perseus or Hercules engines. The final submission was from Supermarine, but they were already overstretched in trying to get the Spitfire into production.

By 9 October the decision had been made to fund seven prototypes, two each from Hawker and Boulton Paul, with two from Fairey as a back-up, and one of the larger Armstrong Whitworth design. Contracts were signed on 4 December, 1935.

Boulton Paul set to work with some urgency, all other projects in the immediate offing being dropped. They were anxious to prove they could build a competitive airframe to which their obviously superior turret could be fitted. By the end of February 1936 they had completed a mock-up of the P.82 at Norwich, and on 21 March metal was cut for the first time for the fuselage construction.

There was a mock-up conference on 14 February, 1936, at which the turret mock-up was almost complete. It was forseen at this conference that a mobile stand would be useful in which to place the turret whenever it was removed from the aircraft, preferably rigid enough for the guns to be tested.

The de Boysson turrets which had been ordered were finally delivered in September 1936 and when the Director of Technical Development came to inspect them on the 9th, he found the first prototype P.82 in a more advanced state of completion than he had expected. He was also pleasantly surprised by what he saw, and the techniques being employed.

The company had devised an excellent compromise between the aerodynamic cleanliness required to overcome the weight and drag of the turret, and ease of manufacture. Most of the aircraft's skin was riveted to Z-section stiffeners on the bench, 'on the flat' and was then wrapped around the structure and the stiffeners were riveted to the frame. As double curvatures were avoided in the main, most of the skin could be applied this way, and there was little need for forming processes, except in minor areas such as the wing leading-edge. The aircraft was also made up entirely of sub-assemblies which were then bolted together.

The aircraft was also of very clean design, with flush riveting in most cases. There were retractable fairings to streamline the turret when not in use, and the undercarriage bay was entirely enclosed by rubber-sealed doors. Compromises were only made where ease of manufacture dictated it. For instance, though a basically elliptical wing form was chosen, it was modified so that it incorporated two linear tapers, to the inner and outer sections, making manufacture far easier than for that of the Spitfire. The engine was to be a Rolls-Royce Merlin I, giving 1,030 hp.

Ground trials of the newly delivered turret were due to take place at Orfordness on 17 October and Boulton Paul requested that de Boysson be allowed to be present so that they could also be considered manufacturer's acceptance trials. The Air Ministry agreed but insisted that he was not allowed to see any part of the F.9/35 prototype. The turret was tested on a truck. De Boysson stated during the tests that an automatic dead-centre for the control had not been found necessary, and that the French Air Force did not have the turret in production, though a SAMM 'turret' fitted with a single 20 mm cannon was in service.

Any lingering doubts the Air Ministry had about Boulton Paul's ability to produce a competitive airframe had been dispelled by the DTD's visit. Doubts about the company's productive capacity were also laid to rest by the imminent move to the new facility being constructed in Wolverhampton, where a plentiful supply of skilled labour was available, not least because of the recent closure of Sunbeam Motors.

The completed parts of the Defiant prototype were moved to Wolverhampton, but by April 1937 only the fuselage was complete. The date for delivery of the prototype had been 4 March, but the rival Hawker Hotspur was even further behind schedule, the Fairey and Armstrong Whitworth designs having been cancelled. To maintain their lead, a night shift was instituted.

Certain small modifications had been made to the original design, and were being applied to the prototype. A fuselage bulkhead was installed to reduce fuselage draughts for the gunner and heating was provided for his turret drawn from the engine radiator which itself had been moved from a position under the nose, to one more akin to the Hurricane's under the centre section. There was a modified aileron balance and a larger rudder. Because of the turret the radio masts could not be on top of the fuselage, and so retractable ones were designed for beneath the fuselage.

The Air Ministry was happy with progress and on 28 April a production order, No.6228849/37, was placed for 87 P.82s, to be serialled L6950–L7036, and the aircraft was named the Defiant. By May the wing of K8310, the first prototype, was mated to the fuselage and the de Boysson turret received from France was being test flown in the nose of Overstrand K8175.

Between 3 July and 28 August, 1937, the turret in K8175 was tested in the air, using a Hart as a target aircraft. Trials were undertaken against a jump card, and then at 2,400 ft both with the aircraft flying straight and level at maximum speed and also manoeuvring and diving at maximum permissable speed, the tests then repeated at 15,000 ft. The firing was against horizontal and vertical flag targets. The conclusion reached was that the turret was satisfactory and would prove practical and reliable in service.

By July K8310 was ready for its first engine runs. As the turret modified to

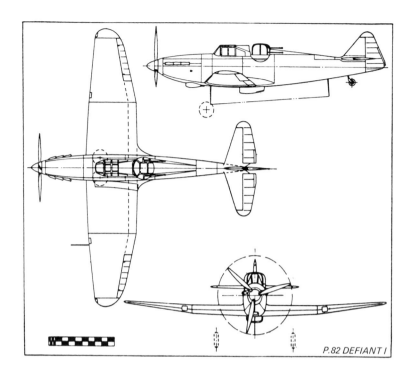

P.82 DEFIANT I

British requirements to fit the Defiant was still in the Overstrand the aircraft was finished as a single-seater. The hole where the turret would be fitted was faired over and ballast was installed. On 11 August, 1937, piloted by Cecil Feather the prototype Defiant flew for the first time, from Pendeford Airport, still in natural metal finish.

The aircraft was found to be a delight to fly, and the performance was excellent, not perhaps surprisingly without the drag of the turret. Trouble was experienced with the Dowty undercarriage units. They often failed to lock in the up position, and in December they were replaced with Lockheed units. The aircraft was fitted with a tailskid, and this was eventually replaced by a tailwheel. The undercarriage bay was entirely closed by flaps attached to the undercarrige legs. The wheels being covered by a circular flap hinged in the middle, the lower part of which folded outwards about 80 deg when the legs were extended, to give ground clearance. The hinged portion of these flaps was later removed.

Between 7 and 31 December K8310 was test flown by a number of Service pilots at the A & AEE, Martlesham Heath, who found it had a sprightly performance. A top speed of 320 mph was achieved, and 10,500 ft was reached in 7½ minutes. A service ceiling of 33,500 ft was predicted. Of course this was achieved, not only without the turret, but also without most of the required military equipment. Without the turret the test programme was restricted to handling, engine cooling and diving trials, and K8310 proved acceptable in all these respects, though neither engine nor oil cooling were perfect. Handling was good in all respects, trim remaining constant when flaps or undercarriage was lowered.

A few small items were criticised by the four pilots who flew the aircraft at Martlesham. Access to the cockpit was difficult without slipping on the wing. This was due to the fact that the cockpit was rather further forward than in other single-seat fighters which gave the pilot a very good view forward and down. The problem was overcome by fitting a piece of non-slip material on the wing centre-section. The cockpit was unheated and there were a number of draughts even with the hood closed. There was adverse criticism of some of the controls. The elevator trim handle tended to creep, and would have been better fitted on the port side. The fuel cocks were stiff and hard to reach, and the undercarriage and flap selector levers were thought to be too complicated.

The ailerons were thought to be too light, and it was suggested that a better balance would cure this. It was also suggested that the flaps should be capable of being depressed to 90 deg to allow a steeper glide approach.

The slippage in completion schedule was only mitigated by the fact that Hawker were even further behind with their Hotspur, both with the airframe and the Nash & Thompson turret which was being designed for it. In January 1938 the Hotspur was cancelled, though Hawker completed the aircraft and later used it for testing work associated with the Henley.

The following month official approval for the Defiant was confirmed when a second production order was placed for 202 aircraft, which would have serial numbers in the N range. Also during February, K8310 finally received its four-gun turret, though it had been test flown with just the cupola fitted.

The turret was designated the A Mk IID, and was only slightly changed from the original de Boysson unit. It was fitted with four .303 in Browning machine-guns, rather than the four Darnes, and each gun had 600 rounds. It was a self-contained unit, with its own hydraulic pump, so that it only had to be lowered into position, bolted down, and then the only connections were the electrical and intercommunication supplies through a slip ring in the base, and the gunner's heating. The turret weighed just 361 lb without the guns and ammunition which weighed a total of 194 lb. The gunner's equipment, sights, oxygen supply, etc, weighed a further 35 lb.

In February 1938 armament trials took place from Martlesham Heath over the Orfordness ranges. The tests were the same undertaken with the Overstrand and 15,167 rounds were fired. There was a problem with the retractable fairings fore and aft of the turret, as the retracting gear had not yet been fitted. Firing trials were undertaken with the fairings fastened down, and then speed tests were undertaken with them fastened up.

Teething troubles with the Merlin I engine delayed its arrival at Martlesham Heath until 18 October for performance tests which lasted until the 28th. These revealed that the top speed was only 303 mph at 15,000 ft with +12 lb of boost. It took 10.1 min to reach 15,000 ft and 15.1 min to reach 20,000 ft. To clear a 50 ft obstacle a take-off run of 870 yards was required. All these figures were disappointing, and though the aircraft was a delight to handle it could in no way compete in manoeuvrability with single-seat fighters. Though the Defiant had been expected to be less agile, the company had hoped that the speed would be as good as the Hurricane's.

On 13 April, 1938, there was a meeting in the DTD's office to discuss new electrical equipment for the turret. It was agreed that the first production turret would go to the RAE for electrical tests and the second production turret would be fitted to K8320.

Though its performance was not as high as expected, the Air Ministry was satisfied enough to place an order in May 1938, for a further 161 production Defiants. Nevertheless, discussions were already under way over ways of improving the aircraft's performance, centred mainly on more powerful engines. Though the new Griffon was suggested, more powerful versions of the Merlin which were being projected were the most likely candidates. The first production aircraft were to be fitted with the 1,030 hp Merlin III engine.

The second prototype, K8620, was having modifications suggested by the test flying of K8310, and was to be fitted with a Merlin II engine. In place of the hinged wheel flaps originally fitted to the first Defiant, separate semi-circular flaps were fitted nearly on the centre line, folding outwards to cover the lower part of the wheels. Just forward of these flaps a wireless aerial post was fitted, with a second aerial post just in front of the tailwheel. These posts retracted when the undercarriage was extended. Landing lights were fitted and there was more glazing between the pilot's canopy and the gun turret. A new windscreen was fitted, allowing the deletion of the central pillar on K8310. Ailerons of increased chord were fitted and finally an enlarged carburettor air intake was also fitted.

The wings of K8620 were not completed until May 1938. The contract had called for its completion one month after the first prototype, that is September 1937, but it did not finally fly until 18 May, 1938. The second prototype was largely representative of the proposed production version, though flight trials revealed the need for a larger rudder.

When K8310 was tested at Martlesham Heath on 30 September, 1938, an unforeseen problem was discovered when the air supply for the pneumatically-retracting turret fairings was found to be inadequate. The pilot's gauge showed a pressure drop of 10 lb/sq in for each rotation of the turret, and the compressor

Production Defiant Is outside the factory.

was unable to replenish the reservoir so rapidly. It was recommended that the turret fairings should be lowered by the gunner at the beginning of an action, using a button provided, and should only be raised again when the action was over. The loss of speed of 5–6 mph with the fairings down was considered acceptable. During these trials it was decided that the radiator fitted would not be suitable for tropical service. The speed trials were limited by the fact that the Merlin kept cutting out, restricting diving trials to a maximum 340 mph IAS.

The first production Defiant, L6950, did not fly until 30 July, 1939, and by the end of September only five production Defiants had flown. On 5 September L6951 went to the Central Flying School at Upavon for the completion of its handling notes, and on 19 September L6950 was delivered to the A & AEE, now at Boscombe Down, for assessment alongside K8620. Both L6951 and L6952 went to the Air Fighting Development Unit at Northolt for comparison with the RAF's other fighters, and for night flying trials.

The loaded weight of the Defiant was 8,318 lb, the loaded weight of the Hurricane I was 6,600 lb, and yet the Defiant had 7½ sq ft less wing area and only the same power. It followed that the Defiant's wing-loading at 33.27 lb/sq ft and power-loading at 8.07 lb/hp were significantly higher than the Hurricane's. Not surprisingly when L6951 and L6952 were flown in mock combat with No.111 Squadron's Hurricanes the Defiants came off rather ignominiously. It is perhaps significant that when the RAF finally got its hands on the Air Ministry's 'bomber destroyer', it chose to pit it in mock combat with a single-engined fighter, probably foreseeing the likelihood of it meeting the Bf 109 in battle.

Tests were also undertaken at Boscombe Down in the tactical use of the Defiant. It was flown in mock-combat with a Blenheim IV, which was intercepted at a height of 12,000 ft. It was found that if the Defiant pilot could get beneath the Blenheim, the bomber pilot could not get rid of him except by diving steeply away, the Defiant would then often be left ½ minute astern. As the Blenheim levelled off at 50 ft, the Defiant pilots' tactic was to dive to a

Boulton Paul's chief test pilot, Cecil Feather, flight testing a production Defiant I over Chillington.

parallel course 6–800 yards away and then to close in. At this altitude no manoeuvres of the Blenheim could effectively lose the Defiant, but the Defiant's gunner found it hard to bring his guns to bear unless the pilot lowered a wing. Boulton Paul technicians did modify this turret during the trials so that it could be depressed 7 deg, but in doing so had to lose 7 deg of elevation. The most damning sentence in the resulting report was 'Every degree by which the field of fire can be extended towards the flight direction is of great value'.

In the meantime Boulton Paul had begun the design of a dual control training version with the turret replaced by a semi-enclosed raised rear cockpit for a pilot instructor. The ease with which pilots converted to the easy-to-handle Defiant obviated the need for this version and it was cancelled when design work was about 80 per cent complete.

Though the gestation period of the Defiant had taken rather longer than first expected, once production got underway the aircraft began flowing off the production lines. This was largely because the structural design of the aircraft made production so simple.

Construction

The construction devised for the Defiant was probably the best of all the three monoplane fighters ordered for the RAF during the 1930s. It was more advanced than the Hurricane's which was simply a development of the Fury/Hart series retaining a fabric-covered fuselage joined to a rather thick wing. The Defiant was very much simpler in construction than the Spitfire, which was also of modern stressed-skin construction, but of a far more complex nature, the mass production of which was not easy.

The beauty of the Defiant's construction was that it was built up of several basic components constructed on the bench, which were then joined together on the assembly line, enabling sub-contractors to be brought into the production programme quickly and efficiently. The main sub-assemblies were as follows: Two outer wings, centre wing, two wingtips, upper and lower engine cowlings, two side engine cowlings, forward fuselage, forward upper fairing, two rear fuselage sides, rear fuselage transition section, rear upper fairing, radiator fairing, ailerons, rudder, elevators and flaps.

Only the control surfaces were fabric-covered, all the rest were metal-skinned, and in the majority of cases no preforming of the skin was required, the alloy sheet simply being wrapped around the assembly. The wing for instance was basically an elliptical design in plan, but modified for ease of production. The one-piece centre-section featured a gradual linear taper, and then the outer wings had a more pronounced taper. The wings were rounded off with detachable tips. As the thickness of the wing was also one linear taper from root to tip the whole surface of the wing could be covered with flat alloy sheets which did not require any forming operations.

In addition the flat sheets were not riveted to the wing structure but to Z-section stiffeners, on the flat. These stiffeners were then riveted to the frame. All the skin plates were drilled two or three at a time on large boiler plate jigs. The skin was dimpled so that countersunk rivets could be used as part of the extensive effort which went into making the airframe as aerodynamically clean as possible; part of the programme of trying to counteract the drag of the turret.

The wing was built with two spars each consisting of upper and lower extruded light-alloy booms connected by webs of vertically corrugated light-alloy sheet. The centre section spars had booms of T section, whereas the outer wing spars were of L section. The lower booms of the centre section spars were bent at the centre to allow for the tapering of the wing thickness, but the other booms were straight. The spar flanges were milled to give a slight taper.

The skin for the upper surface of the wing was riveted on first, the centre section being held vertically on a wheeled trolley. The Z-section stringers ran span-wise, and were cut at the ribs, to which they were attached by brackets, with the skin being directly riveted to the rib boom. The lower skin of the wing was then applied, with pop riveting used to attach the sheet to the ribs and spars. The leading edge of the wing was made of light-alloy sheet, bent on a Pels Press to D shape and attached to light-alloy nose formers, and screwed to the spar flanges top and bottom, with countersunk steel screws. The entire wing leading-edge was thus detachable.

The trailing edge was built up of an auxiliary spar with a corrugated web half way between the rear spar and the trailing edge. This in effect created a box rear spar. Hydraulically-operated split flaps along the trailing edge made up about 18 per cent of wing chord. They did not extend continuously beneath the fuselage as the glycol radiator was sited there. The oil cooler and carburettor air intake were beneath the engine in a single duct.

Because of the cut-out in the lower wing for the inward-retracting undercarriage the wing centre-section was not structurally a box-beam, but on the outer wings the top and bottom skins were continuous, thus forming a box structure, otherwise similar to the centre section.

The outer wings were joined to the centre section by machined steel fittings attached to the spar booms which held ground taper bolts. To close the gap between the outer wings and centre sections a rubber strip was wrapped all around the wing and pulled tight by tightened screws at the trailing edge.

The two 52 gal fuel tanks were housed in the centre section at its outer edge. They were covered with Lynatex to make them leak-proof and to give self-sealing properties. The undercarriage unit was attached to a very stiff beam at an angle to the line of flight. The production undercarriage legs were Lockheed Airdraulic units, which retracted inwards, being entirely submerged within the centre section, and nearly touching on the centre line. The undercarriage when retracted was entirely enclosed, up to the wheel centre line by two flaps attached to the undercarriage legs, and the remainder by two small semi-circular flaps hinged at the central rib of the centre section, and hanging vertically down when the undercarriage was extended. The undercarriage closed on a rubber seal to give an air-tight joint.

The wingtips were built-up metal curved units, and were bolted to the wings with four bolts, which made them easily detachable. They contained the navigation lamp fairings.

The front fuselage was built up of four light-alloy angle section longerons, at the front of which was a braced frame of steel tubes carrying the engine mountings. The lower pair of longerons were curved to the same shape as the upper surface of the wing centre section, which then formed the floor of the pilot's cockpit; the wing being contained within the lower fuselage in the recess thus created. The longerons were connected at the side by light-alloy sheet shaped to the fuselage section and horizontally by light-alloy tubular members supporting corrugated light-alloy sheet decking, as far aft as the trailing edge of the wing, where a flat-topped bulkhead was sited. There were two corrugated light-alloy decks, an upper one, interrupted by the cockpit, and the lower one by the wing recess.

The rear fuselage was assembled from three parts, an upper corrugated deck, and two opposite-handed sides built up on two L-section longerons linked by channel section formers, five of which were braced by tubes creating wing-rib like structures. The intermediate formers between these 'ribs' were just channel sections. The corrugations of the deck which ran transversely were created, intriguingly, on a German Pels press. The fuselage skin was wrapped around the unit and the stringers were riveted to the formers, though the edges were riveted directly to the longerons. The bottom longerons of the two side sections were then bolted together after fitting the control fairleads and guides, and then the top longerons were bolted to the upper deck section.

The short section of fuselage aft of this rear section was a tubular structure to carry the tail unit, and originally to hold and contain a retractable tailwheel, though this was not fitted on production Defiants.

The two near cones which were the front and rear fuselage sections were then joined together by a 2 ft long transition section, on which a certain amount of forming was required. Because there was no double curvature of the rest of the fuselage skin, it could be simply wrapped around the structure as with the wings.

The tailplane and fin were cantilever and built on a series of tapered longerons and covered with a flush riveted metal skin. The elevators, Frise-type ailerons and rudder had metal structures but were fabric-covered. The two elevators were interchangeable, so that the elevator tab control mechanisms were on the upper side of one elevator and the lower side of the other. The rudder also had a trimming tab, and this had some automatic servo action. Both the rudder and elevators were horn-balanced.

The engine oil cooler was contained in a duct cowling integral with the bottom engine cowling panel, which extended further aft than the fire-proof bulkhead forming the lower fairing of the front fuselage section back to the wing. Removable side and top panels extending back to the fire-proof bulkhead completed the engine covering. A duct from the oil cooler led air for cockpit heating. The rear of the forward fuselage had a lower fairing in which was built the radiator duct, lying between the trailing edge and the rear spar. The radiator was supplied with a hinged flap to control the flow of cooling air. Because of the radiator position taxi-ing on muddy ground had to be done with care as it could easily become clogged with mud. The upper fuselage fairing was mainly of light spruce and three-ply in two sections for the two sections of fuselage. The frame of the pilot's windscreen was the exception being a light-alloy casting.

The front part of the upper fairing carried the line of the pilot's cockpit canopy back to the gun turret cupola, the rear part being retractable. The rear part of the upper fairing, behind the turret tapered away to a slightly domed section at the tailplane. The front part of this fairing was also retractable.

The cockpit contained two unusual features compared with other fighters. First of course there were no switches to arm guns, and no firing button. Second the control column was mounted on the seat frame, so that when the adjustable

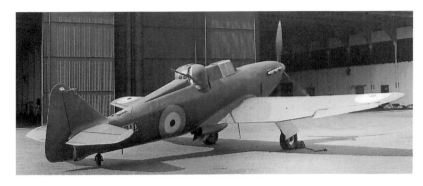

The prototype Defiant, K8310, fitted with the cannon turret, a standard A turret converted to take a single 20mm Hispano cannon. (*Crown Copyright A & AEE*)

seat was moved the column remained in the same relative position to the pilot's hand.

The turret was the standard A type, a self-contained unit, apart from electrical and intercommunication leads and warm air from the radiator, which came in through a slip ring in the base. To try to counteract the high drag of the unit, retractable fairings lay fore and aft of it, which rose and lowered automatically as the turret revolved and the guns passed over them. They were built of spruce and three-ply, and were operated by pneumatic jacks actuated by cams fitted to the turret.

The aircraft's hydraulic system was entirely separate to the turret's and operated the undercarriage and flaps from an engine driven hydraulic pump, with a manual back-up pump. A pneumatic system operated the retractable fairings and the wheel brakes. The pneumatic reservoir was kept at pressure by an engine driven compressor, but this did not work well at idling speed, as a pilot in a No.410 (Cougar) Squadron, RCAF, at Drem was to discover. He taxied his aircraft from one side of the aerodrome to the other, and the low engine revolutions were not sufficient to top up the pneumatic reservoir, which he discovered when he tried to apply the brakes near the hangars he was approaching. The brakes did not work, the Defiant swung with the wind and rolled downhill straight at one of the hangars. It hit the sliding door and knocked it from its channel. As the 20 ft high door slowly toppled forward the pilot hunched down into his cockpit, and the startled mechanics inside the hangar ran for their lives. Luckily the door fell on an upright propeller blade and damage to the aircraft was not great.

From the outset three assembly lines ran through the factory between blast walls. The different sub-assemblies had their own lines, either elsewhere in the factory or at sub-contractors. Redwing Aircraft made fuselage sections at their factory in Heath Town on the Wednesfield Road. Daimler were to start wing manufacture in Coventry, but were bombed two days after receiving the drawings. They moved to the redundant Courtauld's factory in Wolverhampton, and began production there. Boulton Paul also opened their own shadow factories in a policy initiated by the Air Ministry in 1938.

On the assembly line the wing centre-sections were positioned first and then the already complete fuselages were lowered onto them. Engines, turrets, and further components were installed as they moved down the production line, and finally they were moved into the flight sheds. Here the outer wings and propeller were attached, and they were wheeled out for their first test flight.

Day Fighter Operations

The first unit to receive Defiants was No.264 (Madras Presidency) Squadron which had reformed at Sutton Bridge, near Wisbech in Lincolnshire, on 30 October, 1939. The squadron was one of two named Madras Presidency, the other being No.234. Such named squadrons dated from the First World War when the entire complement of aircraft for a unit was purchased by a particular benefactor, usually a distant part of the then Empire, and which was then honoured by having the squadron named after them.

No.264 (Madras Presidency) Squadron Defiants early in 1940.

No.264 Squadron was equipped with Fairey Battles and Miles Magisters until the first Defiants arrived, and moved south to Martlesham Heath in Suffolk to receive them. The first three, L5959, L5960 and L5961 arrived on 8 December, 1939, followed quickly by L5956, L5957, L5964, L5968, L6970 and L6972. The Squadron began familiarising itself with the new aircraft and working towards operational status.

There were numerous teething problems with the Defiants, with frequent engine malfunctions and hydraulic problems. This led to the grounding of the aircraft on 28 January, 1940, while teams from Rolls-Royce and Lockheed worked on the problems. The ban was lifted during the first week in February and flying resumed. The aircraft were finished in the standard day fighter scheme of dark brown and dark green shadow-shading on the upper surfaces with undersides half black and half grey. The squadron letters for No.264 were PS, and these were carried on the fuselage sides together with the individual aircraft letter on the other side of the RAF roundel – which in No.264's case came in several styles.

The Defiant had always been regarded as a fighter for both day and night operations, and No.264 Squadron began night flying training on 15 February. In some ways the Defiant was not ideal for night flying, with a landing speed of over 100 mph, and full control in the air only fully retained at over 120 mph, but it made up for this with its wide-track undercarriage, and the relatively good forward and downward visibility for the pilot, at least compared with the Spitfire and Hurricane. Also, before the days of airborne radar, it had the advantage in night-time interceptions of two pairs of eyes.

The Squadron, and its commander, Sqn Ldr Phillip Hunter, had the problem of not only introducing a new type of aircraft into service, but of also working out novel operational tactics. There had never been a fighter with all its fire-power concentrated in a turret, and for the first time the gunner would control any engagement. Tactics had to be worked out to place the aircraft in the best position for the gunner to fire, and therefore the two men in each aircraft had to co-ordinate their efforts. In addition the tactics of the whole Squadron had to be re-worked. If cross-over attacks were made against enemy bombers it was important to co-ordinate the movements of each Defiant to achieve the best results and to avoid mid-air collisions.

On 20 March two sections, each of three aircraft were declared operational, and were detached to Wittering two days later, with Sqn Ldr Hunter commanding. For the rest of March and through most of April the Squadron flew convoy patrols, without encountering any German aircraft.

On 10 May all that was to change, when the Germans launched their Blitzkrieg upon the Low Countries. No.264 Squadron was moved in its entirety to Duxford and placed on full alert. It was the only Defiant squadron yet in service, as the RAF had only received 56 of the 536 Defiants so far ordered.

Two days later 'A' Flight went into action for the first time, with Sqn Ldr Hunter in command of Red Section, along with POs Young and Whitehouse, and Flt Lt Cooke commanding Yellow section with POs Barwell and Whitley. Their gunners were LAC King, LAC Johnson, Sgt Smalley, Cpl Lippett, Sgt Quinne, and LAC Turner respectively. They landed at Horsham St Faith to refuel, fittingly near the Boulton & Paul factory at Riverside, and then joined up with six Spitfires of No.66 Squadron.

Whitley and Turner returned to Duxford soon after take-off the aircraft having developed a fault, but the others flew on, to patrol off the Dutch coast near The Hague, each Defiant section trailing a Spitfire section. Soon after the patrol began they saw a Ju 88 bombing three destroyers. As it dived to make its escape Red section dived to cut it off and initiated a cross-over attack by each aircraft in turn. The bomber was repeatedly hit and crashed into a field with smoke pouring from both its engines. The Defiant had for the first time proved its effectiveness as a 'bomber destroyer', and a Boulton Paul aircraft had gone into action for the first time.

Meanwhile an He 111 was seen flying at about 3,000 ft. As the Spitfires attacked it from the rear, the two remaining aircraft of Yellow Section made cross-over attacks beneath it from each quarter. The He 111 also crashed into a field, but was credited to No.66 Squadron's account.

The following day 'B' Flight took off for a similar joint operation with No.66 Squadron, with very different results. Intense Dutch anti-aircraft fire caused the formation to change direction over Ijmuiden, only to run into German anti-aircraft fire over Maasluis. Shortly afterwards a large formation of Ju 87s

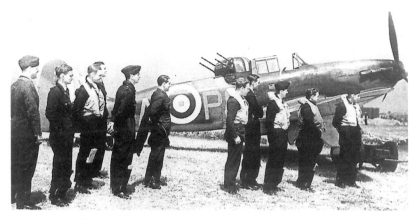

Aircrew of No.264 Squadron at Manston on 29 May, 1940, the day they were credited with the destruction of 37 German aircraft without loss to themselves. (*Wg Cdr E Barwell*)

was seen, and the Spitfires dived from 6,000 ft, followed by the Defiants. In the resulting mêlée No.264 Squadron shot down four of the dive-bombers, but then a large force of Bf 109s attacked, and five of the Defiants were shot down, L6955, L6958, L6960, L6969, and L6977. Only L6974 flown by PO Kay with LAC Jones survived, though their aircraft was damaged in the desperate battle. It landed at Knocke to refuel and then flew home. One pilot, PO Thomas baled out after his gunner was killed, and a gunner, PO Hatfield, managed the difficult feat of baling out from a Defiant turret; both men eventually finding their way back to England. One of the Bf 109s was shot down by the Defiants, so in effect the score was even, with five aircraft on each side lost, but it did not bode well for the future.

The Squadron moved to Manston on 23 May and began flying patrols over the Channel. On the 24th the newly promoted Flt Lt Whitehouse, with his gunner PO Scott shot down a Bf 110 in the Dunkirk region. On 27 May a formation of twelve He 111s was broken up and three shot down, with two others damaged, again proving that the Defiant could be an effective bomber destroyer. Two Bf 109s were also claimed that day, but the following day the German fighters took their revenge. The Squadron was attacked by around thirty Bf 109s and three Defiants were shot down, (L6953, L6959, and L7007), those of Flt Lt Whitehouse/PO Scott, PO McLeod/PO Hatfield, and Sgt Daisley/LAC Revill. Six of the Bf 109s were claimed by No.264 Squadron.

On 29 May twelve aircraft of No.264 Squadron patrolled over Dunkirk with three squadrons of Hurricanes. The Defiants were 'bounced' from behind by six Bf 109s flying out of the sun. The German pilots had obviously mistaken their prey for Hurricanes, and received a rude shock from the concentrated fire of 48 Browning machine-guns. Two of the Bf 109s were shot down, but then No.264 Squadron was attacked by twenty-one Bf 110s. In the mêlée fifteen of the German fighters were claimed, together with a Ju 87 which had strayed into the battle, for the loss of no Defiants. Only the aircraft of PO Kay/LAC Jones was even damaged, though extensively, Jones having baled out when his turret was hit.

The Squadron was refuelled and re-armed, and in the evening flew another patrol over Dunkirk. They came upon forty Ju 87s and three Ju 88s bombing the town. In the ensuing battle eighteen of the Ju 87s and one of the Ju 88s were claimed, again for no losses to the Defiants, though Sgt Thorne's aircraft was badly damaged and he had to land at Manston with just one undercarriage leg down. During the day No.264 Squadron had claimed the amazing total of thirty-seven enemy aircraft destroyed for no loss to themselves, and the following day a congratulatory telegram was received from No.11 Group headquarters. Research into German Quartermaster's records have since shown that a total of only fourteen German aircraft were lost on that day to all sources, but there is no doubt that this was the high spot of the Defiant's career.

The fact that the Luftwaffe had now got the measure of the Defiant was brought home on 31 May. Although No.264 Squadron claimed nine German aircraft shot down, five more Defiants were lost. Two of these, L6961 and L6980 collided, but it must be assumed that the collision was caused by combat circumstances; and all four crew members were missing presumed killed. The other three aircraft lost were L6968, L6972, L6975, and only the crew of L6972 were saved after ditching in the Channel. The Squadron's score was now sixty-five enemy aircraft claimed destroyed for the loss of fourteen Defiants. It had to be withdrawn from the battle of the Channel in order to recover, and it returned to Duxford.

Sqn Ldr Hunter was awarded the DSO, and Flt Lt Cooke the DFC, for the success of the Dunkirk battles. The Squadron received new aircraft to replace those lost, and new pilots including J Bailey, D Hughes, R Knocker and H Percy. The Rotol two-speed propeller units were replaced by de Havilland constant-speed units during this period. Comparative trials at Boscombe Down on L6954 had shown that there was a reduction of climbing time to 10,000 ft from 6.7 to 5 min, to 15,000 ft from 10.1 to 8 min, and to 25,000 ft from 23.8 to 18.2 min; though there was little change to the top speed.

In spite of little contact with the Luftwaffe there were still losses of course, the pilot of L7004 lost control over Linton on 7 June, and the crew baled out, and on the 11th L6970 was stalled while landing at Manston and one of the crew died in the crash. On the 13th the pilot of L6964 suffered considerable embarrassment when he taxied into a gun emplacement at Duxford, causing extensive damage to the aircraft. On 19 July L6963 was being ferried from Farnborough to Duxford by a pilot from No.4 Ferry Pilot's Pool when the tailwheel hit the hedge at Duxford and the aircraft crashed into a field, and this was not the only disaster to strike the Defiant that day.

Another Defiant squadron had come into being, No.141. It had been reformed at Prestwick in February and began receiving its Defiants in April at Turnhouse. It was declared operational on 3 June and moved to West Malling in July with a detachment at Hawkinge. They began flying coastal patrols and on 19 July nine Defiants flew a patrol south of Folkestone at 5,000 ft, led by Sqn Ldr Richardson in the usual formation of Vics of three flying in line astern. They were bounced out of the sun by the Bf 109Es of III JG 51, who had just escorted Bf 110s attacking a trawler and with enough fuel in their tanks had decided to fly a sweep towards the English coast.

They sighted and recognised the Defiants, and were pleased to find there were no Hurricanes or Spitfires around. In the first pass two Defiants were shot

A Defiant of No.125 Squadron being serviced sometime in 1941. (*Wg Cdr E Barwell*)

down. The German pilots then proved they now knew all about the Defiant by attacking from dead astern and below, the aircraft's main blind spot, and four more Defiants were lost. The aircraft lost were L6974, L6983, L6995, L7009, L7015, L7016. In addition L7001 piloted by PO Ian MacDougall was badly hit and the engine stopped. With his cockpit filling with smoke, MacDougall dived the aircraft, told his gunner to bale out and began undoing his own straps. There was no reply from his gunner, and with the sea getting close, MacDougall levelled out, at which point the Merlin spluttered into life. He crashed at Hawkinge village on his return and the aircraft was written-off, the gunner was not in his turret and his body was never found. Only L6999 and L7014 returned to base, and four pilots and five gunners had been killed in all.

The survivors claimed they had shot down four of the Bf 109s, and the Commander of III JG 51, Hauptmann Hannes Trautloft certainly crash-landed in France after being hit. This action had been a devastating blow to No.141 Squadron, and two days later it was withdrawn to Prestwick to recover in an area where it would only meet unescorted bombers, leaving No.264 Squadron as the sole Defiant-equipped day fighter unit during the rest of the Battle of Britain.

No.264 Squadron, after a short spell at Fowlmere in Cambridgeshire from 3 to 23 July, moved north to Kirton-in-Lindsey on 23 July, with 'A' Flight detached to Ringway for the defence of Manchester, and 'B' Flight at Coleby Grange. The first night patrols were flown and PO Whitley/Sgt Turner in L6985 exchanged fire with an He 111, but it escaped into cloud, and though they claimed its destruction, there was no confirmation.

On 22 August they were moved south once more, to Hornchurch, with

Manston as the forward base. With the Battle of Britain at its height the Defiants could not have been more to the fore, and action was to follow quickly. Early in the morning of the 24th nine aircraft were moved forward to Manston, and were refuelling, when Ju 88s dived out of the sun. The Defiants scrambled, seven of them managing to get off the ground, but Sqn Ldr Hunter and two others were trapped against the sea by Bf 109s and shot down.

The aircraft of Flt Lt C Colquohoun was slow in starting and he took off after the others, who were engaging the incoming raid. Visibility was not good, but he sighted two fighters which he thought were the other part of his section, and flew to join up with them. A cannon shell in his fuselage which ignited the Very cartridges revealed his error, and he took evasive action and returned to base. He claimed to have been attacked by He 113s, evidence of the effectiveness of a German mis-information ploy. They had painted the dozen He 100 prototypes which had been built, in fictitious squadron markings, and then released photographs which had convinced the RAF for a time that the fictitious He 113 was in widespread service, when in fact the handful of He 100s built were only ever used for ad hoc defence of Heinkel's own aerodrome.

Just after lunch Hornchurch was attacked by a large force of Ju 88s and Bf 109s, with No.264 Squadron refuelling on the ground. A number of aircraft managed to take off to engage the attackers and three Ju 88s were shot down by Sqn Ldr Garvin, PO Whitley and Sgt Thorne, another being damaged by PO Knocker. PO Barwell shot down a fighter which he claimed was another of the fictitious He 113s. Three of the Defiants were lost. Aircraft lost were L6966, L7027, and N1535. At 15.40 there was another raid of Ju 88s and He 111s escorted by Bf 109s, this time on Manston, and the Defiants rose once more to meet it.

Sqn Ldr Garvin shot down two Ju 88s from the main formation while PO Welsh shot down a straggler, and then had to fight off three Bf 109s which attacked him, damaging one. PO Young also shot down a straggler, an He 111 which he destroyed in an overtaking attack. Flt Lt Banham and PO Goodall both attacked a Ju 88 which they claimed as damaged. PO Easkin and his gunner Sgt Machin in L6965, fought desperately against six attacking Bf 109s, but were finally shot down.

The following day L7002 was returning from an evening patrol over Dover with oil on the windscreen and overshot Hornchurch, severely damaging it. On the 26th a large raid of Do17s was intercepted near Dover. Flt Lt Banham led the formation, attacking the bombers from below. He shot down one and was then attacked by the escorting Bf 109s, his aircraft L7025 was hit by a cannon shell and he and his gunner, baled out into the Channel, where he floated for an hour and a half before being rescued. L6985 was also shot down by the Bf 109s, but when PO Goodall was also attacked by them, he managed to avoid being shot down and went on to destroy a Do 17. PO Hughes shot down two of the bombers as did Sgt Thorne/Sgt Barker, who were then also attacked by a Bf 109. Their Defiant, L7005, was hit and developed glycol and oil leaks, as they tried to reach the coast at low level. The Bf 109 kept attacking, and they managed to shoot it down before making a crash landing in a field near Herne Bay.

On the 27th some of the Defiants moved to Hornchurch's other advanced landing ground at Rochford, near Southend. The following day they were scrambled at around 09.00 to meet a raid heading for Folkestone. The new CO, in L7021, had trouble getting his wheels retracted as they climbed steadily. At 17,000 ft they saw the incoming Heinkels, and turned through 180 deg climbing up underneath them at around 160 mph. As they opened fire on the bombers from below the Bf 109s of Adolf Galland's JG 26 came down to attack. L7021 burst into flames, and though the CO baled out, his gunner, Flt Lt Ash, died. L7026 and N1574 were also shot down, with both crew members dying in each case, one of them Whitley, another of the Squadron's veterans. Among the damaged Defiants was that of PO Bailey who shot down a Heinkel before being hit by a Bf 109 and descending to a successful wheels-up landing in a field.

For the afternoon's sortie there were only three serviceable Defiants. No.264 Squadron had been shattered for a second time, for in four days they had lost eleven aircraft and fourteen aircrew, and were withdrawn the following day to Kirton-in-Lindsey. It was now abundantly clear that the Defiant did not stand a chance against the Bf 109, and could only henceforth be used in sectors out of range of German single-seaters, or on night-time operations. The two Battle of Britain Defiant Squadrons had fought courageously, had destroyed more German aircraft than they had lost, though not to the degree which their confirmed kills would suggest, and were now to be fully committed to another exacting role, at night.

Further Development

A further production order for Defiants was placed in December 1939 for 150 aircraft with serials in the range from T3911 to T4121, and trials were being undertaken to find different roles for the type.

The original specification had required provision for fitting the light series bomb racks under the wings, and, later in February 1940, L6950 was fitted with these and dive-bombing and ground strafing trials were undertaken at Orfordness. Bomb-aiming was found to be satisfactorily accurate below 500 ft but poor above 1,000 ft. The optimum angles were found to be 40–45 deg with a dive from 5,000 ft down to 1,500 ft requiring 800 ft to recover, and a shallow angle of 15–20 degrees from 1,500–500 ft. The maximum angle tried was 60 deg but this required 1,400 ft to recover. The maximum indicated airspeed at 60 deg was 400 mph.

Another Defiant, L6968, was used for trials in the army co-operation role, which must have proved satisfactory to a certain extent, because No.2 Squadron received a few Defiants for this role in August 1940, though they were never declared operational and were quickly withdrawn.

There followed further speed trials of production aircraft, which with all the operational equipment installed suffered higher weights than the prototypes. The Defiants were tested against Hurricanes and the results were disappointing, one aircraft, even with +12 lb of boost and 2,950 rpm, could only manage 282 mph at 10,000 ft and all the others displayed poorer performance than expected.

Though the operational use of the Defiant was still proving a problem for the men required to use it, a further order was placed with Boulton Paul in February 1940, for 50 Defiants which would be serialled V1106–V1141 and V1170–V1183. The events over Dunkirk, which tended to vindicate the turret-fighter protagonists had prompted the largest order yet placed with Boulton Paul. In

July 280 Defiants were ordered to be serialled in batches from AA281 to AA670.

The first 87 Defiants had been fitted with Rotol two-speed propellers, but subsequent aircraft were fitted with de Havilland constant-speed units and some of the earlier aircraft were retro-fitted. The aircraft used at Boscombe Down for trials of the new unit, L6954, had achieved a top speed of 302 mph at 20,000 ft and a service ceiling of 30,000 ft, with improved take-off runs.

Further improvements in performance were sought with more powerful engines, and the Merlin XX giving 1,260 hp at 3,000 rpm at 11,750 ft, was finally chosen. This engine was fitted with a two-speed supercharger, giving 6 lb/sq in boost or 12 lb/sq in by lifting a catch on the throttle quadrant. Boulton Paul converted N1550 to the new specification which also featured a pressurised fuel system and increased fuel tankage with the existing 52 gal tanks in each wing centre-section plus extra tanks in each outer wing, a 27 gal tank to port and a 28 gal tank to starboard. Redesigned engine mounts and a deeper radiator were also needed, together with a longer engine cowling. These changes also required a slightly larger rudder and the weights of the Mk II Defiant, as it was designated, rose to 8,424 lb loaded and 6,282 lb empty.

Defiant Mk II prototype, N1550, at Boscombe Down with tropical oil cooler under the nose. (*Crown Copyright, A & AEE*)

N1550 first flew in its redesigned form on 20 July, 1940, but suffered an unfortunate accident only a week later. On the 27th Cecil Feather was taxi-ing N1550 along the taxiway from the factory to the aerodrome when it collided head-on with N1639 coming the other way! Robin Lindsay Neale had just finished test flying the standard production N1639 and was taxi-ing back to the flight sheds. Neither pilot was hurt but the 'gunners' received slight injuries and had to be taken to hospital. Unfortunately it took three weeks to repair N1550, holding up the Mk II programme as another conversion, N1551, was not ready until later in the summer.

Speed increases were only small, with maximum speeds of 303 mph at 12,000 ft, 315 mph at 16,000 ft, and 313 mph at 19,000 ft, but cruising speed was also improved. Eventually enough Merlin XX engines were found to build 210 of the

Boulton Paul's test pilots (left to right) chief test pilot Flt Lt Cecil Feather, George Skelton, and Robin Lindsay Neale (later also to become chief test pilot).

Defiants ordered in July as Mk IIs, and seven of the Mk I aircraft were converted on the production line, so that only 63 of this order were eventually built as Mk Is.

Further development of the 20 mm cannon mount acquired from SAMM along with the rights to the four-gun turret, also took place on the Defiant. The pedestal mount had been tested in the nose of Overstrand K8176 and in May 1938 agreement was reached with the Ministry of Aircraft Production to fit an enclosed mounting for a single gun on the second prototype, K8320. A standard turret was adapted to take the cannon on the starboard side (when the turret was facing aft). Delays in completion of this aircraft, meant the first trials actually took place on K8310, the first prototype, in July 1939 at the A & AEE.

It was discovered that there was a substantial increase in torque on the turret as it was revolved at speeds greater than 190 mph. H A Hughes decided the drag of the cannon barrel, which was responsible for this undesirable effect, could be alleviated by fitting to the barrel a streamlined fairing, which would align itself automatically in the airstream, no matter where it was pointed. Design studies for such a device had been made in 1935 for fitting to the four-gun turret, but they had proved to be unnecessary. The fairing as fitted proved to be rather unstable, and the problem was shelved for the time being.

A new role was found for K8310 in the days after Dunkirk, Boulton Paul took the aircraft, without the turret, sprayed it in standard day fighter camouflage to serve as a development aircraft for a proposed stop-gap single-seat fighter to be fitted with two .303 in machine-guns in each wing. As deliveries of Hurricanes and Spitfires never became critical the project was not proceeded with, though further work was done on an improved twelve-gun Defiant-based single-seater, the P.94.

A Service modification of the turret was tested in 1941. Thirty-six sets of a sliding clear vision panel for the turret roof were ordered, and distributed to all Defiant squadrons for testing. They were seen as an aid to visibility in bad weather. They reduced head-room slightly, allowed a small amount of dirt and water into the turret, and it was left to individual squadrons whether they fitted them to further aircraft.

A new airframe became available for the cannon mounting early in 1941, N1622. It had crashed after an engagement with a Heinkel He 111 and had been returned to Wolverhampton for repair. One trial was undertaken with the cannon turret fitted to N3397 before that aircraft was delivered to the A & AEE where it was used for various trials. Tests with various barrel fairings fitted to the cannon mounting in N1622 continued into 1942. Fairings designed by both Boulton Paul and the RAE were tested, with actual firings over the ranges at Penrhos. The RAE two-piece fairing broke up immediately firing began, but the BPA fairing succeeded in alleviating the torque generated. The standard hydraulic motor was still incapable of turning the turret beyond 30 deg against the drag of the cannon, at 342 mph and above. Even above 300 mph a slight snaking set in when the gun was moved to the beam. This particular cannon turret was only seen as a development turret, being no more than a converted standard A turret. Once Boulton Paul had finished with it they were ordered, on 17 August, 1942, to clean it up and send it to the RAE for further tests.

Night Fighter Operations

As specialist night fighter squadrons No.264 and No.141 were assigned to 12 and 13 Group respectively. Their Defiants received an all-black paint scheme with low visibility red/blue roundels and grey unit lettering. Other than that the changes to convert a day fighter to a night fighter at that stage of the War were limited. Flame damper exhausts were fitted and the Perspex panel between the pilot's cockpit and the turret was eliminated.

Having being based at Prestwick since 25 July, with a detachment at Grangemouth, No.141 Squadron was moved to Dyce with a detachment at Montrose on 22 August. With the Luftwaffe switching from daytime attacks to the night-time Blitz on London, they moved to Turnhouse on 30 August and 'B' Flight was detached south to Biggin Hill on 13 September. It was not long before they claimed their first victims, PO Waddingham/Sgt Cumbers in N1552 claimed two He 111s, on the night of 15 September, though the kills were not confirmed. The following night Sgt Laurence/Sgt Chard in L6988 claimed a Ju 88 which crashed at Maidstone. 'B' Flight moved to Gatwick on 25 October. Meanwhile 'A' Flight had been operating from Turnhouse, but moved to Drem on 15 October to train in night fighting, and joined 'B' Flight at Gatwick on the 25th, moving on to Gravesend on 4 November.

On the night of 10 November Sgt Hamer/Sgt Hill exchanged fire with an intruder, and claimed it as a probable, but the Squadron's first confirmed night victory came on 22 December when PO Benson/PO Blair destroyed an He 111.

While based since 23 July at Kirton-in-Lindsey, No.264 Squadron operated detachments from Northolt, Luton and Martlesham Heath, at various times, before moving to Rochford on 29 October.

On 23 November PO Hughes/Sgt Gash were on patrol near Braintree when they saw an He 111 momentarily silhouetted by a searchlight. They closed in on the bomber and Gash got in a two-second burst, destroying one of the Heinkel's engines. Then the turret jammed, and Gash could not rotate or elevate his guns!

A Defiant Mk II night fighter, T4037, JT T of 256 Squadron with the turret fairings retracted.

Despite being caught by their own searchlights for a while they continued the attack. Hughes instructed Gash to fire while he attempted to align the aircraft so that the bullets would strike home. He almost collided with the Heinkel, so near were they. The bomber ran for the coast, shadowed by the Defiant, which had to turn back when low on fuel. Hughes and Gash were certain the Heinkel would have crashed at sea, but could only claim it as a probable. For this extraordinary action Hughes was awarded the DFC and Gash the DFM.

A third Defiant squadron formed before the Defiant was totally converted to night operations, No.307 (Lwow) Squadron, a Polish unit, was formed as a day fighter squadron at Kirton-in-Lindsey on 5 September. It moved to Jurby on the Isle of Man on 7 November, with detachments to Squires Gate and Cranage to cover the Northwest. They began night flying training in January 1941, and moved entirely to Squires Gate on the 23rd. Their first combat was on 12 March when an He 111 was damaged over Ruthin, but their first confirmed victory came after they moved to Colerne on 26 March.

On 12 April Sgt Jankowiak/Sgt Lipinski opened fire on an He 111 at 13,500 ft from a distance of only 40 yards. The gunner fired two bursts into the bomber's nose and saw pieces fly off and internal explosions. The Heinkel dived steeply through cloud and was later seen to crash by the Observer Corps. Four days later Flg Off Lewandowski/Sgt Zakrocki attacked another He 111 in the classic Defiant manner. Having seen it 300 yards ahead, they closed to about 50 yards and 75 ft below to open fire. They stayed with the bomber, pouring all their ammunition at it, and the Heinkel was last seen diving to the ground with smoke pouring from the port engine.

Two new Defiant night-fighter squadrons were formed on 23 November, 1940, No.255 re-forming at Kirton-in-Lindsey, and No.256 re-forming at Catterick. No.255 was the first to become operational, on 5 January, 1941, and flew its first operation four days later. The first success was not until 10 February, when two He 111s were claimed as probables over the Humber. The Squadron was dogged by poor serviceability and had a high accident rate. On 2 February N3306 stalled on approach to Kirton and crashed, with one fatality.

A successful Defiant night-fighter crew, Sqn Ldr E C Deanesley DFC and Jack Scott DFM, with their 256 Squadron Defiant in 1941. At least four kills are marked on the fuselage.
(*Wg Cdr E C Deanesley*)

Two weeks later N3334 overshot and collided with N1727. On 4 May the crew of N3333 baled out southeast of Lincoln after explosions in the engine. Hurricanes supplemented the Defiants from March 1941.

Their best night's work was on 8/9 May when the Squadron claimed five He 111s destroyed, though one of them may have been claimed by two pilots. The Luftwaffe had sent a force of 120 bombers against Hull and the first of them was shot down by the CO, Sqn Ldr Smith, flying a Hurricane. This same He 111 might also have been the one attacked and claimed by PO Wyrill in his Defiant, one of four claimed by Defiants. PO Wynne-Wilson also shot down an He 111, which crashed near Patrington in Yorkshire, and Flt Lt Trousdale shot down two bombers, one near Spurn Head and the other southwest of Leconfield. On 15 May No.255 Squadron moved to Hibaldstow, a new station also in Lincolnshire. In July they began re-equipping with Beaufighters.

A detachment of No.256 Squadron became operational in February at Middle Wallop, and the rest of the Squadron on 1 April. They moved to Pembrey in Carmarthenshire on 4 April, and their first victory came two days later when Flt Lt West destroyed a Ju 88 off Southport. On 6 February they moved to Colerne with a detachment to Middle Wallop, and on 26 March they moved back north to Squires Gate with a detachment at Ballyhalbert. On 10 April Flg Off Deanesley shot down an He 111 over Smethwick.

No.256 also suffered a high accident rate. On 20 February N3446 had struck some trees and a stone wall in the darkness near to Colerne and one crew member was killed. On the 26th of the same month N3520 was crash-landed near Upavon due to fuel shortage, the pilot was killed but the air-gunner had baled out. On 12 March, operating from Middle Wallop, N3451 crashed into a hill at Imber. N1694 was abandoned just before midnight on 7 April after the crew became lost on a patrol, and the following night, at 04.50, N3424 lost height just after taking off and both crew were killed in the resulting crash. Three days later another Defiant, N3460, was abandoned in the air at 03.00

when the crew became lost in bad weather, the aircraft crashing near Cannock in Staffordshire. On 15 May T3955 crashed at Bolton-le-Sands after control was lost during a training flight at 01.45. On 27 August No.256 suffered their worst accident when N1745 collided with a Blackburn Botha over Blackpool Station. Both crew in the Defiant and three in the Botha were killed together with fourteen people in the station.

This catalogue of accidents, by no means complete, and by no means restricted to one squadron, shows the problems presented by night flying over a blacked-out countryside in wartime, with few navigation aids to help the crew. Yet the Defiant crews were not only supposed to find their way, they also had to find German bombers in the darkness with nothing but two pairs of eyes to help them, and a ground control which could only put them in the vicinity of the raiders. Furthermore, just to show the dangers they faced were not just from the weather and the darkness of the night, on 7 May N3500 was shot down by a Ju 88 near Widnes, though the crew successfully baled out.

One more squadron received Defiants before the end of 1940. No.151 Squadron had been a Hurricane day fighter squadron which converted to night operations in November 1940. In December it began receiving Defiants at Bramcote, though retaining some of the Hurricanes. On the 22nd it moved to Wittering with a detachment at Coltishall, and its first victory with Defiants came on 15 January, 1941, when Sgt Bodien in N3387 destroyed a Do 17. It was not until 9 April that the next victory took place, when a raid on Birmingham was intercepted and three aircraft were shot down, with one probable. There were six more victories in May.

No.85 Squadron was another Hurricane night-fighter squadron which began to receive Defiants in January 1941. They viewed the arrival of the Defiants and the new gunners with misgivings, the only good aspect of the change seemed to be the chance to give their ground crew a flight now and then. Snow and fog delayed them becoming operational on Defiants while still using the Hurricanes, and they flew only three sorties with Defiants before reverting to being an all-single-seater squadron, just before re-equipping with Havocs. All nine Defiants received by No.85 were passed on to the next long-term user of Defiants which was No.96 Squadron. Again it was a Hurricane squadron which converted to Defiants in March 1941 at Cranage, near Middlewich in Cheshire.

From Cranage they also operated a detachment at Squires Gate, for the defence of the Northwest, and on 6 May scored their first success when Flg Off Verity destroyed an He 111, and then probably destroyed a Ju 88 in a second sortie. In the same raid both Sgt Taylor and Sgt Scott shot down He 111s. The total score for May was seven bombers, but after that the sector went very quiet.

No.141 Squadron also had a successful May, they claimed eight aircraft in the month, operating from Ayr, where they had moved on 29 April, with detachments at Acklington and Drem. No.264 Squadron, after a spell at Biggin Hill had moved to West Malling on 14 April, and began intruder operations. On 8 May they shot down two and damaged three more while on these operations. Like the other Defiant squadrons, they found trade dropped away in the summer, as the Luftwaffe turned its attentions East. May 1941 had been the most successful month with 23 kills recorded by all squadrons, following 14 in April, but there were to be only three more in the final seven months of the year.

As the second summer of the War approached there were thus seven Defiant night-fighter squadrons in operation, No.96 at Cranage, No.141 at Ayr, No.151 at Wittering, No.255 at Hibaldstowe, No.256 at Squires Gate, No.264 at West Malling, and No.307 at Exeter. June and July were to see four more Defiant night-fighter squadrons form, all with Commonwealth connections.

The first of these was No.125 (Newfoundland) Squadron which formed on 16 June at Colerne, becoming operational on 27 September at Fairwood Common in Glamorgan, covering South Wales, Bristol and Bath. The following day another Canadian night-fighter squadron formed at Digby, No.409 (Nighthawk) Squadron, but did not receive its own aircraft until 6 July, and flew its first operation on the 20th. A week later it moved to Coleby Grange and in August began converting to Beaufighters. The third Canadian unit was No.410 (Cougar) Squadron, which formed at Ayr on 30 June. It moved to Drem on 6 August with detachments at Acklington, Ouston and Dyce, though it saw little action. No.456 Squadron was Australia's first night-fighter squadron, forming at Valley in June 1941 though few Australians were actually posted to it. It became operational on 5 September, but began converting to Beaufighters the same month.

Many of the aircraft for these four squadrons came from the other Defiant units, as they began converting to Beaufighters, No.141 in June, No.255 in July, and No.307 in August. The last Defiant night-fighter squadron to form was No.153, which was created from 'A' Flight of No.256 Squadron at Ballyhalbert in County Down on 24 October. In defence of Northern Ireland they operated detachments at Limavady, Ballykelly, Eglinton and St Angelo.

Two Defiant squadrons co-operated in the ill-starred Turbinlite Havoc venture, No.264 from June 1941 and No.151 from August. The use of Defiants as the 'killer' aircraft escorting the Havoc with the searchlight mounted in its nose, was no more successful than using Hurricanes, the targets showing a marked reluctance to stay in the searchlight beam, which effectively destroyed the attackers night-vision. In December No.151 Squadron also developed the 'Flare Burning' tactic with the Havocs. When the Havoc detected a low flying enemy it would drop a flare, and the Defiant would then, in theory move in for the attack. As the flares had no forward velocity, unlike the target, it is not surprising that no victories were recorded using this method.

Improvement in the equipment of the Defiant squadrons was to take two forms. First they began to acquire airborne interception radar. The Blenheims and later Beaufighters were given priority with this equipment, and so equipping the Defiants did not start until the autumn of 1941, though Boulton Paul had received drawings of the installation in November 1940. The sets installed were the AI Mk4 radar, more compact than the AI Mk3 sets which had only gone to the more commodious Blenheims, but still of limited use. It had a maximum range of four miles and a minimum of 600 ft, but was of no use if the distance of the target was less than the height of the fighter above the ground, as ground clutter swamped the signal.

The Defiants were converted by Boulton Paul, with an arrow-type aerial on each wing and a small H aerial on the starboard side of the fuselage just in front of the cockpit. The transmitter itself was sited behind the turret, and the receiver, power-pack and control box were behind the pilot's cockpit. The radar was operated by the pilot, which rather reduced its usefulness in the Defiant.

A Defiant Mk IA at the factory, showing the array of radar aerials.

The pilot's night vision was badly affected by looking at the Cathode-Ray Tube, which was sited to the pilot's left with the control panel to his right. The radar-equipped Defiant was designated Mk IA, and was entering service at the same time that the Mk II was beginning to appear. The Mk II equipped with radar does not seem to have been differently designated, to the Mk II without radar.

The Mk IA served first with No.264 Squadron, and then with Nos.96, 125, 256 and 410. No.264 Squadron began receiving Mk IIs equipped with the AI Mk 4 sets in September 1941. No.151 Squadron also received its first Mk IIs in September 1941, and No.125 Squadron received the first of their's the following month, but also used the Mk IA. No.96 Squadron, however, did not receive Mk IAs until February 1942, and did not receive Mk IIs until April 1942. The fifth and last night-fighter squadron to receive Mk IIs was No.256, which began equipping with them in May 1942, but gave them up the following month as they were acquiring the Beaufighter IF and were re-assigned as a shipping patrol squadron.

An action on 19 February, 1942, probably hastened the Defiant's final demise. Four aircraft of No.151 Squadron intercepted some Do 217s and Ju 88s attacking shipping in the North Sea. Though they claimed a Do 217 shot down and four others damaged, they were unable to catch the escaping bombers. Faster aircraft were now urgently needed, and were soon forthcoming.

In April and May 1942 most of the surviving Defiant units were re-equipped; No.96, No.125, No.256, and No.410 with Beaufighters, and No.151 and No.264 with Mosquitos. Most retained some Defiants until June or July, and the last did not leave No.125 Squadron until September, but the era of the Defiants as a fighter was effectively over, and new uses had to be found for them.

Air-Sea Rescue Operations

Air-Sea Rescue squadrons were a new phenomena at the start of the Second World War, but as the War progressed they became more and more important. Largely equipped initially with Lysanders discarded by the Army co-operation squadrons and Walrus amphibians acquired from the Navy, consideration was given early in 1942 for the use of the Defiant in this role. Boulton Paul modified an aircraft to take an M-type dinghy in a cylindrical container attached to the bomb lugs under each wing. Tests were undertaken in February with both the Mk I and Mk II, and the aircraft proved to have certain advantages over the Lysander. They had a quicker transit time, to the area of any downed airmen, and were better able to protect themselves against German interference, often by Luftwaffe aircraft on similar missions.

In March the decision to use Defiants in the ASR role was taken. No.281 Squadron was formed on 29 March, 1942, in 13 Group, with Defiant ASR Mk Is (converted Mk I fighters). It was based at Ouston, Northumberland, with a detachment at Drem. Four more ASR Squadrons were equipped with Defiants in May, No.275 at Valley with detachments at Andreas on the Isle of Man and Eglinton, Northern Ireland; No.276 at Harrowbeer in Devon, with detachments at Roborough, Porthreath, Warmwell, Perranporth, and Fairwood Common; No.277 at Stapleford Tawney with detachments at Martlesham Heath, Hawkinge, and Shoreham; and No.278 at North Coates in Lincolnshire, later moving to Coltishall.

Of the 76 Defiants used by the ASR Squadrons, by far the largest number went to No.277, which operated over the Channel, and used 31 of them. No.276, further west down the Channel used 20, but No.278 used just 12, No.281 used nine, and No.275 only five.

The prototype under-wing life-raft installation for ASR Defiants.

262

Of course operating single-engined aircraft, over the sea for long periods could be a hazardous business. Among the ASR Defiants which were lost were N3516 of 276 Squadron which failed to return from an ASR mission off Dodman Point, Cornwall, on 7 November, 1942, T4051 of 276 Squadron, which was abandoned in the air in bad weather after an ASR search, at West Stafford, Dorset, on 22 January, 1943, and N3392 of 277 Squadron which ditched 25 miles east of Leiston in Suffolk, while on a search for a bomber crew on 27 January, 1943.

On 19 August, 1942, twelve ASR Defiants of No.277 Squadron provided ASR cover for the Dieppe Raid. On 7 December, 1942, No.277 moved to Gravesend with detachments at Martlesham Heath, Hawkinge, Warmwell and Hurn.

A No.277 Squadron aircraft, V1117, had the dubious honour of being the 48th and last Defiant to be shot down. Operating from Stapleford Tawney on 25 July, 1942, it was shot down 4 miles north of Dunkirk by an Fw 190, both crew members dying. Though no comfort to those unfortunate men, it is perhaps fitting that the last Defiant lost to enemy action should be in the same area where so many others had been lost, and where the Defiant had had its finest hour.

After about six months operation in the ASR role, it was decided that the Defiant was not really suitable after all. It had a much wider turning circle than the Lysander, and more importantly, a much higher minimum speed. After some thought it was decided to replace them in the high-speed search role by Spitfire IIs. Re-equipment began around the turn of the year, but Defiants remained in service with No.277 Squadron until May 1943 and with the other three ASR Squadrons until June.

The Moonshine Operations

One other squadron was to operate Defiants operationally, No.515. The Telecommunications Research Establishment, the cover name for the experimental radar establishment, developed a number of radar jamming devices during the War. Two different pieces of equipment were used in Defiants, code-named Moonshine and Mandrel. The first of these was Moonshine which worked by re-transmitting the signal from German Freya radar, and thus increasing the strength of the apparent echo, giving a spurious return which looked like a large formation of aircraft. The aircraft chosen to carry this equipment was the Mk II Defiant. After tests undertaken at Defford, a number of Defiant IIs were equipped with Moonshine and operated from Northolt by a unit known as The Defiant Flight, or the Special Duties Flight Northolt, which was established on 28 May, 1942. After a protracted development, the first operation was flown on 6 August. Eight Defiants began transmitting from a holding pattern off Portland, and thirty German fighters were scrambled to meet the apparent 'raid'. After this operational test, on 17 August the Defiants went out with a bomber sortie for the first time when they supported a US 8th Air Force raid on Rouen.

The Flight was expanded into a Squadron and given the number 515 on 1 October, four operations being flown the same month. They were known as

Moonshine Operations, and the Defiants involved would operate from a forward aerodrome such as West Malling, Tangmere, Exeter, or Coltishall, where they would have their own ground crew. They would fly ahead of the bombers giving spurious radar signals and causing German fighters to be sent to intercept in the wrong places. Operations were also flown during the day, to cover USAF B-17s and B-24s, as on 9 October when nine No.515 Squadron Defiants provided cover for a USAF raid on Lille. By the end of October thirty Moonshine operations had been flown, by which time it was losing its usefulness as the Germans were beginning to work out what was happening.

Mandrel worked by jamming German radar in the 10 MHz band, thereby cloaking the appearance of an oncoming raid on radar. The installation consisted of a T1408 transmitter, a Type 68 modulator, a Type 300 power unit and a transmission mast. Mandrel became operational on the night of 5/6 December.

On 29 October No.515 Squadron had moved to Heston, but operations were limited over the winter period because of bad weather. In February 58 operations were flown, two of the aircraft having inconclusive combats with German night fighters. In April as many as 144 operations were flown. On 3 April AA542 was shot at by friendly anti-aircraft guns, and hit a balloon cable in taking avoiding action, crashing into a field at Shotley, Suffolk.

On 21 May AA658 crashed into the Channel just before midnight while on an operation, both crew members dying, and on 8 June AA435 flew into Beachy Head in thick fog while returning to base.

On 1 June No.515 Squadron moved to Hunsdon in Hertfordshire, and during the same month began converting to Beaufighter IIFs which offered greater range, more room for new equipment and a greater chance of self-protection. Defiants remained in service until December 1943, but their last major operation was on 17 July, 1943, the last operational sortie by any Defiant unit. In fact the Squadron was considered non-operational from July to December 1943, its aircraft in a sorry state after standing in the open at various aerodromes.

One other unit used Defiants in the radar-countermeasures role, but in a training capacity, No.1692 Flight which was formed in late 1942 as the Radar Development Flight, being redesignated 1692 Flight in June 1943 for Serrate training. Serrate was a device for homing on to German airborne radars. The Defiants served as targets, fitted with transmitters in the 420 and 490 MHz bands, simulating the German AI radar. It operated Defiants (eleven in all) and Beaufighters, though its history is sketchy.

Target-Towing Operations

The use of the Defiant as a target-towing aircraft was first mooted in 1940, but nothing was done until the following year when an order was placed in July for a specialist target-towing aircraft based on the Mk II, with the Merlin XX engine. The order was for 140 aircraft with serials in batches from DR863 to DS159. The turret was not fitted, and the resulting space was occupied by an observer's station with a small canopy. For ground-to-air firing there was a drogue box beneath the fuselage and a large windmill on the starboard side, supplying

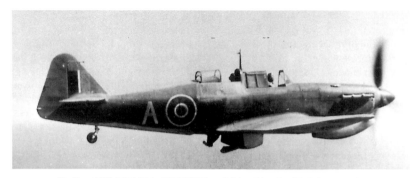

Defiant T.T.I DR977 of 779 FRU, at Blida, Algeria. (*R C Sturtivant*)

power to the Mk IIB winch. For air-to-air firing the Mk IIE winch was fitted with electrical drive. The resulting aircraft was capable of taking all standard targets, 3 ft or 4 ft sleeves, 4 ft or 5 ft 5 in flags, 3 ft astern attack target or high-speed flare. Confusingly, although the aircraft was based on the Mk II fighter, it was designated the T.T. Mk I.

Although the removal of the turret might have been expected to reduce weight and drag, the target-towing equipment more than made up for that, and the resulting aircraft weighed 8,250 lb loaded and could manage only 280 mph. The prototype, DR863, was delivered from Wolverhampton on 31 January, 1942, production of the target-towing version having started in the latter part of 1941.

Production of Mk II fighters in excess of demand was such that there was not enough space at Pendeford to store them, and some had their wings removed and were towed the few miles to RAF Cosford for storage. Forty Mk II fighters were actually built as T.T. Mk Is, *i.e.* AA614–AA633 and AA651–AA670. The last thirty of the Mk IIs with 'AA' serials were cancelled, as well as a further

Defiant T.T.I DS124 of 727 Squadron, Fleet Air Arm. (*R C Sturtivant*)

order for 298 Mk IIs with 'AV' serials. Subsequently 150 Mk II fighters were converted to T.T. Mk Is, many of them before use as fighters.

In view of the weight of the T.T. Mk I, and the resulting loss of performance, consideration was given to fitting the 1,620 hp Merlin 24 and trying to reduce the weight as much as possible. Design work indicated that the loaded weight could be reduced to 7,500 lb. In this form it was designated T.T. Mk II, but it was considered that the effort involved was not worth the improved performance.

Instead a programme to convert redundant Mk I fighters was instituted. Boulton Paul converted N3488 in a similar configuration to the T.T. Mk I, to serve as the prototype conversion. It went to Boscombe Down for testing early in 1942, and then to Farnborough for a further period of development. It had a loaded weight of 8,227 lb and a top speed of 250 mph. In late 1941 Reid & Sigrist of Desford, who were already Defiant sub-contractors, received an order to convert 150 Mk I fighters, and conversions began in 1942.

The prototype Defiant T.T.III conversion, N3488, at Pendeford.

Defiant target-tugs saw widespread service, many being fitted with tropical filters for operation in Africa and Asia. T.T. Mk IIIs were delivered initially to five Anti-aircraft Co-operation Squadrons, all receiving their first Defiants around March 1942. In 9 Group there was No.285 at Wrexham, with detachments at Honiley and Woodvale, moving to Honiley in October, with further detachments to High Ercall and Valley. In 10 Group there was No.286 Squadron at Colerne, with numerous detachments all over the southwest including South Wales, and later moving to Lulsgate Bottom, Zeals and Weston-super-Mare. In 11 Group in the southeast there was No.287 Squadron at Croydon with up to 13 detachments to various aerodromes. In 12 Group there was No.288 Squadron at Digby with detachments at Church Fenton and Duxford, and moving in December to Wellingore. Finally, in 13 Group there was No.289 Squadron at Kirknewton in Midlothian, with detachments in the north of England and Scotland, and moving in May to Turnhouse.

Later on in the War two further Anti-aircraft Co-operation Squadrons were formed, No.667 which was created from No.1622 and 1631 Flights at Gosport, both of which already operated Defiants, and No.691 Squadron which was created from No.1623 Flight at Roborough, though in February 1945 it moved to Harrowbeer.

A number of Anti-Aircraft Co-operation Units (AACUs) also used Defiants, including No.1 AACU at Weston Zoyland in Somerset, No.2 AACU, No.21 AACU which used just six Defiants in West Africa, No.22 AACU which used 54 Defiants at various places in India, No.23 AACU which used just two Defiants, No.25 AACU which used ten in East Africa, and No.26 AACU which used thirty. Also using the Defiant target-tug in India was No.1 Air Gunners School (India) at Bhopal.

A total of over 150 Defiant target-tugs were transferred to the Admiralty for use by Fleet Air Arm Units in many parts of the world. Many were taken from RAF units as they were replaced by Martinets, but others went directly to the Navy. They served in eighteen Fleet Requirements Units, half of them overseas, in such places as Trinidad, Cyprus, Malta, Gibraltar, East and West Africa and Ceylon.

AA327, a Defiant T.T.III in Fleet Air Arm service with No.776 FRU at Woodvale in early 1945. (*R C Sturtivant*)

Operation of Defiants in the tropics was not without difficulty, No.797 FRU in Ceylon, which had four Defiants, found that the heat of the day followed by the cold of the night played havoc with the plywood fairings. Laminations began separating, panel pins had continually to be pushed back in, and the ply often had to be re-covered with fabric.

Two Defiant T.T.Is, DR944 and DR945, were even transferred to the USAF for use by the No.11 Combat Crew Replacement Centre at Bovingdon. Few survived beyond 1945, though DS155 was not struck off charge in India until 1 January, 1947, and DR968 not until 27 February, 1947, serving with 26 AACU.

Training Operations

The first Operational Training Unit to acquire Defiants was No.5 at Aston Down, which later became No.55 OTU, though it never had more than a dozen on strength. Crews for Defiant squadrons were mainly supplied from 54 OTU opening in December 1940 at Church Fenton. This was followed by 60 OTU at Leconfield which opened in May 1941. To begin with both units operated Defiants and Blenheims, but then all the Defiants were concentrated in 60 OTU, and the Blenheims in 54 OTU. Not surprisingly 60 OTU became one of the major users of Defiants, 109 of them passing through its hands, before it started using Blenheims and then Beaufighters to train Coastal Command pilots. After that Defiant pilots received their training at No.18 (Pilots) Advanced Flying Unit, which had 33 Defiants at one time or another, and operated them up to April 1945.

As many as 25 other OTUs, both Fighter and Bomber, had at least one Defiant on strength at some point, often the sole gunnery training aircraft, though No.79 OTU in Nicosia acquired a dozen later in the War. A number of Flights used Defiants for air-to-air training, often for bomber squadrons, including No.1479 at Peterhead, which used N1580, N1693, N3320 and AA304; No.1480 Flight which used a total of fourteen Defiants from N1538 to AA359 at various locations; No.1481 Flight at Binbrook, which used six Defiants from N1796 to AA357; No.1482 Flight at West Raynham, which used N3322, N3434, N3450 and T4103; No.1483, Flight which used L7006, N1634, T3960, T4068 and AA507; No.1484 Flight at Driffield, which used a total of twenty Defiants from L6981 to AA357; and No.1485 Flight which used T3989, T4066 and V1135.

Defiants were also extensively used in Air Gunners Schools, for obvious reasons. No.2 AGS at Dalcross had 108 Defiants pass through its hands; No.7 AGS at Stormy Down had 54; and No.10 AGS at Walney Island used 114, making it the second biggest Defiant consumer after No.264 Squadron. Though initially just having the fighter versions, the Air Gunners Schools also acquired some target-tug Defiants.

Other significant users of Defiants for training purposes were the Central Gunnery School at Warmwell which used thirteen early Defiants; No.9 Air Observers Schools at Penrhos, which had twenty-seven at one time or another; No.2 (Observers) Advanced Flying Unit at Millom, which had seventeen; and No.9 (O)AFU which had just three.

Countless Defiants were lost in accidents at training units, and many aircrew killed, but one Defiant from a training unit was lost due to enemy action. While on a night flight on 26 April, 1940, from Church Fenton, a 54 OTU Defiant, N1568, hit a tree while carrying out evasive action to avoid a hostile aircraft, and both crew members were killed.

Other Defiant Users

The Air Fighting Development Unit at Duxford used a number of Defiants, L6952 and L6955 early on, then N1756, N1765, V1121, AA382 and AA400 later. The GRU at Colly Weston used N1549 and N1674 for gunsight development, and Rotol at Staverton used N3322 and N3430 for propeller vibration tests.

The RAE at Farnborough used a large number of Defiants throughout the War for various experiments. Early in the War L7002 was used in attempts to boost its speed. N3514, with its turret removed, and the hole faired over was used for engine experiments, with a Merlin XLV in June 1941 and later a Merlin XLVI, and for a series of carburettor developments. N3484 was also used for engine research. The Armament Department used L7024 and N3311, and turret modifications were made on AA354. This aircraft also flew with a Martin Maxon twin 0.5 in gun turret. Wing pressure experiments were done on N3331, and DR863, DR895, DR966 and DS139 were used for towed-target trials.

Odd Defiants found there way into some strange uses. No.1566 Met Flight in Khormaksar, Aden, used DR990 for a while, and a slightly earlier Defiant, DR944, one of the two used by the USAF, was seconded to Martin-Baker Aircraft on 11 December, 1944, for the first British ejector-seat trials, at Wittering. The observer's station was rebuilt to take the ejector seat, and on 11 May, 1945, the first ejection, using a dummy was made. On 17 May six more ejections were made at Beaulieu up to a speed of 300 mph. This aircraft was not struck off charge until 31 May, 1948. Another Defiant, AA292, was also used for ejector-seat trials, in this case by the Air Ministry, and this aircraft was not struck off charge until March 1947, nearly two years after the Defiant had been declared obsolete.

P.82 Defiant

One 1,030 hp Rolls-Royce Merlin III (Mks I and T.T. Mk III); one 1,280 hp Rolls-Royce Merlin XX (Mks II and T.T.Mk I.)

Span 39 ft 4in; length 35 ft 4 in; height 11 ft 4 in (Mk I), 14 ft 5 in (Mk II); wing area 250 sq ft.

Empty weight 6,078 lb (Mk I), 6,282 lb (Mk II); loaded weight 8,318 lb (Mk I), 8,424 lb (Mk II), 8,250 lb (T.T. Mk I), 8,227 lb (T.T. Mk III).

Maximum speed 302.5 mph at 16,500 ft (Mk I), 315 mph at 16,500 ft (Mk II), T.T. Mk I 280 mph, T.T. Mk III 250 mph; climb to 25,000 ft 23.8 min (Mk I two-speed propeller), to 25,000 ft 18.2 min (Mk I constant-speed propeller); service ceiling 28,100 ft (Mk I), 33,600 ft (Mk II); range 465 miles at 259 mph (Mk I); endurance 1.78 hr (Mk I).

Armament: four .303 in Browning machine-guns in power-operated turret.

P.92

Though the Defiant prototype was being built by 1936 and had not even yet won a production order against the competition from the other Specification F.9/35 contenders, the Air Ministry was already considering its replacement. There was a widespread feeling that the heavier structures of the new all-metal bombers could withstand swift firing passes by fighters armed with the standard small calibre machine-guns that were in service. It was considered that cannon would be needed to deliver the necessary weight of fire. The Specification F.9/35 aircraft all featured four .303 in machine-guns in power-operated turrets. The next generation of fighters in this class would need to be larger, to carry four 20 mm cannon in a power-operated turret, and would have to have far higher performance.

In March 1936 Specification F.18/36 was issued calling for a twin-engined three-seat aircraft with a four-cannon turret, which would be capable of 375 mph at 15,000 ft. This specification proved quite fluid as discussions were undertaken about the ability of the aircraft industry to meet its performance requirements,

Mock-up of P.92 turret.

with existing engines and technology; and further proposals were aired regarding the best armament layout.

The carriage of 250 lb high explosive bombs to drop on bombers was proposed and then abandoned, and the use of 23 mm cannon was suggested by Hugh Dowding. Concentrating the guns in the turret was still controversial and different layouts with a combination of nose/wing/turret mounted cannon were put forward. The speed requirement was changed several times but eventually settled at 370 mph at 15,000 ft, and invitations to tender were issued in March 1937.

Boulton Paul were immediately interested, not least because they feared their P.82 might be cancelled in favour of this heavier aircraft. Work on the prototype P.82 was well advanced at Norwich, but delays were about to ensue with its transfer to Wolverhampton. The new project was numbered P.92, and was being designed against a re-written Specification F.11/37 issued on 26 May, 1937.

This called for a three-seat day and night fighter armed with four 20 mm Hispano cannon concentrated in a power-operated turret, and able to fire through 360 deg of azimuth including straight ahead, with large angles of elevation and depression. The gunner's view was to be unimpeded in the upper hemisphere, and his seat was to revolve with the turret. The pilot's cockpit was to have an excellent view for night flying. Top speed was to be at least 370 mph at 35,000 ft, with a cruising speed of 320 mph at that altitude. Manoeuvrability and low-speed handling were to be good, and the aircraft was to provide a steady gun platform. It was to be able to maintain 15,000 ft on one engine. Minor considerations were to be adjustable seats for pilot and gunner, an adjustable rudder bar, easy means of exit for the crew in an emergency, and the ability to change an engine within two hours. The whole aircraft was to be designed so that it could be quickly built at dispersed sites.

Apart from Boulton & Paul, five other companies tendered for the project, Armstrong Whitworth, Bristol, Hawker, Short and Supermarine. Matters were confused further in early 1938 when a new Specification F.2/38, called for even higher performance, but it quickly became clear that these requirements were out of reach, and the new specification was abandoned.

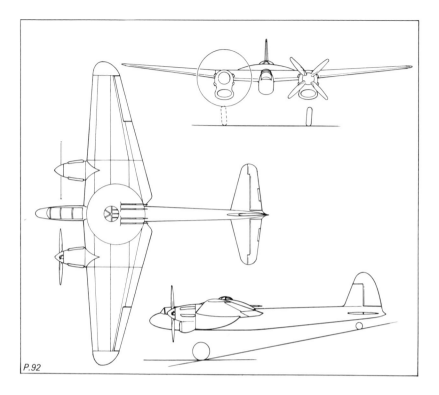

P.92

In March 1938 three prototypes of the P.92 were ordered, one to be powered by Rolls-Royce Vultures, one with Napier Sabres, and the third, powered by Vultures, would be for turret and armament development. Boulton Paul had a mock-up of the aircraft ready for inspection on 31 May, 1938. The design was a three-seat shoulder-wing monoplane of metal stressed-skin construction throughout. The Type L turret was housed almost totally within a very thick centre section of the wings between the spars. A 13 ft diameter revolving cupola contained the four 20 mm Hispano cannon which were housed in recessed slots when not in use, covered by shutters operated by the gun elevating gear. In the first design for the turret, two .303 in machine-guns were also included, outboard of the cannon, but as this was not a requirement, they were later abandoned as an unnecessary complication.

Offset from the centre of the turret, behind the cannon slots, was a small transparent siting hood for the gunner. As most of the turret was buried in the wing, only the shallow dome of the cupola was exposed, and this was very carefully designed and faired to reduce drag.

Realising the difficulties of keeping such a large diameter ring of ball-bearings free from jamming caused by structural distortions of the aircraft in flight, substantial structural stiffening was designed for the area between the spars, and a secondary outer ring was also fitted. The turret was built up of light-alloy skin over braced ribs, and was powered by the electro-hydraulic system used in the company's other turrets.

271

Mock-up of P.92 centre section, incorporating the turret.

The gunner sat between the breeches of each pair of guns on their shock-absorbing mountings. The Hispano cannon were drum fed, and the gunner had the task of replacing the drums. So that he did not have to lift them, the spare drums were located on rails in the turret roof so that he just had to slide them forward into place on the breeches. A total of 120 rounds were provided for each gun.

The sighting hood was 3.2 ft in diameter, and could be jettisoned in an emergency. It was a Perspex moulding attached to a rotating ring, the gun sight being fixed to the same ring. The usual interrupter mechanism was fitted so that the gunner did not shoot off parts of his own aircraft.

The wide-chord wing had a marked gull-shape, the thick centre section sloping down to the engine nacelles, with dihedral on the outer wings, which had an overall span of 66 ft 3 in. Split flaps and Frise ailerons with trim tabs would have been fitted. From ahead the gull shape with the low dome of the turret above gave the aircraft a distinct humpback shape.

The first and third prototypes were to have two Rolls-Royce Vulture IIs giving 1,760 hp, and driving 13 ft diameter variable-pitch propellers. The nacelles were underslung with the main Lockheed undercarriage units retracting into them. The radiators were beneath the spinners in the front of the nacelles which were also fitted with fire-extinguishing and anti-icing systems. The second prototype was to have two 2,055 hp Napier Sabre 1 twenty-four cylinder engines.

The fuselage was to be built in five sections, front, centre, the rear in two halves, and the tail unit. Because the turret had been built into a thickened wing centre-section, the fuselage could be given a very slim cross section. The pilot's cockpit was just ahead of the propeller arcs, giving excellent visibility in the forward hemisphere. Because of his proximity to the propellers special attention was given to its soundproofing, and though the pilot could bale out by jettisoning the canopy in the normal way, the nearness of the propeller tips meant that devising a safer method of egress was considered prudent. By tilting his seat back through 110 deg he could slide out of a hatch in the bottom of the fuselage, upside down. As related previously, this method was tested in the mock-up by John North himself, with some damage to his head.

The P.92/2 V3142, the half-scale P.92 built by Heston Aircraft, pictured at Pendeford.

The navigator's cockpit was behind the pilot's, and extra soundproofing was also a feature of that. The provision of a navigator reflected the endurance of the aircraft, normally 1½ hr with an allowance for 15 min of full-power at sea level. The normal fuel capacity was 328 gal, but with extra tankage a range of 2,000 miles was possible.

For an aircraft with an all-up weight of 19,100 lb Boulton Paul claimed the P.92 would have a very sprightly performance. A top speed of 371 mph at 15,000 ft was claimed, 353 mph at 30,000 ft and a service ceiling of 38,000 ft.

Construction of the first two prototypes began in mid-1939, but an extensive programme to investigate the P.92's aerodynamic properties was already underway. The company's own wind tunnel was only of small-scale and so the RAE tested a ²⁄₇th scale model, of 17 ft 10 in wing span, in their 24 ft wind tunnel during March to September 1939. The model was tested extensively, and was fitted with two 15 hp motors to simulate the propeller effect. There were other tests on the turret's drag in a smaller tunnel, the effect of the movement of the guns on the effectiveness of the tailplane being carefully examined.

It was found that the elevation of the guns to 45 deg, with them turned to 135 deg increased drag by as much as 35 percent, with the lift co-efficient at full-speed being reduced by 25 percent. To further examine the aerodynamics of the design it was decided to build a half-scale wooden flying replica of the aircraft to be powered by two 130 hp de Havilland Gipsy Major II four cylinder inline engines.

As Boulton Paul were no longer equipped to build wooden aircraft, and were pre-occupied with getting the Defiant into production, Heston Aircraft were contracted to build the aircraft. It was designated the P.92/2 by Boulton Paul, and the J.A.8 by Heston Aircraft, and given the serial V3142. The P.92/2 had an all-wooden structure with a ply monocoque fuselage and ply-covered wings and control surfaces, apart from the rudder which was fabric-covered. Metal was used to cover the engine cowlings, nose, and the undercarriage which was non-retractable for simplicity. The turret was represented by a plywood hump but no dummy guns were fitted.

Care was taken to make sure the nacelles of the Gipsy engines matched those of the full-size aircraft, so cooling air had to be ducted in from the undercarriage fairing.

There were certain problems in building to half-scale, not least in finding a half-scale pilot, so the forward fuselage had to be widened to take one of more

A view of the P.92/2 showing the hump-backed appearance caused by the gull-wing and the turret.

normal dimensions. There was further trouble in trying to build a spar to the tiny section required at the aileron tip, and trying to find places to install the camera and the manometer panels. A hole had to be cut in the fuselage which did not do the monocoque a great deal of good.

A means of exit for the pilot in an emergency was even more difficult to achieve than in the full-size aircraft. An emergency exit panel was sited behind the seat on the port side. By depressing a handle the seat collapsed backwards and the panel could be pushed out, the pilot supposedly wriggling sideways and out on his back, hampered by the fact that he had to wear a back-type parachute because of the close confines of the cockpit. His seat was virtually on the floor of the long narrow, cramped, cockpit. Exit by this method was made more difficult by the fact that the handle could not be reached by the pilot from his seat! When the P.92/2 was finally delivered to the A & AAE a piece of string was attached to the handle for the test pilots' peace of mind, but it was considered that the alternative method of exit, by jettisoning the hood and taking the risk of hitting the propellers during the bale-out, was a better bet.

Entry to the cockpit was even more difficult than exit, and it could not be accomplished while the engines were running. The canopy had to be entirely removed in one piece, and could only be replaced with external aid. The pilot then required steps placed between the nacelle and the fuselage in order to climb in.

The wing was fitted with split trailing-edge flaps in three sections stretching outboard to the ailerons. Because of anxiety about the pronounced taper of the wing, built-in slots were fitted to the leading edge of the wings near the tips, though the anxiety was to prove unfounded. Another precaution was to fit an anti-spin tail parachute.

Before the P.92/2 had been completed its purpose had been ended when, on 26 May, 1940, the P.92 project was cancelled. Metal had already been cut on the first two prototypes, and the structure was about 5 percent complete, but the Air Ministry had decided to concentrate on developing fewer basic designs, and the Bristol Beaufighter was already in production with four prototypes flying.

It was decided to complete the P.92/2, and its first flight took place from Heston in the spring of 1941, with Flt Lt Cecil Feather at the controls. After a few flights at Heston the P.92/2 was flown to Wolverhampton and a programme of flights was begun to test the effect of the turret on the aircraft's aerodynamics, for which the centre section and turret were tufted and fitted with pressure pick-up tubes.

In June 1943 the P.92/2 was flown to the A & AAE at Boscombe Down, and was subjected to handling trials during the following month. Interestingly the A & AAE test pilots were not told that the strange domed hump was representative of a gun turret, and assumed it was to house a radar scanner. It was reported that the cockpit was very cramped and stuffy on the ground, but cooling air was ducted in when aloft. Despite the nearness of the propellers it was not thought to be too noisy, but the full-size aircraft would have been excessively so. The view was bad to the rear and side, not a great fault in an aircraft which would have a rear gunner, but was very good ahead, unobstructed to 85 deg. In the case of the P.92/2 the aircraft had to be yawed from side to side when taxi-ing so that the pilot could see if the sky was clear behind.

The aircraft was found to be very pleasant to handle, with hardly any faults. The longitudinal and directional characteristics were very satisfactory, but lateral behaviour was very unpleasant in rough conditions. Though the ailerons and rudder were satisfactory, more upward movement was felt to be needed on the elevators and nose-up trimmer range, for gliding and landing, as lowering the flaps induced a nose-down change of trim. Stalls were gentle and recovery was quick, with the engines on or off.

Single-engined flight was straightforward and turns could be made both with and against the running engine. Dives at both full- and one-third throttle were steady and a slight pull induced a quick recovery. The limited available elevator trim meant the glide on the approach was made rather fast. At 70 mph, the correct gliding speed, the rate of sink was rather high and the glide was flat. A greater area of flap would have induced a steeper and more natural angle of glide. Elevator control was in fact just sufficient for a three-point landing.

It was found that the P.92/2's drag was higher than predicted by the tests on the wind-tunnel models, however the RAE felt that in the full-size machine the values assumed for the wind-tunnel models would prove nearer to the truth than the P.92/2.

On 4 July, 1941, a half-scale dummy cupola complete with dummy guns was ordered to be installed on the P.92/2, with an electric or electro-hydraulic power unit to revolve it. The company stated that it would take 5–6 months to build,

The P.92/2. The Gipsy Major II engines are housed in nacelles shaped to match those of the Vulture.

275

and the DTD considered it likely that a further 5–6 months would be needed to iron the bugs out of the equipment, and considered the expenditure of several thousand pounds would not be worth the information likely to be gathered, so the powered-half-scale cupola was cancelled.

After the programme of tests V3142 was returned to the company and was stored for a while, but it was eventually broken up. It had shown that the P.92 would have made a valuable night fighter, apart from the Vulture engines. As it was the Boulton Paul design staff found itself with no aircraft to work with after development of the Defiant ceased, and it was not until after the War that another of the company's designs flew.

A turret fighter did enter service during the Second World War, which quite closely matched both the specification and performance of the P.92. It was the world's only turret fighter not built by Boulton Paul (if the Blenheim is discounted as a 'turret fighter'), the Northrop P-61 Black Widow. It stemmed from reports received in the USA in 1940 which emphasised the need for a specialised night fighter equipped with a heavy armament and radar, and possessing long endurance and good manoeuvrability and performance.

When it entered service in the summer of 1944, the P.61 had evolved into a three-seat night fighter rather larger than the P.92 at 27,600 lb all-up weight but with the extra power of two 2,250 hp Pratt & Whitney R-2800s to make up for that. As a result its performance almost exactly matched that estimated for the P.92. Its maximum speed was 369 mph at 20,000 ft, its service ceiling was 33,100 ft and its range with auxiliary fuel tanks was 1,900 miles. Its large remotely controlled dorsal turret carried heavy weapons, not the cannon of the P.92, but 0.5 in machine-guns. The one substantial difference to the P.92 was its fixed forward-firing armament of four 20 mm cannon. Though it was also equipped with radar, that would have presumably become part of the P.92's equipment in time.

There is no doubt that the Vulture engines, and even the Sabres would have caused extensive development delays for the P.92, but with suitable engines, and assuming the turret could have been made to work, the aircraft could have evolved into a night-fighter and intruder of similar capabilities to the Black Widow, and might well have also found use as a long-range escort fighter.

P.92

Two 1,710 hp Rolls-Royce Vulture II.
Span 66 ft 3 in; length 55 ft; height 15 ft 3 in; wing area 709.1 sq ft.
Loaded weight 19,100 lb.
Maximum speed 299 mph at sea level, 371 mph at 15,000 ft, 352 mph at 30,000 ft; cruising speed 320 mph at 15,000 ft; climb 3,220 fit/min at 15,000 ft; service ceiling 38,000 ft; endurance 1½ hr (with 15 min at full power at sea level).
Armament: four 20 mm Hispano cannon in power-operated turret.

P.92/2

Two 130 hp de Havilland Gipsy Major II.
Span 33 ft 1½ in; length 27 ft 6 in; height 7 ft 7½ in.
Loaded weight 2,778 lb.
Maximum speed 152 mph; cruising speed 135 mph.

VL892, the first prototype Balliol, as first flown with a Bristol Mercury engine.

P.108 Balliol

In drawing up Specification T.7/45 for an advanced trainer to replace the many wartime Miles Masters and North American Harvards, the Air Ministry introduced three new criteria for the design of the new type. The pupil and instructor were to sit in side-by-side seats, rather than the tandem seats of the aircraft that were being replaced, a feature which was to be a fundamental tenet of British military trainer design for the next 25 years. A third seat was to be provided for a second pupil, who could gain extra experience by watching his colleague, a feature which had been required in the new basic trainer, the Percival Prentice. Lastly, and most dramatically, the aircraft was to be powered by a 1,000 hp propeller-turbine.

It was clear in 1945 that the future combat aircraft of the RAF were to be jet-powered, and it seemed obvious that experience of turbine engine management should be a fundamental part of the advanced flight training curriculum. The engines suggested were the Rolls-Royce Dart and the Armstrong Siddeley Mamba, both of which were under development. As a back-up it was also required that the new trainer could be powered by an improved version of the Bristol Perseus engine.

It was required that the new trainer be suitable for day and night training, armament training, with guns and bombs, glider-towing, and should be readily adaptable for deck landing, with provision for the fitting of folding wings, arrester gear and a strengthened undercarriage.

This Specification was issued on 16 March, 1945, and within a month Boulton Paul submitted their proposals for their P.108 an entirely conventional all-metal low-wing monoplane, powered by a Rolls-Royce Dart, and two weeks later for their P.109 powered by the Perseus. These two designs were more or less identical apart from the engines, but were different in several respects to the aircraft which eventually emerged as the Balliol. The Dart engine exhausted centrally beneath the rear fuselage, and the upper canopy line was continued in the top line of the rear fuselage, so that there was no all-round vision for the

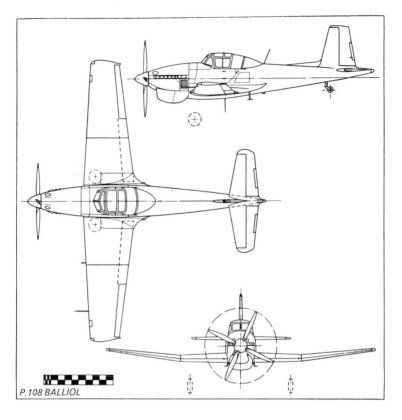

P.108 BALLIOL

crew. The third crew member sat sideways, facing starboard, just behind the side-by-side seats of the pupil and instructor.

The TAS was estimated to be 292 mph at sea level at combat power, 299 mph at 5,000 ft, 304 mph at 10,000 ft, and 313 mph at 20,000 ft. Maximum cruising speed at 20,000 ft was 267 mph. With an initial rate of climb of 2,400 ft/min the time to 5,000 ft was 2.1 min, to 10,000 ft it was 4.4 min and to 15,000 ft it was 6.95 min.

There was a new issue of T.7/45 in August, and the Perseus-engined requirement was deleted, so that the P.109 was abandoned. With the prospect of large orders, numerous manufacturers were anxious to fulfill the requirements of T.7/45, including Avro with their Type 701, Miles with their M.70 and Blackburn with their B.52, but only two were chosen to construct prototypes, Avro with their Athena T.1 and Boulton Paul with their P.108.

At the end of August 1945 an order was placed with Boulton Paul for the construction of four Dart-powered prototypes, VL892, VL917, VL935, and VL954. An early proposal to make VL954 the navallised prototype was abandoned, with the intention of making two of the pre-production aircraft the naval prototypes, and to fit them with Mamba engines, as a back-up to the Dart.

By June 1946 delays in the development of the Dart led to a proposal to fit an 820 hp Bristol Mercury piston engine in the first aircraft so that flight trials would not be delayed. In August 1946 an order for twenty pre-production aircraft was placed, to Specification 29/46P, to be equipped with either turbine. Boulton & Paul planned to fit the Dart and the Mamba to ten aircraft each, but to fit only the Mamba to the four prototypes, as it was by now in a more advanced state of development than the Dart. As VL892 would be completed before even the first Mamba was available, the decision was made to go ahead and fit it with the Mercury for initial flight trials.

A slight setback to the programme occurred when during taxi-ing trials the undercarriage of VL892 retracted. Further delays were expected with the Mamba, and alternative engines were actively considered, including the Mercury 25, the Pegasus 28, the Merlin 24 and the Merlin 32/Special. The prototype's undercarriage troubles were cured and it flew for the first time, from Pendeford, on 26 May, 1947, with Boulton Paul's new chief test pilot, Robert Lindsay Neale, at the controls.

A Balliol covered with DX3 anti-radar material, on 30 April, 1957.

Within two weeks the decision was taken to switch all pre-production aircraft to Merlin engines, under Specification T.14/47, but the four prototypes were still to be powered by Mambas.

VL892 went to Boscombe Down for preview handling trials from December 1947 to January 1948. The aircraft was ballasted to the nominal fore and aft centre of gravity of the Mamba-Balliol, and an auto-observer was fitted in place of the third seat. It was found to be easy and pleasant to fly under all normal conditions, apart from slow rolls and manoeuvring at sustained high 'g', where high stick forces were experienced. A small number of criticisms arose, for instance a walkway not being provided on the starboard side, so that entry for both pilots was from the port side. There was also deemed to be insufficient left rudder trim, and directional snaking in a dive, though this was not unpleasant except when instrument flying, but it did make the aircraft a bad gun platform.

The Mamba engine installation in VL917.

The Balliol T.1

The first of the Mamba-powered Balliols to fly was VL917, on 24 May, 1948, from Wolverhampton, with Lindsay Neale at the controls.

The aircraft was constructed in seven main sections on standard jigs. The fuselage was in three sections behind the firewall, comprising the cockpit, the rear fuselage and the tailcone, the wings were in outer and inner sections, and finally there were the tailplanes and fin and rudder.

Unlike the rest of the fuselage, the engine compartment was built up of light-alloy and steel tube, with detachable side and lower panels for access to the engine and accessories. The engine mounting consisted of three tubular mounting struts extending back from the casing between the compressor and combustion chambers to four anchorage forks on the firewall. Loads were carried into the fuselage structure by similar steel tubes running back to the fuselage longeron anchorages. The jetpipe was angled down beneath the cockpit to exhaust low down on the starboard side of the fuselage. This avoided any interference with the airflow over the tail, and counteracted the torque of the three-blade de Havilland propeller. The jetpipe was surrounded by a duct filled with aluminium foil and cooled by forced air. The jet efflux also contributed 20 percent of the aircraft's total 320 lb static thrust.

The cockpit section was built on four main and two auxiliary longerons, held on several sub-frames including two strengthened arches which comprised the crash structure over the cockpit. The covering was light-alloy stressed-skin. The fuselage fuel tank was fitted just in front of the cockpit in the upper part of the fuselage. There were also fuel tanks in the wings, giving a total internal tankage of 169 gal. Beneath the cockpit section were three crash skids made up of box sections on rubber buffers, so that in the event of a wheels-up landing little damage would be done to the airframe. Also, in the event of a pilot seriously overshooting, there was manual override to the undercarriage safety lock, so that the pilot could retract the wheels on the ground, to avoid more substantial damage caused by careering beyond the runway.

The forward part of the canopy consisted of quite heavy gauge framing, but

VL917, the first Mamba-powered Balliol to fly, taxi-ing across Pendeford aerodrome.

the rear section over the third seat was a curved single blown section. There was a marked step down between the sliding hood and this rear canopy section, to give clearance.

The rear fuselage was a cone built on monocoque principles, joined to the cockpit and to the tailcone with transport joints of angle section hoops. The outer skin was lapped at these two joints. A location for an F24 camera was sited in the rear fuselage just aft of the jetpipe. The steerable tailwheel was non-retracting. A control on the pedestal allowed the pilot to select tailwheel free, steerable, or locked. Control was sufficient for the normal narrow winding perimeter track like the track from Boulton Paul's factory to Pendeford aerodrome, but if movement of more than 45 deg was incurred the tailwheel freed itself automatically. Fitted in the very rear of the tailcone was a glider-towing attachment.

The fin and tailplane sections were interchangeable to simplify maintenance spares holdings—a feature of the P.41 Phoenix many years before—and so were the ailerons, main undercarriage oleo legs and wing tanks. The wings spanned 39 ft 4 in with a gross area of 250 sq ft. The inner sections, which comprised roughly half the span (21 ft 8 in), were attached directly to the fuselage side with four pin-joints, and the outer sections were similarly attached. By withdrawing the lower pair of bolts on each side the outer sections could be manually folded, without disturbing the control runs.

The wings had an aerofoil of NACA 65 and were of two-spar construction with an uninterrupted rigid torsion box created between them, holding the fuel tanks in the inner sections. The spars themselves were light-alloy T-section extrusions, and there was a rear auxiliary spar to which the trailing-edge skinning and the flaps were attached. Light pressed ribs were employed, cut out between the spars to contain the fuel tanks. The forward edge of the wing contained the undercarriage wells, for the inward retracting units, a really strong forged steel box. A single .303 in Browning machine-gun was fitted just inboard of the fold line in the port wing. Folding the wing gave access to the gun, and also enabled the wing fuel tank to be removed, by simply sliding it outwards. A G45 cine-camera was fitted to the starboard wing.

The outer wings contained the dive-brakes, which were simple holed units, curved in shape, and hinged on radius arms, which retracted just in front of the front spar. Conventional split flaps were fitted, extending beyond the fold line to

The cockpit of VL917 after its crash at Pendeford.

the outer wing panels, as far as the ailerons. The large inner flaps were directly actuated, the outer ones being worked through auxiliary actuation.

Because of the high and rough utilisation which is normal at training establishments, the aircraft was designed to be as easy to maintain as possible. Apart from the interchangeable components already mentioned, there were no less than 40 access panels, most of them fitted with quick-release fasteners. The structure was built to be robust, even excessively so in some eyes.

As mentioned earlier a second mishap struck the programme when VL917 experienced engine problems on a test flight. The third prototype, VL935, was moved to Bitteswell, near Coventry, for its first flight on 27 May, 1948, in the hands of Sqn Ldr Price-Owen, chief test pilot of Armstrong Siddeley's engine flight development section, and further trials were flown from there. The first Service pilot to fly the Balliol was Air Marshall Sir Alec Coryton.

The first prototype, VL892, was re-engined with the Mamba, and this version of the aircraft was now designated Balliol T.1. The decision had now finally been taken that the production aircraft was to be Merlin 35 powered, and as such it was designated the Balliol T.2. Specification T.14/47 was issued to cover

The first prototype Balliol, VL892, re-engined with the Armstrong Siddeley Mamba.

this new version. The decision to use the Merlin, was largely because of the large stocks of the engine, and spares that were available, and because of the development problems with the Mamba. A trainer aircraft has to be reliable, above all else. It was now decided not to build the fourth Mamba-powered prototype, VL954. There were now to be four more Merlin-powered prototypes, VW897 — VW900, followed by a new order for only seventeen pre-production aircraft, VR590 — VR606, all Merlin-powered. The reduction in the number of pre-production aircraft reflected the original order for twenty-four prototype/pre-production Balliols. This number would still be delivered, counting the three T.1s.

The Balliol T.2

Boulton Paul were aware that they were involved in an intense competition with the Avro Athena, the orders for which mirrored the Balliol orders. The prototype Balliol T.2, VW897, beat the Merlin-powered Athena prototype into the air, just as the Mamba-powered aircraft had. The first flight of VW897 took

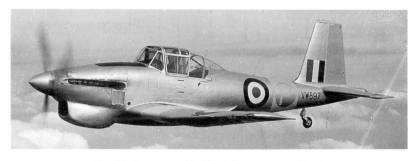

First Merlin-powered Balliol T.2 prototype, VW897.

place from Wolverhampton on 10 July, 1948, flown by Peter Tishaw, with the Athena following it into the air on 1 August. A date for competitive trials between the two aircraft was set for February 1949, but this had to be postponed when VW897 crashed.

It had been discovered that elevator reversal occurred at an indicated airspeed of about 320 mph in an out-of-trim dive. To investigate this, with Peter Tishaw as co-pilot, Lindsay Neale took off on a flight to dive the aircraft at over 400 mph, checking the control responses. During the dive the windscreen disintegrated, possibly due to a bird strike, and the aircraft crashed in a field near Coven, Wolverhampton, killing both men. After this tragedy Flt Lt A E (Ben) Gunn was seconded to Boulton Paul from Boscombe Down where he had been involved in flight testing the Balliol. He eventually left the Service and became the company's chief test pilot.

The control reversal problems were solved or at least its effect delayed beyond the maximum permitted diving speed, by altering the tailplane incidence by 2 deg, and strengthening it.

A factory fresh pre-production Balliol T.2, VR599.

Extensive testing of the Balliol prototypes at Boscombe Down, began with carbon monoxide contamination tests on VW 898 on 10 April, 1949, and the first handling trials took place with VW900 in June 1949, though these aircraft were not fully representative of production aircraft, not having had the tailplane incidence changed and having no dive-brakes or leading-edge spoilers. The aircraft proved to be pleasant and easy to fly, the controls being well harmonised, light and effective, and stability good in all axes. Aerobatics were easy to perform smoothly. Loops were straightforward, with entry speed 220 kt, and sedate slow rolls were possible at 170 kt. The stall warning in the prototypes was found to be inadequate, but leading-edge spoilers in the pre-production aircraft were to cure this and the stall was then gentle and straight, and when the aircraft was held in the stall for a second or two, the left wing and nose fell sharply and abruptly; ideal for a training aircraft.

On 22 April, 1949, VW898 flew to Khartoum for its tropical trials at the Tropical Experimental Unit. The pilot was Sqn Ldr P P C Barthropp DFC with Sqn Ldr D M T McRae as his navigator. The flight, from Boscombe Down was via Istres, El Aouina (Tunis), Castel Benito, Benina, El Adem, Fayid and Wadi Halfa, 3,373 nautical miles in a total flying time of 17 hr 40 min. Forty-five gal Tempest drop tanks were used for these trials. On 14 May VW898 left for Eastleigh, Nairobi, to undertake high-altitude take-off trials, transiting through Malakal and Juba. It was found that the cooling requirements were met in every respect except in level flight at maximum continuous cruising power with the radiator flaps in automatic control, when the coolant temperature was 3 deg above the maximum permissible. The cockpit was found to be 5–13 deg C too hot on the ground and hardly cooler in the air as the punkah louvres did not provide sufficient air. It was recommended that the cabin heating ducts should provide extra air by being able to switch off the heat exchanger. The return flight to Boscombe Down was begun on 12 July, 1949. On this long intercontinental journey, it was noted by the pilots that the relief tube provided was conveniently positioned but not used.

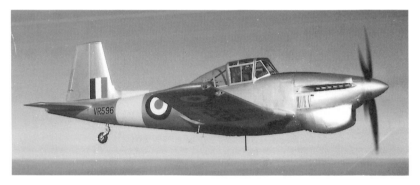

Pre-production Balliol T.2 VR596.

The first of the pre-production aircraft joined the prototypes for spinning trials which were to reveal the only major critisism of the aircraft. The spin was found to be acceptable in two turns, but longer spins to the left subjected the aircraft to yawing and pitching motions making it uncomfortable and complicating recovery, and also suggesting high lateral loads on the tail structure. Spins to the right had the same characteristics but not so pronounced. Recovery depended on the attitude of the aircraft in pitch. At best the aircraft would be in a nose-down attitude ready for a dive out, at worst it would be in a stalled, banked condition at a low airspeed, *i.e.* less than 40 mph. The only consolation for Boulton Paul was that the spinning characteristics of the Avro Athena were found to be even worse. In a four-turn spin its behaviour was very erratic with pitching and yawing oscillations which would easily disconcert a student.

Armament trials with four rockets or eight 8½, 10, 11½ or 25 lb practice bombs had proved satisfactory as had the drop tank jettison trials. The bomb racks were carried beneath the wings inboard of the undercarriage legs, the drop tanks just outboard, with the rocket rails under the outer wings. Though it was not intended for all of these to be carried together, the aircraft was tested in this condition.

One slight problem had been the failure of the tailcone mainframe of VR592

A pre-production Balliol T.2, VR596.

after only 59 hr. The tailwheel oleo swinging link had fouled two fuselage bolt heads, but repairs and modifications on future aircraft were put in hand.

After a prolonged fly-off against the Athena, the Balliol was finally declared the winner in early 1950. The advantages of the Balliol over the Athena were never more than marginal. The Balliol was considered a little crisper, with more effective ailerons and more lightly loaded rudder, making handling more precise. It was praised for its aerobatic qualities, especially its rate of roll. It seems that the Athena was regarded as the better engineered of the two, but that servicing of the Balliol was easier, apart from access to the starter motor behind the engine, and required fewer man-hours, though it was criticised for

The fourth prototype Balliol T.2, VW900.

the design of the undercarriage operating mechanism, which was considered unusual and needing careful attention in service. They also found the chin cowling and details of the tailcone insufficiently robust. Though the two aircraft were very close in overall ability, the outcome was not really in doubt. The spinning characteristics were the final nail in the coffin for the Athena. Whereas the Balliol had been cleared for spinning even up to sixteen turns, the Athena had problems from the outset. On arrival at Boscombe Down, it was rushed into its spinning programme after only a brief handling assessment and Flt Lt Dickie Stoop had the unfortunate experience of losing part of the fin and rudder on only the first turn of a spin. Despite Avro's hurried attempts to strengthen the offending structure, they had lost the order. An initial contract for 100 Balliols was placed in February 1950, disappointing in one respect for Boulton Paul who had expected an initial order for 500.

Nevertheless the production order was welcome news for Boulton Paul who were coming to the end of their Wellington T.10 conversion contract, and needed the Balliol order to fill the factory. This was quite convenient timing, as the factory could be totally cleared, and the Balliol production lines could be well laid out, with plenty of space. There were two main production lines, the fuselage line, in which the Merlin power eggs and three fuselage sections were joined, and the fin and tailplane fitted, and then the adjacent final assembly line at which the inner wing and undercarriage, and then the outer wings were added, and the final fitting out took place. The first production aircraft, WF989, first flew in April 1952.

The Merlin Balliol did not differ signifcantly from the Balliol T.1 but the power egg was revised to contain the 1,245 hp Merlin 35, with a chin air intake, giving the aircraft a more massive nose profile, and slightly reducing the pilot's view ahead while taxi-ing. The T.2 was also 1 ft 4½ in shorter than the T.1. The T.2, because of the extra 830 lb of the Merlin, had its all-up weight increased to 8,175 lb, compared with 7,860 lb for the T.1, despite a saving of 140 lb in the structure and carrying 44 gal less fuel.

The engine mountings were of the conventional kind for piston engines. The

Balliol T.2s of No.7 FTS Cottesmore.

third seat was not fitted, the idea of carrying a pupil/observer had been abandoned and the space was taken over by radio equipment. The canopy over this position was changed to a framed unit, more closely matching the forward section. The dive-brakes were also changed significantly, more substantial units being fitted, which extended hydraulically both above and below the wing. Above the wing they were of heavy slatted design, and below they were solid, and could be opened at any speed allowing controlled descents of up to 5,000 ft/min.

The top speed of the T.2 was less than the Mamba-powered T.1, 288 mph at 9,000 ft, as against 307 mph at 20,000 ft, and service ceiling was less at 32,500 ft against 36,750 ft, but endurance was up from 2½ hr to 3 hr.

In August 1949, for the first time since the P.9s, a Boulton Paul aircraft was entered in an air race, the Air League Challenge Trophy at Birmingham Airport. This was for piston-engined aircraft with a top speed in excess of 250 mph, and amongst the other competitors were a Spitfire, a Firebrand, a Sea Fury Trainer and a Hornet 3. A pre-production Balliol, VR602, flown by Ben Gunn took part, but because of a broken flap could only manage an average 234 mph and was last to finish.

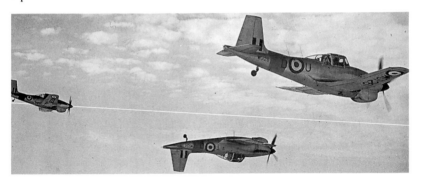

Three production Balliol T.2s, WG126, WG124 and WG128, in a No.7 FTS formation from Cottesmore.

He had better luck in September 1950 when flying the same aircraft in the *Daily Express* International Air Race from Hurn to Herne Bay. There were 74 other entries, with 67 actually starting, and the overall winner was Proctor G-AHUZ. The Balliol was first in the Handicap section of the 3,000–4,500 kg weight category.

By then Gunn had also flown VR602 at the SBAC Display at Farnborough, and the RAF Display had featured two Balliols flying synchronised aerobatics, with spectators making requests for particular manoeuvres over the R/T! The pilots were Flt Lt Byrne and Flt Lt Garner DFC.

In January 1951 further orders were placed for the Balliol T.2, 138 from Boulton Paul, and 120 from a second production line set up with a sub-contract placed directly by the Air Ministry with Blackburn Aircraft at Brough. It was expected that further orders would follow, but once more priorities had changed and 98 of this second order were cancelled, and Blackburn's order was reduced to just 30 aircraft.

The RAF decided it was more appropriate to have a jet advanced trainer, and the Vampire T.11 was ordered in large quantities to fill this role. This was a grave disappointment to the company, which had staked so much on the Balliol, and with the P.119 was hopeful of building its successor. Now the RAF training sequence was to be Provost/Vampire, and Boulton Paul were shut out of the area on which they had hoped their future lay.

RAF Service

Only one Flying Training School was to receive the Balliol T.2, No. 7 at Cottesmore, and that comparatively briefly. It received its first Balliols, three pre-production aircraft in February 1952, but the first production aircraft, WF992, did not arrive until August. Two of the three training squadrons at Cottesmore received the Balliol, the other being equipped with Prentices, in the then current RAF practice of having both basic and advanced flying training at the same establishment. The Prentice squadron was re-equipping with Provost basic trainers even as the Balliols arrived, presaging the Provost/Vampire sequence. The difficulties of operating both slow-moving piston engined trainers and fast jet trainers from the same base soon changed RAF policy and they were separated.

The normal flying training course was 60 hr on the Prentice followed by 120 hr on the Balliol, which was so easy to fly that time to solo was only 5 hr, whereas it had been about 8 hr on the Harvard it replaced. For instrument flying training the Balliol was fitted with amber-tinted screens (with the pupil wearing blue-tinted goggles). The front screens were raised pneumatically, activated by a push-button, and lowered by elastic cable, the runners being part of the canopy structure. The side screens were drawn forward by the pilots, and the upper glazed portions of the sliding hood were permanently amber-tinted.

No.7 FTS had given up its Balliols by mid-1954, most of them going to the

No.228 OCU Balliol WN138 at North Luffenham.

289

RAF College, Cranwell, which became the biggest user of the type, with 56 going through its books. By the end of 1955 Cranwell, too, had retired its Balliols, the end of its RAF service in the training role.

There were other users of the aircraft though, in a variety of roles. It served with No.288 (Control and Reporting) Squadron at Middle Wallop, for radar training duties, two dozen aircraft being used, and most of these were passed on to 3/4 Civil Anti-Aircraft Co-operation Unit at Exeter, nineteen being used. Eight of these were in turn passed on to the School of Flying Control at RAF Sopley.

No.238 OCU at Colerne and then North Luffenham, used over thirty Balliols at various times to fly as targets for Bristol Brigands, and No.228 OCU also used eleven for a while. With over two hundred Balliols available, and Flying Training Command very quickly giving them up, there was an embarrassment of spare aircraft. They were issued as communication aircraft at Benson, Colerne, Kenley, Upavon and Bahrain, and most notably White Waltham where a dozen were operated both as communications aircraft and to give refresher flying to senior officers. Two aircraft were issued to Durham University Air Squadron for a few months, but they were really too powerful an aircraft for this role.

Accidents involving Balliols included a number of collapsed undercarriages, though no more than other trainers, and a reasonable number of engine failures, but it was the torque stall which was the dread of the inexperienced student. When the considerable power of the Merlin engine was applied suddenly during an attempted overshoot, the aircraft would try to revolve around the propeller. The port wing would drop, and if remedial action was not taken immediately the wingtip would hit the ground and a cartwheel result. Seven Balliols suffered crashes in this way, and not all of them at the hands of student pilots. The Balliol was no different to other high-powered propeller-driven aircraft in this respect, but it was no aircraft for a beginner.

Some Balliols were actually tried in an operational role for a while. The Meteor NF.11s of No.68 and No.87 Squadrons in Germany practiced the night intruder role, flying army co-operation missions against 'enemy forces', but were incapable of dropping flares. A number of Balliols and Athenas were sent out to undertake this task. Unfortunately neither aircraft was really equipped for such a role at night and three aircraft were lost, one of one type and two of the other, and they were quickly withdrawn to the United Kingdom.

The last Balliol T.2 was delivered to the RAF in April 1954 and by July 1957, sad to relate, forty of them were sold for scrap. In fact fifteen aircraft never saw any service at all, going to No.9 MU at RAF Cosford for storage, and then being passed to No.22 MU at RAF Silloth where they were scrapped. The last few RAF Balliols were withdrawn by the end of 1961, six serving as instructional airframes at RAF St Athan for a while.

The Mamba-Balliol, VL892, was delivered to Boscombe Down in June 1952 for brief handling trials before going to the Empire Test Pilots School at Farnborough for use in pilot training in handling propeller-turbines. It was found to have the same handling characteristics as the T.2 but the quietness and freedom from vibration made it more pleasant to fly. It was recommended that a service-limiting speed of 270 kt be applied as there was a nose-down change of trim at higher speeds, but otherwise it was found suitable for the role envisaged providing the engine was handled with care.

Arrester hook and tailwheel deflector fitted to the navalised pre-production Balliol VR598.

The Sea Balliol T.21

The Royal Navy required a deck-landing trainer, and the Balliol had been designed from the outset with this in mind. Few further modifications were necessary, the Boulton Paul undercarriage legs had, for instance been stressed to 12–14 ft/sec vertical velocity, and the rebound ratio was 0.25. One of the pre-production aircraft, VR599, served as the naval prototype, first flying in this form in October 1952. Richard Mancus, an ex-Royal Navy pilot, came from Aero Flight at the RAE Farnborough to undertake testing of the naval version.

Deck landing trials on HMS *Illustrious* had already taken place in November

The first Sea Balliol T.21, WL715, awaiting delivery.

291

Sea Balliol WL718 suffering undercarriage collapse on HMS *Triumph*.

1950 with two of the pre-production aircraft, VR596 and VR598, only partially converted, with just arrester hooks being fitted, but the full deck-landing trials with VR599 took place in June 1953 also on HMS *Illustrious*. Forty-five landings were made in daylight and sixteen by night from both the left and right seat, though the view from the latter was considered inadequate. The aircraft was found to be satisfactory and was well-liked by the pilots. It was actually thought that the Mamba-Balliol might have had even better characteristics with regard to engine response and directional changes of trim.

In the full naval version the arrester hook was fitted with a landing wire deflector in front of the tailwheel, a propeller of 9 in less diameter was required, the undercarriage was strengthened, and a positive spring was fitted to the elevator circuit. In addition an external ASI was fitted and a lock was provided to keep the hood open during carrier landings. In this form the aircraft was redesignated the Sea Balliol T.21. An order was placed for thirty examples, WL715–WL734 and WP324–WP333, and the last was delivered on 7 December, 1954. They served with Nos 702, 750 and 781 Training Squadrons and No.1843 RNVR Squadron at Abbotsinch. One of these Sea Balliols later served at RAE Bedford.

Further Development and Sales

The company made extensive attempts to export the Balliol. One of the pre-production aircraft, VR597, went on an extensive sales tour of the Middle East, and was demonstrated in Egypt, Iraq, Lebanon and Syria, with officers of the respective air forces sampling the aircraft. Only two snags developed during the trip, first the port undercarriage leg tended to unlock when the aircraft undertook positive 'g' manoeuvres, and second the fuel booster pump for the main fuel tank failed. Luckily a replacement was borrowed from an RAF Hawker Fury squadron. The operation of the aircraft in hot and dry conditions did not reveal any problems, the coolant temperatures remaining within limits despite ground shade temperatures up to 42 deg C. Because of the large sliding hood, ground cockpit temperatures were also acceptable.

First Balliol T.2 for the Royal Ceylon Air Force, CA301.

No orders were secured from this trip. With large numbers of cheap reconditioned T-6 Texans available from the United States, and Yak-11s from the Soviet Union, no country was prepared to expend its military budget on new basic trainers. Boulton Paul was caught in the same bind that it experienced after the First World War, its aircraft, excellent though they were could not compete with cheap war surplus equipment. There was a brief hope that India would place an order for 198 Balliols, but the RAF had the priority for orders at the time, and so the Indian Air Force opted for Texans, supplemented later by the Vampire T.55.

Balliols being crated for despatch to Ceylon.

One order was won in Asia however, the first Boulton Paul export order since the P.9s which went to Australia just after the First World War. The Ceylon Air Force ordered twelve Balliol T.2s which were drawn from the RAF order. Five aircraft were delivered from RAF stocks (WG226/7, WN155/6/7), receiving the CAF serials CA301–5 respectively. Five more aircraft were built for the RAF to replace these, (XF672/3 and XF929–931). In the Ceylon serialling system, the first number indicated the aircraft type, so that '3' was the designated number reserved for the Balliol. The other seven aircraft were part of the cancelled RAF order and were placed on the British Civil Register by Boulton Paul for flight

The company demonstrator G-ANSF painted maroon with cream trim.

testing before delivery to Ceylon. These were WN164 (G-ANYL), WN166 (G-ANYM), WN147 (G-ANZV), WN148 (G-ANZW), WG224 (G-APCN), WG230 (G-APCO), WN132 (G-APCP), and they received the Ceylon serials CA306–312. After flight-testing they were dismantled and sent to Ceylon in packing cases by sea.

For a time Boulton Paul also operated their own Balliol demonstrator, G-ANSF, registered in August 1954. It was actually WG125 bought back from the RAF, and was painted maroon with cream trim. It was flown at the SBAC Farnborough Air Show of 1954, though its C of A check flight was not until 13 September, 1955. It was withdrawn from use in September 1956, with no likelihood of further Balliol sales. The last Ceylon Balliol T.2 (WN132/CA312) was the last Boulton Paul aircraft ever built, flying for the first time in June 1957, and being delivered to Ceylon in August. Though the P.111 and P.120 were later designs they were built and flown well before this.

A straightforward jet-powered version of the Balliol was drawn up by the company, the P.125. This was to be powered by a Rolls-Royce Derwent, sited in the nose in place of the Merlin, with the exhaust pipe passing beneath the cockpit and emerging beneath the rear fuselage. To give it ground clearance a nosewheel undercarriage was to be fitted, but beyond this the airframe remained largely Balliol. Nothing came of this rather crude conversion, and Boulton Paul were already working on more advanced jet trainers.

The Balliol was an aircraft conceived out of time. It was a competent basic trainer, well able to perform the tasks for which it had been designed, and to perform them well, but it was overtaken by the age of the jet. It has taken the RAF over 30 years to obtain their first propeller-turbine basic trainer, the Short Tucano, this being the concept which gave birth to the Balliol in the first place. The Mamba-powered Balliol T.1 was just ahead of its time, or at least ahead of turbine-engine technology, and the Merlin-powered Balliol T.2 was an anachronism.

Two Balliols survive, one of the Ceylon T.2s, CA310, is preserved at Katunayake in what is now Sri Lanka, and a Sea Balliol T.21, WL732, is

294

preserved at the Cosford Aerospace Museum, fittingly near its birthplace. Three cockpit sections of Balliol T.2s were also rescued from a Salford scrapyard, two going first to the Pennine Aviation Museum at Bacup, WN149 and WN534. Both these were later acquired by the Boulton Paul Society and moved back for restoration to the factory where they were built. The other, WN516, was saved by the North East Aircraft Museum at Sunderland.

P.108 Balliol

One 1,000 shp Armstrong Siddeley Mamba (T.1), one 1,245 hp Rolls-Royce Merlin 35 (T.2 and T.21).

Span 39 ft 4in; span folded 21 ft 8 in; length 36 ft 6 in (T.1), 35 ft 1½ in (T.2); height 10 ft 7 in (T.1), 12 ft 6 in (T.2); wing area 250 sq ft.

Empty weight 6,000 lb (T.1), 6,730 lb (T.2); loaded weight 7,845 lb (T.1), 8,470 lb (T.2).

Maximum speed 307 mph at 20,000 ft (T.1), 288 mph at 9,000 ft (T.2); service ceiling 36,750 ft (T.1), 32,500 ft (T.2); rate of climb 1,790 ft/min (T.2); endurance 2½ hr (T.1), 3 hr (T.2).

Armament: one .303 in Browning machine-gun, four rockets or eight 8½/10/11/25 lb practice bombs.

P.111/P.111A

'Ben' Gunn taking the unpainted P.111 for taxi-ing trials on the grass at Pendeford.

Built to Specification E.27/46 as part of a Government-funded research programme into the aerodynamics of delta-wing aircraft, the P.111 was the first of only two jet aircraft which Boulton Paul built. Design responsibility was assigned to Dr S C Redshaw, chief engineer of the company now that John North was managing director. It was a basic research aircraft unlike the contemporary Avro 707, which was a one-third flying model of the proposed Vulcan bomber. It was designed to investigate the control and stability of a high-speed delta-wing, and alternative wingtips could be fitted.

A Rolls-Royce Nene 3 RN.2 of 5,100 lb st provided the power and to achieve the maximum performance from this limited rating the airframe was designed to be as small as possible, the length being only 26 ft 1 in, not including the nose-probe, and the span 25 ft 8 in without either of the extended tips. The wing had a leading-edge sweep of 45 deg and a chord of 17 ft 2½ in at the root down to 4 ft 8 in at the (non-extended) tip, with zero dihedral. The wing was of stressed-skin construction with three main spars and one auxiliary spar to the rear. The sealed balance type elevons were hinged to the auxiliary spar, and comprised the entire trailing edge of the wing. As their name suggests they acted as both elevators and ailerons, and each was fitted with a tab which could be controlled electrically or manually.

The wings were attached directly to the fuselage in a mid-wing position, with the forward main spars connected within the fuselage, thus forming a single wing structure. There were three flexible fuel tanks in each wing, two forward of the front main spar at the inboard end, and one aft of the rear main spar, also at the inboard end; giving a total tankage of 230 gal. Alternative wing tips were provided, giving spans of 25 ft 8 in, 29 ft 9 in, and 33 ft 6 in, the last of these tips coming almost to a point, and the second being of intermediate planform.

The main undercarriage retracted inwards into the wing between the spars, and had an unusually wide track, for the wingspan, of nearly 14½ ft. The nosewheel retracted aft into the fuselage, and all undercarriage units were of the Dowty Liquid Spring type. Attached to the nosewheel leg was a long door unit, and there were two more sideways-retracting doors to completely cover the nosewheel bay. Likewise the main undercarriage legs had doors attached, with inner doors folding outwards to cover the wheels. Undercarrige retraction and extension was hydraulic, with a back-up air pressure system.

P.111 VT935 at Boscombe Down, showing the blister on the rear fuselage housing the anti-spin parachute.

The fuselage was of all-metal stressed-skin construction, in three basic sections. The forward section contained the intake, the cockpit, nosewheel bay, and an instrument bay just behind the cockpit. The engine intake was a horizontal oval with a centre-body splitter-plate. The cockpit sidewalls were formed by the bifurcated intake inner walls, which terminated in four ducts, created by the main spars bisecting the two side ducts, immediately before the plenum chamber just behind the cockpit.

296

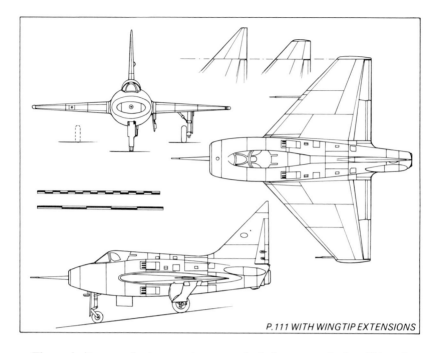

The cockpit canopy had a one-piece curved windscreen, and a hood hinged at the rear, containing three small windows for upward and sideways vision. The canopy was faired into the fuselage spine. The pilot sat on a Martin-Baker ejection seat, and had a conventional rudder bar, adjustable for leg reach, and a vertical grip-type control column. The elevons were fitted with a Boulton Paul hydraulic power-control unit, which could be switched off in the event of the power-control unit failing, for normal manual operation. An automatic electric trimming system was installed so that if the controls reverted to manual, the aircraft would always be in trim. The rudder was also power-operated, and had a small trim tab. The power-control units were some of the first ever installed. All controls were operated by normal push/pull rods. Entry to the cockpit was by an access ladder while the hood was held open by a special support.

A TR.1920 VHF radio was fitted in the fuselage spine just behind the cockpit, and below this was the instrument bay containing an automatic-observer panel recording twenty engine and control parameters. The aircraft also contained trace and voice recorders.

The centre fuselage section contained the engine bay, and the electro-hydraulic generators for the powered flying controls and undercarriage operation system, as well as other electrical equipment packed round the jetpipe. The rear fuselage section was integral with the tall triangular fin. The whole rear section could be removed for access to the engine.

The fin was constructed with three main spars, like the wings, and had a leading-edge sweep of 45 deg, the trailing edge being vertical. The triangular tip was made of fibreglass, and was designed so that it could be removed, like the extended wingtips, to test a different fin profile, but there is no record of this

The substantial rear fuselage structure of the P.111.

ever having been done. The VHF aerial was fitted to the fin tip, and there was a GSAP camera installed in the leading edge.

A 7 ft diameter anti-spin parachute was housed in a bulged fairing at the base of the fin on the port side of the fuselage. There was a substantial bumper beneath the tailcone to protect it in the event of the rear fuselage touching the runway, though this was unlikely as the aircraft sat on the ground at a natural angle of 17 deg to the horizontal, and had a comparatively tall undercarriage.

Construction of the P.111, VT935, started in 1947 and the aircraft was complete in the autumn of 1950. The first flight could not take place from Pendeford because it only had short grass runways, so after taxi-ing trials there the P.111 was dismantled and taken to Boscombe Down. It was still in bare metal finish, with just a black anti-glare panel in front of the cockpit, RAF roundels above and below the wings, and on either side of the nose, and fin

The P.111 taking off from Boscombe Down.

298

flashes. Boulton Paul's chief test pilot, Ben Gunn was not entrusted with the first flight as the aircraft was an RAE project, and Sqn Ldr Smyth, the CO of the Aero Flight undertook it.

The aircraft was found to be highly sensitive in all axes, because of the lack of feel in the power-control units, and the pilots had the impression of flying 'on a knife edge' all the time. Although they did get used to it to a certain extent, the rudder remained too slow in operation during cross-wind landings. This was made worse by the fact that landings were already quite tricky, and not only because of the sensitivity of the controls. With the clean lines of the aircraft, and the need to keep the engine turning at at least 7,000 rpm to keep the generators operating, pilots had trouble decelerating for landing, and approaches were normally made very fast and flat.

During the first few flights there were many problems with the undercarriage retraction system, resulting in several flights being made with the undercarriage locked down. Also, when the undercarriage was retracted the loss of drag from the nosewheel door caused an unacceptable trim change. There were also problems with the one-piece blown windscreen, and in July 1951 a new framed windscreen was fitted, together with a spring-loaded 'feel' system for the powered flying controls, and the rudder control was converted to manual operation.

The P.111A.

The P.111 appeared at the SBAC Displays at Farnborough in 1951 in a new silver respray with a blue cheatline. Two slight accidents occurred on 29 October, 1951, and 5 January, 1952, but the aircraft resumed flight test after only a short time. On 29 August, 1952, the P.111 suffered a more serious accident, a wheels-up forced landing, resulting in extensive damage.

While the damage was being repaired at Wolverhampton the opportunity was taken to make extensive modifications to the airframe, which were to result in it

The P.111 undergoing fuel flow tests, showing the later air brakes, sited at existing inspection panels.

being redesignated P.111A. A long probe was fitted to the intake splitter-place, the undercarriage doors were modified to ease the change of trim problem, and most important of all four air-brakes were fitted around the fuselage centre section to help deceleration on the approach. The inner surface of these air-brakes formed the intake duct wall just in front of the engine, so that when the air-brakes were extended, there were four rectangular holes in the intake walls, disturbing the airflow and causing loss of engine power. As a result of the crash of Boulton Paul's other delta-wing research aircraft, the P.120, caused by an undetected flutter in an elevon tab, the P.111A's elevon tabs were modified. As the P.111 had already flown at Mach 0.75 it would seem this alteration was just precautionary. The most striking change in the P.111A was a new all-yellow paint scheme.

The aircraft was taken back to Boscombe Down by road, and the first flight of the modified aircraft was on 2 July, 1953. The air-brakes worked well, but landing speeds were still high, and so the anti-spin parachute was strengthened

Now designated P.111A, VT935 wearing its new all-yellow paintwork at Boscombe Down.

300

The P.111 VT935 at Boscombe Down.

so that it could be used as a braking chute. The control system was still deemed to be too sensitive, so a pilot-controlled fully-variable system was installed. a 'Feel Strength' dial was added above the upper left hand side of the control panel. It was found to be possible to control the aircraft up to a speed of about 400 kt, but above this power assistance was essential, as the controls became too heavy.

In general the aircraft was pleasant to fly, and hardly justified its nickname *Yellow Peril*. It achieved Mach 0.93 (622 mph) at 35,000 ft and Mach 0.96 in a shallow dive. Top speed at sea level was 650 mph, and initial rate of climb was 9,400 ft/min with a maximum weight of 11,400 lb. Boulton Paul undertook the first 40 test flights, and then the aircraft was taken on charge by the RAE once more. Flight trials continued until 20 June, 1958, and all three wingtip configurations were tested.

On completion of its testing VT935 was donated to the College of Aeronautics at Cranfield, whence, it went by road. After many years there, in use as an instructional airframe, it was placed on permanent loan with the Midland Air Museum, at Coventry Airport, arriving on 13 July, 1975. During 1990/91 its pristine yellow paint scheme was restored, and it was displayed under the wing of a much larger delta, the Avro Vulcan, though it played no part in the design of that aircraft, or the other main RAF delta, the Gloster Javelin.

P.111/P.111A

One 5,100 lb st Rolls-Royce Nene 3 RN.2.

Span 25 ft 8 in (29 ft 9 in and 33 ft 6 in with detachable wingtips); length 26 ft 1 in (31 ft 6 in in P.111A with nose-probe); height 12 ft 6 in; wing area 269.25 sq ft (284.16 and 290.13 sq ft with detachable wingtips).

Empty weight 7,517 lb; loaded weight 10,217 lb (with 570 lb ballast, forward cg), 9,787 lb (with 230 lb ballast, aft cg).

Maximum speed 564 kt at sea level, 554 kt at 20,000 ft, 550 kt at 30,000 ft, 540 kt at 35,000 ft (Mach 0.93); rate of climb 9,400 ft/min.

The P.120 as first flown in natural metal finish.

P.120

The P.120 was purely a research aircraft built to Specification E.27/49 as part of a large Government programme to investigate the aerodynamic characteristics of the delta-wing form. It differed from the P.111 primarily in having a swept fin and rudder and a horizontal tail surface near the tip of the fin to improve longitudinal and directional stability. It was also fitted with movable wingtips, rather than the interchangeable wingtips which had been one of the features tested on the P.111.

The fuselage was identical to that of the P.111A back to frame 290.88, apart from the pitot tube being moved from the intake splitter-plate and the mounting of a VHF whip aerial on the spine just aft of the canopy. The same type of engine was fitted, a Rolls-Royce Nene RN.2 of 5,100 lb st. The rear fuselage was considerably modified and strengthened with extra formers to accommodate a swept fin and rudder, which replaced the P.111A's upright triangular unit. The fin leading-edge was swept 55 deg 50 min, and the trailing edge 39 deg 45 min. There was a main spar at about mid-chord with front and rear auxiliary spars,

The P.120 under construction at Pendeford.

302

the power-operated rudder being attached to the rear spar. In the tip of the fin there was a cine camera for recording airflow investigations when the port wing was tufted. The 7 ft diameter braking/anti-spin parachute was housed in a bullet fairing below the rudder and projecting back above the jetpipe, which itself was slightly lengthened.

A horizontal tail surface of delta planform was mounted about two thirds of the way up the fin. The leading-edge sweep was 45 deg, with a root chord of 5 ft 9 in, tapering to 10 in at the tip. It was not a tailplane in the accepted sense, pitch control remaining with the elevons as on the P.111A, but acted as a trimming surface activated by a switch on the left hand side of the cockpit. It was an all-moving slab surface of 30.74 sq ft area.

'Ben' Gunn with the unpainted P.120 VT951 at Boscombe Down.

The wing was identical to that of the P.111A apart from bulges over each outboard undercarriage door, the siting of the pitot head on the port wing and fitting of semi-elliptical fences at the wing/wingtip junction, to control span-wise flow. The interchangeable wingtips of the P.111A were replaced with movable wingtips of the same planform as the pointed, *i.e.* largest span, tips of the earlier aircraft. They were for pitch and lateral trimming, being activated by switches on the same port side cockpit panel as the tailplane control. There were three switches, one being a simple on/off switch, one operating the tips in unison for pitch trimming, and the other moving them in opposition for lateral trimming. They were operated by actuators mounted in the fuselage, in a bay housing the electro-hydraulic flying control actuators.

The P.120 was taken to Boscombe Down for its first flight, and it was to have a very short, but chequered flying career. It was given the serial VT951 and delivered unpainted. Boulton Paul's test pilot 'Ben' Gunn was to make the first flight on a bright morning on 6 August, 1952, and expected no problems following his experience with the very similar P.111A.

One of the few changes was to give him immediate difficulties. The horizontal tailplane had been set at what would later prove to be an incorrect, over-cautious, angle, requiring a much higher speed for take off than would otherwise have been necessary. Gunn discovered this when he had consumed three-quarters of Boscombe Down's very long runway and was still firmly on the

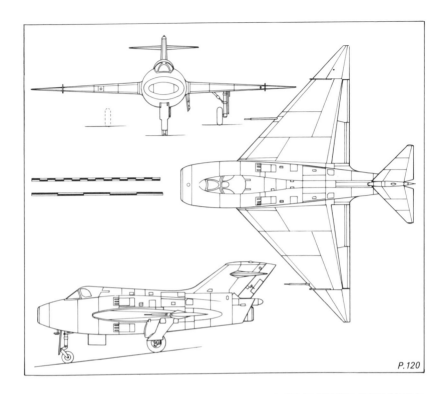

P.120

VT951 at Boscombe Down.

ground despite travelling at 175 kt. In his own words 'I shall never forget the look of startled amazement on the faces of the fatigue squad picking potatoes at the end of the runway as this dark shape scraped over their heads clawing frantically for altitude.'

After this alarming start to its flying career, the P.120 proved to be very pleasant to fly, without the sitting on a knife edge feeling of the P.111A at high speeds. After its first flights, a week before the Farnborough Show of 1952, it was given a gloss all-black colour scheme with yellow trim, which was to earn it

The P.120 newly painted all-black for the Farnborough exhibition and displays.

the immediate prophetic nickname Black-Widowmaker. It had flown a total of only 11 hr, all spent on investigations of its control characteristics, when it crashed.

On 28 August, Gunn was flying at around 4,000 ft undertaking a series of tests. He reached the highest speed so far achieved with the aircraft, about 450 kt, when he heard an intense buzz and saw the tab position indicator flicker. Because there was no feedback system in the power controls, he had been unaware that a severe flutter had occurred in the port elevon, there being no vibration transmitted through the control column. There was a loud bang, the test pilot's nightmare, and immediately the aircraft rolled to port.

The P.120 near the end of its short flying career.

After two complete rolls Gunn managed to resume level flight by the use of full starboard aileron and rudder. With continued judicious use of the remaining elevon and the trimming tailplane he was able to control the aircraft to some degree and began a slow climb to 12,000 ft. As the pitot tube had been bent back by the wing vibration before the elevon had parted company, the air-speed indicator was useless. Gunn continued to gingerly try different controls to discover what he was able to do. He found that if power were reduced or if he moved the control column or rudder from their fully starboard positions, the port wing immediately dropped.

He made a gentle descent to 6,000 ft and then jettisoned the cockpit canopy,

The remains of the P.120 after its crash.

which seemed to help stabilise the P.120. With the canopy gone he was now able to see that the entire port elevon and tab assembly had been ripped away. When he descended further to 3,000 ft, he encountered some turbulence which engendered violent lateral oscillations, which he was unable to control. With the angle of bank 60 deg, he gave up the unequal fight and ejected. Gunn thus had the dubious honour of being the first pilot to eject from a delta-winged aircraft, and the P.120 smashed into Salisbury Plain.

Subsequent investigations found that a lack of stiffness in the tab control mechanism had caused the tab to be forced down some 45 deg, and the elevon

Test specimen of the P.120 tailplane preserved at the Midland Air Museum, Coventry. (*Author's photograph*)

306

up some 60 deg, causing the fracture. Further tests showed that only half the design load was able to produce the effect, whereas test specimens at Boulton Paul had taken 1.36 times the design load.

Little of the P.120's planned testing had been done in its 11 hr flying, of course, and little was learned, apart from the elevon flutter itself. Plans were formulated to convert the P.111A to the same layout, but these never came to fruition. One outcome of the accident was that Martin-Baker were given priority by the Air Ministry for the development of automatic ejection seats!

As the last Boulton Paul design to fly, it was unfortunate that the P.120 came to grief in this way. Amazingly a test specimen of the trimming tailplane still survives. Used for instruction purposes for many years at Hatfield Polytechnic, it now resides in the Midland Air Museum, Coventry.

P.120

One 5,100 lb st Rolls-Royce RN.2 Nene.
Span 33 ft 5½ in; length 29 ft 7½ in; height 9 ft 6½ in; wing area 290.13 sq ft.
Empty weight 10,656 lb; loaded weight 12,580 lb.
Performance unrecorded but presumed similar to P.111.

Production Details

Boulton & Paul P.3 Bobolink

Three aircraft ordered under Contract A.S.37485 dated 1.12.17., (to Specification A.1a), powered by Bentley B.R.2 radials. One built, C8655, largely complete by December 1914. First flight at Mousehold by Capt F T Courtney, delivered to Martlesham Heath week ending 9.3.18 for comparative trials with rival A.1a fighters. Remaining two, C8656 and C8657, cancelled 9.4.18.

Boulton & Paul P.5 Hawk

Three aircraft ordered 1.12.17 to Specification A.1a. Serials C8652, C8653, C8654. Order cancelled before any built.

Boulton & Paul P.6

One aircraft only, first flown late 1918, with special serial X.25. Registered K-120/ G-EACJ on 20 May, 1919.

Boulton & Paul P.7 Bourges

Two aircraft only built to Contract 35A/909/C730, dated 24.4.18 to Specification A.2(b). First prototype, F2903, delivered week ending 12.7.18, designated Mk IIA with Bentley B.R.2. Re-engined with ABC Dragonflies during 1919 and re-designated Mk IA. Entered civil register as K.129/G-EACE. Second prototype, F2904, delivered 1919 with Dragonfly engines, and gulled upper centre section, designated Mk IB. Crashed Mousehold, early 1919. Entirely rebuilt as the P.8 Atlantic prototype.

Boulton & Paul P.7b Bourges

Third Bourges, F2905, the sole P.7b with Napier Lions built to Contract

35A/909/C730, dated 24.4.18 to Specification A.2(b). Delivered 21.3.20, later G-EAWS.

Boulton & Paul P.8 Atlantic

Two aircraft, company-financed for nonstop transatlantic flight and prototype airliner/mailplane powered by Napier Lions. First aircraft (built from structure of P.7 Bourges F2904), crashed on maiden flight at Mousehold April 1919. Second aircraft, G-EAPE. First flight 10.5.20.

Boulton & Paul P.9

Eight aircraft, all with RAF.1a engine. First aircraft exported to Australia mid-1919. Subsequent aircraft slightly modified. Second aircraft, G-EAPD, 21.4.20, to company. Cancelled Nov. 1920. Third aircraft, G-EASJ, 15.7.20 to J.G. Weir at Renfrew. To South Africa March 1929 as G-UAAM. Fourth aircraft, to Australia, as G-AUBT in June 1921. Fifth aircraft, to Australia, as G-AUCP in June 1921. Sixth aircraft, as G-AUCT June 1921. Seventh aircraft, G-EAWS, used by Boulton & Paul. Eighth aircraft, G-EBEQ, first flight 4.9.22.

Boulton & Paul P.10

Sole aircraft built 1919. Unregistered and possibly unflown. One wing and fin/rudder preserved by Bridewell Museum, Norwich.

Boulton & Paul P.12 Bodmin

Two aircraft, J6910 and J6911, built to Contract AM 305919/20 dated 16.8.21 against Specification 9/20. First flight of J6910 during 1924.

Boulton & Paul P.15 Bolton

One aircraft, J6584, built in 1922 to Contract AM 232562/20 dated 7.7.20. The first aircraft with an all-metal structure delivered to the RAF.

Boulton & Paul P.25 Bugle I

Five aircraft to Specification 30/22. First two, J6984 and J6985 with Jupiter II/III, to Contract AM369336/22 dated 19.12.22, first flown 25.7.23. Third aircraft, J7235; with Jupiter IV, shorter span and increased fuel capacity to AM 439250/23, dated 25.9.23, completed in 1924. Two further prototypes built in 1924, to Contract AM 454262/24, dated 21.1.24, J7259 and J7260.

Boulton & Paul P.25a Bugle II

Two aircraft, J7259 and J7260, to Contract AM 469837/23, built in 1925 with Napier Lions and fuel tanks inside fuselage instead of beneath upper wings.

Boulton & Paul P.29 Sidestrand I

Two prototypes built to Specification B.9/24, J7938, first flown from Mousehold in 1926, second, J7939, flown later in the year. Bristol Jupiter VI.

Boulton & Paul P.29a Sidestrand II

Six production aircraft to Contract 789943/27, with Jupiter VI ordered in July 1927 to equip No.101 Squadron. J9176–J9181.

Boulton & Paul P.29a Sidestrand III

Twelve production aircraft to Specification B.10/29. Jupiter VIII and VIIIF, altered fuel tanks and bomb-aimer's position. Ordered in three batches of five (April 1928, Contract 789943/27), four (November 1929, Contract 921961/29) and three aircraft (Contract 92429/31). J9185–9189, J9767–9770, K1992–1994. J9186 Testbed for Townend Ring development. Re-engined with Jupiter XF and then Pegasus I.M.3s. Converted to Specification B.29/33 as prototype Sidestrand V, later re-designated prototype P.75 Overstrand. J9770 used for engine development work, later converted to Overstrand.

Boulton & Paul P.31 Bittern

Two aircraft, J7936 and J7937, to Contract 617051/25, Armstrong Siddeley Lynx. First machine had fixed guns, second machine had revolving barbettes. J7936 first flown in 1927. Second aircraft differed in having strut bracing to outer wings, engines lowered and fitted with Townend rings, redesignated P.31A.

Boulton & Paul P.32

Prototype only, J9950, to Specification B.22/27, under Contract 796097/27. Three Bristol Jupiter XF. First Flight 23.10.31.

Boulton & Paul P.33 Partridge

Prototype only, J8459, to Specification F.96/26, under Contract 693450/26. Bristol Jupiter VII. First flew in 1928.

Boulton & Paul P.41 Phoenix I

One aircraft with wooden airframe and an ABC Scorpion, registered G-AAIT on 11.6.29. Experimental model only, totally rebuilt in proposed production form.

Boulton & Paul P.41 Phoenix II

G-AAIT totally rebuilt with Salmson radial, metal fuselage and revised undercarriage. Production plans abandoned.

Boulton & Paul P.64 Mail-Carrier

Prototype only G-ABYK, built to Specification 21/28. Two Bristol Pegasus I.M.2. First flight 23 March, 1933. Wrecked on 21.10.33.

Boulton & Paul P.71A Feederliner

Two only for Imperial Airways, G-ACOX *Boadicea* and G-ACOY *Britomart*. Two Armstrong Siddeley Jaguar IV. G-ACOX crashed and written off 25.10.35 at Hàren, Brussels. G-ACOY lost over English Channel 25.9.36.

Boulton Paul P.75 Overstrand

Four Sidestrands were converted to Overstrands. J9186 prototype, converted Sidestrand to Specification B.29/33, originally designated Sidestrand V. J9185 converted Sidestrand. J9179 Converted Sidestrand. J9770 Converted Sidestrand.

Production batch of 19 aircraft ordered to Specification B.23/34 to replace No.101 Squadron's two flights of Sidestrands, and to enable a third flight to be formed, with 50 percent spare aircraft to allow for attrition. K4546–4564. Five production aircraft ordered as replacements in 1935, K8173–8177.

Boulton Paul P.82 Defiant

Two prototypes built to Specification F.9/35 issued on 26.6.35, and ordered on 4.12.35. Construction of first prototype begun at Norwich, but completed at Wolverhampton. K8310 first prototype, first flight 11.8.37 from Wolverhampton. Not fitted with a turret initially. Became 2783M. K8620 second prototype, first flight 18.5.39. Crashed at Portcawl, 13.7.40.

Boulton Paul Defiant Mk I

First production batch of 87, aircraft, L6951–L7036, under Contract 622849/37 placed 28.4.37. Aircraft delivered between August 1939 and May 1940. L6950 first production aircraft flown 30.7.39. A & AEE, performance and handling trials. Tested with bomb racks August 1939. Became 2980M.

A further 202 production aircraft ordered in February 1938, followed by 161 more in May 1938 both under contract 757867/39, with the following batches of serials. The first 202 aircraft were delivered between June and October 1940. N1535–N1582, N1610–N1653, N1671–N1706, N1725–N1773, N1788–N1812, N3306–N3405, N3421–N3460, N3477–N3520. Batch of 150 aircraft ordered, December 1939 under Contract 34864/39 with the following serials. T3911–T3960, T3980–T4010, T4030–T4076, T4100–T4141. Aircraft were delivered between February and August 1941.

Fifty aircraft ordered February 1940 under Contract 34864/39 with the following serials, V1106–V1141, V1170–V1183. Aircraft were delivered between April and June 1941.

Final order for Defiant Mk Is, for 300 in July 1940 under Contract 34864/39. Only the 63 with the following serials, AA281–AA330, AA350–AA362, were built to Defiant Mk I standard, and delivered between May and July 1941.

Boulton Paul Defiant Mk II

Seven aircraft of the previous order were converted to Defiant Mk II standard on the production line, and subsequently to Target Tug T.T.1s. AA363–AA369.

The last 230 aircraft from the last order for Defiant Mk1s under Contract 34864/39, order changed to Defiant Mk II standard. Delivery began in July 1941, and was completed January 1942. AA370–AA384, AA398–AA447, AA469–AA513, AA531–AA550, AA566–AA595, AA614–AA633, AA651–AA670.

The last 30 aircraft of this order were cancelled, AA671–AA673, AA687–AA713.

A further order for 298 Defiant Mk IIs with the following serials was cancelled, AV508–AV557, AV571–AV605, AV633–AV682, AV698–AV742, AV768–AV787, AV805–AV839, AV863–AV892, AV910–AV944.

Boulton Paul P.92

Three aircraft ordered in March 1938 to Specification F.11/37, two powered by Rolls-Royce Vultures and one with Napier Sabres. Order cancelled 26.5.40 when work on first aircraft was 5 percent complete.

Boulton Paul P.92/2

Half-scale wooden replica of P.92 built by Heston Aircraft, V3142. Completed in the spring of 1941.

Boulton Paul P.108 Balliol T.1

Three aircraft only built, from four prototypes and 20 pre-production aircraft ordered in August 1945 under Contract 6/Acft/5623/CB.9(a) to Specifiction T.7/45 issued August 1945. The aircraft to be powered by either Rolls-Royce Darts or Armstrong Siddeley Mambas. The latter engines were chosen.

VL892 First flown 26.5.47 from Wolverhampton. Powered by Bristol Mercury due to late arrival of the Mamba.

VL917 First flown 24.3.48. Powered by the Armstrong Siddeley Mamba. The world's first aircraft powered by a single propeller-turbine.

VL935 First flown 27.5.48.

VL954 Unbuilt, replaced by first Merlin-powered prototype.

Boulton Paul P.108 Balliol T.2

Amended order for four prototypes and 17 pre-production aircraft powered by Rolls-Royce Merlin 35 to Specification T.14/47, replacing the balance of the Balliol T.1 order. Ordered in August 1946 under Contract 6/Acft/175/CB.9(a). Pre-production aircraft originally ordered as propeller-turbine powered, VR587–9 cancelled with the switch to Merlin engines to maintain the total of 24 prototype/pre-production aircraft. VW897–900, VR590–606.

VW897 First Merlin-powered prototype. First flown 10.7.48.

VW898 AAEE, CO2 contamination tests, tropical trials Khartoum and Nairobi. Performance tests, engineering appraisal.

VW899 AAEE, CO2 contamination tests, towed-target tests.

VW900 AAEE, handling, spinning, hood jettison trials.

VR590 First pre-production aircraft.

One hundred production aircraft ordered under Contract 6/Acft/4869/CB.9(a). Four aircraft released as part of a Royal Ceylon Air Force order for 12 Balliols, WF989–WF998, WG110–WG159, WG173–WG187, WG206–WG223.

WF989 First production aircraft, first flown April 1952.

Second production order for 138 aircraft under contract 6/Acft/6281/CB.9(a). Only 40 built, the final 98 being cancelled. Eight aircraft released as part of a Royal Ceylon Air Force order for 12 Balliols. WN132–171. Cancelled aircraft WN172–WN181, WN196–WN234, WN255–WN303.

Five aircraft, XF672, XF673, XF929, XF930, XF931, ordered as replacements for RAF Balliols delivered to Ceylon. The remaining seven Ceylon Balliols being offset from RAF cancellations.

Thirty Balliols built by Blackburn Aircraft to an order for 120, the remaining 90 being cancelled. WN506–WN535 Delivered to Royal Air Force. (Cancelled WN536–WN555, WN573–WN601, WN634–WN674).

Boulton Paul Sea Balliol T.21

First batch of 20 aircraft for the Fleet Air Arm ordered under contract 6/Acft/5971/CB.5(c). WL715–WL734 Delivered to Fleet Air Arm.

Second batch of 10 aircraft for the Fleet Air Arm ordered under Contract 6/Acft/6347/CB.5(c). WP324–WP333.

Total Balliol production		
Balliol T.1 prototypes	Boulton Paul	3
Balliol T.2. prototypes	Boulton Paul	4
Balliol T.2 pre-production	Boulton Paul	17
Balliol T.2. RAF	Boulton Paul	133
Balliol T.2 RAF	Blackburn	30
Balliol T.2 Ceylon	Boulton Paul	12
Sea Balliol T.21	Boulton Paul	30
Total		229

Boulton Paul P.111

One aircraft only, VT935, to Specification E.27/46, first flown 10.10.50. After landing accident 29.8.52 it was modified with four large air-brakes and other minor changes and redesignated the P.111A. First flight in this form was on 2.7.53.

Boulton Paul P.120

One aircraft only, VT951, to Specification E.27/49. First flown 6.8.52. Crashed 29.8.52, after inflight failure of port elevon. Pilot ejected.

Unbuilt Projects

The drawings in this section were prepared by Colin Penny, with minimal alterations, from various original company drawings and therefore vary in style and detail.

Boulton (&) Paul designs for complete aircraft were assigned project numbers from P.1 to P.147, though P.13 was not apparently used. Of these, 23 designs were actually built, including the P.92/2, which was a half-scale P.92, and the P.93 which was the Blackburn Roc. Surviving details for the first 15 unbuilt projects, *i.e.* up to P.24, are very sketchy, as they are for a few of the subsequent projects.

P.1, P.2, P.4

There are vague indications that the first five Boulton & Paul designs were all layouts for fighters. The P.1 *or* the P.2 was a single-bay biplane fighter design with a Bentley B.R.2, and one of these three project numbers might well have been assigned to a design referred to as the N.F.1 (Night Fighter 1) on a drawing list. This was a biplane equipped with an Eeman gun mount, a mounting for three Lewis guns angled upwards at 45 deg.

P.5 Hawk

Though three prototypes of the P.5 were ordered (C8652–4), no details of the design survived their cancellation, though it is possible that the P.5 would have been an ABC Wasp powered fighter. Specification A.1a which outlined the so-called Sopwith Camel replacement, attracted designs powered by both the Wasp and the Bentley B.R.2, and Sopwith produced both the B.R.2 powered Snipe, and the Wasp-powered Snail, the former being the eventual winner of the production contract, and the latter being ordered in only prototype form. It seems unlikely that Boulton & Paul would have received orders for two B.R.2–powered types, unless they were very similar.

P.11

This aircraft is referred to on the surviving drawings as the Type XXI, which actually refers to the RAF Specification XXI, which was issued on 20 May, 1919. The Type number P.11 has been inferred, as this is the only unknown Boulton & Paul project number before the P.12 Bodmin, whose specification was issued in 1920. Specification XXI called for a two-seat amphibian which could be operated from land or sea, or from the decks of carriers.

The P.11 emerged as a two-bay biplane powered by a 475 hp Napier Lion V. The crew were seated close together beneath the upper wing, in which there was a large circular cut-out for the pilot's ingress, and upper hemisphere visibility. There was also a long cut-out at the rear of the upper wing to give the gunner sufficient clearance to operate his Scarff ring mounted Lewis gun. The pilot was provided with a fixed forward-firing Vickers machine-gun on the port side of the upper fuselage firing through the four-blade propeller. The fuselage, which was carried above the lower wing on struts, had a marked hump in the centre section to give the pilot better forward visibility.

Boulton & Paul went to the trouble of building an elaborate mock-up of the aircraft, but no prototype order was forthcoming. The rival Fairey Pintail received an order for three prototypes, but no production order followed, though the Imperial Japanese Navy ordered three.

P.13

(Designation thought not to have been used.)

P.14

Possibly a biplane design dating from 1922.

P.16

A troop carrier with drawings dated in October 1920, built to official Specification 5/20. The Armstrong Whitworth Awana and the Vickers Victoria each received orders for two prototypes, the latter winning the production order.

P.17

A fleet spotter with the pilot forward of the engine, and a second P.17a layout with the engine forward of the pilot.

P.18

A preliminary scheme only for a reconnaissance aircraft, dated June 1921.

P.19

Designed to Specification 15/21 for a twin-engined bomber, which was abandoned, details of which do not seem to have survived.

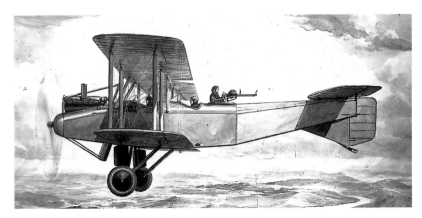

Impression by Geoffrey Watson drawn in 1921 of an all-steel military biplane, most probably the P.20.

P.20 (All-Steel Military Aircraft)

The only information surviving about this aircraft are two photographs of artist's impressions with this title, by Geoffrey Watson, who made a number of such pictures for the company in the early days. They are dated 1921, so the likeliest project number is P.20, which was a Corps reconnaissance aircraft. The most likely specification to which it was designed would be Specification 5/21 which was for an Army Co-operation aircraft to replace the D.H.9A, a requirement eventually fulfilled by the Fairey Fawn, though that was a two-seat aircraft. There was also another specification which started as 'The D of R Type 3A' and was later re-issued as Specification 10/21. This called for an Army-Co-operation aircraft capable of gunnery spotting, general reconnaissance and unit liaison, and the Hawker Duiker and Armstrong Whitworth Wolf were the prototypes resulting from this requirement.

The All Steel Military Aircraft was a three-seater, and is interesting because its fin and rudder are below the tailplane, in the manner of the Fairey Pintail. This would give the rear gunner, with his single Lewis gun, a much wider field of fire. The powerplant appears to have been the Armstrong Siddeley Puma, supporting the view that the design might have been a 'Nine-Ack' replacement. The aircraft also features a very wide-track, split-axle undercarriage, also indicating that it was an Army Co-operation design. The streamlined overwing fuel tanks are a rather unusual feature, emanating from a feeling within the Air Ministry at the time that fuel tanks should not be carried within the fuselage of such aircraft.

P.21

This was a high-altitude photographic-reconnaissance aircraft dating from October 1921.

P.22

A Coastal torpedo aircraft also from October 1921.

An amphibian.

No details survive.

A further development of the Bolton/Bugle theme. A twin-engined medium day bomber, powered by Napier Lions.

A single-engined day bomber landplane to Specification 10./23 powered by a Typhoon.

A single-seat fighter powered by a single Lioness, which was a projected inverted unsupercharged version of the Napier Lion to give better forward visibility. The engine was test flown in a Fairey Fawn, but got no further, so the P.30 was stillborn.

A monoplane powered by two Lynx engines.

The P.34 was navallised version of the P.33 Partridge for Specification N.21/26 for a Fairey Flycatcher replacement, in competition with the Fairey Flycatcher II, Hawker Hoopoe, Gloster Gnatsnapper and Vickers 123/141. Dates on the drawings suggest changes required for the P.33, were incorporated in the P.34 from the outset, so that the final version of the P.33 could be more truthfully said to be a landplane version of the P.34. No prototype order was forthcoming, and there were no production orders for this Specification.

The prevailing doctrine between the wars in RAF circles was that 'the bomber would always get through'. Obviously those planning the defence of this country had then to make plans to see that this doctrine was negated. One of the persistent ideas for destroying bombers was the upwards-firing gun as embodied in the P.31 Bittern, but the twin-Lewis guns of that design were deemed insufficient fire power and so the use of cannon was also advanced. The two concepts were combined in Specification F.29/27 which called for a bomber destroyer armed with a Coventry Ordnance Works 1½ pdr cannon (COW Gun) firing obliquely upwards.

The first Boulton & Paul design drawn, in February 1928, to fulfill the requirements of this Specification was a large two-seat biplane, to be powered by a Bristol Jupiter VII. The pilot sat just in front of the unstaggered wings, for good forward visibility during night flying, and the gunner was located in the rear fuselage, with the COW gun pointing obliquely up over the centre section. The rear fuselage and tail seem to have been basically taken from the P.33 Partridge. The potential performance of this design seems to be moderate to say the least, which is perhaps why Boulton & Paul's submissioon for F.29/27 was a totally different design, the P.35 single-seat monoplane.

This P.35 was to be powered by a Rolls-Royce F11 supercharged engine driving a two-blade propeller. Rolls-Royce were soon to change the designation of this and other engines using the Roman system of numerals, so that the F11 became the FXI, shortly to be named the Kestrel. The wings were strutted and wire-braced, untapered and with the markedly square-cut tips which were a Boulton & Paul trademark. Surface cooling radiators were recessed in the inner wings. The 8-ft long COW gun was sited in front of the pilot, just to his right, and he was tasked with loading it as well as flying the aircraft against hostile targets. For the requirement to operate at night the P.35 was given a very wide-track non-retractable undercarriage. Because of the weight concentrated in the forward fuselage, not least the 200 lb gun plus its ammunition, a markedly long fuselage was drawn, to increase the moment of the tail surfaces.

The P.35 did not receive approval for F.29/27, two other companies receiving orders for prototypes, Westland with a version of their Jupiter-powered monoplane Interceptor, and Vickers with an extraordinary pusher, reminiscent of their First World War Gunbus and Vampire. By the time that these aircraft were ready the Air Ministry seemed to have cooled towards the whole concept. Certainly a fighter armed with the very slow firing COW gun would have been lucky to hit a bomber not in the plane of its flight. When the Luftwaffe adopted the idea during the Second World War it was with faster-firing weapons.

P.36

The P.36 was basically an airliner version of the P.32 heavy bomber. It featured the same wings of 100 ft span and the same engines, three geared Bristol Jupiter VIII, allied to a new fuselage, with provision for 14 passengers. The meagre passenger capacity compared to the size and power of the aircraft must have mitigated against it ever being ordered. The contemporary Handley Page H.P.45 of similar size, could seat 38, though it did have four engines.

P.37 'Streamline'

This was an extraordinary design for a high-speed day bomber. The design had a long gestation as drawings were dated September 1929, nearly a year after the project was initiated. It was basically a sesquiplane layout, with the large upper wing, of nearly 72 ft span and 12 ft chord, carried well above the fuselage on a substantial streamlined pylon. This was to reduce interference drag between wing and fuselage. The lower wing was very much smaller both in span and chord (Only 3 ft), and there were just single V interplane struts on each side. The fuselage was very streamlined and the crew were carried in an enclosed cockpit. The most extraordinary feature of the design however was the retractable skid undercarriage, with small outriggers under the lower wings. Presumably there would have been a jettisonable bogie for take off. With the single large skid occupying much of the fuselage's lower surface, it is unclear where the bombs would have been stowed. There was little ground clearance beneath the small lower wing.

There does not appear to have been provision for gun positions, presumably the high speed of the aircraft being its only protection, presaging the concept of

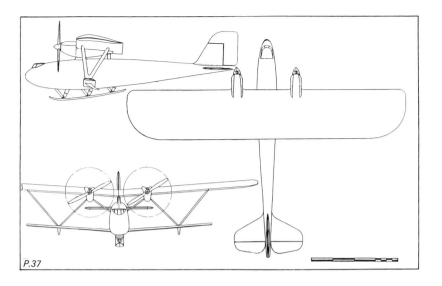

P.37

the unarmed day bomber so notably achieved by the Mosquito. It was to be
powered by two Rolls-Royce F.IIS engines mounted on the upper wing.

P.38

This was an aerial survey monoplane with three de Havilland Gipsy engines,
designed in December 1928.

P.39

Though the company did build Felixtowe hulls during and after the 1914–18 war,
this is the only Boulton & Paul design for a flying-boat project. Obviously
believing that if they were going to enter a new sphere of interest they would do
it in a big way, then P.39 was a very large monoplane flying-boat powered by six
Rolls-Royce F.11 engines in three tandem pairs carried on pylons above the

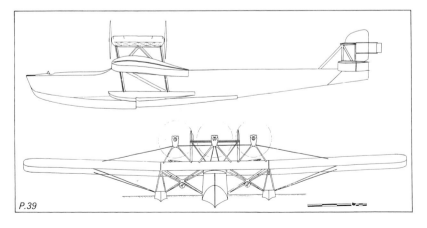

P.39

wing. Though clearly Dornier influenced, it featured inboard wing floats rather than sponsons.

Span was 125 ft, and length 115 ft 1 in including the rudder servo. If it had been built at land-locked Norwich, just transporting it to the sea would have been an interesting exercise.

P.40

This was a biplane troop-carrier designed in January 1929 to Specification C.16/28, and powered by three Bristol Mercury V geared engines. Two prototypes were ordered to this Specification, the four-engined Gloster T.C.33, and the three-engined H.P.43, a close relative of the H.P.42. No production orders resulted.

P.42

This was a civil general purpose landplane to Specification 6/29 powered by three supercharged Armstrong Siddeley Lynx engines. Two layouts were offered, the P.42 which was a biplane, and the P.42A which was a monoplane with the third engine on a pylon. Interestingly the monoplane drawings were dated June 1929, a month before the biplane's.

P.43

This was a four-seat cabin aircraft powered by three Cirrus Hermes engines and reminiscent of the Westland Limousine IV, which was powered by the same engines. The P.43 design appeared in October 1929, when the Westland Limousine was already flying.

P.44

This was a four-seat light aircraft reminscent of the de Havilland Puss Moth, and powered by a single ADC Airsix engine. It had 53 ft span, and the design appeared in September 1929.

P.45

In November 1929 a further design for a small airliner appeared, or 'saloon' as they were referred to in those days. This was a twin-engined aircraft, with five seats, for Imperial Airways. A choice of engines was offered, either Jupiter XIFs or Jaguar VIs or Lion Vs.

P.46

This was a version of the P.45 saloon, but with two geared Lynx engines.

P.47

This was a high-speed mail-carrier developed from the sesquiplane P.37 bomber, in December 1929, and powered by two Rolls-Royce 'F' type engines. The high-speed mail-carrier, a concept the Air Ministry continually toyed with, was an obvious way to exploit Boulton & Paul's expertise in high-speed twin-engined bomber design.

P.48

This was a four-engined airliner for Imperial Airways for the same requirement which was to be filled by the Handley Page H.P.42 and the Short L.17 Scylla. It was to be powered by four Jupiter XIF or Jaguar VI engines, and the drawings were dated February 1930.

P.49

This was a further version of the P.37/P.47 sesquiplane layout, but was a single-seat high-speed racing aircraft. It was powered by a single Gipsy engine mounted centrally on the upper wing. The retractable skid idea was replaced by a single retractable mainwheel with castors on the tips of the lower wings.

The pilot was seated in the torpedo-like fuselage, behind the wing, with what would have given an abysmal view, a not unusual aspect of racing aircraft of the day.

P.50

In April 1930 this two-seat general-purpose monoplane appeared on the drawing-boards at Boulton & Paul. It was to be powered by an Armstrong Siddeley geared Panther. The Panther had started life as the Jaguar Major, basically a slightly enlarged Jaguar giving 525 hp. The P.50 was the first of a whole series of projects to be designed around it.

P.51

At the same time this six-passenger monoplane, also powered by the Panther appeared, and it must be assumed they were closely related.

P.52

This was a twin-engined bomber powered by two Panthers.

P.53

A further illustration of Boulton & Paul design department's tendency to produce a whole family of designs based on one theme, this was a reconnaissance seaplane version of the P.50 also powered by the Armstrong Siddeley Panther.

P.54

Another 'Saloon' for Imperial Airways, the P.54 was a five-passenger, twin-engined biplane, with two Panther engines. Unusually it featured a biplane tail unit. The design appeared in May 1930.

P.55

This was designed in July 1930 against Specification 26/28, for a civil aircraft to operate from confined spaces. It was a single-engined biplane, powered by a Panther engine. The pilot sat in front of the wings for good visibility and there was provision in the cabin for four passengers, a toilet, and baggage. Span was 49 ft 9½ in, length 38 ft 4 in and height 15 ft. It might well have made a useful bush aircraft.

P.56

This was another streamlined mail-carrier of the same sesquiplane layout as the P.47, powered in this case by two Armstrong Siddeley Panthers.

P.57

The P.57 was drawn in August 1930. This was a development of the P.29 Sidestrand for the Irish Free State, for use as a general purpose aircraft/bomber. It featured extra streamlining and two geared Jaguar engines, but unusually had a biplane tail unit.

P.58

This was designed to Specification S.9/30 which called for a three-seat fleet spotter, with optional wheels or floats. The P.58, designed in September 1930, was an equal-span biplane with single-bay staggered wings. It was powered by a supercharged Panther or an inline Rolls-Royce F12 in alternative P.58A form.

The pilot sat just behind the wing, in a slightly raised portion of the fuselage so that his head was above the upper wing, which was carried over the fuselage on inclined N-struts. The other two crew members sat in tandem in a large bath-tub like cockpit just behind the pilot. A single fixed forward-firing Vickers machine-gun was fitted, together with a Lewis gun for the observer.

The company went to the extent of offering a more radical alternative airframe, the P.58B. This bore the hallmark of the P.37 project in that it was a sesquiplane with a narrow-chord cranked lower wing. In the wheeled version it was to be fitted with large spats, the design of which was to appear later in the P.64. The P.58B was also offered with either engine. The only prototypes emanating from S.9/30 were the Gloster FS.36 and the Fairey S.9/30 and no production orders were forthcoming.

P.59

Yet another three-engined transport for Imperial Airways, the P.59 was offered with either geared Jaguars or Panther M.S. engines.

P.60

Another development of the P.29 Sidestrand, the P.60 was a photographic aircraft for the Royal Canadian Air Force. It was powered by two geared Jaguars.

P.61

This was the third streamlined mail-carrier designed by Boulton & Paul. It was powered by two Jupiter XFBs.

P.62

Another attempt to exploit the moderate success of the Sidestrand, this was in effect a cross between the P.61 mail-carrier and the Sidestrand, produced in two versions. There was the P.62 streamlined day bomber, with optional use as a torpedo bomber, and there was the P.62A, a civil transport version. Both of them were offered with either Jupiter XF or Panther engines.

P.63

This was the final metamorphosis of the sesquiplane layout started with the P.37. It was a high-speed interceptor fighter powered by two Napier Rapiers. The Rapier had been designed in 1928 by Frank Halford, and was a H configuration sixteen-cylinder air-cooled engine giving 340 hp.

P.65

This was a seaplane version of the P.64 Mail-Carrier for AB Aerotransport of Sweden. It was offered with a variety of engines, either Jupiter XFA or XFAM, or Panther M.S. A great deal of work was done in designing an upper cargo hatch for lifting cargo out, and in mooring methods. No order was forthcoming however.

P.66

This was designed to Specification G.4/31 issued in June 1931 and amended three months later, for a replacement for the Gordon/Wapiti general purpose aircraft, of which about 700 had entered service, so there was intense competition from most manufacturers. The aircraft had to fulfill an almost impossible combination of roles, including army co-operation, casualty evacuation, dive-bombing, light bombing by day and night, photography, reconnaissance over land and sea, and torpedo bombing.

Wind-tunnel model of the P.66 to Specification G/4/31.

The P.66 was a very advanced looking shoulder-wing monoplane, offered with a Jupiter FFAM or XFBM or a Panther engine shrouded by a Townend ring. The pilot sat just in front of the wing for good forward visibility, with the gunner just aft of the wing. It featured interchangeable surfaces, the horn-balanced rudder and elevators being identical, for ease of maintenance. A P.66 prototype was not ordered for evaluation, and the eventual competition winner was the Vickers 253, but this was not given a production order either. Vickers suggested a more advanced design they had on the drawing board, and that was ordered as the Wellesley.

P.67

Specification F.7/30 was issued to produce a fighter which would exceed the performance of the Siskin still in service and the Hawker Fury which was about to replace it. It called for a top speed of at least 250 mph, and corresponding improvements in ceiling, rate of climb and manoeuvrability. As a check on all-out performance it was also to be able to be operated by day and night, which usually meant excellent forward visibility for the pilot and a wide-track undercarriage. It was also to be armed with four Vickers machine-guns rather than the usual two, the first step towards acknowledging the greater fire-power that would be needed as speeds increased. The preferred engine was the evaporation-cooled Goshawk, though this was not mandatory because of the problems the engine had been having.

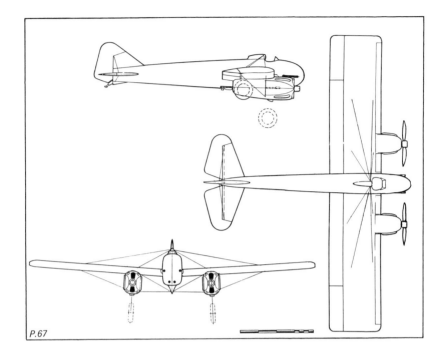

P.67

John North's submission, the P.67, resurrected the twin-engined, single-seat monoplane layout of the P.31 Bittern. Bristol, Supermarine and Vickers also submitted monoplanes, whereas Hawker, Westland, Armstrong Whitworth, Blackburn and Gloster offered biplanes. The P.67 was to be powered by two Napier Rapier engines underslung on a wire-braced low wing of 40 ft span, with the square-cut tips which were still a Boulton & Paul trademark. The undercarriage retracted rearwards into the engine nacelles, and a fixed tailskid was to be fitted.

The pilot, seated well in the nose of the aircraft had the excellent forward visibility which night-flying called for, and the landing speed was less than 60 mph. The tail was very similar to that of the P.66, and may well have been identical, with interchangeable rudder and elevators. The overall length was 29 ft 4 in.

Estimated top speed was 227 mph at 12,500 ft and service ceiling of 30,000 ft. It could climb to 12,500 ft in 6.55 min and 20,000 ft in 11.5 min.

The P.67 did not receive a prototype order and F.7/30 was another specification which did not lead to a production aircraft. The requirement was eventually filled by the Gloster Gladiator, an utterly conventional biplane fighter, in stark contrast to some of the unusual layouts which attempted to meet all parts of Specification F.7/30.

P.68

The P.68 was an eight-seat passenger aircraft with four Pobjoy engines and a span of 53 ft.

P.69

Specification C.26/31 was issued to provide for a bomber/transport aircraft. The P.69 was based on an enlarged P.64 Mail-Carrier with two Pegasus engines. It featured a biplane tail with twin fins and rudders. There were gun positions, with Scarff rings in nose and tail.

Three prototypes were ordered for this Specification, all monoplanes, the Armstrong Whitworth A.W.23, the Handley Page H.P.51 and the Bristol Bombay which secured the order. The H.P.51, adapted as a bomber became the Harrow.

P.70

This was also loosely based on the P.64 and was designed to Specification B.9/32. It is important in that it was the first Boulton & Paul new design to feature power-operated gun turrets. The company was at the time in the process of developing the power-operated turret for the nose of the Sidestrand, in a modification which led to the Overstrand, and this same nose turret was also included on the P.70 project.

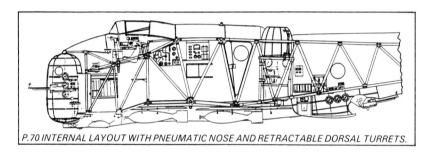

P.70 INTERNAL LAYOUT WITH PNEUMATIC NOSE AND RETRACTABLE DORSAL TURRETS.

In addition the P.70 featured a retractable power-operated dorsal turret. There was room within the fuselage for a retractable turret because it filled the space between the wings, therefore being deeper than the Overstrand's fuselage, though there were features borrowed from that contemporary design. The same sliding canopy was supplied for the pilot, and the same ventral tunnel for a Lewis gun position was fitted.

The rear gunner also acted as wireless operator and this position was just forward of his turret, with a large circular window to give it light. The navigation position was between this and the pilot's cockpit, between the wings. The recessed bomb bay was further forward, because of the weight of the dorsal turret, the forward part of it being beneath the pilot's cockpit.

The Wellington and Hampden bombers finally emerged from Specification B.9/32, so it can be seen that the biplane P.70 was not nearly advanced enough to receive any official interest.

P.72

This was a twin-engined two-seat fighter, powered by two Bristol Pegasus radials.

P.73

Aimed at a Hawker Hart replacement Specification P.27/32 called for a light bomber able to carry a 1,000 lb bomb load over a range of 1,000 miles. Not surprisingly there was intense interest around the industry for this requirement. The eventual winner, of what were to be large orders, was the Fairey Battle. Little detail of Boulton & Paul's submission, the P.73 survives, other than a mention that it was powered by a Rolls-Royce Griffen [sic] engine, a cancelled engine project, not the later Griffon of the Second World War.

P.74

Designed against Specification F.22/33 the P.74 was another of several Boulton & Paul twin-engined fighters, but this one was the first to be designed with a gun turret. F.22/33 called for a three-seat fighter armed with a turret. Rivals were the Armstrong Whitworth A.W.33 and the Bristol Type 141, which was powered by two Aquila engines and housed its spherical turret in the nose. The P.74 was offered in four versions, the P.74A and P.74B with Napier Rapier engines, the P.74A with basically Overstrand turrets in nose and dorsal positions, the tail carried on a very narrow rear fuselage, and the P.74B with the dorsal turret more akin to the P.70, and a wider rear fuselage.

The P.74C and P.74D had Pegasus IV engines, with the same turret options. Because of the greater power they were much larger, with a span of 60 ft as against 48 ft for the lower-powered versions, a length of 44 ft 9 in against 39 ft 3 in and an all-up weight of 9,035 lb against 6,147 lb. All designs were deemed too slow by the Air Ministry. The P.74A/B/C/D were estimated to achieve respectively 195/203/226/232 mph at 15,000 ft.

P.76

Yet another twin-engined fighter, also to be equipped with a gun turret. It was designed for Specification F.5/33, which called for a two-seat fighter with a turret. The P.76 was offered with either two Napier Rapier H inline engines, or Bristol Pegasus radials. Curiously it was aimed at an earlier specification than the P.74, though given a later project number. The two designs were almost certainly closely related. Rivals for the specification were the Armstrong Whitworth A.W.34 and a Gloster project, both of which were conventional twin-engined monoplanes, and the Bristol Type 140, which was a pusher powered by a single Perseus engine, with its spherical turret in the nose.

P.77

This was a version of the Overstrand converted for coastal reconnaissance duties.

P.78

The P.78 is described as a day and night bomber powered by two Pegasus engines, and may well have been similar to the following P.79.

P.79

This twin-engined heavy bomber, with an all-up weight of 19,000 lb, was designed to Specification B.3/34, the Specification which produced the Wellington and the Hampden. It was a low-wing monoplane powered by two

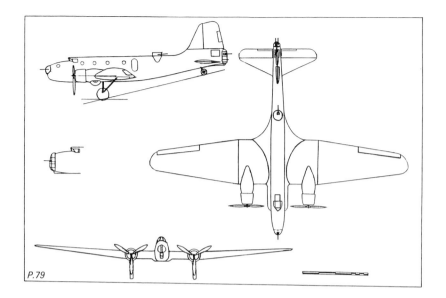

P.79

Bristol Perseus sleeve-valve engines, of all-metal stressed-skin construction throughout. It had a very large, thick wing spanning 97 ft, with a broad chord of 14 ft 6 in just outboard of the engines and an area of 925 sq ft.

It had a deep fuselage much narrower at the top, and because of the sloped-back pilot's windscreen, was very reminiscent of the Boeing 247. It was offered with alternative noses, either with a full-length turret, housing a single Lewis gun, as in the Overstrand, or a much smaller unit, only glazed in its upper half. The navigator's position was just behind the pilot, but an alternative, raised seat could be fitted there with dual controls, and an all-round vision canopy protruding above the fuselage line, for training purposes. There was a dorsal position for a retractable turret equipped with a single Lewis gun, and another turret behind the tail with its very large bluff fin and rudder. The compact tail turret was fitted with twin Lewis guns and a mock-up of this was constructed.

There were two fully-enclosed bomb bays both fore and aft of the wing spars, with the bombs on revolving bomb-carriers, four per bay. There was a further compartment for flares and smaller bombs aft of the bomb bay. The main undercarriage was fully retractable but the tailwheel was not retractable.

The whole layout of the P.79 is reminiscent of contemporary Douglas and Boeing aircraft practices, and Boulton Paul certainly studied American designs. A catalogue of photographs of features of the DC-2 testify to that. Though a massive advance in Boulton Paul bomber design, it would have had to have been exceptional to have overcome the competition from the expected heavy bomber experts, Handley Page and Vickers.

P.80

Strangely the P.80 was a twin-engined bomber from the previous era to the P.79, an extensive development of the Overstrand, which had even acquired a name,

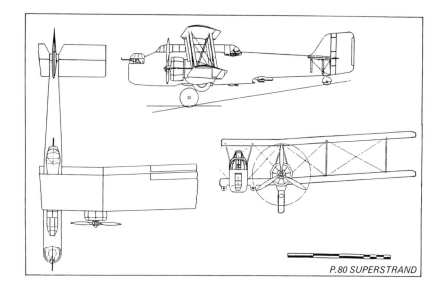

P.80 SUPERSTRAND

the Superstrand. The logical further improvement for the Sidestrand/ Overstrand theme, was to fit more powerful Pegasus IV engines with variable-pitch propellers, and a retractable undercarriage to take advantage of the extra power, but there were further changes beyond that.

The Overstrand nose turret was replaced with one only glazed in its upper hemisphere, like the alternate nose turret on the P.79. The single Lewis gun in the ventral gun position was retained but the dorsal position was completely covered by a transparent folding hood. The fuselage was deepened by filling in the area between the upper line of the pilot's canopy and this dorsal gunner's hood.

It was hoped that the changes would give the Superstrand an improved top speed of 191 mph at 15,000 ft, and a service ceiling of 27,500 ft. The range at 150 mph at 15,000 ft was estimated to be 1,050 miles, and an increased bomb-load could be carried.

With even Boulton Paul designing modern monoplane bombers, the Superstrand was an anachronism which had little chance of being built, but interesting in that it was the last development of a line of the company's biplane bombers which stretched back to the Bourges.

P.81

Specification A.39/34 was issued to find a replacement for the Hawker Audax army co-operation aircraft, which was then entering service. The requirements were a wide speed range, good low-speed handling coupled with what now would be termed STOL capabilities, good visibility from the cockpit for reconnaissance over the battlefield, and the ability to undertake the sundry duties the army co-operation pilots found themselves involved with.

There seems to have been little interest in this requirement within the industry at the time, which is surprising when the winning Westland Lysander eventually received orders totalling over 1,400. Few details of the P.81 survive, other than it was a monoplane with a single Pegasus engine.

P.83

This was a shore-based torpedo bomber designed to Specification M.15/35, for which the Blackburn Botha was a rival, and ordered into production.

P.84

This was a shore-based general reconnaissance aircraft to Specification G.24/35. The Bristol Beaufort was designed to fulfill both this requirement and the one outlined by Specification M.15/35, and Boulton Paul were also to offer an aircraft to cover both Specifications, the P.86.

P.85

The Fleet Air Arm developed an interest in the new fad of the turret fighter, and in an attempt to obtain one for themselves Specification O.30/35 was issued. Boulton Paul put forward a navallised version of the P.82, which was to become the Defiant, but equipped with a Bristol Hercules HE-ISM engine instead of the Merlin. This proposal was rejected in favour of the Blackburn Skua equipped with the Boulton Paul A type gun turret. The resulting aircraft, the Blackburn Roc, was manufactured by Boutlon Paul at Wolverhampton, and they did all the detail design work to convert the Skua to take the turret, and gave it one of their own project numbers, P.93.

In hindsight the decision to order the Roc seems a strange one. It was never more than useless as a fighter, whereas a naval Defiant would have been the fastest fighter the Fleet Air Arm had in service in 1939, given that removing the complication of building the Roc would have meant the Defiant could be produced in all forms a little earlier. The Navy would then have had the option of ordering the single-seat Defiant, with forward-firing guns which was offered to the RAF, an aircraft more than a match for the Fulmar, Martlet or Sea Hurricane.

P.86

This was Boulton Paul's equivalent of the Bristol Beaufort, for a general reconnaissance/torpedo bomber to Specifications M.15/35 and G.24/35. It was powered by two Bristol Aquila AES-SM engines.

P.87

This was a heavy bomber powered by two (modified) Merlin engines.

P.88

The growing awareness in the thirties that future fighters would have to be armed with the quick-firing cannon which were in the process of being developed resulted in Specification F.37/35. This called for a single-seat fighter armed with four 20 mm cannon. Boulton Paul submitted two proposals in May 1935. The P.88A was a conventionally configured single-engined fighter powered by a Hercules HE-ISM, with an alternative P.88B with the newly proposed Rolls-Royce Vulture.

The P.88A had an estimated top speed of 337 mph at 15,000 ft and service

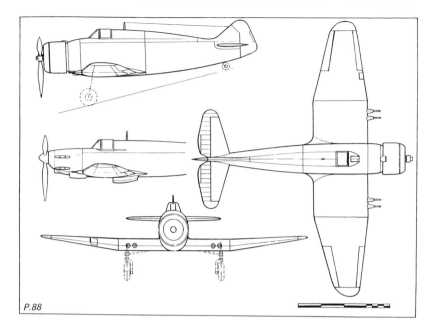

P.88

ceiling of 39,500 ft, with a maximum rate of climb of 3,500 ft/min at 15,000 ft. The P.88B would have been a slightly larger aircraft with a wingspan of 44 ft as opposed to 39 ft 6 in, and a length of 36 ft 3 in as opposed to 32 ft 8 in. Performance would have been significantly better with a top speed of 358 mph at 15,000 ft and 326 mph at 30,000 ft though the service ceiling was estimated to be slightly less at 38,000 ft and the maximum rate of climb 3,400 ft/min at 15,000 ft.

In each case the 20 mm Hispano cannon were fitted on their sides either side of a specially designed beam fitted between the wing spars in the parallel chord inner wing section, the outer wings being tapered. Magazines holding 60 rounds per gun were to be provided. The undercarriage retracted inward giving a wide track, and the tailwheel was also retractable.

Rivals included the Bristol Type 153, powered by the Hercules, the Supermarine Type 313 twin, a twin Peregrine powered aircraft from Westland and a cannon-armed Hurricane from Hawker. The Type 88A was the preferred single-engined design, with a quoted price of £20,500 for the first prototype and £17,500 for the second, and Westland's was deemed the best twin, with a quoted price of £27,500 and £18,000 for the second aircraft. Provisional orders were placed for two prototypes of each of these. Finally it was decided that there was no powerplant yet available of sufficient power for a single-engined design and on 11 February, 1937, Boulton Paul's P.88A was cancelled and the production order went to the Peregrine-engined Westland Whirlwind.

P.89

Another cannon-armed fighter project, the P.89 was designed to Specification F.9/37 which required a twin-engined two-seater armed with four 20 mm cannon. It was to be powered by two modified Rolls-Royce Kestrel XVI engines. The main rival, which was ordered in prototype form only was the Gloster G.39, powered by two Taurus or two Peregrine engines.

P.90

This and the next Boulton Paul project covered the two famous Specifications which produced the RAF's three heavy bombers for the Second World War. The P.90 was designed to Specification B.12/36 which produced the Stirling, and was powered by four Rolls-Royce Kestrel KV26 engines.

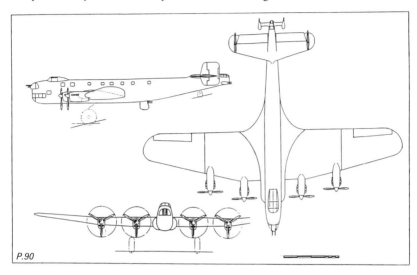

P.90

Like the Stirling it was designed to fit the standard RAF hangar, and therefore had a 100 ft wingspan. It was armed with twin-gun nose and retractable ventral turrets, and a very unusual tail turret behind the twin fins and rudders. A mock-up of this turret was built at Mousehold, and it featured twin guns in pods on the ends of articulated winglets either side of the gunner's position. This arrangement gave the gunner a huge arc of fire, but the movement of the pods would surely have caused substantial control inputs.

A further unusual feature was the cylindrical cheek-mounted bomb bays, containing revolving racks for bombs of up to 1,000 lb, and a total of up to 14,000 lb. This layout kept the fuselage cross-section to a minimum. Estimated top speed was 290 mph at 15,000 ft, with a cruising speed at two-thirds power of 248 mph. Interestingly, considering the Stirling's appallingly low service ceiling, that of the P.90 was estimated at an optimistic 35,000 ft.

P.91

This was designed to Specification P.13/36, which led to the Manchester/ Lancaster and the Halifax. Like the Manchester it was designed to be powered by two Vulture engines. It was very similar to the P.90. Though both these designs were promising, it is hard to believe that the Air Ministry would have considered placing quantity orders for either of these large bombers from a production unit as small as Boulton Paul's, which at the time was still in the

329

process of moving from Norwich to a factory only half the size it was later to attain, and was heavily engaged on the Defiant.

P.93

This number was assigned to the Blackburn Roc, for which Boulton Paul did all the detail design work, and produced all the prototypes and production examples.

P.94

This was a company proposal for a single-seat version of the Defiant, able to be built quickly using standard Defiant jigs. Not to be confused with the simple conversion offered during the Battle of Britain, basically the Defiant in its turretless prototype guise with four forward-firing guns, the P.94 was a little more radical. It featured a lower fuselage line behind the cockpit, a Merlin XX engine, and alternative wings adapted to carry twelve forward-firing machine-guns, or four 20 mm cannon. In yet another example of John North's interest in movable gun mountings, the cannon were designed to point ahead in the plane of flight, or to be depressed by the pilot at an angle of 17 deg for ground attack. Estimated top speed with the twelve-gun wing was 380 mph at 23,500 ft. At a time when the RAF was still crying out for turret-equipped Defiants, the P.94 had little chance of being ordered.

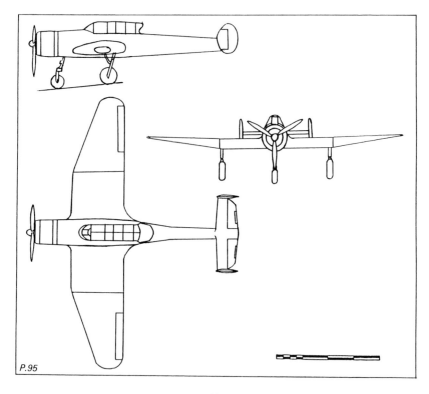

P.95

P.95

This was a single-engined two-seat bomber to Specification B.20/40, capable of close-support bombing and tactical reconnaissance. It was powered by a Bristol Hercules VI. It was a low-wing design with a parallel chord centre section but a marked sweepback of the leading edge of the outer wings. The crew were housed under a long transparent canopy, the gunner's end being in the open, so that he could operate his twin .303 in Browning machine-guns on a Scarff ring-like mounting. The tail had twin fins and rudders to improve the gunner's field of fire aft. Armour plating for the crew was heavy, and so was armament. There were fixed forward-firing Hispano cannon in each wing together with four Browning machine-guns. The bomb load was housed in fuselage and wing bomb-bays, each capable of holding a 250 lb bomb or alternative weapons. An F.24 camera was fitted in the centre fuselage, with a flare launching tube for night reconnaissance. Other aircraft offered for this specification were the Hawker P.1006, a version of the Henley, and the Bristol Type 162. The nearest equivalent to this aircraft that ever saw service was the Russian I1-2 Stormovik.

P.96

In looking for a night-fighter replacement for the slow Blenheim and the less than ideal Beaufighter, Specification F.18/40, issued in August 1940, called for a two-seat aircraft armed with six 20 mm cannon. It was to have a speed of 400 mph at 20,000 ft, a 3-hour patrol endurance at 15,000 ft and a ceiling of 35,000 ft. Take-off run was to be less than 500 yards and landing run less than 650 yards. An alternative armament could be four cannon and six machine-guns.

A model of the P.96 night fighter with turret and Napier Sabre engine.

Boulton Paul submitted project P.96, a scaled-up Defiant with a variety of engine and armament options. It was offered with a standard Defiant A turret plus either two or four fixed forward-firing cannon, or with no turret and a long canopy housing the pilot and observer, and six fixed-forward firing cannon. It could be powered by a Rolls-Royce Griffon, a Bristol Centaurus CE4SM or a Sabre NS6SM. With the last of these they forecast a speed of 367 mph at 21,000

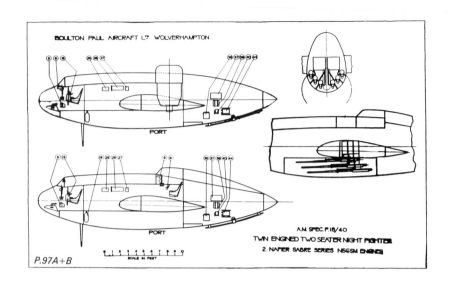

BOULTON PAUL AIRCRAFT L^{TD} WOLVERHAMPTON

PORT

PORT

SCALE IN FEET

A.M. SPEC. F.18/40

TWIN ENGINED TWO SEATER NIGHT FIGHTER

2. NAPIER SABRE SERIES NS6SM ENGINES

P.97A+B

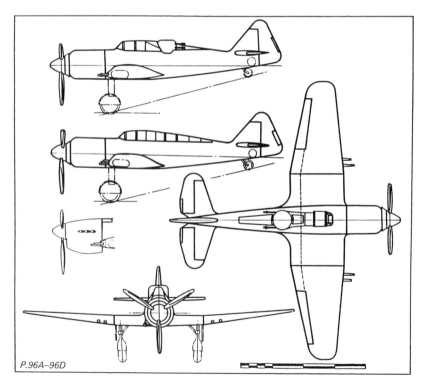

P.96A–96D

332

ft, or 389 mph if a turret were not fitted. With a Sabre NS6SM, high-altitude engine, top speed rose to 392 mph and 415 mph at 34,000 ft respectively.

The various designations are confusing, some of the surviving drawings even being contradictory but seem to be, P.96A – Sabre-powered with no turret, P.96B – Sabre-powered with a turret, P.96C – also Sabre-powered with a turret, P.96D – Centaurus powered with or without a turret.

Fairey also offered a turret fighter, a version of the Firefly, and other rivals for this requirement were a development of the Gloster G.39, the Hawker P.1008 and the Miles M.22A. Work on the P.96 continued into February 1942, but no order was forthcoming for any of the contenders.

P.97

This aircraft was drawn up to the same specification as the P.96, but as were some of the rival contenders was a twin, powered by two Napier Sabres or two Vultures. It was a twin-boom aircraft, and like the P.96 was offered both with and without the four-gun A turret, with forward-firing armament in both versions. In the P.97A, the version without the turret, the observer was housed in a stepped up extension of the canopy, to the rear of the nacelle. In the P.97B this position was taken by the turret.

The nacelle was very deep, with a mid-mounted wing, beneath which was an enclosed weapons bay. This housed a battery of six 20 mm Hispano cannon, but two 550 lb bombs could also be carried in place of four of the cannon, giving the aircraft a substantial ground attack potential.

In concept the P.97 featured an identical layout to and was contemporary with the design of the Northrop P-61 Black Widow. It was deemed too futuristic by the Air Ministry.

A model of the Sabre-powered P.97 night fighter without turret.

P.98

A Specification issued in 1942 for a lightweight, fast climbing fighter-bomber was F.6/42, requiring an armament of four 20 mm cannon with ammunition for 15 sec firing, and under-wing attachment points for bombs or extra fuel tanks. Internal fuel capacity would be sufficient for 10 min maximum climb, 15 min of combat, and 30 min for return at cruising speed.

The P.98 project, was for a Griffon-powered aircraft in a tail-first layout, with the engine driving contra-rotating pusher propellers. Further versions were offered with the Sabre and the Centaurus. The all-up weight of the Sabre version was estimated to be 9,892 lb hopefully giving a wing loading which would match the Fw 190. Its top speed at 20,000 ft was estimated to be 446 mph.

P.99

The P.99, also to F.6/42, was a Griffon-powered aircraft with a twin-boom layout. The engine was a pusher driving contra-rotating propellers, leaving the nose free for the armament. Two armament layouts were proposed, a 47 mm cannon flanked by two 20 mm cannon, or two 20 mm cannon flanked by two 40 mm cannon; and provision for two 500 lb bombs or eight rockets under the wings. There was a tailwheel at the base of the single fin and rudder, placed centrally on the horizontal tail surface, with mainwheels at the front of the booms, retracting rearwards.

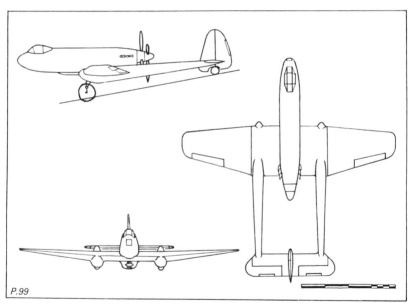

P.99

The pilot sat right in the nose of the fuselage with a bubble canopy, giving him an excellent all-round view, compared with conventional fighters of the day. In order that the pilot was not killed by the propellers when baling out, a downward escape mechanism was designed. The lower forward fuselage on which his seat was mounted, fell away, and after 0.4 sec the pilot would fall from

his seat and then use his parachute in the normal way. This was basically the
escape system which had been designed for the P.92.

P.100

The P.100 was another tail-first design, to F.6/42, with the pilot once more
seated right in the nose, just in front of the shoulder-mounted canard
foreplanes. The same baling out mechanism was incorporated as in the P.99.
The swept wing was mounted on the lower rear fuselage with the twin fins and
rudders on the tips. Three armament layouts were offered, two as for the P.99 or
a more conventional four 20 mm cannon. A tricycle undercarriage layout had to
be adopted because of the tail-first layout.

The loaded weight was estimated to be 13,450 lb giving the required wing
loading of 40 lb/sq ft. Maximum sea level speed was 298 mph rising to 435 mph
at 17,000 ft.

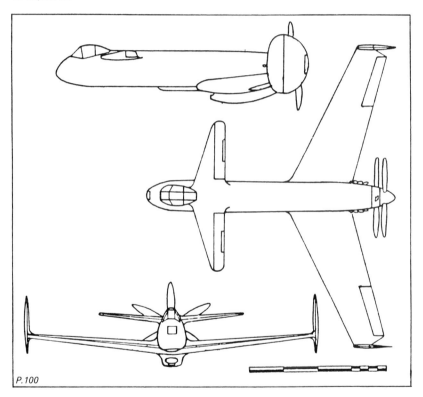

P.100

P.101

The P.101 was an even more unorthodox layout for F.6/42 being a staggerwing
biplane with a non-retractable undercarriage! The fuselage filled the gap
between the cantilever biplane wings, which were staggered in the manner of the
Beech 17 to give the pilot a better forward and downward view for the attack
role. The large bulbous spats which housed the undercarriage also contained the

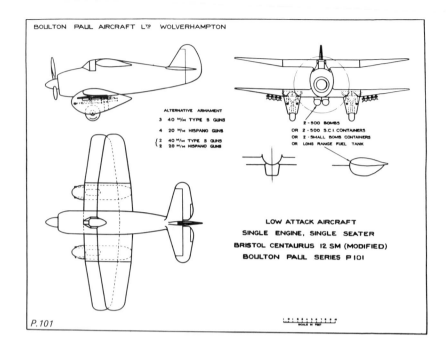

ALTERNATIVE ARMAMENT
3 40 ᴹ/ₘ TYPE S GUNS
4 20 ᴹ/ₘ HISPANO GUNS
{ 2 40 ᴹ/ₘ TYPE S GUNS
  2 20 ᴹ/ₘ HISPANO GUNS

2 - 500 BOMBS
OR 2 - 500 S.C.I. CONTAINERS
OR 2 - SMALL BOMB CONTAINERS
OR LONG RANGE FUEL TANK

LOW ATTACK AIRCRAFT
SINGLE ENGINE, SINGLE SEATER
BRISTOL CENTAURUS 12 SM (MODIFIED)
BOULTON PAUL SERIES P 101

P.101

fixed forward-firing guns. Alternative armament was offered, either four 20 mm Hispano cannon, three 40 mm Type S guns, two of each, or one 47 mm and two 20 mm Hispano cannon. Two 500 lb bombs could be carried beneath the fuselage, with small bomb containers or a long-range slipper tank as alternatives. Four rockets could be carried under each of the outer wings. The airframe was heavily armoured and the three fuel tanks were housed in the central fuselage, behind and beneath the pilot.

This was a large aircraft, height to the canopy top was 11 ft 10 in, length was 33 ft 7 in and span 36 ft 7 in. There was a single tractor propeller, powered by a Bristol Centaurus 12 SM (Mod). True air speed was estimated to be 285 mph at sea level, 300 mph at 10,000 ft, and 317 mph at 18,000 ft. Despite the considerable work done by the company on all these F.6/42 proposals, orthodox and otherwise, the result was just more disappointment.

P.102

This began as a request from the Naval Staff to fit a jet engine to an existing naval aircraft. They had in mind the Fairey Firefly, but John North naturally chose the Barracuda as they were flowing through the production shops at the time. To begin with the Barracuda II was redesigned to take a Whittle W.2b/37 turbojet as a power egg in the rear fuselage, and then the project was re-drawn at official request using the Barracuda V as a basis.

A request to halt the project and restart it using the more powerful Whittle W.2/700 engine, was one delay too many, and the Jet Barracuda project faded away.

P.103

Specification N.7/43 called for a lightweight naval fighter, designed to arrest the ever growing size of combat aircraft. A radial engine was preferred for this new aircraft, though an alternative would be considered, but the creation of a new design was not desirable, leaving two options for any interested manufacturer, to redesign one of their existing aircraft, or to redesign the product of another manufacturer. Boulton Paul succeeded in getting the Specification uprated to a Design Study with weight, performance and an outline drawing submitted by 24 April, 1943, and to be based on the Griffon engine.

The P.103 was loosely based on the Defiant and was offered with alternative engines, the P.103A with the Griffon RG5.SM and the P.103B with the Bristol Centaurus CE 12 SM, both driving contra-rotating propellers. An all-round vision bubble canopy was fitted. The wings folded by being revolved through 90 deg and then folded back against the fuselage sides. Provision was made for assisted take-offs by rockets mounted above the wing centre-section pointing obliquely outwards. Incorporated in this design submission were carrier layouts showing how many extra aircraft of this layout could be carried.

The design featured a number of other unusual aspects. The undercarriage was shorter when retracted, in order to give adequate ground clearance for the propellers when extended, and also to allow inward retraction in the narrow centre section. Automatic electric trim tabs were fitted to the elevator, and a 'dive-brake' propeller was to be fitted.

A proposal from Hawker that their Tempest, wth the centre section omitted, would meet the requirement met with official approval, and the Fury, and Sea Fury resulted, and work on the P.103 was halted on 20 May, 1943. This was unfortunate as there is little doubt that this was the most attractive design ever to emanate from the drawing boards at Boulton Paul.

P.104

Despite the fact that N.7/43 had stipulated that an existing aircraft form the basis for submissions, Boulton Paul also drew a completely new radical design, the P.104. This was a tail-first aircraft powered by the Griffon RG5 SM driving a pusher propeller.

P.105

Early in 1944 the P.105 crystallised all John North's research into naval aircraft, and produced a naval strike aircraft which could be built in different configurations to perform different tasks, much as the Douglas Skyraider was being formulated in California.

It was offered in four layouts, all powered by the Bristol Centuarus CE 12 SM driving contra-rotating propellers. There was a fighter, a torpedo bomber, a reconnaissance aircraft, with ventral glazing for the observer, and a dive-bomber. It was also drawn both with and without rear armament, and it featured a cranked wing, much like the Chance Vought Corsair, to reduce the length of the main undercarriage legs.

The fighter version was offered with four fixed 0.5 in machine-guns or 20 mm cannon, and the other versions with a third alternative of just two fixed 0.5 in machine-guns. All versions had the option of a pair of rearward-firing 0.5 in machine-guns. The range at a maximum take-off weight of 14,000 lb varied from

1,300 to 3,320 miles according to version and equipment specified. At a more normal gross weight of 12,500 lb it could carry a 1,650 lb torpedo, two 1,000 lb bombs, or two 70 gal underwing tanks.

The P.105 was a very aggressive looking design, much more attractive in all its forms than the Barracuda, which it was attempting to supercede, but remained a paper project.

P.106

The RAF operated a varied collection of elementary trainers, the bulk of them being Tiger Moths and Magisters. Specification T.23/43 was issued to find an aircraft to replace them. Unusually it called for a three-seat layout, with side-by-side seating for instructor and pupil, with a third seat behind them to take another pupil who might learn from watching his colleague's performance. The P.106 was offered in three versions however, the P.106A which offered just two side-by-side seats, the P.106B which featured the three-seat layout, and the P.106C which was a more normal tandem two-seat layout with a much narrower fuselage, and the instructor in a slightly raised position in the rear cockpit. A choice of powerplants was also offered, either the Gipsy Queen II or the Gipsy Queen III.

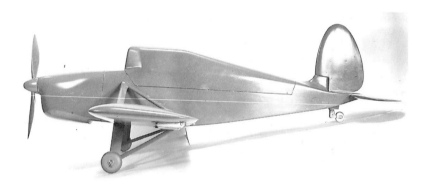

A model of the P.106 elementary trainer, side-by-side seating version.

Top speed at sea level for the P.106B was estimated to be 141 mph with the Gipsy Queen II or 145 mph with the Gipsy Queen III. In the two-seat side-by-side layout, 1.5 mph could be added to these figures, and in the tandem seated layout 3.5 mph could be added. Initial rate of climb with the Gipsy Queen II was 195, 210 and 220 ft/min respectively. Time to 5,000 ft with the same engine was 6.1 min for the three-seat version, 4.8 min for the side-by-side version, and 4.5 min for the tandem seater. With the Gipsy Queen II engine these times were 4.9, 4.00 and 3.8 min respectively.

It was a very simple low-wing monoplane with square-cut wings braced by V-struts above them, and further V-struts bracing the non-retractable undercarriage. There was a large greenhouse canopy with a flat windscreen on a short fat fuselage. The Percival Prentice was the aircraft ordered to fulfill the requirement.

338

P.107

This was a two-seat long-range escort fighter powered by a single Bristol Centaurus CE 12 SM driving contra-rotating three-blade propellers. The crew sat almost back to back under a short all-round vision canopy. The gunner operated a pair of remotely controlled 0.5 in machine guns which had 3 deg of depression and 45 deg of elevation, the breeches sinking into the aircraft's fuselage to achieve this, rather than the barrels being raised, and so upsetting the airflow. To give the gunner a good field of fire astern, the P.107 had twin fins and rudders mounted on a tailplane with marked dihedral. The aircraft had a cranked wing to minimise the length of the undercarriage legs.

P.109

This was the Perseus-engined version of the P.108 Balliol, required in the first issue of Specification T.7/45, but deleted in the second issue.

P.110

This was Boulton Paul's last design for a civil light aircraft, and the first since the P.41 Phoenix. It was a three-seat pusher very reminiscent in overall layout to the Republic Seabee amphibian. The cockpit was sited ahead of the low-wing with large doors on each side. The Cirrus Minor Series II engine was behind the cockpit over the wing and driving the pusher propeller above the narrow boom which formed the rear fuselage and carried the tailplane. Pictures of models seem to indicate the fin was an all-moving horizontal tailplane on each side. This would not be out of place on a John North design as he had used this idea before. Experience with the lack of sales of the P.9 after the First World War may have stopped North putting the P.110 into production, with the prospect of many surplus Messengers/Proctors/Tiger Moths being available very cheaply.

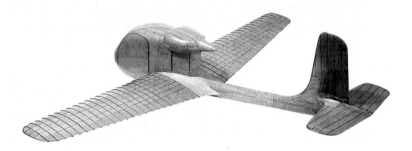

Wind-tunnel model of the P.110 three-seat light aircraft.

P.112

Anxious to exploit the success of the Balliol, Boulton Paul produced a three-seat elementary trainer based on the Balliol fuselage with new, higher aspect ratio, wings of 45 ft 9 in span, and a non-retractable undercarriage. It had more powerful engines in its two versions than generally accepted for elementary trainers at the time, the P.112 with the Alvis Leonides IVM and the P.112A with the Pratt & Whitney Wasp R-1340. This was the only Boulton Paul design ever offered with a foreign engine. The spatted undercarriage had a wide track of 15 ft 2 in. An elaborate full-scale mock-up was built, but there was no official interest.

The RAF fulfilled its elementary trainer requirements with the de Havilland Chipmunk.

P.113

This was a design study for a supersonic aircraft powered by a single Rolls-Royce Avon engine in P.113A form and an Armstrong Siddeley Sapphire in P.113S form. It featured a highly swept wing, with the wing tapering almost to a point, and a swept tail, with a fin-mounted tailplane, but the most unusual

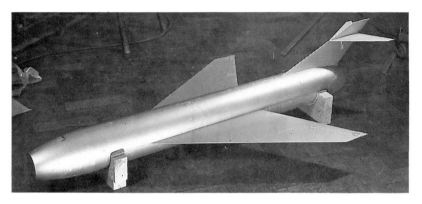

A model of the P.113 transonic research aircraft.

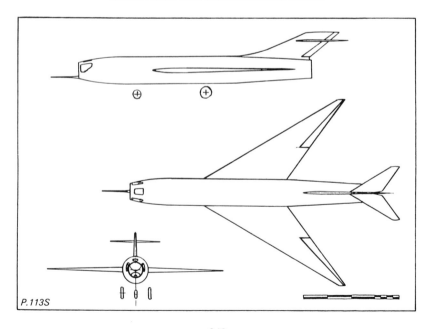

aspect of the design's layout was the cockpit location. The pilot sat in a very reclined chest-down position actually inside the nose air intake, with limited view provided by three windows in the intake walls, one on each side, and one above. Forward view being out through the circular intake. Emergency ejection could have involved the pilot being thrust into a slightly more vertical position and then downwards, feet-first, from the aircraft.

P.114

This was a design study for a twin-engined transonic research aircraft powered by two Avons with reheat, as the P.114A or two reheated Sapphires as the P.114S. Like the P.113 it featured highly swept wings and tail, but the wings were not so tapered. The pilot's cockpit was in the circular forward fuselage just ahead of the air intakes, the remainder of the fuselage being oval in section. Unusually for a research aircraft there was provision for twin 30 mm Aden cannon with 200 rounds per gun, sited in the fuselage just below the intakes. The tricycle undercarriage was all fuselage mounted, and there were four large air-brakes mounted in pairs above and below the rear fuselage just in front of the fin.

The P.114A, with reheat switched on at 30,000 ft was estimated to have a climb to 45,000 ft in a fraction over 6 min.

P.115

The RAF decided they needed a new piston-powered basic trainer to replace the Percival Prentice and Specification T.16/48 was issued to cover this requirement, with the Armstrong Siddeley Cheetah being the preferred engine. Boulton Paul drew up two designs, the P.115 with a de Havilland Gipsy Queen 71, which was a new engine, geared and supercharged to give 400 hp; and the P.116.

The P.115 had a top speed of 160 mph at 5,000 ft, a cruising speed of 141 mph at the same height, and took 10 min to climb to 10,000 ft.

P.116

The other submision for Specification T.16/48, this one was powered by a Gipsy Queen 50, also a new engine, supercharged to give 295 hp. Like the P.112 it owed much to the Balliol layout, but had a shorter fuselage of 30 ft 9 in, but a slightly larger span. There would probably have been a certain degree of commonality in the structures, but in the case of the P.115/116 the main undercarriage legs retracted to the rear. The seating arrangement was side-by-side.

Top speed of the P.116 was 154 mph at 5,000 ft, cruising speed 136 mph at that height and time to 10,000 ft was 13½ min.

The Percival Provost won the order after competitive trials against the Handley Page H.P.R.2., both these aircraft being offered initially with the 375 hp Cheetah, but subsequently with the 550 hp Alvis Leonides, and therefore having better performances than the P.115/116, the Provost having a top speed of 200 mph.

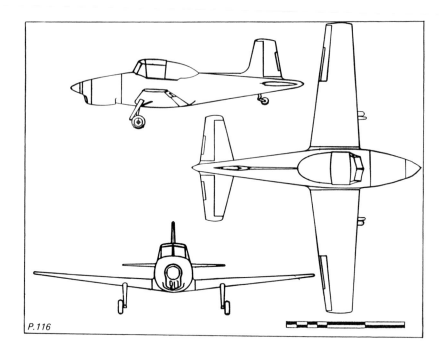

P.116

P.117

This was a project for a wing-controlled aerodyne. It was not a specific aircraft but a series of studies to see if an aircraft could be controlled by an articulated wing, rather than separate control surfaces.

P.118

This was an aircraft with a highly swept wing, powered by a Rolls-Royce Nene.

P.119

As it became increasingly obvious that Britain, and the world's air forces, would need a jet-powered advanced trainer, rather than the piston-powered Balliol which the company was building, Boulton Paul initiated a private-venture jet trainer, the P.119. It was seen as very important in the future of the company as an aircraft manufacturer, and an expensive full-size mock-up of the aircraft was built in August 1951.

The P.119 was an attractive design with moderately swept wing and tail, and was to be of light-alloy stressed-skin construction. It featured side-by-side seating, with ejector seats and a jettisonable hood over a pressurised cockpit. All controls were duplicated and provision was made for amber or blue screens to simulate night flying.

The Rolls-Royce Derwent was to be the standard powerplant giving a top speed of around 475 mph and a duration of 1 hr 45 min at 30,000 ft, at around 400 mph (with an allowance for taxi-ing, take-off, climb, and landing). A Nene could also be fitted for higher performance, giving about 555 mph. The engine mounting was to the forward fuselage just aft of the wings, so that the entire rear fuselage and tail could be removed for ease of servicing the engine. It was estimated that the entire engine could thus be replaced within an hour. The engine intakes were rather unusual, being cheek mounted and inset of a NACA design, more normally used for small air vents. Such intakes were concurrently being tested on a Sabre in the USA. The fuel tanks were fuselage mounted at the cg between the intakes.

Practicality and ease of maintenance were a general feature of the design. For instance, the under-fuselage panels, which might be damaged in a crash landing, were easily replaceable. A crash protection frame was located just behind the seats. Pneumatics replaced the more normal hydraulics for all services, such as flap operation, for ease of service.

The aircraft was designed both for advanced jet training and armament training, being equipped to carry two 20 mm cannon, bombs and rockets. It was also foreseen that the aircraft could be used in what would now be termed counter insurgency tasks. In fact the Nene-powered P.119 makes an interesting comparison with the BAe Hawk, given that the P.119 suffered aerodynamically from having side-by-side seating. A deck-landing trainer, designated the P.119N, was also offered, with wing-folding at about mid-span.

The 38 ft 9 in span wing had square-cut tips and housed the inward retracting mainwheels.

The P.119 was never built, the Vampire T.55 and Lockheed T-33 were easily available, and with the RAF and Fleet Air Arm not requiring the aircraft, no foreign power was going to take a serious interest. It would have made an excellent trainer, which might have given sterling service in many roles, and should have been the advanced trainer ordered from Boulton Paul rather than the anachronistic Balliol.

Span 38 ft 9 in; length 42 ft 5 in; height 12 ft 3 in; wing area 298.5 sq ft; loaded weight 9.650 lb. With Derwent maximum speed 475 mph at 22,500 ft; climb to 20,000 ft 7½min, to 30,000 ft 14 min; service ceiling 41,000 ft. With Nene maximum speed 555 mph at 10,000 ft; climb to 20,000 ft 4½ min, to 30,000 ft 8 min; service ceiling 51,000 ft.

P.121

The P.121 was a single-seat supersonic fighter to Air Ministry Specification ER.110T, powered by two Rolls-Royce RA.8 engines buried side-by-side in the fuselage with a nose intake and exhaust pipes beneath the rear fuselage. It was offered in two basic versions with a fixed highly swept and with a variable-sweep wing. In both cases there was a conventional swept tail. It was armed with a single 30 mm cannon beneath the pilot's cockpit, and was equipped with an arrester hook.

P.122

This was a rocket-propelled interceptor, powered by an Armstrong Siddeley Screamer of 8,000 lb st. The Screamer was developed as a successor to the 2,000 lb st Snarler, which used as its propellant a combination of methanol, water and liquid oxygen. The Screamer became Britain's first variable-thrust rocket, and formed the basis for most submissions to F.124T for a small rocket-powered interceptor to counter the threat of high-performance Russian bombrs which were under development. The interceptor would be fast reacting, with a

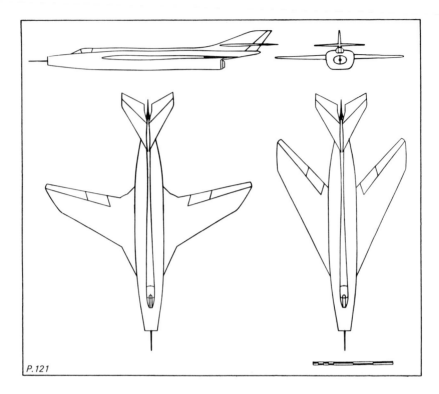

P.121

high-altitude performance capable of meeting the perceived threat. After attack the aircraft would glide back to earth, much in the manner of the wartime Me 163B.

The P.122 was a diminutive aircraft, 36 ft 7 in long, with a span of only 21 ft 7 in. It had a twin-boom layout, with the booms extending ahead of the wings and containing the cannon armament. Take off was from a jettisonable trolley, and no wheeled undercarriage was fitted, landing being on a central stabilising skid.

Not surprisingly the P.122 was estimated to have a startling climb performance. Time to 10,000 ft was 1.4 min, to 40,000 ft 2.3 min and to 60,000 ft, only 3 min. Being rocket powered the rate of climb increased with height from 12,000 ft/min at sea level, to 20,000 ft/min at 20,000 ft, 29,000 ft/min at 40,000 ft and 34,000 ft/min at 60,000 ft.

One of the few companies not invited to tender for this specification was Saunders-Roe, who had been undertaking research in just such an aircraft, but considered the inclusion of a small turbojet so that the aircraft could fly back to base, would be advantageous. When appraised of Saro's work, the Ministry invited the other manufacturers to submit similar proposals, but two prototypes of the SR.53 were the only outcome.

P.123

Both the United States and the Soviet Union developed air-breathing guided missiles during the forties and fifties, what would now be called cruise missiles,

344

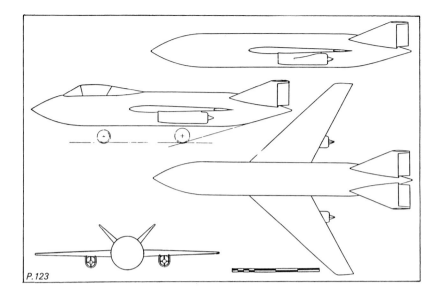

P.123

though without the degree of accuracy of the modern Tomahawk. The US Martin B-61 Matador was just such a missile, representing a logical development of the wartime V 1 flying bomb. The British also considered such a weapon, and on 9 February, 1951, issued Specification UB.109T, for what was decribed as a short-range expendable bomber. There was seen to be an immediate need for such a weapon as the RAF strategic bomber force was equipped with Lincolns and borrowed B-29s, and the V-Bombers would not become operational for at least five years.

The weapon was to be a radio-controlled unmanned bomber for the destruction of small or large targets over a large area, and with a radius of action of 400 miles. The unmanned bomber with a 5,000 lb warhead would be launched from a ramp and have a cruising speed of 450 kt at 45,000 ft. The production run was likely to be in the region of 20,000 units, for a missile which was intended to be launched in barrages.

Boulton Paul's submission, the P.123, was a swept wing, V-tailed aircraft powered by two wing-mounted Rolls-Royce RB.93 expendable turbojets of 1,750 lb st. It was adaptable for two missions, either the Blast version with two 2,000 lb charges, in forward and rear fuselage, which would be exploded simultaneously at the end of the final 800 kt dive, or the Multi-bomb version with eight 500 lb bombs, which would be released in the same way as from a manned bomber.

In order that the centre of gravity remained virtually constant in flight the fuel was not housed in the wings but was in one central tank, of the same diameter as the fuselage, creating the frames to which the wings could be attached. The wings were of 21 ft span with a leading-edge sweep of 45 deg at ¼ chord, and a chord at the root of 8.33 ft. The two engines were underslung at about one third span. There were to be no ailerons, all control being vested in the combined elevators/rudders of the V-tail. remarkably Boulton Paul intended to develop

345

glass-fibre wings and tail surfaces, for the missile, provided design strengths could be met. Obviously cheapness and ease of manufacture were imperative, so that mass-production could take place.

The fuselage was 30.33 ft long and built in three distinct sections, so that the explosive sections could be stored separately to the fuel tank section and the wings/engines. There were seven sections in all, including alternative Blast and Multi-bomb versions, so that the missile could be assembled at the launch site according to the mission envisaged.

With a wing loading of 84 lb/sq ft a method of accelerating the P.123 to its minimum flying speed of 200 kt was needed. At first Boulton Paul suggested a railway track mounted trolley, containing a booster rocket which would launch the missile after a run of 580 yards in still air. The trolley would then arc round a curved, banked track of 100 yards radius and return through a braking section to the launch site/loading bay. Obviously such a large facility was rather inflexible and vulnerable to attack, even if sections of commercial railway track were used. After the Martin Matador had shown the possibility of launching the missile on the back of a large booster rocket, from an inclined ramp which could be fully mobile, this method was adopted for the P.123.

For flight testing the P.123, Boulton Paul envisaged a piloted version, like the piloted version of the V 1. This version would be of all-metal construction with a retractable nosewheel undercarriage. Conventional ailerons would be fitted, though they could be locked to test the 'ruddervators'. Trailing-edge flaps would also be fitted. There would be a simplified form of engine throttle control, and the cockpit, in the nose, would contain an ejection seat, normal flight controls and instrumentation. The test pilot would first fly the aircraft in the normal way, to test its flying characteristics, and would then in turn test the automatic pilot, radio control, and automatic evasion device, until complete flights were made without the pilot intervening, unless necessary. All-up weight of this version was envisaged at about 6,000 lb, so that ballast would have to be carried to test at the operational all-up weight of 9,297 lb.

Two companies, Bristol and Vickers actually began work on their UB.109T proposals. The Bristol version, termed Type 182R Blue Reaper, was quite similar to the P.123. It was a swept wing design with a span of 20 ft 10 in, a length of 33 ft 10 in and an all-up weight of 9,500 lb, but would be powered by a single turbojet under the fuselage. It would have been all plastic in its production form, apart from the steel wing-spar, but the two prototypes ordered were to be aluminium, powered by a single Armstrong Siddeley Viper, and fitted with a de Havilland Venom undercarriage. The Vickers design was called the Red Reaper, and would have been built of light alloy and powered by three Rolls-Royce Soar turbojets. Work on both aircraft/missiles ceased when the project was abandoned in 1953, in favour of getting the Valiant into service as soon as possible.

P.124

The P.124 was a rival to the Jet Provost for a basic jet trainer for the RAF. In general layout and appearance it resembled the P.119, but was in fact a completely new design. It was a side-by-side two-seat aircraft powered by an Armstrong Siddeley Viper ASV.5 of 1,640 lb st. The wings and horizontal tail, which was sited two thirds of the way up the fin, were both of moderate sweep-back, the fin and rudder much more sharply swept. The wing spanned 32 ft and was of 235 sq ft in area, fitted with split flaps.

The engine intakes were sited, unlike the P.119, in the wing roots, but the Viper was attached just behind the wing in the same way as in the P.119. The nose of the aircraft contained a G.45 camera and the VHF 1985/1987 ILS receiver. The crew were each provided with ejector seats and sat beneath an all-round vision canopy with a sliding hood. The main 150 gal fuel tank was sited in the centre fuselage at the centre of gravity.

One 0.5 in machine-gun was fitted to the wing, and there were bomb racks for two 250 lb bombs, or eight practice bombs. Alternatively six 60 lb rockets or two 100 gal drop tanks could be carried.

The P.124 was another attractive looking aircraft which was destined not be be built.

One 1,640 lb st Armstrong Siddeley ASV.5 Viper. Span 32 ft; wing area 235 sq ft. Loaded weight 5,400 lb. Maximum speed 302 kt at sea level, 330 kt at 30,000 ft; crusing speed 278 kt at 30,000 ft; service ceiling 41,000 ft. Armament: one 0.5 in machine-gun. Racks for two 250 lb bombs or eight practice bombs or six 60 lb rockets.

P.125

This was a straightforward jet-powered version of the Balliol, with the Merlin engine in the nose simply replaced by a Rolls-Royce Derwent. The circular intake was in the nose of the aircraft, and the long jet-pipe passed beneath the cockpit and exhausted under the rear fuselage. A tricycle undercarriage was substituted for the Balliol's tailwheel, the nosewheel being offset to port to accommodate the engine. Four fuel tanks were fitted, two wing tanks each of 50 gal, a 105 gal fuselage tank just in front of the cockpit and a 35 gal fuselage tank just behind the radio bay.

P.126

This was not so much an aircraft as a project for developing a very thin, stiff wing, though applications for it were sketched out. It was thought that to cope with speeds of Mach 2 and above, when very high surface temperatures, in the order of 150 deg C applied, a wing with a thickness only 3 per cent of chord was required, and that it had to be made very rigid.

A process was devised for building up a wing of thin strips of L65 light alloy so as to form the aerofoil section in a series of flat surfaces, as in the sides of a cone. The final shape of the curve was then created by milling the surface, bringing it to within 0.0005 in of the theoretical curve.

A fighter aircraft sketched to show the use of this wing bore a startling resemblance to the Bristol Type 188 high-speed research aircraft, with a long thin pointed fuselage, a straight thin wing with two underslung engine nacelles at mid-span projecting well forward and slightly aft of the wing, and unswept tail surfaces.

P.127

This was a supersonic interceptor, but no details survive.

P.128

This was a projected research aircraft for Air Ministry Specification ER.134T issued in February 1953 to investigate the effect of kinetic heating on airframes at speeds in excess of Mach 2. It was to be powered by two Armstrong Siddeley Sapphire engines mounted on the tips of a short, constant-chord wing which featured the thin-wing construction process. The unswept tailplane was mounted half-way up the unswept fin. Length 63 ft 8 in, span 28 ft 11 in including engines. The Bristol Type 188 was the aircraft chosen to fulfill the Specification.

P.129

Another projected research aircraft, the P.129 was to be a mixed powerplant aircraft, contemporary with the Saunders-Roe SR.53. It was to be powered by two Viper ASV.5 or Turboméca Marboré turbojets and a Snarler lox/alcohol rocket of 2,000 lb st. The basic layout was similar to that of the P.128 (for which it may have been a development aircraft) with wingtip-mounted turbojets, and the rocket motor in the extreme tail, but there were fundamental airframe differences, centring on alternative wingtips.

The Marboré-powered version seems to have been intended for phased development of the airframe layout. Phase 1 looked in plan form like a Meteor, with straight outer wing beyond the underslung Marborés, giving an overall span of 32.5 ft and a wing area of 245 sq ft. Phase 2 had delta-shaped tips giving the same span but an area of only 232 sq ft. In both Phase 1 and 2 the tip extensions were fitted with ailerons. Phase 3 had the same delta tips as Phase 2 but without ailerons outboard of the engines. Finally Phase 4 was without tips at all, featuring the same layout as the P.128, a span of only 18 ft and a wing area of 150 sq ft.

The Viper-powered version was drawn with the engines both underslung and centrally mounted on the wings, both with and without delta-shaped tips. Without tips the span was 20.5 ft, with an area of 167.1 sq ft. With tips the span was 28.75 ft with an area of 216 sq ft. Only drawings of the Viper-powered version are shown with the rocket motor fitted. The alcohol fuel tank just behind the cockpit was separated from the liquid oxygen tank by two jet fuel tanks and the main undercarriage bay.

In concept and layout the P.129 was very similar to the French SO.9050 Trident II, a point-defence interceptor powered by two wingtip-mounted Vipers and a two-stage SEPR rocket.

P.130

This was a group of proposals formulated in late 1954/early 1955, and designated Mk 1 to Mk 12, for VTOL aircraft having fanlift. Details of only two of them survive. The Mk 6 was a fairly conventional delta-wing aircraft with a centrally-mounted 54 in diameter contra-rotating fan, and powered by five Rolls-Royce RB.108 engines. The Mk 8 was a more radical delta powered by two Bristol Orpheus engines, and featuring a 75 in diameter contra-rotating fan, with three smaller balancing fans in the wings and the nose. The twin fins were underslung and supported the mainwheels of the tricycle undercarriage. This layout was to give adequate ground clearance for the large mass airflow from the

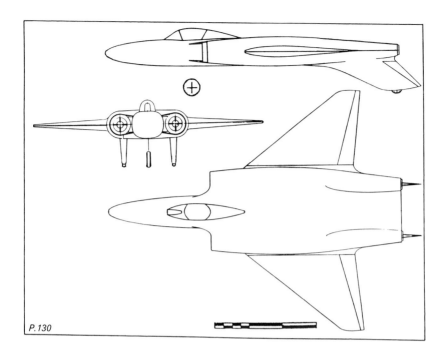

P.130

fans. The Mk 8 design had folding wings and a cannon mounted in each wing inboard of the balancing fan, and outboard of an underwing pylon.

P.131

This was the P.124 advanced jet trainer adapted for the requirements of the Royal Australian Air Force. The RAAF eventually bought Vampire T.34s and T.35s.

P.132

This was a definitive proposal in January 1956 for a VTOL aircraft, one of a number from Boulton Paul which used fan lift. It was a swept-delta wing aircraft, designed to Ministry of Supply Specification ER.166D, with the fuselage egg not extending much further back than the wing leading-edge. It had twin fins and rudders and was powered by four Armstrong Siddeley Viper turbojets in two nacelles slung beneath the wings. In this proposal vertical lift was provided by two large fans centrally placed in the wing, hence the abbreviated fuselage, or alternatively by three fans, in a triangular layout in the wing, the central one being just behind the fuselage 'egg'. It was to lead to a fighter version with the twin fins below the wing, to serve also as the main undercarriage members. This was to avoid undercarriage legs which were very long to prevent ground effect problems.

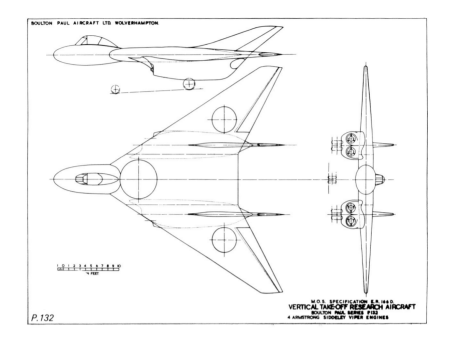

M.O.S. SPECIFICATION E.R.166 D.
VERTICAL TAKE-OFF RESEARCH AIRCRAFT
BOULTON PAUL SERIES P132
4 ARMSTRONG SIDDELEY VIPER ENGINES

P.132

P.133

This was a proposal for a very potent fighter, for both RAF and Naval service. It was a VTOL aircraft powered by two de Havilland Gyron Juniors with afterburners, supplemented by a Spectre rocket engine. In its initial version, the P.133 of June 1956, it was a single-seat fighter, dart-shaped overall, with the turbojets near the wingtips, and six fans in all, providing lift. Its P.133A form of August 1956 incorporated an equipment rearrangement and only four lift fans. The P.133B, in November 1956, was a more radically different layout specifically for a two-seat naval search and strike aircraft, with only the Gyron Junior engines and no rocket. In this form three different weapons stowage schemes were explored. Case 1 was for five rocket packs to OR.1126 or eight packs to OR.1099. Case 2 was for two 2,000 lb bombs or one target marker and Case 3 was for four 1,000 lb bombs.

P.134

The P.134 was a single-seat VTOL aircraft powered by two fuselage-mounted Bristol Orpheus B.OR.II turbojets, though in the first version formulated in September 1956 the engine layout was close to that of the P.133, i.e. near the tips of the dart-shaped delta wings. In the final version, drawn in January 1957 it was a slightly more conventional design, though retaining the radical thick dart-shaped wings of the earlier designs, and four lift fans. Top speed was expected to be Mach 1.25 at 35,000 ft.

P.135

This was a development of the P.132 VTOL research aircraft projected in May

350

1957. It was to be powered by two Bristol Orpheus B.OR.12 engines, buried in the wing roots, and with four lift fans, the main two centrally mounted in the forward fuselage and two smaller ones outboard in the wings. There were two projected versions, the P.135A and P.135B, the former having a double-delta wing, and the latter a highly-swept delta, with no tailplane in either case.

P.136

This was a single-seat research aircraft, drawn up in August 1957, powered by two Orpheus engines, and very similar in size and layout to the P.135B, but with six Rolls-Royce RB.108 ducted fans in a central row. This entailed moving two fuel tanks to the wing.

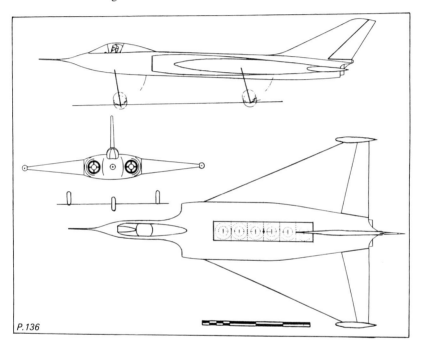

P.136

P.137

Another VTOL research aircraft with two de Havilland Gyron Juniors, the P.137 was to further explore the Naval NA.39 requirement for a two-seat strike aircraft. It retained the basic layout of the P.133B, but incorporated ten lift fans, mounted in two rows inboard of the engines.

P.138

The first of a number of civil VTOL proposals, this one was for a 32-seat airliner powered by four Bristol Orpheus engines.

P.139

Possibly related to the P.138 proposal, this was a single-seat research aircraft drawn in November 1957 for a VTOL airliner layout, powered by two Bristol Orpheus, mounted near the roots of the swept wings. Unlike earlier layouts it featured a conventional tailplane. The three lift fans were to be placed in the outer wings and forward fuselage.

P.140

Drawn in October 1957 this was obviously a larger version of the same theme. This was a proposal for a 72/80-seat VTOL airliner powered by eight Bristol Orpheus B.OR.12 engines, slung in four pods beneath the swept wings. The twelve lift fans were to be mounted two in each outer wing, and two rows of four in the wing roots. In essence it was an 80-seat VTOL Boeing 707.

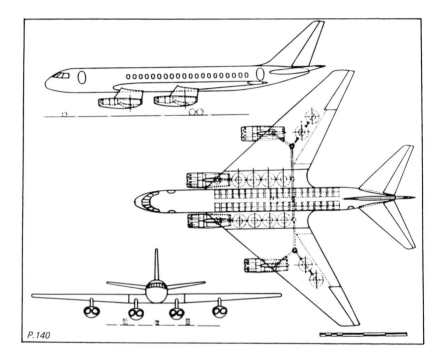

P.140

P.141

This was another VTOL transport with air-driven fan lift, but was radically different from the P.140, and appeared much later in January 1960. It was a 40-seat straight wing design with six RB.108 engines in two slightly underslung triple pods for forward propulsion, and four engines in tip pods driving the 24 lift fans. These were mounted in batteries of six in the outer wings, forward and rear fuselage.

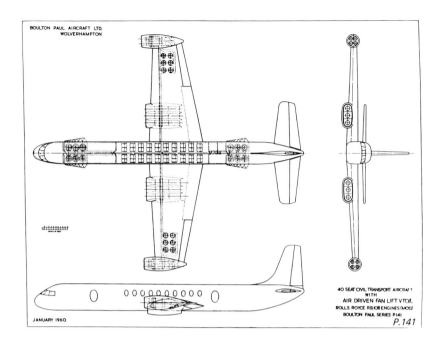

40 SEAT CIVIL TRANSPORT AIRCRAFT
WITH
AIR DRIVEN FAN LIFT VTOL
ROLLS ROYCE RB.108 ENGINES (MOD)
BOULTON PAUL SERIES P.141

JANUARY 1960

P.141

P.142

This was a VTOL research aircraft to investigate fan lift with reheat. Interestingly it was drawn in April 1958, well before the drawings for the P.141. It was to be powered by a battery of six Rolls-Royce RB.108 engines mounted vertically at an angle of about 70 deg in the central fuselage, with a rearward-facing thrust nozzle in each wing root. The engines powered eight Rolls-Royce 25.8 in diameter fans in the wings and forward and rear fuselage, but also provided lift themselves, through swivelling lower louvre doors. This was an extremely unusual application for the RB.108, which was the world's first purpose-built lift jet, with a thrust of between 2,150 lb and 2,550 lb. A battery of five RB.108s provided the power for the Short SC.1, four for lift and one for thrust. It was designed for vertical installation, with the facility of being pivoted on trunnions by 30 deg fore and aft.

P.143

This was to be a VTOL 46/52-seat civil transport powered by ten Rolls-Royce RB.144 engines, an engine which was never built, with forty Rolls-Royce 25.8 in lift fans, six mounted in triple pods near the tip of each straight wing and the remaining four were buried in the lower rear fuselage. The span was to be 85.5 ft with a wing area of 916 ft and the fuselage length was 100 ft. The payload over a range of 400 nautical miles was 10,513 lb but went up to 12,640 lb over half that distance.

P.144

This was a VTOL airborne vehicle, drawn in February 1959 and powered by two

353

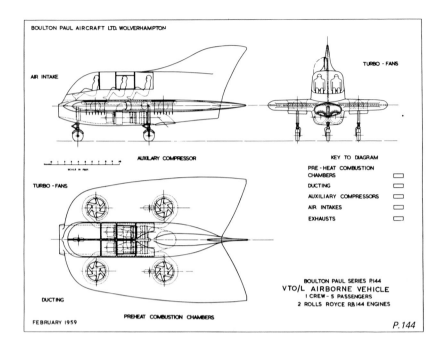

Rolls-Royce RB.144 engines, with lift provided by four fans, two in each of the wings, which were of greater chord than span. Its length was 27.75 ft and width (a term more appropriate than span) was 17.5 ft, with an overall height of 13.5 ft. It carried a pilot/driver and either five passengers or a cargo payload of 1,000 lb. Top speed with 160 kt with an endurance of 50 min, giving a range with a reserve fuel allowance of 120 nautical miles. Its fully loaded weight was 10,050 lb.

A second scheme, more easily recognisable as a car, was the P.144A. This was to be powered by a single RB.155 with four nozzles for flight and a 3.6 litre piston engine on the ground. It had an overall length of 16.5 ft, a width and height both of 7 ft. Its payload was 1,100 lb and it had five seats plus provision for two stretcher cases. Fuel capacity was 110 gal for the lift engine, giving an endurance in the air of 15 min, and 25 gal for the piston engine, giving a range on the ground of 300 miles.

P.145

This was a VTOL twin-boom transport powered by four Rolls-Royce RB.154 engines and twelve Rolls-Royce RB.155 lift engines. The RB.154 was never built but the RB.153 was a 6,850 lb st engine originally designed for the German VJ 101D. The P.145 was in effect a VTOL Argosy, with a wingspan of 100 ft and a length of 70.5 ft. The RB.154s were sited in pairs in pods underslung beneath the outer wing, with the lift engines in the booms which projected forward of the wing. It could carry a payload of 19,366 lb over 200 miles, or 15,550 lb over 500 miles.

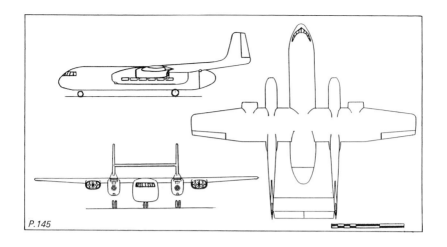

P.146

This was a 96-seat VTOL civil airliner with tandem swept wings and powered by three modified RB.163 bypass engines with eighteen RB.155 lift engines. This was the most astonishing of all the Boulton Paul VTOL designs. The propulsion engines were mounted around the rear fuselage, and the lift engines in four pods on the tips of both the main wings and the forward canard wings. It is hard to see how Boulton Paul could ever have seriously considered an airliner of this size going into production, even if anyone had thought it commercially viable.

Model of the P.146 VTOL airliner project.

355

P.147

This was a design study for Project Prodigal, a Fighting Vehicle Research and Development Establishment requirement (No.9258), dated 21 March, 1960, for a ground-borne military vehicle having a limited airborne capability, that is the ability to leap large obstacles in a single stride, (*e.g.* canyons).

P.148

The P.147 was to be the last Boulton Paul aircraft design, the P.148 was a road vehicle, a low profile fuel tanker, able to be transported by air.

Appendix I

Aircraft Built under Licence

Beginning with the Royal Aircraft Factory's F.E.2b Boulton (&) Paul built 3,485 complete aircraft of other organisations' designs. The history and Service career of these types is to be found in great detail in other Putnam publications, and it would be inappropriate to repeat such information here, beyond their serials and basic details of the Boulton (&) Paul contracts. The numbers of each type were as follows:–

F.E.2b/d	550
Sopwith Camel	1,575
Sopwith Snipe	425
Hawker Demon	106
Blackburn Roc	136
Fairey Barracuda	692
Hawker Sea Fury	1

F.E.2b

250 aircraft built, under Contract 87A 658. First aircraft completed (5201 *City of Bombay*), first flight 4 October, 1915, delivered to Farnborough 8.10.15. A further sixteen were delivered by the end of the year. The bulk of the remaining deliveries were completed before the end of 1916, but a few aircraft were delivered through 1917, both during and after the deliveries of F.E.2ds – 5201–5250, 6928–7027, 7666–7715, A5438–A5487.

F.E.2d

An order was placed for 300 aircraft under Contract 87A 658. All nacelles were supplied by Garrett & Sons Ltd of Leiston. Delivery began week ending 20.1.17 and was completed week ending 18.8.17, – A6351–A6600, B1851–B1900.

Handley Page O/400

One hundred were ordered from Boulton & Paul on Contract A.S.22434, but they were cancelled on 20 September, 1917, in favour of an order for Sopwith Camels.

Sopwith Camel F.1

An initial contract for 100 was placed on 2 August, 1917, (Contract No.AS.7737, under Req. 187.65.121). Further batches of 200, 100 and 300 Camels were ordered under this contract, making 700 in all, covered by the following serial numbers – B5151–B5250, B9131–B9330, C1601–C1700, D6401–D6700. The first aircraft was delivered in week ending 15.9.17, and all 700 had been delivered by week ending 11.5.18. Highest week's production was week ending 30.3.18 when 47 were delivered.

150 Camels ordered on 29.12.17 (Contract AS37028 under Req.273.245), and in a clerical error were allotted the serials D9231–D9380. This was soon corrected and the following correct serials were allotted – D9381-D9530. They were delivered from week ending 27/4/18 to week ending 1/6/18.

250 Camels ordered on 23.3.18 (Contract AS.2164 under Req.305) – F1301-F1550. Delivery was from week ending 15.6.18 to week ending 3.8.18.

100 ordered under Contract 35a/224/C416, (Req.375) – C3281–C3380. Delivered between week ending 24.8.18 and 7.9.18.

75 ordered (Contract 35A/587/C680 under Req.452) – F1883–F1957. Delivered between week ending 24.8.18 and week ending 7.9.18.

200 Camels to Contract 35A/1302/C1293 had the following serials allocated – F6301–F6500. Largely delivered between week ending 7.9.18 and week ending 26.10.18.

A further two orders were placed for Camels. The first for 200 aircraft, allocated the serials F9496–F9695, was cancelled. The second for 100 to Contract 35A/2046/C2343 on 16.7.18, with the following serials – H2646–H2745. Last delivered by 18.11.18.

The totals ordered were 1,775, with 200 cancelled, leaving 1,575 actually built. This made Boulton & Paul equal-first with Ruston Proctor as the largest manufacturer of Sopwith Camels.

Sopwith Snipe

400 ordered 20.3.18 (Contract 35A/436/C303 under Req.407) – E6137–E6536. First delivered during week ending 23.11.18 and the last delivered in September 1919. Highest weekly production was 26, during week ending 11.1.19.

100 ordered 19.9.18 (Contract 35A/3070/C3532 under Req. 666) – J451–J550. 75 were cancelled in December 1918 leaving only J451–J475 which were delivered to store between 28.1.19 and October 1919.

Vickers Vimy

150 ordered 30.8.18. Serials H4046–H4195 allocated but the order was cancelled at the end of hostilities before work had begun.

Martinsyde F.4 Buzzard

Two orders were placed for the Buzzard for 350 (Contract 35A/2861/C3245 placed 4.9.18) allocated serials H8763–H9112, and for 150 (Contract 35AQ/3386/C3979 placed 11.10.18. Allocated serials J1992–J2141, but both orders were cancelled on 19.12.18.

Royal Airship Works R101 Airship

The complete structure of G-FAAW was built by Boulton & Paul for assembly at Cardington.

Hawker Demon

Production of the Demon was transferred to Boulton Paul beginning with a batch of 59 under Contracts 176937/32 (for the first three aircraft) and 246236/33 for the other 56. They all had Kestrel VDR engines and many were subsequently fitted with Frazer-Nash turrets. Construction of them began in Norwich, but the first one was not completed until after the move to Wolverhampton. First flew on 21.8.36 at Pendeford. Further batches of 10 and 37 were ordered, making 106 in all. These were largely fitted with Frazer-Nash turrets, and they were variously fitted with Kestrel VDR, VI. X, and XRD engines. The last aircraft was flown in December 1937 and delivered in January 1938 – K5683–K5741, K5898–K5907, K8181–K8217.

Blackburn Roc (Boulton Paul P.93)

Detail design work to convert the Blackburn Skua to take the Boulton Paul four-gun A Turret, and the total production of 136 aircraft was sub-contracted to Boulton Paul. The first three production aircraft served as prototypes. The Roc was given the Boulton Paul Project No. P.93, reflecting the design input. Serial numbers were – L3057–L3192. L3057 first prototype, first flown 23.12.38 at Wolverhampton.

Bristol Beaufighter

250 ordered 25.2.40 under Contract 68420/40/c.23a and later cancelled. Allocated the following serials – W6089–W6126, W6140–W6185, W6200–W6249, W6265–W6300, W6316–W6360, W6376–W6410.

Handley Page Halifax

On 25 March, 1941, the decision was made that Boulton Paul should build the Halifax jointly with Fairey, the latter company doing the final assembly, and receiving an initial order for 100. Boulton Paul's involvement was latter cancelled in favour of the Barracuda.

Fairey Barracuda

300 initially ordered under Contract Aircraft/1066/c.20(b). The first flew during 1943. They were allotted the following serials. Fairey Barracuda II, DP855–DP902, DP917–DP955, DP967–DP999, DR113–DR162, DR179–DR224, DR237–DR275, DR291–DR335.

Follow-up order for 600 Barracuda IIIs, but only 392 were delivered before the order was cancelled. Fairey Barracuda III, MD811–MD859, MD876–MD924, MD945–MD992, ME104–ME152, ME166–ME210, ME223–ME270, ME282–ME293, RJ759–RJ799, RJ902–RJ948, RJ963–RJ966.

208, serials RJ967–999, and RK111–323 cancelled.

Hawker Sea Fury

The third prototype Sea Fury, VB857, was built by Boulton Paul as the first aircraft in an order for 100. It and the Hawker-built SR666 were the first true Sea Furys, with folding wings. The first prototype, SR661, was a navalised Fury with fixed wings. The order was cancelled at the end of the War and VB857 was assembled by Hawker at Langley and first flew 31.1.46.

Appendix II

Surviving Boulton Paul Built Aircraft

Despite the fact that Boulton Paul built 4,795 complete aircraft, only five survive of which only four are of Boulton Paul design. There are parts from several more, many of which are being worked on, and might well, one day be restored to virtually complete condition.

In the 1950s there were three Defiants in the United Kingdom and during that decade some Sidestrand wings were taken out of the lofts at Pendeford, and thrown on the scrapheap. By the early 1960s Balliols and Sea Balliols were being scrapped en masse.

Sopwith F.1 Camel – Royal Air Force Museum, Hendon, F6314. Ex-Nash Collection. Once marked H508.

Boulton & Paul P.10 – Bridewell Museum, Norwich. The frame of one wing and the tail, are held in store. The only Norwich-designed relics left in existence.

Hawker Demon – Aero Vintage Ltd, East Sussex. K8203 fuselage, tail, engine and some wing parts. Long-term rebuild to flying condition.

Boulton Paul Defiant I – Royal Air Force Museum, Hendon. N1671. Modified to Mark II standard. Displayed in No.307 Squadron' colours and coded EW-D.

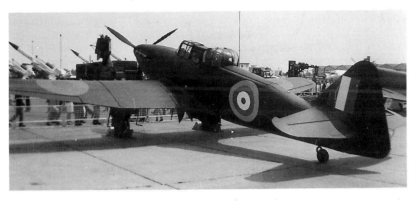

The sole surviving Defiant, N1671, at RAF Abingdon in 1969, now in the Battle of Britain Museum, Hendon. (*Author's photograph*)

Fairey Barracuda II – Fleet Air Arm Museum, Yeovilton. DP872. Crash remains salvaged from a Lough Enagh bog, Northern Ireland. Crashed 29.8.44 with 1796 Squadron. Being restored off-site for eventual display.

Boulton Paul Balliol T.2 – Katunayake, Sri Lanka. CA310. One of a small

P.111A in the Midland Air Museum, Coventry, with the author in the cockpit.

number of preserved aircraft at the home of the Sri Lanka Air Force's No. 4 Helicopter Wing.

Boulton & Paul Sea Balliol T.21 – Cosford Aerospace Museum, Wolverhampton, WL732. Ex-Anthorn, Lossiemouth and Boscombe Down.

Boulton Paul P.111A – Midland Air Museum, Coventry Airport, VT935.

In addition, in May 1993 the Boulton Paul Society began the restoration of two Balliol T.2 front fuselages, WN149 and WN534, in the factory where they were built. A further T.2 cockpit section, WN516, is in store at the North East Air Museum at Sunderland.

Boulton Paul D Type tail turret with AGLT on Avro Lincoln at Aerospace Museum, Cosford. (*Author's photograph*)

Appendix III

Major Sub-contracts

Felixstowe F.3/F.5 flying-boat
In 1917 Boulton & Paul won an order to build F.3 flying-boat hulls, and went on to build a total of 70, some of which were completed as the slightly different postwar F.5. All of them seem to have gone to Phoenix Dynamo in Bradford for final assembly. Allocating serials to the 70 built by Boulton & Paul is difficult as Phoenix Dynamo built a total of 100 F.3/F.5 flying-boats. All of them were ordered as F.3s but some of the last batch were eventually built as F.5s. The three batches of serials allocated are as follows:– N4160–N4179, N4400–N4429, N4180–N4229.

Blackburn Bluebird IV
Boulton Paul built 55 sets of wings for the all-metal Bluebird IV, using their spot-welding process. The aircraft were built by Saunders-Roe.

Blackburn Shark
Boulton Paul supplied 246 steel wing spars for the Blackburn Shark.

Saro A.27 London
Boulton Paul manufactured the wings for the Saro London flying-boat. The prototype's wings were built by Saro, but the production wings were designed and built using Boulton Paul's steel locked joint system, the contract being initiated at Norwich and completed at Wolverhampton. Ten Mk Is were built followed by 38 Mk IIs.

Fairey Sea Fox
Boulton Paul manufactured the tail assemblies for the Fairey Sea Fox shipboard biplane, of which there were 64 production examples.

Douglas Boston/Havoc
Sister firm status for various modifications and installations for RAF service, including gun packs.

Vickers-Armstrongs Wellington T.10
Between January 1946 and 20 March, 1952, 270 Wellington B.X. bombers were converted to T.10 trainers. They were completely stripped, overhauled, and re-covered with fabric, before refitting as Navigation trainers.

de Havilland Hornet
Target-towing equipment installed on one aircraft, serial not known.

Fairey Spearfish
A de-icing rig was fitted.

de Havilland Vampire

Redesign of intakes and installation for a Rolls-Royce Nene on Vampire F.1, TG276.

Target-towing equipment installed on another aircraft.

A survey unit was fitted to Vampire FB.5, VX985.

Gloster Meteor T.7

'Window' ejection apparatus was fitted to Meteor T.7 WL377 at Defford.

Supermarine Swift

Boulton Paul undertook the manufacture of the wings of the Swift, including the dog-tooth leading-edge modification.

English Electric Canberra

Boulton Paul were the main contractor for experimental and production modifications of Canberras from 30 June, 1952, to 1965. They also designed and manufactured the four-cannon belly pack. Some of the major modifications were as follows:

1953–4 Canberra B.2 WH671 Methanol and hot-air engine de-icing systems.

1954 Canberra B.2 WE146 Radio compass fitted.

1954 Canberra B.2 WF914 Venezualan Air Force prototype.

1954 Canberra B.2 WF915 RNZAF prototype.

1954 Canberra B.2 WJ730 Trial installation of night photographic cameras in the bomb-bay, with photoflash discharge crate (400 1.75 in photoflashes). Supplied to India for B.58.

1955 Canberra B.2 WK128 Trial installation of 'Window' dispensing crate in the bomb-bay.

1954–5 Canberra B.2 WJ565 Trial installation of gun-pack, containing four × 20 mm Hispano cannon and 16 photoflashes. Used on B(I) Mk 6 and B(I) Mk 8.

1955 Canberra B.1 VN828 Section forward of Frame 12 replaced by a B.8 front fuselage, but with a nose radome carrying GEC AI Mk 18 radar units. Power supplied from an inverter pack in the bomb-bay. First flight 25.5.55.

1955 Canberra B.2 WJ646 Converted for radar systems trials.

1955 Canberra PR.3 VX181 Modifications for the PR role. Two F.97 cameras fitted, later fitted to most PR.3s and PR.7s.

1956 Canberra B.2 WK123 Converted to T.T.18.

1956–7 Canberra B.6 XH567 Bomb-bay modifications for specialist load-carrying role for ATDU Culdrose. Bomb doors were removed and a special mine carrying beam fitted to carry four 1,000 lb mines or two 2,000 lb mines.

1956 Canberra B.8 WT327 Modified to carry AI.23 radar with associated units, for Lightning. Used by Ferranti for trials.

1957 Canberra B.2 WG789 Installation of GEC AI.18 radar and computer. Used extensively by GEC.

1957 Canberra B.8 XH232 Prototype for Indian B.58.

1957 Canberra PR.7 WH780 Trial installation of two F.89 Mk 3 high-altitude cameras, later fitted to most PR.7s.

1957–63 Canberra B.2 WK161 Selected parts of the aircraft covered with DX3 material in four stages, and radar reflection measurements taken. A Radio Dept RAE Farnborough project.

1958 Canberra B.2 WH903, WJ610, WJ975, XA536 Converted to T.11.

1958 Canberra B.2 WH724, WH904 Converted to T.19.

1958 Canberra B.2 WJ734 Prototype for Canberra T.11, fitted as an AI.17 trainer. Nose modified forward of Frame 1 for radar units, scanner and dielectric radome.

1958 Canberra PR.7 WT541 Prototype for Indian PR.57.

1958–9 Canberra B.8 WT329 Prototype for RNZAF B.12.

1959 Canberra B.2 WH711 Royal Swedish Air Force prototype.

1959 Canberra T.4 WE190 Prototype for RNZAF Canberra T.13.

1959 Canberra B.2 WV787 Modification of nose for 'Blue Parrot' including radome. Used by Ferranti for radar trials for Buccaneer. Sapphire-powered.

1959–62 Canberra B.6 WT305 Nose modifications for radar trials at CSE Watton.

1963 Canberra B.8 WT327 Further modifications to incorporate FLR equipment for radar trials by Ferranti of the TSR.2 system.

1963 Canberra B.15 WH967 Installation of Nord AS.30 missile.

Gloster Javelin

Boulton Paul undertook a number of modification and trials work with the Javelin. XA561 F.(AW) Mk1. Undertook spinning trials – the aircraft crashed 8.12.55. XA562 F.(AW) Mk1 Trials aircraft for the installation of a Rolls-Royce Avon RA.24. XA567 F.(AW) Mk1 Undertook radar trials.

English Electric Lightning

Work on the Canberra was followed by a small amount of conversion work on the Lightning, before this was taken on by other branches of the British Aircraft Corporation. In particular a number of pre-production Mk 1 aircraft were converted to Mk 3 standard in 1960/61, and weapon system trials were undertaken.

Beagle 206 Basset

Boulton Paul undertook the complete structural testing of the Beagle 206 and built all the 206 wings for Beagle Aircraft.

Appendix IV

Boulton Paul Gun Turrets

Turret	Aircraft	Position	Armament	Rnds/guns	Ring Dia
–	Overstrand	Nose	1 Lewis		
–	P.70/74/79	Mid-upper	1 Lewis	–	
–	P.79	Tail	2 Lewis		
AMkIID	Defiant	Mid-upper	4 × .303 in	600	43 in
AMkIIR	Roc	Mid-upper	4 × .303 in	600	43 in
AMkII PB1 & PB2	Patrol Boats	As Reqd	4 × .303 in	600	43 in
AMkII S1	Short G Class	Nose	4 × .303 in	600	43 in
AMkII S2	Short G Class	Mid-upper	4 × .303 in	600	43 in
AMkII S3	Short G Class	Tail	4 × .303 in	600	43 in
AMkII S4	Short C Class	Mid-upper	4 × .303 in	600	43 in
AMkII S5	Short C Class	Tail	4 × .303 in	600	43 in
AMkIII	Albermarle	Mid-upper	4 × .303 in	600	43 in
AMkIV	Liberator	Mid-upper	4 × .303 in	600	43 in
AMkV	Baltimore	Mid-upper	4 × .303 in	600	43 in
AMkVa	Baltimore	Mid-upper	4 × .303 in	600	43 in
AMkVI	Ventura	Mid-upper	4 × .303 in	600	43 in
AMkVII	Halifax	Mid-upper	4 × .303 in	600	43 in
AMkVIII	Halifax	Mid-upper	4 × .303 in	600	43 in
BMkI	Halifax		4 × .303 in	600	43 in
CMkI	Halifax	Nose	2 × .303 in	1,000	38.3 in
CMkII	Hudson I	Mid-upper	2 × .303 in	1,000	38.3 in
CMkIIa	Hudson II	Mid-upper	2 × .303 in	1,000	38.3 in
CMkIV	Ventura	Mid-upper	2 × .303 in	1,000	38.3 in
CMkV	Halifax	Mid-upper	2 × .303 in	1,000	38.3 in
DMkI	Halifax	Tail	2 × .5 in	1,110	36.95 in
DMkIc	Halifax	Tail	2 × .5 in	1,110	36.95 in
DMkI Series 2	Lincoln	Tail	2 × .5 in	1,110	36.95 in
EMkI	Halifax	Tail	4 × .303 in	2,695	36.95 in
EMkII	Liberator	Tail	4 × .303 in	2,445	36.95 in
EMkIII	Halifax	Tail	4 × .303 in	2,445	36.95 in
FMkI	Defiant	Mid-upper	1 × 20 mm	n/a	43 in
FMkI GMk1	Lincoln	Nose	2 × .5 in		
HMkI	Lincoln	Mid-upper	2 × 20 mm	300	38.25 in
HMkII	Stirling/ Halifax	Mid-upper	2 × 20 mm	300	38.25 in
HMkIII	Lancaster	Mid-upper	2 × 20 mm	300	38.25 in

Field of fire in degrees			All-up	Ordered	Remarks
Rotate	Elevate	Depress	Wt Lb		
360	near 90	n/a	n/a	13.8.32	World's First
360	n/a	n/a	n/a	–	Unbuilt
n/a	n/a	n/a	n/a	–	Mock-up only
360	84	nil	821	4.37	Based on SAMM turret
360	84	nil	821	4.37	
360	74	10	820		
180	74	10	798		three a/c only
360	84	nil	804		three a/c only
180	74	10	798		three a/c only
360	84	nil	804		two a/c only
180	74	10	798		two a/c only
360	84	nil	804	11.1.39	
360	84	nil	804		
360	84	nil	804	16.6.41	
360	74	10	804		
360	74	10	804	15.11.41	
				7.7.42	Not completed
360	84	2½	784		
360	65	20	n/a		Modified A turret
200	60	45	679	Mid-1938	
360	60	45	755	Late 1938	
360	60	45			
360	60	30	755		
360	60	30	755		
180	45	45	728	14.12.42	
180	45	45	n/a		With AGL (T) radar
180	45	45	n/a		Optional AGL (T)
180	56½	50	679	Mid-1938	
130	56½	50	679		
180	56½	50	679		
360	n/a	n/a	n/a	22.9.43	One only. F re-used
90	50	9	1,350	30.5.42	Not completed
n/a	n/a	n/a	n/a	19.5.39	Not completed
360	70	20	n/a		Not completed

Turret	Aircraft	Position	Armament	Rnds/guns	Ring Dia
KMkI	Halifax	Ventral	2 × .303 in		
KMkII	Albermarle	Ventral	2 × .303 in		
LMkI	P.92	Mid-upper	4 × 20 mm		
LMkII	H.P.58	Ventral	4 × 20 mm		
NMkI		Tail	1 × 20 mm		
OMkI	Stirl ing/ Halifax	Mid-upper	2 × 20 mm		
RMkI/II	Halifax	Ventral	2 × 20 mm		
SMkI	USA	Tail	2 × .5 in	350	
TMkI	USA	Mid-upper	2 × .5 in	600	41.25 in
UMkI		Ventral	2 × .5 in		
VMkI		Nose	2 × .5 in	350	
YMkI		Ventral	2 × .5 in		
BA	Lancaster	Mid-upper	2 × 20 mm	200	
BB	Lancaster	Ventral	2 × 20 mm	200	
–		Side	1 × .5 in		
Pillar- Mount		As reqd	1 × 20 mm		
L Mount ing	Shackleton 1	Nose	2 × 20 mm		
N Mount ing	Shackleton Mks 2/3	Nose	2 × 20 mm		

| Field of fire in degrees | | | All-up | Ordered | Remarks |
Rotate	Elevate	Depress	Wt Lb		
360	nil	60	n/a	25.5.38	Retractable
360	nil	90	n/a	11.1.39	Retractable
360	n/a	n/a	n/a		Mock-up only
360	n/a	n/a	n/a		Unbuilt
n/a	n/a	n/a	n/a		Not completed
n/a	n/a	n/a	n/a	19.5.39	Not completed
360	2	60	684	22.10.40	Periscope sight
200	70	50	1,088	25.10.40	Prototype for USA
360	85	20	1,584	9.4.41	Prototype for USA
360	10	85	n/a	9.4.41	Not completed
200	70	50	n/a	28.6.41	Not completed
360	10	85	n/a		
45	70	7	838	10.4.43	Elec barbette
45	2	70	n/a	10.4.43	Elec barbette
n/a	n/a	n/a	n/a	13.1.44	GGS Mk IIc sight
180	70	30	309		SAMM. Test in Overstrand
nil					Prototype only
nil					Production models

Appendix V

The Boulton Paul Association

In 1991 a group of mostly ex-employees of the company formed the Boulton Paul Society, with the simple aim of preserving the history of Boulton Paul Aircraft in all its forms. Later, anxious to preserve the initials BPA, the Society decided to change its name to the Boulton Paul Association.

Their first project towards this aim was to create an extensive mobile exhibition of the company's history. Both Dowty Aerospace, and its former parent, Boulton & Paul Ltd, of Norwich, providing sponsorship, and the first location for this exhibition was the Aerospace Museum, Cosford, suitably near the factory.

In May 1993 the Society obtained the cockpit sections of two Balliols, WN149, and WN534, which had been rescued from a scrapyard by the Pennine Aviation Museum, and taken them back to the factory where they were built. In a workshop made available by Dowty Aerospace these will be restored to exhibition standard, one as an RAF T.2, and the other hopefully as a Mamba-engined T.1. A target date of March 1997 has been set for the completion of the first, the 50th anniversary of the Balliol's first flight. Many of the members working on these, such as brothers Brian and Jack Holmes, helped build the aircraft in the first place. As boys they had been brought to Wolverhampton by their father, Billy, who began working for the company in Norwich, in the 1920s; and they later became apprentices.

Also in May 1993 the Boulton Paul Society took over the administration of the Dowty Boulton Paul archives, including a collection of around 20,000 negatives. They began the huge task of cataloguing them, and handle all queries relating to the company's history.

General Index

The name J D North appears throughout the pages of this book almost as frequently as the name of the company to which he devoted most of his life. It is therefore deemed inappropriate to include it in the index.

371

Index to Aircraft

This index refers only to the main text. Further reference to Boulton (&) Paul aircraft can be found in the Production Details section. Extensive information on the unbuilt projects can be found in their own section. Both sections are largely self-indexing.

373

Index to Aero-Engines

Index to Gun Turrets